Star of Destiny

STAR OF DESTINY

The Private Life of Sam and Margaret Houston

by Madge Thornall Roberts

Foreword by Randolph B. Campbell

University of North Texas Press

©University of North Texas Press

10 9 8 7 6 5 4 3 2 1

Requests for permission to reproduce material from this work should
be sent to:
Permissions
University of North Texas Press
P. O. Box 13856
Denton, Texas 76203

The paper used in this book meets the minimum requirements of the
American National Standard for Permanence of Paper for Printed Library
materials, Z39.48.1984.

Library of Congress Cataloging-in-Publication Data

Roberts, Madge Thornall, 1929–
Star of destiny : the private life of Sam and Margaret Houston / by
Madge Thornall Roberts.
p.   cm.
Includes bibliographical references.
ISBN 0-929398-51-3
1. Houston, Sam, 1793–1863. 2. Houston, Margaret Lea, 1819–1867. 3.
Governors—Texas—Biography. 4. Governors' wives—Texas—Biography.
5. Legislators—United States—Biography. 6. Legislators' wives—United
States—Biography. 7. United States. Congress. Senate—Biography. I.
Title.
F390.H84R6   1993
976.4'04'092—dc20
[B]   92-31587
CIP

To *my* grandmother who told me the story of *her* grandmother

Table of Contents

Foreword

"I see with great pain the marriage of Genl. Houston to Miss Lea!" Barnard E. Bee wrote to Ashbel Smith on June 5, 1840. "I had hoped it would never have been consummated—in all my intercourse with life I have never met with an individual more totally disqualified for domestic happiness." Bee's fears are easy to understand: Sam Houston had led a spectacularly unsettled life for most of his forty-seven years and hardly seemed a candidate to become anyone's husband, let alone that of a twenty-one-year-old woman from a genteel Alabama family. Bee apparently did not know, however, just how much Houston wanted to settle into family life, a longing he frequently expressed to close friends. If the Republic could just be at peace, he wrote his friend Robert Irion in 1837, "I would retire to East Texas, get a fair, sweet 'wee wifie,' as Burns says, and pass the balance of my sinful life in ease and comfort, (if I can)." Perhaps Bee also did not recognize that, for all his life of seemingly reckless adventure, Sam Houston was an eminently sensible and practical man. He knew Margaret Lea was special when he saw her, and he would do everything in his power to win and keep her.

Nancy Moffette Lea, Margaret's mother, probably shared Barnard Bee's fears concerning the marriage, but for different reasons. Her intelligent, cultured daughter was marrying a hard-drinking, twice-divorced (if the marriage to Tiana Rogers during his years with the Cherokees in the Indian Territory counted), heroic but always controversial man who was more than twice as old as the bride. What Nancy Lea may not have realized, however, was Margaret's deep love for Sam Houston and her determination as an ardent Christian to reform his drinking, bring him to the church, and make him a happily married man.

ix

Fortunately, the fears of friends and family concerning the marriage of Sam Houston and Margaret Lea proved totally groundless. The match was a blessing for the husband. He never led a life of "ease and comfort," but he enjoyed all the happiness of family life with few of its tragedies. For example, all of the eight children Margaret bore between 1843 and 1860 lived to adulthood, a true blessing in that age of high infant mortality. Margaret accomplished her objectives; for Houston stopped drinking, became an advocate of temperance, and joined the Baptist Church in 1854. Above all, Sam and Margaret built and maintained a close and loving relationship of the sort attained in few marriages. When apart, as they frequently were due to his political career, they wrote letters virtually every day, confiding in each other their love and innermost thoughts.

In *Star of Destiny*, Madge Thornall Roberts, a great-great-granddaughter of Sam and Margaret Lea Houston, tells the story of their marital partnership in detail never before available. The Franklin Williams collection of private Houston family letters, only recently donated to the Sam Houston Memorial Museum at Huntsville, provides the heart of her research. Using these materials and many other sources provided by the Houstons' numerous descendants, Roberts greatly enhances our understanding of the private life of the couple who could well be called "the First Family of Texas" from their marriage in 1840 until Sam Houston's death in 1863. *Star of Destiny* is both significant history and a wonderful human-interest story.

Randolph B. Campbell
University of North Texas

Acknowledgements

This work could not have been completed without the help and encouragement of many persons. One of the first to encourage me was Dr. Llerena Friend, who long ago read my first manuscript and checked it for historical accuracy. Then my friend Jane Monday, former mayor of Huntsville, discovered I had begun the work. She insisted that I stay with her while I did research and convinced me to show it to Fran Vick, director of the University of North Texas Press. Fran put my efforts in the hands of the very competent editor, Charlotte Wright. These three were responsible for turning my little manuscript into a book.

The libraries of Texas have a wealth of materials and are staffed with wonderful people to help the researcher. I am greatly indebted to the staff at Sam Houston Memorial Museum, especially to Lois Pierce and Kathy Shute, who spent many hours locating and copying letters for me, and to Richard Rice and David Wight, who were always available to help me locate information. Paul Culp of the library at Sam Houston State University helped me locate information there. James Patton, Walker County Clerk, located the legal documents I needed in Huntsville, and shared his wealth of knowledge with me.

In Liberty, at the Sam Houston Regional Library, Robert Schaadt helped me locate information on photographs, and Darlene Mott searched for materials for me. Mary Beth Fleischer of Barker History Center, Nancy Boothe of the Woodson Research Center of Rice University Library, and J. C. Martin of the San Jacinto Museum of History were also helpful.

In Independence, Madora McCorcklin, who lives on the old Houston farmstead, and Frankie Slaughter, who with her husband Gene restored Margaret's home, furnished me important documents. Jay Belew and Paul Sevar of the Baptist Museum at Independence were helpful in locating photographs for me.

The staff of the Daughters of the Republic of Texas Library where I did volunteer work were never too busy to help me when I went back as a researcher or when I called on the telephone with a question. I am indebted to Linda Edwards, Rusty Gamez, Charline Pavilska, Jeannette Phinney, Warren Stricker, and Martha Utterback.

My cousins were also helpful. Mary Louise and Robert Teasdale furnished family records, and Meredith Spangler gave me permission to quote from her master's thesis, and Margaret Houston's album. Charlotte Darby Taylor furnished me material from her family, and her mother, Charlotte Williams Darby, encouraged me to use her father's collection.

Within my immediate family I found encouragement. My sister Nancy Burch gave me bed and board while I was researching in the Houston area. My mother-in-law, Mildred Crawford, tracked down information from her cousin, Douglas Howser. Last and probably most important, my husband Charles insisted I get a computer, and my son-in-law, Bryce Jacobson patiently taught me how to use it. All of these people have shared with me in telling the story of Margaret and Sam Houston.

Madge Thornall Roberts

Introduction

Throughout her lifetime, Margaret Lea Houston shunned publicity and attempted to stay in the shadow of the husband she adored. She and Sam Houston kept their private life separate from his political career. She shielded her eight children so successfully that most were grown before they knew who Houston's political enemies were.

When they were apart Houston wrote Margaret daily, and on some occasions twice in one day. Each carefully saved the other's letters to be reread many times. Possibly because of the way they were raised, the Houston children had a sense of family privacy which carried through to the next generation. While children and grandchildren usually co-operated with authors in historical matters, they rarely released family letters to the public. Historians knew very little about Margaret, but her story was kept alive within the family.

It is amazing to me that any letters still survive today. Toward the end of her life Margaret burned untold numbers of letters. When she died in 1867, her Independence home was purchased by her daughter and son-in-law, Maggie and Weston Williams, and the home remained filled with Houston artifacts. Santa Anna's saddle was in the upstairs hall, the San Jacinto sword hung over the mantle, and trunks of documents sat unattended in the barn for nearly forty years.

Maggie and Wes were my great-grandparents. My grandmother, Madge Williams Hearne was born and raised in this home along with her brothers, Houston, Franklin, and Royston, and her sister Marian. Around the turn of the century the home was sold and clean-up was begun for the new owners. Many papers went into the trash barrel to be burned. Franklin Williams and Madge Williams Hearne rescued as many of the Houston documents as they could.

xiii

These documents were divided among descendants, some-times with disastrous results. Madge Hearne once decided that, as the last surviving Houston child, Andrew Houston should have some of his parents' letters and many of Margaret's poems. This proved to be a tragic mistake, as his home in La Porte later burned to the ground, taking the documents with it.

Family members aided Amelia Willliams and Eugene Barker in preparing the eight volumes of *The Writings of Sam Houston*, but they released only a few of Houston's letters to Margaret. Mean-while, although some letters were preserved in museums and libraries, many traveled with various relatives from house to house. In 1964, when my family home was sold, a huge metal box full of Houston documents was found in a crawl space in a closet beneath the stairs. This was the first that my sisters and I knew of the existence of the box and its hiding place. I often wonder if similar circumstances might have occurred with other relatives.

There were over thirty Houston grandchildren. Many lived well into their eighties, and along with Andrew Houston were still very much alert when I was a child. Most of them remained close and frequently enjoyed family get-togethers. Since my grandmother lived with us I was often present. How I wish I had asked more questions and kept a journal! They all enjoyed telling family stories, with each person trying to relate a more interesting incident. I grew up listening to family history related by Andrew Houston, Jennie Morrow Decker, Maggie Morrow John, Margaret Bell Houston, Franklin and Royston Williams, Marian Williams Whittemore, and especially Madge Williams Hearne.

As a teenager I served as grandmother's secretary, typing her many letters, speeches for historical occasions, and family records. Some years after her death in 1955, I set out to organize all her records, notes, and photographs into a collection I refer to as the Hearne Papers. I then decided to write down all the family stories I could remember. I began reading and adding material from published sources. The result was a manuscript, originally in-tended as a record for my children, which I continued to add to through the years.

In 1991, I agreed to help the Sam Houston Memorial Museum by transcribing to typescript the Franklin Williams collection of private letters which it had recently acquired. There were several hundred letters in the collection and very few had been made public. With each letter I read, a clearer picture of the relationship between Sam and Margaret fell into place. When I read a letter written by Sam Houston on December 21, 1841, I felt that perhaps he felt that one day their story would be told. In it he wrote Margaret that he was in the habit of carrying her letters in the breast pocket of his hunting shirt for handy reference. He told her that he feared this habit would "have a tendency to destroy the delectable manuscript and disappoint the novelist in a specimen of very pretty epistolary correspondences."

While some of the letters *were* hard to read, I was not disappointed and I had the feeling that at last it was time for me to write their story. This book was the result. I have preserved the original punctuation and spelling of all the letters, and retained the underlining of certain words that Houston underlined for emphasis, as well as the colloquial spellings and the mistakes that were made when he wrote too hurriedly. I have attempted to tell the story as much as possible in their own words and in the words of those who knew them. I have rechecked family sources for accuracy in the hopes that this book will at last give the story of two people, one famous and the other unknown, who together dared to follow their "Star of Destiny."

Madge Thornall Roberts.

Chapter I

I have a strange feeling that someday I shall meet this man.

Margaret Lea, New Orleans
May 22, 1836

On May 22, 1836, a dirty little trading schooner, the *Flora*, sailed into the Mississippi River port of New Orleans. Throngs of people lined the levee and the wharf. Rumors had spread that the little vessel carried Sam Houston, the hero of San Jacinto, on board. He was, some said, a dying man. The crowd had come to catch a glimpse of him. They came in buggies, on horseback, or in boats on the river. A group of young girls from Professor McLean's School had ridden the stage from Marion, Alabama, on a school outing, and when they heard of General Houston's pending arrival, came to watch.

General Houston lay on a pallet on the open deck, his shattered ankle covered with blood. One of the first to reach him was William Christy, an old friend who had served with him in the United States Army. A band struck up a welcome march as the crowd surged forward to help carry the wounded man off the ship. Houston told Christy to hold back the crowd and he would get off by himself.[1]

With the aid of crutches Houston managed to stand. Ever the politician, he stopped to make a short speech. Among other things he said, "What Texas needs is large recruits of pious women and ministers of the Gospel."[2] Little did Sam Houston suspect that

1

among the crowd was a pious young lady who would later come to Texas with him and change his life forever. In the group who had come with Professor McLean was Margaret Lea, a seventeen-year-old student from Alabama. Margaret was particularly impressed with the wounded hero and the speech he made. Moreover, she felt a strange premonition. Aside to one of her friends she confided, "I have a strange feeling that one day I will meet this man."[3]

Margaret Moffette Lea came from an Alabama family of distinguished men that included soldiers, lawyers, and laymen active in the state government, so it would not seem impossible that she could be introduced to so famous a man. Still, because of the differences in their ages and states of residence, it did not seem highly probable. Throughout her life Margaret would have flashes of clairvoyance. However, history was later to prove this particular premonition right in a way that she could hardly have imagined.

Sam Houston was one of the strangest and most mysterious figures in America at this time. He was born on March 2, 1793, in Rockbridge County, Virginia, to Major Samuel Houston and Elizabeth Paxton Houston. He was the fifth of five boys, and would be followed by one more brother and two sisters. Sam disliked school intensely and was truant every chance he got. Yet he became an avid reader and devoured every book in his father's library.

His father, who was away in the army for much of the time, died when Sam was ten years old. Just before his death Major Houston had sold the family farm with the intention of relocating in Tennessee. One of his last purchases had been a new wagon for the trip. Elizabeth Houston had no choice. She moved her family into the wilderness of Tennessee. They settled on four hundred acres of land that her husband had selected a few miles north of Maryville on the branch of Baker's Creek. While their house was being built and the farm being established, Elizabeth and her brood stayed with Major Houston's cousin, James Houston, on his fort-like plantation.

With the exception of Sam, whose talents did not lean toward agriculture, and James, who became a shopkeeper in Maryville, the Houston brothers worked diligently to establish the farm. Sam suffered his mother's reproofs in silence, but he argued constantly with his brothers. Soon it became apparent to all that securing Sam's help in clearing and planting the land was a losing battle, and the family decided that he should go to work for James in the shop.

Sam did not fare any better in the store. He rebelled and solved the problem by disappearing. Elizabeth was frantic. After weeks of searching, the family learned that Sam had crossed the Tennessee River into Indian country and was living with the Cherokees. Elizabeth sent James and John to bring him back. They found Sam at the wigwam of Chief Oo-loo-te-ka. When his brothers asked him to come home, Sam replied that he "preferred measuring deer tracks to tape" and "the wild liberty of the Red Men better than the tyranny of his own brothers."[4]

Sam would stay with the Cherokees for the next three years. He became a favorite of the chief, who gave him the name of "The Raven." He became close friends with James and John Rogers, the sons of the chief's brother-in-law, who was part Scot. Sam returned home a few times, mostly to purchase supplies on credit. When his purchases reached one hundred dollars it became necessary to find a way to pay the bill. Much to everyone's surprise and amusement he announced that he was going to open a school. With about twenty students he opened the school in May, 1812. It was successful for nearly a year and as a result Sam paid off his debts.[5] Years later when asked which office had afforded him the greatest pride—governor, senator, commander-in-chief of an army or president of a republic—Houston would reply that it was teaching where he "experienced a higher feeling of dignity and self-satisfaction than from any office or honor. . . ."[6]

His teaching days ended on March 24, 1813, when a Regular Army party came to Maryville on a recruiting mission. Sam took the silver dollar, the token of entry into military service, and became a part of the War of 1812. Since he was not yet twenty-one Sam needed his mother's consent. Elizabeth gave it, along with a musket and his father's ring with the inscription "honor" engraved on the inside. She also gave him some advice: "Take this musket and never disgrace it, for remember, I had rather all my sons should fill one

3

honorable grave than that one of them should turn his back to save his life. . . . [R]emember, too, that while the door of my cabin is open to brave men, it is eternally shut against cowards."[7]

Sam entered the army as a private, quickly rose to the rank of ensign, and found himself fighting at the Battle of Horseshoe Bend alongside Andrew Jackson. Ensign Houston was one of the first men wounded in an attack against the Creek Indians. An arrow pierced his thigh. He tried to remove it, but the arrow was barbed. Ensign Houston asked for help and finally had to brandish his sword and command a lieutenant to yank it out. When the fighting subsided the ensign sought medical aid from the surgeon. Sam was resting on the ground when he heard General Jackson call for volunteers to rout the last of the enemy entrenched in a ravine. Ensign Houston arose and ordered his men to charge. When the fight was over, it was discovered that a musket ball had smashed Sam's shoulder. His bravery did not go unobserved by Andrew Jackson. It would be almost a year before he recovered, and the shoulder wound remained a running sore until the day of his death.[8]

After Sam left the army he served briefly as an Indian agent, then decided to become a lawyer. In Nashville, Judge James Trimble prescribed the eighteen-month law course. Sam completed his reading in one third of the time and passed the examination to be admitted to the bar. In short succession he became a colonel and then adjutant general of the state militia. He was elected attorney general of the Nashville district and in 1823, was elected as congressman to serve in Washington, D. C., with Senator Andrew Jackson. In a few more years Jackson was president and Sam Houston was governor of Tennessee.

Houston was thirty-five when his career hit its peak in 1828. There was talk now that he was being groomed by Jackson to be the next president. It would seem that his life was complete, but he longed for a home and family. He was in love with Eliza Allen of Gallatin. President Jackson was overjoyed because his protégé had picked the daughter of one of his old friends.[9]

Eliza Allen was just nineteen and was not at all sure of her feelings. She was dazzled by family pressures and the thought of

4

becoming the first lady of Tennessee and perhaps of the United States. Eliza finally consented to marry him, and thereby took part in changing the course of American history. On January 22, 1829, Sam and Eliza were married by the Reverend Mr. William Hume in a wedding attended by most of the notable families of Tennessee.[10]

Three months later the Houstons separated. The governor refused to discuss it except to defend Eliza's honor. On April 16, 1829, he resigned as governor. Eliza returned to her family, and Sam Houston left for a second life of exile among the Cherokees. In all probability his hasty actions cost him his fondest dream, the presidency of the United States. It appeared to all that Houston's public life had ended forever in mystery.

On April 23, Houston left Nashville on the packet *Red Rover*. When the boat stopped at Clarksville two men from the Allen family came aboard, and Houston asked them to publish in the Nashville papers that he would return to Tennessee and kill anyone who questioned Mrs. Houston's honor. The Allens departed and wisely refrained from giving the newspapers anything more to write about.[11]

Houston next made a curious trip to visit his friend, Thomas Howser, who lived nearby. The two old friends talked late into the night discussing the question of Houston's staying in Tennessee and making a fight for re-election to the governorship. Finally Howser went to sleep and Houston sent orders to have the horses ready for his departure at 3:00. He then sat down and wrote a letter. He sealed it and on the outside wrote, "Relying upon your better judgment, I am leaving this manuscript with you to be opened only when you think my honor requires it."[12]

Houston left to continue his journey down the Cumberland and Thomas Howser put the sealed letter in a safe place. He would never see his friend again, and he never saw fit to break the seal and read the contents. It was speculated that because of his friendship with Houston, Howser may have felt that he knew about what the contents of the letter were and saw no need to reveal his friend's secret to the world. In any event he did not discuss the matter even with his family. In 1896, his grandson, W. D. Howser, placed the letter in a safety deposit box at his bank. Through the years there were offers of as much as one thousand dollars from people who wanted to read the letter, and even President Theodore Roosevelt once tried to purchase it. The family refused all offers.

In the 1930s, W. D. Howser was writing a book about Tennessee history. His son convinced him that the letter should be read and used in the history if the matter was suitable. On May 2, 1933, the two removed the letter from the bank. By the time they reached home it was late and the matter was deferred until the next day. Early the next morning a fire occurred and the house and its contents burned to the ground. The Howser family believed that Divine Providence had intervened because it was not predestined that the contents of the letter should be given to the world.[13]

Houston continued his journey until he reached the land of the Cherokees. Here he was reunited with Chief Oo-loo-te-ka and James and John Rogers. He was adopted by the tribe and no longer considered himself a citizen of the United States. Soon he had his own wigwam on the Neosho River. He then, in an Indian ceremony, married Tiana Rogers Gentry, the widowed half-sister of James and John. He remained with the Indians for three years, at which time Andrew Jackson persuaded him to leave his life of oblivion. In December of 1832, he left for Texas after bidding Tiana farewell. Their relationship was dissolved according to Cherokee custom, and Tiana had given him a power of attorney which identified her as the "widow of David Gentry."[14]

On December 2, 1832, Houston crossed the Red River into the new land of Texas. It was Jackson's consuming wish that Texas would one day become a part of the United States. On his first trip to this land Houston felt at once that Jackson was right and that his life was to be devoted to bringing about this end.[15]

By 1836, Texas had declared its independence and Houston had been chosen to lead a small army to win freedom for Texas from the Mexican dictator, Santa Anna. On April 21, 1836, during the eighteen-minute Battle of San Jacinto in which General Houston led a small band of Texans to victory over the huge Mexican army, three horses were shot out from under him. Only fourteen Texans had been seriously wounded, but Houston was one of them. A musket ball had shattered the bones above his ankle. The Texas surgeon, Dr. Ewing, could not repair the damage done to the leg and insisted that the general must go to New Orleans immediately for an operation. Aside he whispered to Houston's aides his fears that lockjaw would develop before the general could reach New Orleans.

The only ship available was the *Yellowstone*, which was commanded by Thomas Grayson and had been used to ferry Texas troops across the river before the battle. When it was time to sail to Galveston with the new government officials on board, Houston was not present. Captain Grayson refused to leave the general wounded on the field of San Jacinto and would not sail until Houston was put on board by Thomas Rusk and his brother, David.[16]

Dr. Ewing accompanied the wounded hero to Galveston and there secured passage for him on the *Flora*. The ship sailed through heavy storms with Houston unconscious much of the time. And so it was that he finally reached New Orleans on Sunday, May 22, 1836,[17] where Margaret Lea first caught sight of the man who would become her husband.

He had been without proper medicine and poultices for over a month. By all laws of nature, Sam Houston should have been a dead man, but once again medical science had to deal with the spirit and will that guided the man whom the Indians called "The Raven." Dr. David C. Ker, who had treated him for his wounds at Horseshoe Bend years ago, and Dr. Augustus H. Cenas, both prominent Louisiana physicians, removed over twenty pieces of bone from Houston's leg. The wound would remain a painful reminder of the Battle of San Jacinto until the day of his death twenty-seven years later, but in just three weeks he was back in Texas despite the fact that he was still seriously ill.[18]

By the spring of 1836 when Margaret first saw the hero of San Jacinto, she was already showing signs of becoming one of the most eligible young ladies of the South. By her own description her height was "about five feet seven inches."[19] Even years later she was described by her daughter as slender of figure with small dainty feet, and possessed with a simple beauty, quiet and serene. Her eyes were of so deep a blue that sometimes they appeared to be violet. Her hair was light brown with just a few streaks of gold around her forehead, and she wore it parted in the middle and held back by combs.[20]

Margaret carried the name of one of the most distinguished families of the South. Her father was Temple Lea, a zealous Baptist clerk and lay minister of the church. Her mother, Nancy Moffette, was descended from a family of Huguenots who fled from persecution in France and settled in South Carolina. Ancestors on both sides had fought in the American Revolution. Temple and Nancy married in South Carolina in 1797 and moved to Alabama. They settled in Perry County about twelve miles from the town of Marion. Here, near the Cahaba River, they managed a successful plantation and bore six children: Martin, Varilla, Henry, Vernal, Margaret, and Emily Antoinette.[21]

The fifth child, Margaret Moffette Lea, was born on April 11, 1819, and was named for her mother's younger sister who had married Green Lea, the brother of Margaret's father. There was a twelve-year difference in age between Henry and Vernal, and the three older Leas had children who were almost as old as Margaret. Despite the age span there was much warmth between brothers and sisters. The parents saw to it that all the children received strict religious training. At an early age Margaret joined the Siloam Baptist Church in Marion and was baptized by the Reverend Peter Crawford.[22]

From her mother Margaret received full instructions in the social graces necessary for a young lady of her time. From her father she received her first training in education and the religious structure that would influence her life as well as the life of her future husband. This close relationship with her father ended before Margaret's fifteenth birthday, when Temple died on January 28, 1834. A tribute to Temple Lea was written by the Reverend Hosea Holcombe:

Temple Lea . . . was many years an efficient member (a Deacon) able in discipline, a man of great intelligence of sterling worth and a humble follower of Jesus. He was strictly benevolent; his soul was alive in the missionary cause; he was looked up to as an able instructor in the affairs of the Lord's house; he wrote and published an "Essay on Church Government" and at last died in full assurance of faith.[23]

When his will was read it was found that Temple had left Margaret four slaves, among them Joshua and the young girl, Eliza.[24] Margaret had always had a special place in her heart for Eliza, whose tragic story became a part of the Lea legend. One afternoon when Margaret was a small child Temple took her with him on a trip to Mobile. As they passed the village square they saw a small black girl on the slave block. She appeared to be just about Margaret's age. Margaret took a fancy to Eliza and begged her father to buy the little girl. After Temple heard Eliza's sad story he agreed to Margaret's request, although the girl did not know her age, place of birth or family name. Eliza, who had been playing by the roadside of her Mammy's cabin when some slave thieves invited her to "take a ride," was kidnapped and ended up on the slave block. Eliza was to become Margaret's most trusted servant and companion. She helped raise all of Margaret's children, most of her grandchildren and was separated from her mistress only by Margaret's death.[25]

In the spring of 1836 Margaret Lea was a teenage school girl at home in Alabama and Sam Houston was the leader of the tumultuous political affairs of Texas. Plots were being made to murder the former Mexican dictator, Santa Anna. Houston was doing everything in his power to protect him. He wrote, "Santa Anna living may be of incalculable advantage to Texas in her present crisis. Santa Anna dead would be just another dead Mexican."[26]

It was time to elect a president for the Republic of Texas. Houston had expressed the opinion that Thomas J. Rusk would make a fine president. However, Rusk's youth was against him and Houston's name was mentioned all over the Republic. Seven days

9

before the election Houston consented to run. He was elected by a tremendous majority.

In Alabama, Margaret no doubt heard the news with more than a little interest. However, she certainly had no thoughts of romantic interest at this time. Among other things she knew that Houston was still married (although it was said in name only) to Eliza Allen of Gallatin, Tennessee. Eliza had still not asked for a divorce and she went by the name of Mrs. Eliza Houston. Many times her family had pressed on both sides for a reconciliation. As late as October 6, 1836, her cousin, John Campbell, wrote to the General: "Some of her friends wanted her to git [sic] a divorce and she positively refused; and said she was not displeased with her present name; therefore she would not change it on this earth; but would take it to the grave with her."[27]

If Houston answered Campbell's letter his reply was not preserved for history. However, to his cousin Bob McEwen he confided that reconciliation was not possible. Houston finally took the initiative, and in 1837, in San Augustine, Texas, the Houstons were finally divorced. The President's petition was presented by his attorneys before District Judge Shelby Corzine. Eliza's lawyers were present too but did not protest the action. Houston still refused to make public the reasons for leaving Eliza, but now he was free.[28]

While Houston was running the affairs of Texas, Margaret was blossoming into a young lady. After attending Professor McLean's School she joined the first class of the newly formed Judson College for young ladies in Marion. Along with others, Margaret's brother Henry Clinton Lea had organized the college and was a member of its board of trustees. Margaret lived with Henry and his wife Serena in their big house on Greensboro Street while she was attending the college. No doubt the Lea family contributed financial help to the young Baptist school.

Margaret played the piano, harp and the guitar, [29] and was developing her literary talent. A Judson teacher said of her, "Margaret will take her place in the galaxy of the great and learned writers of her day."[30] Before she was twenty she had demonstrated a talent for writing poetry. Before her twentieth birthday a number of her earlier poems were published in Alabama newspapers and in the *Mother's Monthly Journal* in Philadelphia. Her interest in writing continued throughout her life.[31]

In Margaret's "Original Album of Poems, Verses, and Diary Entries," many of her poems express her personal thoughts. On June 19, 1839, she wrote a long tribute to her father. It began:

> Beneath a tall and widely spreading tree,
> Beside a cottage door at hush of even,
> A father sat. A young girl clasped his knee,
> And talked with him of God and heaven.

The poem told of her love for him and her grief at his death.

> . . . e'en her father's dying words awhile,
> Lay hushed, but still their memory was not flown,
> For when her spirit sighed to wing its flight,
> From scenes that chained its weary pinions down,
> Then from the clouded past, a beacon light,
> Her father's image rose within her heart,
> And bade the world's soft witcheries depart.[32]

In many of her poems she showed her keen observance of nature. In "Thoughts During a Storm," written on June 23, 1839, she described a hurricane and its aftermath:

> Oh what a night is this! So earth and heaven
> In battle met! Whilst through the heated air,
> In dark confusion wrathful clouds are driven,
> And even now among a lurid glare
> Reveals the trees low bending 'neath the wing
> Of the dread hurricane that sweeps along
> The brightened earth, a furious maddened thing . . . .

She went on to contrast the appearance of the earth when the storm had abated:

> Soft! soft! the rain descends, the clouds do bow
> And weep as if in sorrow for the past.
> The earth looks up in mild forgiveness now,
> No longer fearful of the cruel blast. . . .
>
> And now the moon smiles from a cloudless sky,
> In sympathy upon the flowers beneath,
> That on their softened couches gently lie,
> So lately shrinking from the gale's rude breath.
> Nature thou'rt beautiful and bright again,
> As if no storm had e'er disturbed thy rest,
> In vain its threatened vengeance—all in vain
> Its darkest bolts were hurled against thy breast. . . .[33]

Margaret had many suitors, and at one time the family encouraged her to accept the attentions of a young Baptist minister.[34] The Reverend Dr. W. C. Crane visited Marion in August of 1839 and met the twenty-year-old Margaret. He reported that two of his associates in the ministry were captivated by her charms. He described their meeting: "It is no wonder that she attracted young hearts. Her manner was winning, her appearance fascinating, and her language indicated high intelligence."[35]

None of the gentlemen suited Margaret's fancy, although she had once seemed to favor a young man by the name of Joseph whom she met in the winter of 1837. However, the romance ended when he returned home to Virginia. Just before he left he wrote her a letter, which she saved:

> Just as our acquaintance begins, we are called to part. After beholding only the magnificent outlines of the Temple of Truth, we must shake hands in the vestibule. . . . Shall our acquaintance cease on parting? No—tho distance may separate us and social intercourse never be renewed, the present occasion shall still live

in our memories and meditation shall after receive the pleasures now enjoyed. [36]

No one seems to know why Margaret saved this letter. Perhaps it was just a pleasant memory, but it may have been because of the prophecy with which the letter concluded. Joseph went on to remind Margaret that as the waters of the James and the Cahaba Rivers both flowed into the same great ocean, so the streams of their influence all turned toward eternity and "so may the tree of Life, thru [sic] your instrumentality . . . scatter her leaves for the healing of nations."[37]

The older Leas had by this time established their families. Henry remained in Marion and became a state legislator. Martin and his wife Opphia had moved to Mobile, where he became a successful merchant. Varilla had married Temple's ward, Robert Royston, and they had established a farm near Marion. Vernal left to study law at the University of Georgia. When he returned he brought a wife, Mary, with him. Margaret frequently visited her brothers. In their homes, although she showed no interest in politics, she became socially comfortable with those who did. It was said that when the legislature was in session she was introduced to many distinguished men who visited Mobile for pleasure or business, as well as those who visited Tuscaloosa to make laws or give their suggestions to law makers.[38]

The brothers and Varilla had always been protective toward the younger sisters Margaret and Antoinette. Margaret received their special attention because of her serious nature and frail health. From infancy she had suffered with terrible attacks of asthma. Many times the family had watched as she wheezed and fought for breath, and many times Margaret had called upon her strong religious faith to bring her through dangerous illnesses.[39]

The Reverend Dr. Crane was impressed by Margaret's strong faith. During his visit to Marion in 1839, he saw Margaret often and reported that each time he felt a higher regard for her graces and virtues. He characterized her as "a faithful member of the Marion Baptist Church, and while enjoying with keen zest the pleasures of

13

society, she ever felt and proved that her highest allegiance was to God."[40]

Margaret received much teasing when the vivacious Antoinette married a Mobile merchant, William Bledsoe, on February 12, 1839, only two days after Antoinette's seventeenth birthday. Margaret took the teasing with a smile; she would not think of considering marriage until she was sure she had found the one of her choice. It would not be long before the Bledsoes would be responsible for bringing about the meeting between Margaret and the man who would be that choice, Sam Houston.

---

[1] Marquis James, *The Raven*, (Indianapolis: Bobbs-Merrill, 1929), 258–59.
[2] Joseph Henry Harrison Ellis, *Sam Houston and Related Spiritual Forces*, (Houston: Concord Press,1945), 26.
[3] Jennie Morrow Decker, family story.
[4] James, *The Raven*, 19.
[5] Ibid., 23, 27.
[6] Alfred M. Williams, *Sam Houston and the War for Independence in Texas*, (Boston: Houghton-Mifflin Co., 1893, 9.
[7] Sam Houston,*The Autobiography of Sam Houston*, ed. Donald Day and H. H. Ullom, (Norman: University of Oklahoma Press, 1954), 9.
[8] Some sources erroneously report that it was the thigh wound which never healed. However, family sources agree that the shoulder wound was the serious one, and Houston himself mentions this in letters written in his later years.
[9] James, *The Raven*, 73.
[10] Ibid., 73–75.
[11] Llerena Friend, *Sam Houston, The Great Designer*, (Austin: University of Texas Press, 1954), 23.
[12] James R. Howser and H. Harris, *The Howser Family History*, (n.p.: printed privately, 1986), 21, and W. D. Howser letter to Madge Roberts, July 29, 1991.
[13] Howser and Harris, 21.
[14] M. K. Wisehart, *Sam Houston: American Giant*. (Washington D.C.: Robert B. Luce, Inc., 1962), 84.
[15] Madge W. Hearne, family story.
[16] Hearne Papers, San Antonio, "Notes on the Battle of San Jacinto."
[17] *Commercial Bulletin*, (New Orleans), May 23, 1836.
[18] Hearne Papers, San Antonio, "Sam Houston's Wounds," Dr. P. I. Nixon, n.d.

[19] Margaret states in a letter (Franklin Williams Collection, Huntsville, May 28, 1846) that she is five-foot seven inches tall. Houston's height is estimated to be six -feet three inches based on studies done with one of his crutches by David Wight of the staff of Sam Houston Memorial Museum, Huntsville, Texas, personal communication with author, March 26, 1992.

[20] From a poem by Nettie Houston, "My Father's Picture"; and James, *The Raven*, 30; and Rebecca Hightower, *Houston Chronicle*, April 22, 1923.

[21] Hearne Papers, San Antonio, "The Lea Family."

[22] Ellis, 54.

[23] Hosea Holcombe, *A History of the Rise and Progress of the Baptist in Alabama*, (Philadelphia: King and Baird, 1840), 152.

[24] Hearne Papers, San Antonio, "Temple Lea's Will."

[25] Madge W. Hearne and Marian W. Whittemore, family story.

[26] Sam Houston, *The Writings of Sam Houston*, vol. 1, ed. Amelia Williams and Eugene Barker (Austin: The University of Texas Press, 1943), 264. Sam Houston to the General Commanding Army of Texas, July 26, 1836. (Hereinafter these volumes will be referred to as *Writings*.)

[27] James, *The Raven*, 278.

[28] Wisehart, 325.

[29] Hearne Papers, San Antonio, notes by Maggie Houston Williams.

[30] Meredith Madison, "Margaret Lea Houston," (Master's Thesis, University of Texas at El Paso, 1960), 7, quoting from Mrs. Robert Boling.

[31] William Carey Crane, "Sam Houston's Wife," *The Houston Post*, August 28, 1884.

[32] Madison, 136–37.

[33] Ibid, 139–40.

[34] Hearne Papers, San Antonio, Samuel A . Gordon to Madge W. Hearne, March 7, 1940, Marion, Alabama.

[35] Crane, "Sam Houston's Wife."

[36] Hearne Papers, San Antonio, Joseph _____ to Margaret, March 1, 1837, Marion, Alabama.

[37] Ibid.

[38] Crane,"Sam Houston's Wife."

[39] Marian Williams Whittemore, family story.

[40] Crane,"Sam Houston's Wife."

Chapter II

Last night I gazed long upon our beauteous emblem, the star of destiny, and my thoughts took the form of verse.

Margaret Lea to Sam Houston,
July 17, 1839, Marion, Alabama

Houston's first term as president of the Republic of Texas ended on December 10, 1838, and he returned to private law practice. One of his first projects was to help plan the details of laying out a city to be located at the mouth of the Sabine River near the border of the United States. He was among the stockholders of a development company for Sabine City.[1]

In the spring of 1839, Houston decided to visit the United States to seek capital for Texas enterprises and to buy some blooded horses for himself. When his business was complete he then planned to spend some time with Andrew Jackson in Tennessee. One of his first stops was Alabama, where at the Hickman Lewis stock farm he bought several horses, including a chestnut filly, Proclamation. He paid for his purchases with script from the city of Sabine and made arrangements to have the horses delivered there.[2]

His next stop was Mobile, Alabama, where he called on a local businessman, Martin Lea. Mr. Lea introduced Houston to his brother-in-law, William Bledsoe, a tobacco and merchandise broker, who had capital to invest. Bledsoe expressed interest in the Sabine City project. He confided to Houston that his mother-in-law,

Nancy Lea, was a shrewd business woman and that she had heard of the project and might be interested.

Bledsoe also offered to arrange for General Houston to make some speeches concerning the annexation of Texas and its promising land developments. Martin Lea invited Houston to visit his stately country home, Spring Hill, on the outskirts of Mobile, to meet his mother. When Houston, Bledsoe, and Martin arrived at Spring Hill they discovered that Antoinette Bledsoe and Opphia Lea were having a church social on the lawn in honor of Antoinette's sister, Margaret, and their mother, who were both visiting from Marion.[3]

Houston was introduced to both sisters and promptly became confused. He was immediately attracted to Margaret and confided to another guest, "If she were not already married, I believe I would give that charming lady a chance to say no."

The guest hastily replied, "But that's not Mrs. Bledsoe. That's the older unmarried sister. So you are free to give her that chance, General."[4]

Antoinette, hearing of the remark, took matters in her own hands. Margaret was passing a dish of strawberries. Taking the general by the arm, Antoinette presented him to her sister. He bowed low, took her hand and said, "I'm charmed." That he really was charmed was evident to all those present, who saw that he had eyes for no one else.[5]

Houston left Margaret's side only for his business meeting with her mother. Nancy Lea had recently sold the family plantation in Perry County and expressed interest in investing her money in Texas land, but she would have to see it before she could make up her mind. As soon as the interview with Nancy was completed, Houston returned to Margaret's side. From the garden he picked a carnation (or as they were called in those days, a "pink") and presented it to her. Margaret put it in her hair.

Margaret asked the General if he had fully recovered from his San Jacinto wounds. When he showed a great astonishment at her knowledge, she explained that she had been on the dock in New Orleans three years ago. She did not confide to him at this time, however, that she had been incapable of dispelling the notion that sometime they would meet and that this meeting would somehow shape her destiny.[6]

That evening Margaret played the piano and sang. Years later Margaret's youngest daughter, Nettie Bringhurst, was interviewed and reported how the scene had been described to her by a Mrs. Ketchum, who as a young girl had been present at the Lea home that night. The visitor pictured Margaret as "tall and slender with a queenly bearing dressed in the fluffy tarlton dress of that period . . . seated at the piano, the soft candle light gleaming on her dark hair and mild blue eyes. Immediately upon the entrance of the General their eyes met in a flash of mutual happiness. It was as if only those two were in the room. The others made no effort to claim his attention."[7]

Later in the evening they walked in the moonlit azalea garden. There was a lone star shining brightly in the sky. Houston pointed to it and called it a "star of destiny." He asked Margaret to gaze at it after he was gone and let it remind her of him and the lone star emblem of Texas.[8]

After all the guests had left and Margaret was alone in her bedroom she did exactly that. Then she held the flower that the General had given her. As her candle burned low, Margaret was writing a poem entitled "Lines to a Withered Pink." In the eight stanzas of verse she told how she would cherish the flower because he had given it to her. It began:

Why have I sought thee out—loved flower?
To gaze upon thy radiant bloom?
Or doth some tranquilizing power
Breathe in thy rich perfume?

Tis true, no beauty now doth dwell
Within thy leaflets sere
But—ah—for me a holy spell
Doth ever linger there.

> He placed thee in my hand, that friend
> Who now doth distant roam.
> I took thee—little thinking then
> How dear thou wouldst become.
>
> That joyous eve, upon my brow
> Thy fresh young leaves I wore.
> Thou wert beauteous then tis true, but now
> Poor flower—I love thee more. . . .

The poem concluded:

> Time onward flies and swift advance
> The years when friends are few,
> The years when I shall live perchance
> Like thee to wither too.
>
> Thou sweet memento! Gentle flower!
> Say will he cherish me,
> And love me in that dark hour
> As now I cherish thee?[9]

It would be over a year before Margaret would show him the poem, on their first wedding anniversary.[10]

By Houston's own admission in later life, he had fallen in love at the first sight of Margaret. In a letter to her some time after they were married, he described his feelings on the night they met:

> Twas there, I saw, admired, and loved my Margaret. Our meeting, our jesting, our promenade, our converse, our gazing on the "Lone star," my confession, and the seal of my penitence!! Then our walk to the flower Garden. . . . Oh my Love, all those scenes I recur with extatic [sic] pleasure.[11]

Many varied thoughts must have passed through his mind on this evening as they strolled in the garden. His colorful life had been filled with strife. Personal happiness had always eluded him, and more than anything else he longed for a happy home life and family. It had been ten years since his tragic first marriage had ended, and there had been times when he had paused to consider his hasty decision. Tiana had died several years earlier and he had closed the chapter on his life of exile with the Indians. Houston was now forty-six years old and realized that he was completely charmed by the girl with the violet-blue eyes who was twenty-six years younger than he. He knew she must have led a sheltered life and obviously knew nothing of the hardships of frontier life. Little did Sam Houston know then that under Margaret's beautiful delicacy there was a will stronger than any he had yet encountered, and that Margaret too was falling in love.

Many years later the Reverend William C. Crane, an old family friend, was writing the first biography of Sam Houston. He asked Margaret how she had dared to make such an important decision on such a brief acquaintance, to commit herself to life in a wild country, and to risk unhappiness and misfortune by linking her destiny to a man given to such excesses. Margaret replied to him that "not only had he won her heart, but she had conceived the idea she could be the means of reforming him and meant to devote herself to the work."[12]

She had heard all about his history, and the romance of it fascinated her. The courtly bearing, the gallant and heroic speech, the fund of anecdotes, and the many exciting incidents in his life all conspired to invest Sam Houston with an irresistible glamour. As she debated in her mind, Margaret came to the conclusion that the highest happiness of her life would be in making one of the most remarkable men of the age a happy man in a kind of life to which he was then a stranger [13]

Margaret was swept into action, and she seemed to be possessed with the feeling that it was God's will that she would be an instrument in saving a life that seemed at times to sink to hopeless depths. Her faith was unshaken and she would attempt anything that she believed God wanted her to do.[14]

But this was not the only reason she would agree to become Sam Houston's wife. She was hopelessly in love. Many years later their daughter Nettie asked to hear the story of how her mother and father met. According to family legend Margaret told her the story of the betrothal and the wedding. Nettie inherited her mother's talent for poetry and later wrote a poem to preserve the story Margaret had told her.

Then she told me, in tones like low music,
The story that measured her life,
Her girlhood, its beauty, its triumphs,
Ere the love-crown had made her a wife.

And she painted a picture so vivid,
I fancied it dawned on my view,
Of the evening my father first met her,
When the old life was lost to the new.

She told how her dress, white and spotless,
And the curls of her dark flowing hair,
How her blue eyes, her fresh simple beauty,
Chained his heart in a lifetime of snare.

She told me the scene of betrothal,
In a beauteous garden of flowers,
Of the lovely enchanted Bay City,
Where glided her girlhood's bright hours.

Then she pictured the eve of her bridal,
When leaving behind every tie,
She followed her heart's chosen ruler,
To dwell 'neath a far distant sky.

Then my mother's sweet face kindled proudly,
And she said, in a low earnest voice,
"When I married your father, my daughter,
Of the whole world, I wedded my choice."[15]

In Mobile, business was all but forgotten as Houston spent the next week courting Margaret. Her mother was horrified. While completely charmed by Houston herself, Nancy could in no way condone a romance between her daughter and a man of such questionable character as Sam Houston. His reputation for drinking and swearing was enough to draw opposition immediately. She was also concerned about the differences in their ages and backgrounds. Then the mystery of his first marriage was certainly not in his favor. Finally, Nancy had heard rumors of there being an Indian wife. All this was just too much to merit Nancy's approval.

None of these things mattered to Margaret. Sam Houston had asked her to come to Texas as his wife. Margaret had made a decision; at last she had met her choice. Houston regretfully left her for his trip to the Hermitage to visit Jackson. While there he wrote letters pouring out his love for her. The mails were very slow, and he agonized as he awaited her answer. Patience had never been one of Sam Houston's virtues and now that his heart and soul were aflame he was more impatient than ever. Finally the letter he had been waiting for arrived in the mail.

It was dated July 17, 1839, and was a long letter in answer to the one he had written to her from Nashville. He had promised to write her from Columbus, and she was very disappointed that the letter was never received. She went on to tell him, "However, I have heard from you and the tidings are truly welcome I assure you. My answer may be taken as strong evidence of that, for it is the first I have addressed to any gentleman." She told him that she was happy to be back in the beautiful surroundings of her native country among her childhood friends, but she could not be completely happy "because there are those absent whose station within [her] heart remain[ed] unfilled," and she suffered from "constant dread of severing some link in this beautiful chain." She was writing him from her favorite room in Henry Lea's home, the library, but her mind was not on any of the characters found in the books on the shelves. "My heart is like a caged bird whose weary pinions have been folded for . . . months—at length it wakes from its stupor, spreads its wings and longs to escape." She had not forgotten his words and assured him, "Last night I gazed long upon our beauteous emblem, the <u>Star of my Destiny</u>, and my thoughts took the form of verse, but I will not inscribe them here, for then you might call me a romantic starstruck young lady."[16]

No doubt this is exactly what Houston had hoped she would be. He had told her that she was his Esperanza (Spanish for "the one hoped for"). Margaret told him that the Bledsoes and her mother were planning to go to Texas in the fall but were unwilling for her to make the trip unless the General had been to Marion to visit her home and meet the rest of the family. If he could not make the trip on his way home she told him he would not see "his Esperanza for <u>ages</u> to come."[17]

Houston felt that this letter was an answer to his proposal. Margaret would be his wife, and he hoped they could marry in Mobile. His reply has been lost, but apparently he urged Margaret to meet him in Mobile rather than Marion, pleading as an excuse urgent business in Texas. She replied in a letter addressed to "Dear Sir": "We learn from your letter that it is impossible for you to return by Marion. Your reasons are good, yet we can but regret the necessity of your declining the visit. I stated to you in my last, that it was the wish of myself and relations that you should visit Marion before our departure for Texas. With regard to that our opinions are unchanged." She also told him that she had always depended upon guidance in great measure from her relations, and in this case she would rely entirely on their discretion. As far as his business in Texas was concerned she advised him, "If she [Texas] requires your presence, go without delay! I would scorn to call him friend who would desert his country at such a time. Go[,] and when her cries of oppression are hushed we will welcome you again to my native state. Let the time of your return depend entirely on the state of your country. It is my wish that you should do so."[18]

Nancy Lea was probably hoping that Houston could not make the trip to Marion, for she had no intention of letting Margaret make the trip to Texas, but the General arrived in late August at the home of Margaret's brother, Henry Clinton Lea. He had come by boat to Selma and then ridden horseback across the countryside to Marion.

He brought to Margaret an engagement gift. It was a cameo brooch of his likeness which he had ordered from the Galt Jewelers in Baltimore to be made in Italy. Joyfully Margaret pinned it to her dress and wore it proudly.[19]

Houston visited in the Lea home for several weeks and did his best to charm Margaret's family out of their opposition to the marriage. At some point during the visit he became ill with a bad cold. Nancy insisted that he go to bed until he was fully recovered and ordered two servants seated by the bedside to insure that he remained there. While the General was thus detained Nancy read him selections of the Scriptures which she thought he should hear.[20]

Nancy finally did admit that Houston was one of the most charming and courteous men she had ever met. In spite of her better judgment she could not help liking the man, but she still opposed the marriage. However, nothing her mother could say or do would sway Margaret's convictions. Before the General left, Margaret had promised to become his wife.

Houston returned to Texas where he received the sad news that his law partner, John Birdsall, had died of yellow fever. On a more pleasant note, he learned that his friends in San Augustine had elected him to a term in the Texas House of Representatives. However, he also learned that Houston City would no longer be the capital. It was being moved to the western frontier. The new capital would be named for Stephen F. Austin.[21]

From the new capital Houston shared the happy news of his coming marriage with his friends. To his friend Robert Irion he wrote describing Margaret as a "clever gal" and added, "I hope to show her to my friends as such."[22]

The mails were frequently delayed, but he was never disappointed when he finally received a letter from Margaret. It was always full of love, devotion, and a determination to join him in Texas and make a home for him there. He was overjoyed when the Bledsoes and Nancy Lea finalized plans to come to Texas in the early spring on a business trip. He flooded the mails with letters to Margaret begging her to come with her family and marry him then.

Margaret agreed and named the ship they would take from Mobile to Galveston.[23]

Houston arranged to have "business" in Galveston on the day the ship docked. Rumors were flying all throughout the Republic that the General was waiting to meet his bride. When the vessel anchored in the harbor he took a dory out to board it. A cannon salute was fired from the post on the island. The Bledsoes and Mrs. Lea were on deck, but Margaret was nowhere to be seen. Houston had not counted on the strong will of Nancy Lea. When he asked for Margaret, her mother told him firmly, "General Houston, my daughter is in Alabama. She goes forth in the world to marry no man. The one who receives her hand will receive it in my home and not elsewhere."[24]

Nancy had finally accepted the fact that the marriage would take place, but she was still in control. Margaret had bowed to her mother's wishes. She had written Houston that she would not be making the trip, but the letter was never received. He hid his disappointment and set out to court the favor of Margaret's family. He spared no effort to show his most charming side, and Nancy was greatly impressed with him and with Texas. She and the Bledsoes made a decision. They would make investments in East Texas lands and move to Texas. While her mother and brother-in-law were taking care of business, Margaret was making a wedding dress and working on a trousseau. She wrote to her mother, "I have made me a white satin dress, a purple silk, and a blue muslin. I have not gone to any expense which I thought you would object to."[25]

Margaret was also writing a poem which expressed her feelings about leaving her home and family and journeying to a new place. It was entitled "To Sarah Ann" and was dedicated to Margaret's favorite niece.

> Sweet girl, whenever of early days
> I muse, and recollections roam
> O'er merry childhood's sunlit ways,
> 'Tis then thy gentle image comes.

And point to many a well loved scene,
Far—far removed, but ne'er forgot,
The mount, the stream, the rustic green,
To each prefixed some hallowed spot.

Come hither, let us speak once more,
Of those sweet hours that came to past,
Like fairy dreams, that glimmered o'er
Our paths each brighter than the last.

Ah me! those joyous hours are gone,
And with them many a cherished friend
And now the hour is hastening on
That other ties as dear shall rend.

Yes, I must leave the household band
That e'en in childhood loved me well.
Far—far within the stranger's land,
Midst unfamiliar scenes to dwell.

And yet the beauteous West I love
O'er its broad plains bedecked with flowers
Of glowing buds, the wild deer rove
And sleep within its moonlit bowers.

Farewell e'en now my spirit sighs
To wander where the "Lone Star's" light—
Gleams out from pure cerulean skies
And gilds a land of verdure bright![26]

The wedding was set for May with the date depending on when the groom would arrive. It was to take place in the Henry Lea home in Marion. Margaret began packing the Lea linens and silver she had been given. Among the wedding gifts was a quilt that Nancy had recently made for Margaret to take with her to Texas.[27]

Because his law practice was not bringing in many fees at this time Houston was short on funds. He had to borrow money to finance his trip. He asked his close friend Ashbel Smith to accompany him and take part in the wedding as a groomsman. Smith regretfully had to decline explaining to another friend, "He [Houston] urged me warmly to accompany him and I was willing enough, but Alas, the unsentimental obstacle to my going—I had no funds and I knew the Old Chief had none."[28]

Houston left the affairs of the Texas Republic to others and went to Alabama for his bride. He took a ship to Mobile where he changed to a steamer which would take him to Selma. No doubt Houston recalled his illness upon his last visit to the Lea home and wanted to make sure he could hold his own in a conversation with Nancy. When the boat stopped at Montgomery, the Reverend Dr. William Carey Crane was on the wharf. He later reported that at this time some of the passengers told him that the General had brought a pocket Bible with him "to enable him to hold a biblical conversation with Nancy Lea."[29]

Houston arrived in Marion on May 7, 1840, and registered at the Lafayette Hotel. Two blocks away in a sheltered grove of oak and elm trees on Greensboro Street stood the home of Henry Clinton Lea.[30]

As a member of the Alabama State Legislature, Henry often entertained some of the most important people of Perry County, and as a trustee of Judson College he sometimes offered his home as a meeting place for the Board of Trustees. By the standards of 1840 the house, with its Virginia Colonial architecture, was a mansion. Although greatly changed, it is still standing today.[31] The L-shaped house stood on the right hand corner of an oblong lot of nearly two acres. The first story of brick rose over a semi-basement that was entered by downward steps. The second story was reached by twin stairways starting on the lawn and meeting to form a landing whose door opened into the reception hall. A formal parlor was on the left, and on the right was the large reception room. It was in this reception room that the wedding was planned for May 9, 1840.[32]

The guests had begun arriving and the musicians were ready to play when an incident took place which almost prevented the marriage. Serena and Henry suggested that Houston owed the Lea family an explanation of the failure of his first marriage or else the ceremony could not proceed. Houston was furious but he held his temper and replied that the subject was closed and that he had nothing more to add to what he had already said. He further suggested that if Margaret's family held such a feeling that they might as well "pay the fiddlers" and stop the wedding now.[33]

Henry's son Sumpter was present, and later reported that Houston instructed the family to tell Margaret that "it would be a mockery for me to seek to take leave of her, but please bear this message to her, that amidst all this desolation, my love for her is the holiest thing that was ever in my poor broken heart."[34]

Margaret, suspecting what might be causing the delay, took matters into her own hands. She appeared in the room and nodded to the violinists, who quickly took up their bows. The wedding proceeded without incident. The ceremony was performed by the Reverend Peter Crawford of the Siloam Baptist Church. In reciting her wedding vows, Margaret did not promise to "obey" her forty-seven-year-old groom. For some unknown reason, this word was omitted from the ceremony as she became Houston's wife.[35] Her friend and former teacher at Judson, Sarah Kittrell Goree, was matron of honor, and her two young cousins, Anne Jane and Mary Helm Moffette, were the flower girls.[36]

At what point in history Houston revealed the story of Eliza Allen to Margaret has caused much speculation. Most family sources believe it was before the wedding. Several months later he mentioned it in a letter when he wrote assuring her that what he had told her of the subject "was correct. You may think of the matter— but let it be kept a profound secret—be always guarded. You are 'Houston's Wife' and many would joy to dash our cup of bliss. My joy is in your life!"[37]

Margaret did keep the information "a profound secret" between the two of them until after Houston's death, and it never seemed to be a problem between them. Toward the end of her life she passed the story on to her older daughters. It seems Eliza Allen had been a very young girl when she fell in love. The young man was suffering from consumption and was forced to go to another climate for his health. He died without ever seeing Eliza again. When Eliza was pressured by her family to marry Governor Houston, she agreed even though she felt that she would never get over her first love. Needless to say, Houston was unaware of all this. One night when Houston was away on business, Eliza took out her loved one's letters. Houston returned unexpectedly and found her crying over the letters as she burned them in the fireplace. When Houston demanded the truth, Eliza told him. [38]

Houston asked Eliza why she had married him if she didn't love him. She replied that it was for the position he afforded her of being the governor's wife. At this Houston strode into another room, grabbed a quill, and scribbled out his resignation as governor. He then handed it to her and said, "Here, Madam, is your position!"[39]

Houston biographer Marquis James found in his research that "after General Houston's death she [Margaret] briefly explained that her husband had said that Eliza had confessed to him that she loved another, and to one of Houston's vast pride this was insupportable."[40]

Regardless of what the circumstances of the past marriage were, it never seemed to be a problem between Houston and Margaret. They were devoted to each other and their union, though not free from strife, was destined to be a happy one. It was reported by historian John Henry Brown that Houston had married Margaret Lea, "a lady eminently fitted by sound judgment, the most substantial graces, quiet but sincere affections, aversion to pomp, and of the strongest domestic attachments, to fill the void which must have existed in the recess of his heart in former years."[41]

---

[1] Friend, 93.

[2] Sam Houston, *Writings* vol. 2, 313–14, contract with Hickman Lewis for Blooded Stock, May 10, 1839.

[3] Hearne Papers, "A Short Biography of Margaret Lea" by Maggie Houston Williams. Some sources refer to Spring Hill as the Bledsoe home but family

sources and a Mrs. Ketchum who was present agree that it was the home of Martin Lea.

[4] Jennie Morrow Decker, family story.

[5] Olive Branch White, "Margaret Lea Houston, Wife of General Sam Houston," *Naylor's Epic Century Magazine*, April, 1936, 28.

[6] Madge W. Hearne, family story.

[7] White, 29.

[8] Madge W. Hearne, family story.

[9] Hearne Papers, "Lines to a Withered Pink," May 31, 1839.

[10] Madge W. Hearne, family story. See also Sam Houston Papers,Barker History Center, University of Texas, Madge W. Hearne, Notes. on "Lines to a Withered Pink."

[11] Franklin Williams Collection, Huntsville, Houston to Margaret Houston, n.d., circa 1841.

[12] William Carey Crane, *Life and Select Literary Remains of Sam Houston of Texas*, (Philadelphia: J. B. Lippincott Co., 1885), 253.

[13] Crane, "Sam Houston's Wife," *Houston Post*, 1884.

[14] Ellis, 30.

[15] Hearne Papers, San Antonio, "A Garnered Memory" by Nettie Houston Bringhurst, n.d.

[16] Franklin Williams Collection, Huntsville, Margaret Lea to Sam Houston, July 17, 1839, a first draft. This document uses the phrase "star of my destiny." The actual letter disappeared, but a typescript copy of it at the Sam Houston Memorial Museum, Huntsville,Texas, uses the phrase "star of destiny."

[17] Ibid.

[18] Franklin Williams Collection, Huntsville, Margaret Lea to Sam Houston, August 1, 1839.

[19] Madge W. Hearne, family story. The cameo was inherited by Maggie Houston Williams and is now in the San Jacinto Museum of History, La Porte, Texas. See also donation records of the San Jacinto Museum of History, La Porte, Texas.

[20] Madge W. Hearne, family story. See also Daughters of Republic of Texas, *Fifty Years of Achievement*, (Dallas: Banks Upshaw & Company, 1942), 335.

[21] Wisehart, 344–45.

[22] Robert Irion Papers, Barker History Center, University of Texas, Austin, Houston to Robert Irion, January 27, 1839.

[23] Madge W. Hearne, family story. Houston's letters of this period apparently did not survive.

[24] Jennie Morrow Decker, family story.

[25] Sam Houston Papers, Barker History Center, University of Texas, Margaret to Nancy Lea, May 9, 1840.

[26] Madison, 25. Sarah Ann Royston, also called Sallie, was the daughter of Varilla Lea Royston.

[27] Sam Houston Memorial Museum exhibit, Huntsville, Texas.

[28] Ashbel Smith Papers, Barker History Center, Smith to Radcliff Hudson, June 1, 1840.

[29] Crane , "Sam Houston's Wife," August 28, 1884.

[30] Sam Houston Papers, Barker History Center, University of Texas, Sumpter Lea, untitled manuscript dated Aug. 9, 1912, University of Texas Archives. Sumpter Lea was the son of Henry Lea and Margaret's first cousin.

[31] Frances Youngblood, *Historic Homes of Alabama and Their Traditions*, (Birmingham, Alabama: Birmingham Publishing Company, 1935), 294.

[32] Sumpter Lea, n.p.

[33] James, *The Raven*, 313–14.

[34] Sumpter Lea, n.p.

[35] Franklin Williams collection, Huntsville, Margaret to Houston, February 7, 1842.

[36] Hearne Papers, San Antonio, Dr. Samuel Gordon, president of Judson College, to Madge Hearne. October 13, 1936. The girls were the daughters of Gabriel Moffette, Nancy Lea's brother.

[37] Franklin Williams Collection, Huntsville, Sam Houston to Margaret Houston, September 13, 1840.

[38] Madge W. Hearne, family story handed down by Maggie Houston Williams.

[39] Peggy Everitt. This story was handed down through the family by Nannie Houston Morrow.

[40] James, "Epic Sequel," *American Legon Weekly*, 8 (March 5, 1926): 13.

[41] John Henry Brown, ed., *Encyclopedia of the New West*, (Marshall, Texas: United States Biographical Publishing Company, 1881), 34.

Marriage license of Margaret Lea and Sam Houston.
Courtesy of Sam Houston Memorial Museum, Huntsville, Texas.

The engagement cameo–circa 1839.
Now in the San Jacinto Museum of
History, La Porte, Texas. Courtesy
of Sam Houston Regional Library
and Research Center, Liberty, Texas.
It was purchased from Galt Jewelers
in Baltimore.

Home of Henry Clinton Lea in Marion, Alabama, where Margaret and Sam Houston were married, May 9, 1840. Photographed circa 1939. In the possession of the author.

Earlier Margaret had written her first letter to Sam Houston from this house. On July 17, 1839, she wrote:

"I have taken my seat in the library . . . Now in the early morning it looks out upon a range of wild hills, still slightly obscured by the mists of the night, and in the evening, the sunset rays will beautifully gild their rich verdure."

Earliest known photograph of Margaret Houston, about age twenty-one. Taken in Galveston shortly after her marriage. Courtesy of Sam Houston Regional Library and Research Center, Liberty, Texas.

Chapter III

My mind . . . fixes itself on the bright hour in which we first met and loved. Ah, how sweetly the lone evening star shone upon our village home! . . . there was a strange joy in my heart. . . . I would rather suffer misfortune with him than enjoy prosperity with another.

Margaret to Sam Houston,
December 7, 1840

After the ceremony the Lea family entertained the guests with a reception for the newly married couple. The best family silver and china had been set out on magnificent table linens and the Goree and Lea servants had prepared the refreshments.[1] A group of Margaret's friends had collaborated to write an original ode in honor of the groom which they sang to the tune of "The Old Oaken Bucket." It concluded with a lofty comparison:

Our Washington's name has been hallowed in story,
    As founder of Freedom's retreat in the West.
Another has risen to share in his glory—
    The Texian Patriot—our honored guest![2]

Before leaving for Texas, the Houstons stayed for a few days at the Lafayette Hotel in Marion. Several parties were given in their honor. The town of Marion organized a public dinner which was held adjacent to the Baptist Church in a large oak grove. Houston made a speech to a crowd which filled the church and overflowed outside. Numerous toasts were made by the town officials and dignitaries to Texas, the General, and the newly married couple.

Perhaps the most unusual toast was made by an old friend of Margaret's father. Major Townes, who had been designated "President of the day," brought cheers from the crowd with his eloquent tribute:

> I presume our honored guest will not deny in spite of all his San Jacinto and other victories, that he has been compelled to trail his banner and bow a suppliant knee at the feet of our fair townswoman. I give you therefore, gentlemen, if not of a better man than General Houston, that of one whom he himself will admit to be his "better half,"—the Conqueress of the conqueror—Mrs. Margaret M. Houston.[3]

No doubt Houston enjoyed the toast. In just a few years he would write to a cousin, "You have, I doubt not, heard that my wife controls me, and has reformed me in many respects? This is pretty true."[4]

The Houstons left Marion by carriage and traveled to Mobile, where they took a steamer to New Orleans. Here at almost the exact place where their paths had first crossed, Margaret and Sam Houston boarded the *New York* bound for Galveston and the new frontier of Texas. This ship was a far cry from the *Flora*, on which Margaret had first seen her husband. It was described as "built for strength and the finest work that had ever come out of New York" by another traveller, Mary Austin Holley, who wrote her daughter:

> The boat is so beautiful. . . . The cabin of the *New York* is on the upper deck like the river boats, the whole of it is of mahogany & marble polished like the finest piano—drapery . . . of blue satin damask, & dimity. The windows of painted glass representing the Texas arms. The table china is white, with a blue device in the center of each plate representing the *New York* at sea with the Texas eagle hovering over her. Every article was made express for the boat—ivory knives, polished to the highest degree, & the silver forks & spoons (not German silver) have the steam boat *New York* engraved on them.[5]

Thus the Houstons' marriage began surrounded by grandeur. During the luxurious trip in such a beautiful setting, and while the first breath of romance was still fresh, Margaret seized the opportunity to make clear her views on temperance. Knowing her background and religious beliefs, Houston could not have been completely surprised. Margaret was to learn one of the Houston traits too, when he refused to make her a promise of immediate abstinence, since he feared he might not be able to keep it. He did, however, agree not to drink to excess. That Houston had not abstained completely was shown when, at the last dinner aboard the *New York*, he arose and proposed a toast:

> Ladies and Gentlemen: I wish to give a toast, hoping that all may agree with me and with my sentiments also. I drink to the long and vigorous life of the Republic of Texas, to the wisdom of her rulers, both now and in the future, to the success of all finding homes within her borders, to the happiness and content of her citizens, and last but not least, to the beauty and virtue of her daughters.[6]

While Margaret's ultimate objective was total abstinence, she was prepared to spend much of her lifetime achieving it. Margaret Houston was a patient woman; she knew that she could not accomplish her task overnight, and she was happy to have made a good beginning.[7]

Houston's old friends did not share Margaret's enthusiasm. When his companions in Texas first heard reports that a marriage was being planned, they did not actually believe that it would come about. Ashbel Smith and Barnard E. Bee had begged him not to marry. They argued that his temperament and his habits ill-fitted him for happiness in wedlock.[8] When word was received that the event had occurred, they feared that it would end as disastrously as his first marriage. George Hockley wrote Smith that he feared this marriage would be the General's death warrant, and could well imagine what a second failure would do to Houston.[9] Bee wrote, "I see with great pain the marriage of Genl. Houston to Miss Lea! I had

hoped it would never have been consummated—in all my intercourse with life I have never met with an individual more totally
disqualified for domestic happiness."[10]

But the shy, quiet young lady was to astound her husband's
friends within just a short while. Years later the historian Amelia
Williams wrote that "a happy married life of twenty-three years was
to prove that good and wise men can be poor prophets."[11]

The Houstons reached Texas in June as the *New York* steamed
around the Gulf Coast to give Margaret her first glimpse of the
Republic. She was pleased to discover that it was not unlike the
Alabama shores she had visited many times in her childhood. The
air was filled with the smell of salty sea breezes. Sea gulls were
everywhere. The summer sun sparkled on the blue waters of
Galveston Bay, and then the color changed to a sandy olive as the
ship dodged the sand bars and rounded the island to dock on the
side facing the mainland.

Landing with the Houstons and viewing Texas for the first time
were Margaret's personal servant Eliza and a young black man
named Joshua who had belonged to Margaret's father. Joshua
would become the most trusted Houston servant and would remain
devoted to both Houston and Margaret to the end of their lives.

Antoinette and William Bledsoe, as well as Nancy Lea, had
relocated in Texas and were staying in Galveston, and in late June
the couple visited with Margaret's relatives. During this time they
hired a small boat and sailed across Galveston Bay to Cedar Point.
Here, in 1837, Houston had purchased a tract of land from Tabitha
Harris. On the farthest point which projected out into the bay he
planned to build a home, and he wanted to show it to Margaret. He
had named the place Raven Moor.[12]

At that time there was only a simple one-room cabin, but by
spring he hoped to have a summer cottage completed. Margaret
would be able to furnish it then. His plans had been hindered by his
financial state, a fact of which his bride was ignorant. Until he could
resume his law practice in earnest, Houston lacked the adequate
funds with which to build and furnish a permanent home. Houston
left Margaret in Galveston for a few days while he was away on

business. It was then that he wrote her for the first time since their marriage, "Like one of your old Beaux, I am at a loss how to address you when a Wife!"[13]

The next day he wrote again to tell her that he had received a fee of $1,000, but "if it wou'd detain me from you, I might hesitate as to its acceptance. . . . I can not remain from <u>one to whom I am so much devoted</u>."[14] The following day he continued to tell her how miserable he was without her: "The heart that only throbs for one must be retched when absence separates them."[15]

He was back in Galveston within a few days and the couple made plans to visit Houston City. They went in a small boat up Buffalo Bayou to the former capital. On the short trip they passed by the fields where the Battle of San Jacinto had been fought. The boat passed quite close, and the tree under which Houston had lain wounded as the captured Santa Anna was brought to him could be viewed quite clearly.[16]

The little boat continued on until it reached a small landing on the bayou and Margaret viewed her first sight of the city which had been named for her husband. The main street in Houston City extended out from the landing. On this street were two large hotels, and the building which had served as the former capitol was located about one-fourth of a mile from the landing. Some other streets were built parallel and at right angles to Main Street, but they were chiefly designated with stakes.[17]

All of the important Houstonians were eager to entertain the General and his lady. The first party that Margaret was invited to in Houston City took place in the home of Colonel Williamson. To Margaret's horror, she discovered that her trunks containing her best clothes had not yet arrived. She had with her only two calico dresses, one of which she was obliged to wear to the party. The other ladies were dressed in their best finery, but the twenty-one-year-old Margaret was described by one guest as being "as regal in calico as if she had been crowned in cloth of gold."[18]

It was possibly during this visit that Margaret was introduced to many Texans who would become close friends for many years, including John and Eugenia Andrews, James and Ellen Reily, and

Colonel George and Catherine Flood. After a short stay in Houston City, the couple began a trip to the little town of San Augustine in the redlands of east Texas. It was from here that the General had been elected to the Texas House of Representatives and it was here where he had set up his law office. On route the couple stopped at Nacogdoches. No doubt they made a striking appearance. Although Margaret was five-foot seven-inches tall, she would have appeared tiny on the arm of her towering husband. Margaret's natural warmth and genuine pleasure at meeting her husband's old friends completely won over the people.[19]

Ashbel Smith was forced to admit that perhaps his earlier opinions were wrong when he saw an apparent change in his old friend. He wrote a description of Houston to Barnard Bee:

> His health is excellent, as good or better that I have ever seen it. ...[he] is a model of conjugal propriety. I had dreadful misgivings as to the propriety of his taking this step—thus far I have been most agreeably disappointed. His health and ways are infinitely mended. Will it last? I always hope for the best.[20]

Hockley agreed and was astonished by the General's total abstinence, commenting that he drank only cold water even though liquor was plentiful. Hockley noted that Houston did not drink even when Margaret was not with him. He wrote Smith, "All agree that if permanent reformation <u>can</u> be effected his estimable wife will succeed in doing so."[21]

In Nacogdoches they attended many barbecues, dinners, and meetings where Houston spoke. It was here that Margaret had her first glimpse of what it was like to be the wife of a public official. She was also exposed to her first taste of raw frontier humor. At one party she was introduced to N. D. Walling, who asked, "Mrs. Houston, have you ever been in Shelby County?" When Margaret answered in the negative, Mr. Walling suggested, "You ought to go there, Madam. General Houston has forty children in Shelby County." After a decided pause while Margaret looked questioningly at her husband, Mr. Walling continued, "That is forty children named after

40

him." The General good naturedly suggested that he would be obliged if Mr. Walling would connect his sentences more closely.[22]

While the Houstons were visiting in east Texas, Antoinette and William Bledsoe were in the process of making a new home just outside the town of Grand Cane. Here on the Trinity River they hoped to establish a sugar plantation. When Margaret became ill with malaria toward the end of the summer, Houston took her there to recuperate. He had to attend to business matters, but he wrote her from Crockett that he grew more lonely each day: "To see you engrosses my greatest desires."[23]

A week later he wrote from San Augustine that he felt he was deprived of his "<u>better part</u>," and that he was as miserable as if she "were across the ocean." He had begun to worry that business would infringe upon their domestic happiness:

> I never did realize the hope while single that I wou'd find in a wife a perfect companion and one who wou'd be capable by her wisdom and prudence to sustain me, or one who wou'd endear life to me and blot out the [sorrows] of the past. I deplore the situation of our country that requires my absence from you. . . . I am inclined to believe that public station will not promote our individual happiness.[24]

The plan was for Margaret to return to San Augustine as soon as her health would permit. The Bledsoes would accompany her, but Houston was worried about their safety on the trip. He sent a list of equipment they would need and cautioned Margaret that she and Antoinette must "get out at all bad places." He instructed her to tell Captain Bledsoe to "inquire at Cincinnati for the nearest and best road when he crosses the River." He told her that he had never passed any difficult part of the road without feeling solicitude for her safety.[25]

Margaret received letters from her husband, but because of poor postal service, it was very difficult to get hers out to him. Houston wrote suggesting that Bledsoe try to find someone traveling East with whom they might send letters instead of using the mail, which was uncertain and not to be relied upon. His letter had been brought by an old friend from Tennessee, Mr. Vance, who also brought Margaret one hundred dollars in Texas money, and Houston's regret that he could not send her a million in gold. He was anxious to see her and wrote, "My affections burn to see you. You are the light of my path; and the only being that can . . . cheer my heart."[26]

On September 7, 1840, Houston was re-elected to serve in the Fifth Congress of Texas, and a few days later he received his first letter from Margaret which told him that she was not able to make the trip. He received the news with great relief. "It was best that you shou'd not come. Indians are killing people within 28 miles of Nacogdoches residing on the main road by which you wou'd be compelled to travel. . . . Wait for my return with patience—my entire love is with you." His return was being delayed as he had been offered some very large fees for a court case, and they needed all that he could make. The money he had sent by Vance was all that he had—"the last and only cent."[27]

Houston planned to give most of the fees to Margaret for expenses for the Cedar Point home. Nancy Lea was such a good manager that Margaret had suggested she go to Cedar Point and oversee the hands, as word had reached the family that the workers were "doing no good." When Nancy boarded the steam boat for Galveston, she was surprised to find Dr. Smith on board. The doctor wrote the news to Houston with the promise that he would give assistance and protection to Mrs. Lea while she was there.[28]

Rumors about Houston's conduct had begun to reach Margaret. It was believed that some had been started by Memucan Hunt, an old Houston enemy. Stories reached Margaret that Houston had again been drinking to excess. Hastily she wrote him what she had heard. Houston had never minded criticism, true or not, but they had only been married for five months, and he was fearful of Margaret's reaction to slander.[29]

He answered her saying:

My Love, I do sincerely hope that you will hear no more slanders of me. It is the malice of the world to abuse me, and really were [it] not that they reach my beloved Margaret, I would not care one picayune—but that you should be distressed is inexpressible wretchedness to me! . . . do be satisfied . . . if you hear the truth you shall never hear of my being on a 'spree.'

He went on to assure her:

Every hour that we are apart only resolves me more firmly not again to be separated from you. . . . This morning while the chill was upon me, I felt as though I would yield everything and fly to you.[30]

Houston's letters during the next few weeks revealed the personal agony he was suffering. Although desperate to be with Margaret he could not afford to abandon the legal fees he was earning. He wrote Margaret that every day seemed like an age, and that he felt miserable not being able to share his feelings in person. He promised that he would not "wait an instant longer here, than what duty to you and myself will compel me to stay." He had begun to have a few regrets about staying in politics, "Were it not that the election was over I shou'd not run. I can not do more than I have done for Texas, and you wou'd be better satisfied to see me at home." He also cautioned her to ignore any rumors which she might have heard or might hear in the future. "Should you regard them, you will be miserable and I must be forever destroyed in my hopes and happiness."[31]

Houston was detained by business for a few days longer than he had planned. He wrote Margaret that "a trial is now before the court of great importance, and I am the leading counsel in the case. . . . My love, I wou'd give millions to see you at this moment." He assured her that he would indulge in no shade of intemperance.[32]

The next day he received a letter from Bledsoe informing him that Margaret was seriously ill and weakened from malaria. He wrote to Margaret promising to leave in four days. He lamented the fact that "Bledsoe thinks that I have nothing to do but to mount my horse to start from this section of the country." He continued, "I wish that I had never left you,—I wou'd have eschewed ten thousand pangs of anguish and wou'd have been more happy, no matter what my losses might have been!"[33]

Houston reached Grand Cane by mid-October. When Margaret was well enough to travel, she and her mother went back to Galveston where Mrs. Lea had rented a home in the spring of 1840. Margaret would remain here with her for the winter. Houston left his twenty-one-year-old bride and traveled alone to Austin for the Fifth Congress.

Margaret and her mother stopped in Houston City, where Margaret wrote to her husband that if she could only see him she would throw her arms around him and tell him "again and again how much I love you." She reminded him that "there is a heart whose every fibre is entwined around you." She told him of her loneliness, and that the world was cold and desolate without him. She expressed her hopes for their future:

> Perhaps the day will soon come when dreary distance shall not thus intrude between us, but each hour shall bring its own bright joy, and day after day shall pass on and find me still with him I love, gazing fondly upon him, and listening to his soft endearing voice and __, will you finish the picture, Love? A thousand fancies are flitting across my mind, but you will readily imagine what they are. [34]

Houston wrote frequently and his letters were filled with his devotion and his loneliness at being away from her. "No mortal can apprehend how much I love you and the anxiety which I cherish to see you."[35]

Margaret replied by telling him how much she missed him:

My mind . . . fixes itself on the bright hour in which we first met
and loved. Ah how sweetly the lone evening star shone upon our
village home! I trembled to think that there was one dearer to me
than all the hallowed ties of kindred . . . yet there was a strange
joy in my heart . . . I thought not of disappointment except to
know and feel that I would rather suffer misfortune with him than
enjoy prosperity with another.[36]

Houston continued to worry about the effect of rumors being
circulated about him. He again warned Margaret not to believe the
falsity of idle reports which might reach her, and assured her that
the only pleasure he had was in reading her letters over and over
again. "You will believe this when I tell you, that all my evenings and
nights are passed in my room! To be sure I have much company, but
they are sober men, and my room is a dry one, for there is [sic] no
spirits in it."[37]

He lamented the fact that there were "two General Houstons" in
Austin at that time. Felix don Houston was in town, and when it had
been reported "Gen'l Houston was on a spree last night," it was often
the case that Sam Houston was home "in his bed." His shoulders
were broad, but he worried that such reports would reach Margaret's
ears.[38]

Houston wrote that his room, besides being dry, was also a
lonely one, because: "I wou'd rather be with you than to wear a
crown or wield a scepter without thee!" He sought to calm any fears
she might have for his safety: "I have many assailants, but do not
be distressed at the news!"[39]

What he did not tell her was that he had narrowly escaped death
two nights before when one of the "assailants," a Colonel Jordan of
the late Federal Army, had come at him with an axe. Adolphus
Sterne reported in his diary that had he not interfered, General
Houston would probably have been killed.[40]

Houston did acknowledge to Margaret that, although he wanted
her with him, it was best that she had remained behind because of

the deplorable living conditions in a city that he detested. On January 18, 1841, he wrote her that it was snowing and firewood was scarce. Although he had a large fire, it was so cold that he could hardly write, and he had to keep his ink beside the fire or it would freeze.[41]

He described his room as "less comfortable than a stable." While he was paying high for board and lodging, he was compelled to lie under his own blankets—even his saddle blanket.[42] As for the city itself, he described it as a place "savages wou'd not live in!" However, history would prove his prophecy wrong when he wrote, "As a city its days are number'd and its glory will pass away!"[43]

Houston was longing to see his bride and wrote, "How fondly wou'd I fly to you, were it not that duty detains me, and were I to leave I might be regarded as a deserter from the interest of my country!"[44] He reported his fears for the country and the "fuss" being caused by "panic makers" who were urging an invasion of Mexico:

> To hear all the fearful talks of war wou'd make the sweet blood of your gentle heart curdle, and run chills thro' your veins. . . . Texas at this time is in a worse dilemma than it was on the 20th of April 1836. . . . We are so poor as a nation that we can not procure stationary [sic]. How then can we invade a nation with mines and eight million souls?[45]

On January 19, 1841, Houston wrote Margaret that he feared for "the ability of our Government! But Texas must be saved!!!"[46] A few days later he explained that out of forty members in the House of Representatives, there were only seven who had served in the former Congress. What was worse, many members had not even been in Texas for two years:

> This is a strange conviction of things. Men ignorant of the history, wants, and facilities, are to determine what has to be done for its benefit and salvation. . . . I always believed that Texas wou'd be capable of achieving her Independence, but I doubted the capac-

ity of those into whose hands the Government might be confided to sustain free institutions. This I now realise! The universal distrust in the administration [is] prognosticating its downfall. It can not remain—It must sink or dissolve![47]

No doubt Margaret could see where their path was going and probably did not rejoice when her husband let it be known that he was thinking of running for the presidency: On December 17, 1840, Houston had written her, "Oh yesterday I was dared to become a candidate for the presidency." He had, he told her, made the mental reservation only to do so if she was willing. "Do not let what I have said induce you to yield any objections which you may entertain. For myself, I have flung away ambition. I wish to retire to quiet and rural life where I can live and love my dear, dear Margaret."[48]

Houston's letters during this period clearly show that he was torn between two loves—Texas and Margaret. Unable to sleep one night, he wrote to her:

> Thru my window I beheld the solitary moon coursing thru the sweet Heavens. I gazed upon it with melancholy pleasure! I contemplated the blue canopy, and smiled upon the bright stars! (for you know why I love them!!!) . . . they all presented the purest lustre and . . . such is the pure association in which the Wife of Houston should appear! His beloved and adorable Margaret. . . . You are the beacon light of happiness!!! You are a talisman of life to me! and I cherish you in my very heart's core![49]

The same thoughts were in his mind on the next day when he wrote of the trip to the United States when he first met her and "when I learned from you to love the bright star of evening." He described his feelings as he gazed at "their" star:

> Oh, how bright and beautifully did it shine on last night! I contemplated its purity and fancied that I again felt your gentle pressure upon my right arm! But when I was wrapped in thought and my soul was all fire, I realized that I was far distant from my

beloved Margaret. I hate this common world, and only wish that I cou'd enjoy a world where <u>you</u> wou'd be the bright and only orb to which my eye wou'd turn.[50]

Margaret may have been expecting a baby by this time. Houston's letters during December hint at the possibility. On Christmas Eve he alluded to it: "In your <u>situation</u>, my love, I feel the most intense anxiety to be with you, and sustain you!"[51] In letters a few days before he had expressed regret that she was not well, but pointed out:

> I hope when the spring renders its mild and genial influences that many blessings . . . will come with it! Oh how tender are the anticipations of future hopes and joys, and <u>little cares</u>!!![52]

> I felt some little regret as you were not well, but as you said that your illness was not serious, but to be "expected" I felt not so much distressed as I otherwise wou'd have done. . . . From day to day, I read and peruse your letters. They are to me a solace, and when I peruse them, I feel, at moments, as tho' I were in sweet communion with you. . .[53]

With the departure of her husband Margaret's spirits had sunk to the lowest level since they had been married. The Texas coast was experiencing a severe winter storm, which was also contributing to Margaret's depression. On January 18, 1841, she wrote to Houston:

> It is a gloomy day, cold dark clouds are hovering above this city and the streets are covered with ice. . . . When I look back over the long sundry days that have passed since you departed, I can scarcely realize my own identity or believe that the pale melancholy face that the glass reflects is the same [one that] a few weeks ago was the happy wife of Houston and blessed with his society.

She was making an effort to raise her spirits by thinking of the future that awaited them at Cedar Point:

> Then . . . how happy will we be in that sweet place! You shall assist me in planting my flowers and training my vines and we will wander through those sweet groves and be as happy as the spirits of some enchanted isle.

She expressed the hope that he was not vexed with her for urging him so much to come home. She assured him, "Do not let the fear of meeting a moping wife detain you from me, for I can not be sad when you are with me."[54]

Much of Margaret's sadness was probably due to her bouts with malaria and bronchitis and the fact that a tumor discovered in her breast over a year ago was growing.[55] On January 27, 1841, she wrote of her regrets at complaining of ill health:

> If you have rec'd my letters, I fear that you are vexed at my urgent entreaties for you to come home. You must not be, my Love, for indeed, I am very lonely without you. I ought to have known, however, that it would disturb you and that the prudent course would have been to conceal my illness & low spirits from you. I confess that selfishness and the desire of being with you prompted me against my better judgment to tell you everything. But my husband will surely forgive this weakness which originated in devoted love for him!

She went on to tell him how much his letters helped to raise her spirits, but the letter also shows that the severe strain of such a long separation was taking its toll:

> My love, do write to me oftener. I am so happy when I get a letter from you! But when days & weeks pass away without one cherishing word, my heart feels as if it would burst with grief. Oh shall I ever be with you again and see you and hear you speak! I shall be wild with joy. I am sure if my heart was probed at this

time, there would not be found much patriotism in it, for I almost
hate the duties that keep you from me.[56]

This letter had been written on the anniversary of her father's
death, and on the outside of the envelope Margaret acknowledged
that "this day always brings to me a loneliness of heart that nothing
can dissipate."

The next day Margaret wrote a poem entitled "Musings" which
expressed her feelings of deep despair. She wrote of how her love
of her husband had rescued her from the throes of depression:

> Oh I would linger yet awhile
> Upon the green earth's shore
> The stream of death is dark and wild
> Its dismal waters roar.
>
> Yet in my heart that scene of gloom
> No terror can awake
> Nor is it earth with all its bloom
> That draws my spirit back.
>
> No, there's an eye that fondly beams
> Upon me in my sleep,
> A form beloved that haunts my dreams
> I think on him and weep.
>
> Oh I would linger with him yet,
> Who knows the dark snares now
> That may his lonely path beset
> The grief, the tearless woe!
>
> Yes, I would linger yet awhile
> His lonely heart to cheer,
> And break the artful tempter's wile
> That would his soul ensnare.[57]

When he received her poetry, Houston wrote that he had "taxed" his own muse, but "it was all in vain." He knew that she would prefer prose and wrote her he had exhausted all his "rhetoric of love" in courting her:

> At all events, I have used none since! Yes I have. I have courted you ever since, and wish very much to make my personal address to you again. Oh the beautiful "soft things" that I propose to say to you will make you smile prettily. You will think you are again a Belle! You are my Belle of all events. . . .

His "prosing" continued with this assurance: "My feelings are more tender, and my admiration as vivid as it was the first evening that we met in Sommerville." He described his feelings of that night:

> These were days of vast idleness . . . but they were to me days of hope and happiness. 'Twas there I saw, admired and loved my Margaret. Our meeting . . . our gazing of the "Lone star," my confession. . . . Then our walk to the flower Garden. . . . Oh my Love all those scenes I recur with [ecstatic] pleasure. You too, may sometimes think upon those days with pleasure and delight. We may yet enjoy days . . . equally pleasing to us mutually!!![58]

As Houston grew more lonely, his letters expressed his feelings at being apart from Margaret:

> Oh! but I am weary of public life. How hateful are even its honors! I feel my love, that I can only be happy when I will be with you. I feel my only love, as tho' I cou'd only be calm, intelligent, and happy when I cou'd hear your voice and enjoy the admonition of your wisdom! I wou'd then be a rational, cheerful, and happy man.[59]

On January 14, 1841, he wrote Margaret that to see her "cheerful, smiling and approving my acts and conduct" and to make her happy was all he desired. He cut the letter short lest she think he was intending to court her again, telling her, "One courtship and eternal love! This is my motto."[60]

A week later he was again writing a love letter:

The sun is setting over our beautiful western hills. The day has been mild, and the evening is serene, and the sunset is calm and sweet! I turn my face to the east when I worship because my Margaret is there! My heart turns to the smiles of my Margaret, as the fire worshipers [sic] turned to render their homage to the centre of light.[61]

On January 31, 1841, he wrote Margaret, "You are my sum and substance of existence. You are my leading star! But now my love, you are the lone star of Texas." His letter went on to explain the comparison:

I find that every thing here changes more or less except my love of you, and that you will find fellowed my one object only, and that is North stars. It was the only comparison that Shakespeare cou'd find for the decision of Julius Caesar! So I chuse [sic] to compare my love of you![62]

Two days later he made another comparison when he wrote her:

My Love! It really seems to me if I do not see you soon that I will become crazy. Even now, I hardly know what I write. I do know what I feel. I feel that I am the husband of Margaret, and that I do love her almost to madness. Certainly delirium! Nor do I wish to see the day when I shall love her less. The passion flower blooms but once in the season. So I am doomed to love but once in the season of life.[63]

Houston continued to write frequently. As he explained,

I would not write to you so often as I do were it not for two reasons. One is that my love can only be gratified by communing with you!! . . . The next is that you . . . might suppose that I was on "<u>spree</u>" and could not write you.[64]

He continued to assure Margaret that he was not drinking, but he worried about false rumors reaching her. He sent her a newspaper with the comment:

> You will be amused at the various slanders against me . . . Tis a source of great distress to me that you may hear so many <u>fibs</u> upon me! that you will in your present situation be distressed, and it may influence your happiness. . . . If I could only be with you I would be the happiest of men.[65]

A few days later he wrote that he had attended a wedding reception and drank one cup of coffee but not even one glass of wine. He explained:

> I find that total abstinence will make me all that I ever was in point of health and constitution. . . . But there is more than this to be considered. The feelings of my dearly beloved Maggy—whose only dread is that I may abandon myself at some time to intemperance . . . <u>when we meet you will be satisfied</u>![66]

In another letter Houston gave Margaret the news that his health and energy, since he had quit drinking, had been restored "to what it was six years ago." He gave her his reason for abstaining: "The first is you demand it, and my first objective is to see you happy. It is not that you demand it in words, but the sacred relations which bind me to you demand this much of me!"[67] He wrote that he greatly regretted the weakness from his earlier years:

> It plagues me much when I reflect that my habits in other days shou'd have been such as to require double caution at this period of life. 'Tis past, and let it go! . . . My health is restored and my colour is returning![68]

Houston had also written to Margaret earlier that he was controlling his habit of swearing, which he knew had caused her grief. To this she replied:

> Dearest, one portion of your letter gives me more pleasure than any others. It was that you were striving to rise above the dreadful practice of swearing. Oh continue those efforts! I entreat you Love, by all the sacred happiness we have enjoyed together . . . do not profane the name of him who has been so merciful to us. . . . And oh do not in return ask his name as an expression of anger or to embellish the unjust![69]

It was approaching the time for Texas to elect a new president and Houston's name was being mentioned as a candidate. He had been evasive because he wanted to discuss it first with Margaret. He sent her a newspaper showing that he had not yet consented to run. He enclosed it with a letter:

> The affections and happiness of my endeared Margaret are more to me than all the Geegaws of ambition, or the pageantry of Royalty. Shou'd she desire me to do so, I will consent but not otherwise. My love must decide. And let her regard her own happiness. . . . The determination of my Love I will abide by.[70]

Margaret made a decision which established a pattern she would follow for the rest of their marriage. Although she would have much preferred to have him all to herself, she realized she could not place any limitations on her husband's political career. She would never directly stand in his way.[71]

The legislative session ended the first week in February and Houston hurried back to Margaret. They had been apart for six months. Together they journeyed to Galveston and then to Cedar Point to check on the progress of the house. Margaret made one request. She wanted a grove of oak trees planted and this was done. Since the cottage would not be finished until late spring, they visited with Nancy Lea. Here Houston hoped that the sun and salty bay breezes would help improve Margaret's condition, weakened by malaria as well as the chronic asthma from which she suffered.[72]

Margaret remained in Galveston with her mother while Houston traveled to East Texas on business. He was in San Augustine when he received the unhappy news that there would be no baby. Margaret had been very ill and Nancy sent for Dr. Hawkins. On April 1, 1841, Margaret wrote that the doctor "seems to think from my appearance that it is all a mistake about my situation." She was worried that her illness might interfere with Houston's law practice and continued,

> I hope you will not be uneasy about me . . . [here the letter is torn] your absence or leave your business unfinished on my account for if things should result as we first anticipated, I shall do doubt have every necessary attention. I trust therefore that your mind will be free and undisturbed about me.[73]

In early April, 1841, Houston was once again nominated for the presidency of the Republic of Texas. While he was gone Margaret busied herself getting things ready for the move to Cedar Point. She wrote to her husband that she had "been busily employed in preparing our things for house-keeping (for I shall not consider myself a housekeeper until we get to our own house) and that is the most agreeable amusement I can have at present." She wondered if he "could possibly be as anxious to get settled" as she was.[74]

In the same letter she enclosed the poem she had written in his absence. It was entitled "My Husband's Picture."

Dear gentle shade of him I love,
   I've gazed upon thee til thine eye
In liquid light doth seem to move,
   And look on me in sympathy!

And oh that smile! I know it well.
   It minds me of the eve in May,
When soft the rising starlight fell
   Upon the flowers at close of day.

And first my trembling lips did own
    Thy love returned, that holy hour.
Sure Nature smiled in unison,
    Through every tree and vine and flower.

As now I gaze upon that form,
    Against those clouds of threatening mien,
In bold relief, as if no storm,
    Could ever scathe that brow again.

An image starts within my mind,
    As if a shadow from the past,
On some sweet dream of olden time,
    Has suddenly my heart o'ercast.

Yes—yes, it must be so! The same
    Proud form of majesty, the one
That o'er my girlish vision came,
    And that my heart hath loved alone.[75]

When Houston returned from San Augustine, he wrote his friend Robert Irion, "I found my wife with chills and fevers and she is worse. I hope to leave in a few days for the 'Point'." He also added the sad postscript, "No Name-sake."[76]

In June of 1841, the Houstons moved into their home at Cedar Point. It was a two-room house with a lean-to and a separate unfurnished shed for the servants. It was meant to be a summer cottage, very plain, but it was their first home and would become a favorite with the Houston children in later years. Margaret disliked the name "Raven Moor" and decided to call her home "Ben Lomond." At last she was able to take over the role of homemaker. It would become Margaret's primary interest, and she would shun the public eye for the rest of her life, content to be in the shadow of the man she idolized.[77]

The cottage faced a beautiful view of Galveston Bay. There was excellent spring water and the salt air seemed to improve Margaret's health. The furniture which Margaret had brought from Alabama was trucked overland from Galveston by ox cart, along with some pieces that Nancy Lea had contributed. Houston bought a few pieces with money he had collected from legal fees. A bed arrived with a mattress filled with Spanish moss. Margaret had brought her guitar and the piano was on the way from Alabama.[78]

Houston was short of money, but he concealed this fact from his wife, not wishing to put a damper on her obvious happiness with her new home. The new furnishings had taken all of his ready cash, and he had been forced to borrow $500 from William Harding, an old friend in Nashville. He was worried about repaying the debt and on July 17, 1841, wrote of his regrets:

> I have upward of twenty-five thousand dollars due me and some of it for years and I can not collect as much as will pay one fourth of my land Tax! . . . I hope soon to be able to pay all my cash debts. If any person in the meantime should be coming to Texas, in whom you can confide, send the note if you think well of it, and I will let you have property (warranted) at any price rather than not pay you![79]

A few days later he wrote to Samuel Williams that by the 15th of August he hoped to set out for San Augustine and remain until court was over. There he hoped to collect some money owed him. As he explained it, "I must have it." In the meantime he asked Williams for a loan of sixty or eighty dollars to purchase a one horse buggy and some trunks. He explained that he would like to go to Galveston, but "a want of cash forbids me."[80]

Margaret seemed unaware of the concerns Houston was facing. She was completely happy in their bay home and expressed her feelings in a poem entitled "Ben Lomond."

> Yes dearest, we are happy here
>   In this sweet solitude
> Of ours, no heartless ones come near
>   Or tiresome scenes intrude.

The Mock-bird on our green yard tree
   Sings through the live-long night,
And greets the moon, his heart less free
   Than ours, his hopes less bright!

At eve beside our cottage door
   We watch the sky's last hue
And listening to the ocean's roar
   Our thoughts the day review.

Would that we thus might ever be,
   Far from the world's dark snares!
Mid nature's wildwood purity,
   Untrammelled by earth's cares![81]

All too soon Margaret would find out that it was not the fate of the bride of Sam Houston to be "far from the world's dark snares" and "untrammelled by earth's cares."

---

[1] Sam Houston Papers, Barker History Center, University of Texas, Austin, Sumpter Lea, August 9, 1912, n.p.

[2] *Marion Herald*, May 16, 1840.

[3] Joan Hartwell, "Margaret Lea of Alabama, Mrs. Sam Houston," *The Alabama Review* 17 (October 1964): 276.

[4] Fran Dressman, "Victorian Lady Tames Texas Hero," *Beeville Bee-Picayune*, August 21, 1986.

[5] Mattie Austin Hatcher, *Mary Austin Holley*, (Dallas: Southwest Press, 1933), 79.

[6] Annie Doom Pickrell, *Pioneer Women in Texas*, (Austin: The Steck Company, 1929), 304.

[7] Franklin Williams and Madge W. Hearne, family story.

[8] Amelia Williams, *Following General Sam Houston*, (Austin: The Steck Company, 1935), 148.

[9] Ashbel Smith Papers, Hockley to Smith, June 1, 1840.

[10] Ibid., Bee to Smith, June 5, 1840.

[11] Amelia Williams, 148.

[12] Jewel Horace Harry, "History of Chambers County," Master's Thesis, University of Texas, 1940.

[13] Franklin Williams Collection, Huntsville, Houston to Margaret, June 30, 1840.

[14] Ibid., Houston to Margaret, July 1, 1840.

[15] Ibid., Houston to Margaret, July 2, 1840.

[16] Madge W. Hearne, family story.

[17] Hatcher, 70.

[18] *Houston Post*, March 26, 1936.

[19] Wisehart, 361.

[20] Ashbel Smith Papers, Smith to Bee, July 27, 1840.

[21] Ibid., Hockley to Smith, August 17, 1840.

[22] Friend, 98. A later version of the same incident was credited to Colonel John Forbes of Nacogdoches, and an Indian version of the same story was also told *(Houston Press*, April 17, 1924).

[23] Franklin Williams Collection, Huntsville, Houston to Margaret, August 22, 1840.

[24] Ibid., Houston to Margaret, August 28, 1840.

[25] Ibid.

[26] Ibid., Houston to Margaret, September 4, 1840.

[27] Ibid., Houston to Margaret, September 13, 1840.

[28] Ibid.

[29] Wisehart, 362.

[30] Franklin Williams Collection, Huntsville, Houston to Margaret, September 23, 1840.

[31] Ibid., Houston to Margaret, September, 1840.

[32] Ibid., Houston to Margaret, October 3, 1840.

[33] Ibid., Houston to Margaret, October 4, 1840.

[34] Ibid., Margaret to Houston, November 10, 1840.

[35] Ibid., Houston to Margaret, December 3, 1840.

[36] Ibid., Margaret to Houston, December 7, 1840.

[37] Ibid., Houston to Margaret, December 12, 1840.

[38] Ibid., Houston to Margaret, December 17, 1840.

[39] Ibid., Houston to Margaret, December 9, 1840.

[40] Harriett Smither, ed.,"Diary of Adolphus Sterne," *Southwestern Historical Quarterly*, 31(July 1927), 80.

[41] Franklin Williams Collection, Huntsville, Houston to Margaret, January 18, 1841.

[42] Ibid., Houston to Margaret, January 22, 1841.

[43] Ibid., Houston to Margaret, January 25, 1841.

[44] Ibid., Houston to Margaret, January 7, 1841.

[45] Ibid., Houston to Margaret, January 12, 1841.

[46] Ibid., Houston to Margaret, January 19, 1841.

[47] Ibid., Houston to Margaret, January 22, 1841.

[48] Franklin Williams Collection, Huntsville, Houston to Margaret, December 17, 1840.
[49] Ibid.
[50] Ibid., Houston to Margaret, December 18, 1840.
[51] Ibid., Houston to Margaret, December, 24, 1840.
[52] Ibid., Houston to Margaret, December 17, 1840.
[53] Ibid., Houston to Margaret, December 22, 1840.
[54] Ibid., Margaret to Houston, January 18, 1841.
[55] Ibid., Houston to Margaret, September 13, 1840; December 14, 1840; n.d., circa January, 1841.
[56] Ibid., Margaret to Houston, January 27, 1841.
[57] Madison, 33.
[58] Franklin Williams Collection, Huntsville, Houston to Margaret, n.d., circa January, 1841.
[59] Ibid., Houston to Margaret, January 8, 1841.
[60] Ibid., Houston to Margaret, January 14, 1841.
[61] Ibid., Houston to Margaret, January 22, 1841.
[62] Ibid., Houston to Margaret, January 31, 1841.
[63] Ibid., Houston to Margaret, February 2, 1841.
[64] Ibid., Houston to Margaret, December 31, 1840.
[65] Ibid.
[66] Ibid., Houston to Margaret, January 16, 1841.
[67] Ibid., Houston to Margaret, n.d., circa January, 1841.
[68] Ibid., Houston to Margaret, January 26, 1841.
[69] Ibid., Margaret to Houston, January 3, 1841.
[70] Ibid., Houston to Margaret, February 3, 1841.
[71] Madge Williams Hearne, family story.
[72] Ibid.
[73] Franklin Williams Collection, Huntsville, Margaret to Houston, April 1, 1841.
[74] Ibid., Margaret to Houston, April 15, 1841.
[75] Ibid.
[76] Sam Houston, *Writings*, vol. 2, 367.
[77] Jennie Morrow Decker, family story.
[78] Wisehart, 369.
[79] Sam Houston, *Writings,* vol. 3, 10.
[80] Sam Houston, *Writings*, vol. 2, 370.
[81] Hearne papers, San Antonio, "Ben Lomond," June 1, 1841.

Chapter IV

Long after the lights had been extinguished through the town, and sullen, desperate armed men gathered in secret meetings, the gay voice of his wife, mingling with tones of her harp and piano, was heard coming forth from the open windows of Houston's dwelling.

Sam Houston, 1842, *Memoir*

Houston may have given some of his reasons for becoming a candidate for the office of president when he wrote a friend in Nashville about the sad state of affairs existing in Texas. He complained:

> We ought to have been most prosperous and happy, had our Rulers acted wisely. . . . [T]he evils of which Texas has now were brought upon her by ignorance and corruption. . . . If the next administration shou'd be composed of men possessing patriotism, integrity, and talents, Texas will again lift up its head, and stand among the nations. It ought to do so, for no country upon the Globe can compare with it in natural advantages.[1]

Houston continued to live up to his temperance pledge to Margaret. He managed to taper off his drinking habits with the help of an old Texas formula for orange bitters. He wrote to his friend Samuel Williams, "Things move on with me . . . very dryly—dryly because we have had no rain for the last nine weeks, and dryly because we have no liquor, and I do not taste one drop of it."[2]

Houston's friends continued to be amazed at the change that marriage had made in him, and they did not view the change with disappointment. His enemies chose to ignore it. He was running against his old enemy, David G. Burnet in a bitter campaign. Houston's political enemies hurled charges based on his reputation for drunkenness. A pro-Burnet newspaper professed doubt of Houston's ability to survive this addiction.[3]

Margaret was getting her first experience as the wife of someone actively engaged in a political campaign. She withstood the rumors well and was not worried about her husband's drinking. While she would have much preferred that Houston retire from public life, he seemed to be taking an almost malicious joy in the campaign he was waging, so she resigned herself to silence.[4]

A newspaper battle between the two candidates was raging. Burnet had published a series of libelous articles in the *Houston Telegraph and Texas Register* under the pen name of "Publius." The General promptly retaliated by sending a series of letters for Ashbel Smith to have published in the Galveston paper. Houston sent them by his trusted servant Frank, and the letters were signed "Truth." He enclosed a note for Smith: "I send you a sketch as I promised. . . . It will provoke this court, most fearfully—[Burnet] will feel it, if feel he can.[5]

In one of the letters, Houston had referred to Burnet as an ex-hogthief. This was a little more than Burnet could stand. He sent Branch T. Archer to challenge Houston to a duel. When Houston asked Archer upon what grounds Burnet based his demands, he replied that the General had abused Burnet beyond forbearance. Houston answered, "Hasn't he abused me to an equal degree? He has done so publicly and privately until I am constrained to believe that the people of Texas are thoroughly disgusted with both of us." Archer returned the challenge to Burnet unopened.[6]

Margaret was greatly relieved that the episode had been resolved peacefully. She had been frantic that Houston might actually agree to fight the duel. He would receive other challenges during his long career, but he promised her that he would never be provoked. Once in his youth, he told her, he had fought a duel and seriously wounded a man. He vowed then that he would never again duel, and devised many ways to keep his promise.[7]

Once, for instance, a challenge came from Albert Sidney Johnston, a soldier who had been offended by Houston's criticism. Houston was sitting in his office with his secretary, Washington D. Miller, when Johnston's friend brought the challenge. Houston studied it for a few minutes, handed it to his secretary and said, "Miller, please see that this challenge is filed in its proper place; it is number sixteen." Houston then told Johnston's friend, "Go tell your friend that angry gentlemen must await their turn if they duel with me, and say that there are fifteen ahead of him." Naturally Houston's enemies labeled as cowardice his refusal to fight, but it is doubtful that even they themselves believed their charges.[8]

Toward the end of the campaign a more serious charge against Houston was brought. On August 26, 1841, the *Austin Texas Sentinel* published an article which intimated that Houston had turned from drink to opium. Houston showed the article to Margaret, who handed it back to him without comment.[9]

Apparently the voters in Texas also chose to ignore the rumors. Margaret, at the age of twenty-two became the first lady of Texas when her husband was elected president of the Republic on September 6, 1841, by a three-to-one margin over Burnet. Edward Burleson was elected vice-president. Margaret was happy for Houston, but she cared very little for the "social position" afforded the president's wife.

The Houstons were immediately extended numerous invitations. The president-elect, while agreeing to make speeches, declined offers of a public dinner or barbecue in both San Augustine and Nacogdoches. He explained, "Owing to the general condition of our country, I have no wish to add to the pressure of our circumstances, by incurring any unnecessary expenses, to those unavoidable outlays of money, which the citizens have been compelled to pay for the support of the Government."[10]

Washington County, however, insisted on giving the couple a victory dinner. The crowd ate over thirteen barbecued hogs and two sides of beef. Many of the people were astounded because only cold water was served. They were even more astounded that no one saw the General take a drop of anything stronger during the couple's entire stay.[11]

The Houstons visited east Texas. The president-elect made his speeches and Margaret charmed the crowds. The San Augustine newspaper reported that Mrs. Houston in her journey to the redlands had "won a popularity, by her kind and Ladylike manner, greater if possible than that which clings to her patriotic husband."[12]

When the couple returned to Houston City on November 6, 1841, the entire town turned out to meet them. It was described as the most festive social event to take place in the city since the San Jacinto Day celebration of 1837. Cannons roared throughout the day, and there was a parade with martial music. This was followed by a reception at the home of Mayor and Mrs. J. D. Andrews. That night Margaret was entertained by Houston society at an invitational ball held at the City Hotel where she and her husband were the guests of honor.[13]

The couple briefly visited Cedar Point and then returned to Houston. Since few people would make the four-day journey to the capital, Houston decided to make a speech at Houston City where he would have a much larger audience. For all practical purposes this speech, given on November 25, 1841, served as an inaugural address. He spoke in glowing terms of both the virtues and problems of Texas. He pointed out that the history and the position of Texas were before the world and that Texas was being courted by the crowned heads of Europe and being welcomed into the community of nations. Perhaps thinking of Margaret, he then paid great tribute to the women of the Republic of Texas:

> It is woman that makes the hero. It is she that instills the fire of patriotism. . . . A nation that possesses patriotic women, must ever boast of her gallant sons, brave defenders and successful generals. What is it that guides the soldier's hand, and nerves his arm in battle, but the anxious desire to defend the near and dear? . . . [I]t is woman who blesses her country while she blesses those

about her. . . . We must expect many evils to be corrected in the formation of society.

He went on to explain his own position:

In promoting the interests of my country, I feel that I am promoting my own individual happiness. All that I have, either in reputation or in property, is in Texas. Texas is my abiding place; this is my home, my nation, the home of my friends. . . . When my country calls, I have ever deemed it my duty and my privilege to peril my life upon the issue of her glory.[14]

During their marriage, Margaret would have many opportunities to reflect on the words "my country calls." The day after his speech, Houston bid Margaret good-bye and journeyed to the capital. She did not accompany him to Austin because there was no presidential mansion to accommodate them, and she was again fighting off malaria. Houston expected only a short session when he left and probably did not want to expose his wife to the tiring journey. There was still the danger of Indian raids on this western frontier city, and Houston had not given up hope that the capital would be removed to a more desirable site.

The "President's House" in Houston City had been finished a few weeks before the end of Houston's first term and was available for Margaret, but it was a small crude cottage. She received invitations to stay with John and Eugenia Andrews and with Mr. and Mrs. Francis Lubbock, in their spacious homes. Margaret gratefully accepted. She spent time with both families and became close friends with Eugenia Andrews and Anna Lubbock.[15]

The city of Houston was still a far cry from the spacious and elegant city which its founders, the Allen brothers, had planned. The streets which they had laid out and named for the Texas heroes were often described as too muddy for travel. On one occasion when Margaret was visiting Ellen Reily's home she was detained for two days after a rainstorm rendered the streets so muddy that it was impossible for her to return to the Andrews' home.[16] A square of land had been chosen for the capitol building, and Capitol Avenue led to its bare expanse. An uncompleted frame building had been the only space available for official offices when the seat of the government was moved.[17]

On the way to Austin the President was greeted cordially but it was difficult for him to remain cheerful. He commented on his situation when he wrote Margaret:

> When I feel that my absence must be for weeks or months from you . . . I am truly unhappy. When these anticipations are contrasted with the last few months and the felicity which I have enjoyed in your society, I must confess that my destiny seems any thing but enjoyable.[18]

He wrote of their happy summer spent at Cedar Point, and in speaking of enjoyments of the past he assured her that those of the last few months were valued by him more than any of his past existence. He described them as "hours of bliss to me because you seemed happy, and I was really blessed." He acknowledged the effect of temperance on their happiness:

> Thus you will perceive that I appreciate properly the influence of sobriety upon our happiness, and the necessity of my adherence to a principle which can place us in the possession of every earthly blessing, and from which a departure cou'd promise nothing but misfortune and wretchedness! Affection for you, my love, has produced this change and conviction which must and will remain while affection maintains a place in my heart, or reason can direct my actions.[19]

As before, Margaret was depressed at being left behind. On December 6, 1841, she wrote of her unhappiness at being separated from her husband:

> Dearest this is the 9th day since we parted. More than a week! Can it be that I have passed so long a time away from him who has

made the sun-shine of my existence for many a happy day! Oh my Love, the world looks dreary around me. Day and night pass away alike to me, and the sun's cheering rays bring no more life to my soul.[20]

She wrote that she had lost all relish for her favorite amusements and even her "loved guitar was laid aside." She had changed since he left her, and she could not imagine how she could entertain or amuse anyone. She had not left her room since they had parted.

It was difficult for Houston to get his letters mailed, and before Margaret could receive his on the subject of their summer at Cedar Point, she was writing on the same subject:

Dearest, do you ever think of our sweet woodland home! Oh what happy days we have passed there! I remember in one of our evening rambles when we had paused to survey the grandeur of the scenery, that I looked up and beheld in your countenance a reflection of joy that filled my own soul.[21]

When Houston received that letter he answered, assuring Margaret that her letters:

. . . whisper the sweet accents on thought, as well as impress the recollections of other days! Days which will ever be sacred to me, to us! They are days of "wildwood" memory. You can not, my Love, cherish those hours of holy love and affection with more lively sensations than myself. I was delighted with . . . the sweet description of past hours.[22]

During his first days in the capital, Houston wrote of his loneliness at their separation:

To be absent from you renders me a solitary being—not a person, for I am pressed with company, but my spirit is lonely. . . . I assure you that I meet no one of either sex who can respond to opinions, notions, and feelings in a manner like you—I feel proud, and at the same time grateful to my creator for such a boon and my devotion of heart is the holy testimony.

He also made known his feelings on drinking:

I feel but one influence, and that is my desire to make you happy ... and then preserve it by the most perfect temperance ... the desire and power to preserve my pledge and save you the sorrow and mortification of seeing a man who is devoted to you fall a victim to the influence of degrading habit! I can see others drink & pass my time with them and not [have] the least inclination to participate with them! And if I were even to feel the desire for a glass, I wou'd only have to recall the image of my beloved wife and fancy her boundless agony at such as announcement.[23]

He assured her that if the session of Congress was long it would not be his fault, for he had resolved that the moment it adjourned, he would fly to her side "never again to leave you on this globe. I have lived for mankind. I will try and live for ourselves."[24]

On December 11, 1841, Margaret expressed her joy in receiving letters from her husband:
She also expressed her loneliness:

Oh my love, I could not live without your letters! They impart new energy to my lowly spirits and after reading them again and again through the long day ... and at night fall to sleep with the image of him I love fresh upon my heart. Dearest, I am lonely and desolate without you! My thoughts never wander from you one moment. . . . I can not bear to think of the time that must pass before we meet. I will think of it as little as possible and try to be cheerful.[25]

But by the next evening she had added to her letter that it was becoming increasingly difficult to remain cheerful and the "day creeps on to day and the only joy that mingles with the passing hour is the thought that [your] return is so much nearer."[26]

Houston was worried that because of his present financial state he had not provided enough funds for Margaret's comfort. In her answer, she reassures him, but she also used the occasion to let him know exactly how she feels about their frequent separations:

Dear noble husband . . . entertain no uneasiness about me! My wants are abundantly supplied, and I have never suffered myself to indulge any whim or caprice that would entail unnecessary expense. Oh how willingly would I resign all the honours of our station and retire into some obscure forest if I could have you, my beloved, always with me. . . . It is no romantic picture for, oh my love, the vain plaudits of the crown can not repay us for the severe trials and disappointments which we are compelled to endure, the painful parting, the agonizing fears and the long, long dreary hours of absence![27]

The inauguration ceremonies were set for December 13, 1841. Margaret could not be present, but she expressed her thoughts to her husband:

Oh how intensely I will think of you tomorrow! May heaven strengthen your arm and direct your heart for our country's good! It will be a solemn occasion, and I know you will feel deeply the responsibility that shall be thrown upon you![28]

That evening, as soon as he returned from the Ball, Houston sat down to write Margaret a description of the day's festivities. He reported that the people of Austin all seemed to feel happy on the change from an unpopular administration for "one which seemed to promise well to the nation." The letter also expressed his personal feelings:

There was one alone who felt that he was lonely and cheerless, tho' he wore smiles on the occasion—I mean your devoted husband. . . . If you were present, I have but little doubt but what you wou'd rival me in popularity.[29]

Houston informed her a few days later that his friends were amazed at the change in his character:

> 'Tis generally believed here, that you are entitled to all the credit of my reformation; and that's a most famous work, for it was more than all the world beside could do. And for the sake of my dear Maggy, I will not act the scamp lest it might tarnish her deserved renown.[30]

Concerning his personal feelings on the subject of his changed character he wrote:

> I thank you as the kind and ministering angel in the hand of Heaven that has restrained me from vicious habits and rendered me the rational husband of my amiable and lovely wife! Tis possible that others might have possessed the charms, but upon this subject, I will remain a skeptic! For this simple reason—you are the only dear object that I ever loved with my whole heart and existence![31]

As Houston took over as chief executive in December of 1841, he began what would become a lifelong habit of sharing the political news with Margaret. Often in letters noting that the information was "sub rosa" he described his dealings with various politicians and gave her information which he did not wish to make public. At this time he also shared with her his fears for Texas: "She now gasps for life, for she has been long strugling [sic] in the throes of corruption."[32] Houston had only been in office two days when he sensed that Congress would be hostile to his efforts. He described the situation to Margaret:

> My Love, my task is more than I can perform, but my failure shall incur no censure. I would rather resign and retire to our home. A Congress, sent to aid me, you will see, has placed every embarrassment in my way. My destiny is a queer one, and I must see it out.[33]

On December 22, 1841, he went on to explain his feelings about his destiny:

> I am now placed in the midst of circumstances untried in their character, for no country has ever been similarly situated with Texas. If my exertions, united with those of my friends . . . should prove triumphant in combatting the difficulties which surround us at this moment, it will at least illustrate two things: first, that Texas is fortunate, and second, that I will be to some extent instrumental in the illustration of her good.[34]

Houston wrote on Christmas Eve that if he had control of the Government, he could save the country, but now he really distrusted the effort.

> It does appear to me that no mortal power can avert the ruin impending over Texas. Every convulsive throw only leaves her more prostrate in her condition. Her resources are wasted and the body politick [sic] is weakened so much that even my sanguine hope is beginning to languish![35]

In the same letter Houston again made reference to resigning, but advised Margaret that he would not decide upon his course until he could have her "sage advice."

As the year drew to a close, Houston's mind was on the adjournment of Congress. He had made an attempt to "raise the muse" and had set his feelings about returning home to poetry though not in rhyming form:

> A heart which beats with kindest love
> Must ire [sic] recur to the shrine
> Of all his hopes and cares!
> There true devotion, will it offer up
> To the bright Star which guides
> Its destiny—(which is my dear Maggy)[36]

When Houston's letters were delivered to Margaret, with them came the news that Congress would not adjourn any time soon. Her spirits sunk to the lowest level since her husband had left. Late in the night of January 3, 1842, she wrote that she could not sleep. She felt as if she could write to him until "the east again puts on her brilliant morning garb." She described her loneliness:

> It is no exaggerated picture. I do feel as if my heart was bursting & deep midnight stillness is reigning around me. My own one thou are not here, and oh how silent is the spot in which thy voice is not heard! How dark and dreary the scene if I behold thee not! . . . Dearest talk no more [of] sacrifices for your country. It must not be. you are mine and mine alone and you must not—oh no, you can not leave me again! I am constantly surrounded by friends, but oh I feel desolate for you are not with me and oh what solitude is like the loneliness of a crowd! Write often dearest and oh do hasten home.[37]

Like many of her other letters during this time, this letter shows her doubts about being able to withstand the trials of being a politician's wife. Perhaps influenced by her husband's doubts and his talk of resigning she wrote:

> Surely my love, your patriotism is undergoing a severe test and doubtless will come out like the refiner's gold. Mine has been pretty much shaken by recent events and I must confess that my predominant thought has been that my husband was wasting his time and energies upon an ungrateful people! But perhaps it is wrong to indulge such feelings.

She was hoping that the seat of government would be moved to a place where it would not be necessary for them to be separated, and commenting on what Houston had written her about living conditions in the city of Austin she said:

> If you are to serve the people for nothing, I think you ought at least to have the privilege of performing the labour in safety and in some civilized spot. But dearest, if you are satisfied it will be all right with me, for your happiness is mine.

Then, perhaps with the feeling that she might have upset her husband, she wrote in a more penitent vein, explaining her feelings and saying that she was almost sorry to have said so much:

> I know that it is my duty to soothe you in your deep disappointments and trials as much as possible, but at this moment I am so indignant at the recent acts of congress that I can not restrain my feelings. If the seat of government should not be moved, I must confess to you candidly that I wish you to resign immediately. Of course, this will not decide your course of conscience in a case of such importance, but I need to say what I think and feel![38]

It would be over two months before she was with her husband again Houston had promised to write to her every day that mail could be sent out, and his letters during this period clearly reflect his loneliness and frustration over their separation. In them, he calls her his "dear Maggy" and says that thinking of her is his "only happiness."[39] He praises her as the "bright star of [his] hopes,"[40] and says "none but [you] can ever warm this heart."[41] On January 25, 1842, he wrote a letter which showed her that his mind was also on religion:

> 'Tis true of late my mind has dwelt with more reflection . . . upon this vast and boundless theme of eternity. . . . I do believe my Beloved, that you are intended by Heaven as the dear being, who is to call home my heart, which has been so long estranged from God, to a sense of great dependence upon His goodness and His almighty power! . . . You have to me been the Star of hope, the guide to happiness and peace.[42]

As Houston began to develop a sense of inner peace, he also began to have more confidence in his ability to control the government. On January 21, he wrote that with the men he had chosen for his cabinet he moved on "most harmoniously," and, he hoped, "beneficially for the country, if it is not too far gone to save it!"[43]

Houston wrote that he had given up swearing and felt more tranquil. He told her that he was constantly busy and usually did not leave his office to sleep until two o'clock in the morning. He described Austin as a "most awful city" where he could not get a decent bed and had to ride out of town to get a decent morsel to eat. He expressed his fears for "our poor dear Texas." He was still hoping for an early adjournment but had no idea of when "our wise men will get tired of earning $8.00 per day in good funds." He was keeping his horse Saxe well shod, in the city and by the door ready "to be off with the first to depart" when adjournment finally came.[44]

Margaret expressed her delight that her husband had given up drinking and swearing:

> Dearest, I have never attempted to give you a full expression of the happiness which your recent sacrifices of habit have conferred upon me, for how could I express it. . . . Perhaps you would think it an unreasonable degree of joy for such a cause—for no human being can appreciate my feelings in this case . . . [45]

Margaret was also delighted to hear that her brother Henry had written Houston a letter full of "expressions of esteem and affection." She decided that she liked her brother "a little better" for that. The same letter told Houston of a ball planned in honor of Eugenia Andrews' daughters and of a meeting with an Englishman, Mr. Charles Power, which amused her:

> The gentlemen are getting up a ball . . . I was very much amused at Mr. Power last night. He requested the honour of attending me to the ball, and when I replied that I would not think of going to any party without my husband, he exclaimed, "Why Victoria would go without Albert!" It was said with so much seriousness

and sincerity that realy [sic] I had not the heart to laugh at the ludicrous comparison, and embarrass the poor fellow by revealing the absurdity of his English notions.[46]

Margaret did not realize it at the time, but Charles Power and his "English notions" would be playing a large part in her family's future within a few years, as he was to become her brother-in-law.

Houston's friends were beginning to pressure her to influence her husband concerning where to move the capital. On this subject she wrote:

> I suppose there is not [a] prospect of moving the seat of government immediately. What are we to do? I can form no plans for the future in the event of their retaining it in Austin. Maj. Reily desires me to say to you that your friends in Houston do not want you to bring censure upon yourself by any attempt to have it brought to this place independent of congress. I suppose you saw Maj. Western's letter to me. He wishes me to use my influence with you in favor of Harrisburg. This I can not do for I would not like to see Houston put down.[47]

During the first few days of 1842, rumors were flying that Mexico might be planning to recapture Texas. Public sentiment was high for recruiting a Texan army to send to the border. One story claimed that Houston had made a secret agreement with the United States. In Houston City, Margaret heard the rumors and wrote her husband, "I am told they [the United States] only await your permission to send an army through Texas into Mexico. I hope you will not oppose it, but I know your course will be right."[48]

Houston immediately answered her:

> My Love, You wish me to say if we are to have war, and that you will rely upon my opinion, or say so. I can only say, my dear, that Mexico is in a better situation to invade Texas, than she has been since 1836. Now whether she is yet in a condition to make a campaign against us must be determined by ourselves. . . . No

application has been made for leave to march troops through Texas from the U. States, nor to invade Mexico, or if it has been done, I have not heard of it.[49]

While wanting to avoid a conflict, Houston was hoping that the threat of war would turn public opinion toward relocating the capital in a less remote place. He wrote Margaret:

> Nothing has yet been done about the seat of Government, but one thing you may rely upon! I will never occupy any situation that will require me to remain apart from you! Separation from you is the most painful of all my endurance. If spared to embrace you my dearest, I will not leave you again until you bid me go! . . . and say "your country demands you services in the field! Go and defend her" This event I hope will never occur.[50]

He was just as adamant eleven days later, when he wrote, "To live apart from you Love, I will not submit to if I have only left to me the power to resign the office I now hold."[51] Two days later he had further news:

> As to the removal of the seat of Government, I am told it has been submitted to Congress by various applicants representing differ-ent places—That they have all been referred to a committee which will report on the subject in a day or two. I have no idea what the report will be, as I take no part in the matter.

Before he could even send the letter, he learned that "the seat of Government [would] be removed. . . . The power of removal may be accorded to the president."[52]

Back in Houston City, Margaret had met a historian who so impressed her that she wrote him a letter of introduction:

> I take great pleasure in presenting to my dear husband, Mr. William Kennedy, whose work on Texas has interested us so much. He has my assurance of the high estimation in which you

hold him and the gratification it will afford you to form his acquaintance. I hope the very favourable impression he has produced abroad with regard to Texas, will be bourn in remembrance by the citizens of Austin, and that they will render his visit as agreeable as possible.[53]

The next day she wrote Houston a personal letter on the subject:

I have a boon to ask of you. Can you not give Mr. Kennedy a line about the task which we once assigned to Dr. Irion? As you may not understand me—in a word, I wish him to write your biography! I have set my heart upon it, Love. Do not suffer me to be disappointed. I know no pen that could so richly portray the thrilling incidents of your life.[54]

When Houston received her letter he replied:

I will "not refuse your request" about the items of History for Mr. K., but I will defer a compliance with it, until we can meet, & then my dearest we will determine as to the most delicate and dignified mode of doing the thing.[55]

A week later Houston was writing Margaret of his enthusiasm in working with the historian:

I must tell you, that I am pleased with W. Kennedy,—he is a gentleman of very correct moral feelings, and clearly intellectual! Today I placed some papers in his hand, which have never met the public eye! They were in relation to Santa Anna's liberation by me. One was a veto upon a Resolution, the other was a letter from Santa Anna to me and his autograph with which W. K. was much pleased. He will see other papers here important to the history of those times! I will show him my prophesy about the Alamo & Goliad.[56]

Houston said he had been delighted to receive a letter from Margaret's brother Vernal Lea, but he was distressed to learn that Vernal was planning to settle near Liberty. He wanted him to locate at Cedar Point. He felt Liberty was an unhealthy location. He planned to write Vernal that even though it was a pretty place, it was also the last county seat in Texas where Houston would choose to reside. As Houston described it, "I have seen more sickness there in one day than I ever saw in an Army for the same time."[57]

Toward the end of the congressional session, Houston seemed happier and his sense of humor returned. He had been criticized for not wearing formal attire to his inaugural and he assured Margaret that her husband would preserve his honor and maintain the dignity of his station "if not in Dress he will in ad-dress!" He described his progress with the government:

> With those which I have in the cabinet, I move on most harmoniously and hope beneficially for the country, if it is not too far gone to save . . . Arduous as the duties are, I feel much pleasure in their performance when I can suppose they result in advantage to the public good. . . . With good temper, and temperance added, I will try and move on as calmly as possible.[58]

While Houston's spirits were improving, Margaret's were not, despite the fact that her friends were very attentive. Margaret wrote that almost every day she had an invitation to dine out, but she rarely accepted.[59] She described her state of mind as "a continual weariness at heart" in which the very sight of company was irksome to her. While in the company of others she "conversed without knowing what [she] was saying and smiled without feeling joy." She had remarked to her friends that she felt oppressed with the same gloom that she had felt on the week he had left for Austin. Since that time she had lived upon "hope with the assistance of some fortitude," but now, she wrote Houston, she was without either:

> It seems cruel to tell you so much of my sorrow, although it is caused by my absence from you, but dearest I must pour out my

full heart to you. If not to you—who is there in this wide world that can feel my grief![60]

Margaret's spirits were raised somewhat when a packet of letters arrived from Austin brought by Judge Hart, who informed Margaret of the rumor that Congress was adjourning. Margaret did not put too much faith in the hope, as she did not feel she could bear to be disappointed. Margaret wrote that her heart was beating "almost to suffocation" when she thought of his return. She knew she must appear as a "silly child" but promised to try "to act with becoming dignity."[61]

Houston had written that he was having trouble expressing his affection for his young wife. To this Margaret replied that if he really loved her more than he expresses, that she was indeed blessed. She claimed to also have trouble expressing her feelings, and to often feeling "a sad dearth of language." When she reviewed her letters she felt that they "fall so far short of my devotion to you that they seem cold and lifeless." She regretted that her letters of late had been so gloomy, and had probably depressed instead of cheering him. However, such letters were inevitable, for as she explained, "How would I be gay when separated from my beloved husband?"[62]

She had expected him home before the end of January, so was very disappointed to receive a letter which, as she described it, "put to flight the sweet hope of seeing you immediately":

> I thought at first my courage would have failed me, but after reading your dear letter again and again, my spirits revived and I determined not to yield. . . . My heart pines for quiet and retirement. This busy world with its boisterous scenes of mirth and its wily snares is no home for me. My spirit is tuned to the murmur of wild streams and song of forest birds! . . . Oh my Love, I wish you would come home!

Her letter of January 29 continued with the confession that she feared she had written too much on the subject and was ashamed:

. . . but the truth is—I have nothing else to write for my mind is in such a state that I can barely read or think. Sometimes I almost forget every thing except that you are not with me and that my heart pines for you. . . . surely another week will not pass before you are with me. Come home if the country must be sacrificed by it for I do not see how you can save the people against their will.[63]

Houston had sent word to Margaret not to write him after the first of February, as he hoped to be on the way home by then. On hearing that a friend was leaving for Austin, however, she decided to send one last letter on February 7. She was in good spirits and her sense of humor had returned, as her description of a meeting with the former president of the Republic shows:

You commanded me not to write to you any more, but recollect Mr. Crawford did not make me promise to obey you, so that you can not charge me with rebellion. . . . I . . . returned in time to see Gen. Lamar . . . He looks like a great clumsy bear. Poor fellow! . . . I was polite enough to conceal my amusement from the company, and I think I deserve some credit for that.[64]

The Congress finally adjourned on February 5, 1842, and Houston left immediately, although not on his sturdy horse Saxe. He was trying out a new mode of transportation, a recently purchased chestnut-haired mule named Bruin. He decided that Bruin had more sense and intuition than most horses. This enabled the animal to travel through difficult places without much guidance from his master, leaving Houston free to relax and consider his problems while he gave Bruin a free rein. Houston surprised Margaret by returning to Houston City on February 9, which was earlier than she had expected him. He attributed his speed to the mule, and bragged in a letter to his secretary, Washington D. Miller, that he was able to make the trip in "two hours less than four days" and that he "left and passed all company on the way." [65]

Things were not going well with the young Republic. War with Mexico was threatening. In March, a small Mexican army invaded

Texas. They took possession of San Antonio, stayed there for two days, and then for some reason returned home. Houston seized this opportunity to order the removal of the public archives from Austin to Houston City, but because some outraged Austin citizens protested the order with arms, the archives remained there.

In April, Margaret was still exhausted with malaria and suffering from frequent attacks of asthma. Martin Lea had been visiting the Bledsoes at Grand Cane, and Houston encouraged Margaret to return to Alabama for a visit, in hopes the change would benefit her health. Margaret was reluctant to make the trip, but her husband and brother finally persuaded her to go. Houston included the news in a letter to William Henry Daingerfield, who was in Nashville:

> She [Margaret] will go to Alabama with her Brother Col. Martin A. Lea by the *New York,* which will sail on the 1st of May. Her visit will be short. By the last of July, she will return as I devoutly hope with health improved. She is reluctant to go as she has some fears that I may take a fancy for the Rio Grande and "dodge" her until the war with Mexico is ended. Now this is groundless so far as my intentions are concerned. . . . [66]

Houston took Margaret to Galveston and put her on the steamer. he wrote her that he had gazed after his "departing love" until "objects on the Boat grew small & dim." He tried to calm her fears about the threatening war with Mexico: "You need not fear that I would be willing to play you the slip & break off to war. . . . Whilst you are on earth, my leading star, you need not fear that I will act regardless of your happiness."[67]

Margaret wrote from the steamer that she had talked with Colonel Gillespie about the removal of the capital to another location: "He seems to think that the western people would be satisfied with Washington [on the Brazos] as a location." The captain of the steamer had told her about a political meeting he had attended in Galveston a few nights before and Margaret related the story:

He says he never before took part in any political meeting, but as it was expected your name would be handled pretty roughly, he and his clerk, Mr. Philips, both attended armed with bowie knives and pistols intending to use them if the scoundrels gave them the slightest provocation. This spirit should not be encouraged, yet I can not but prize the friendship that is willing to risk everything for you.[68]

When the ship docked at New Orleans, Margaret was already missing her husband and pleaded: "My Love, do write to me constantly. My heart is very heavy. I can not live long away from you. Do not condemn me to a long absence. I would implore you not postpone my return past July. . . . "[69] She arrived in Marion on the second anniversary of their wedding, but was happy to be in her childhood home for the first time in two years. She wrote in her first letter from there:

We arrived here on . . . our wedding day, as I predicted. I devote to you the first moment that I could claim from my friends, for we have had a constant jubilee ever since we arrived. . . . Marion is a perfect earthly paradise. I have never seen anything so beautiful as its green hills and blooming gardens. Oh that my beloved husband were here to share with me the happiness that is around me! But he is far away, toiling and oprest [sic] with cares, and I wish I was with him, for it is nonsense to think of being contented without the presence of him who engrosses every thought and wish of my heart.[70]

The next day Houston wrote noting that the anniversary, which should have been a day of celebration, was a sad one for him: "You will perceive that I did not celebrate the '9th of May' as cheerfully as I cou'd have desired. I can only pray that hereafter such occasions may be more in keeping with their original cause." Knowing how much Margaret wanted to be in a place of their own, Houston rented a house from Mr. Bagby in Houston City. He made arrangements to have their furniture taken out of storage and put in the house, but he told Margaret that until her return he had no desire to live there. He also wrote that if it were possible, he would retire and never again be heard of except as a private citizen. he expressed his regrets that he felt it was too late for this:

> That day has passed by, and I am in for the plate! While you are my counsellor, I have no fears of your sensible and friendly advice, and sustain myself, if you will only keep your temper. But you know my dear, that you will get provoked at the unruly folks of Texas.[71]

In the hopes of preventing loneliness, Margaret had brought some of her husband's previous letters with her. She read parts of them aloud to Varilla and shared with Houston how happy it had made her sister to hear "every expression of tenderness." She again emphasized her wish to keep the trip short:

> I can not stay longer than July. . . . I believe I would go mad! In reviewing your dear letters from Austin, I discovered your frequent promises never to leave me again. And can it be that I have left you![72]

She also included the news that Henry and Serena might be coming for a visit in the fall, and expressed her hope that the Republic of Texas might provide the Houstons with a home in which to entertain their relations.

Physical problems continued to plague Margaret. Dr. and Mrs. Nathaniel Fletcher planned a supper party to entertain her, but she suffered an asthma attack and was too ill to attend. Among the treatments prescribed by Dr. Fletcher on this occasion were Fowler's Solution of Arsenic, Balsam of Toler, and a tonic of Assafoetida to "strengthen the nervous system." For preventing asthma attacks and difficulty in breathing, he advised her to smoke dried stramonium leaves as it "aids expectoration, soothes the nervous system, and relaxes the pectoral and other muscles engaged in respiration." Dr. Fletcher also expressed the regret that she had visited Alabama in a season which he described as "the most deleterious we possible could have for pulmonary infections."[73]

Houston wrote describing his situation as being "alone in society." He could not be happy because "My Wife, My Love, My Friend is not here!" His thoughts were of her and their first meeting:

> I can assure you that when the declining sun casts its rays eastward . . . I view with rapture our favorite star. It is still the star of affection to me, for it seems to grow more bright and beautiful with time. It is the pure emblem of our affection. It is the Banner of our nation. I hope the one will shine throughout Eternity while the other will only survive with things temporal![74]

Margaret soon began making plans to return to Texas. On June 3, 1842, she wrote:

> I assure you my spirit pines to be with you, and in my present state of anxiety about you, I do not think that my health could be improved by a longer absence. To be candid, my Love, I hardly think this climate agrees with me so well as that of Houston.[75]

Houston's letters at this time are full of praise for his wife:

> You are the light of my path, and the sunshine of my hopes! or rather you are the star of my existence. You lend light to my Hopes as "the bright star of Sommerville" gave lustre to our western horizon! In Texas we have again gazed upon its sweet brilliance. May it long shine in its peerless purity, and render bright the twilight of life's evening.

The same letter turned to politics, and Houston asked for some input from Margaret:

> [I] wish you would give me your calm and solemn opinion as to my commanding in the approaching invasion. I wish to know something from you, while absent, on this important matter.

. . . To be sure I hope kind Heaven will grant us many interviews before such could be the case, but I should like to know what you think while Texas is far from you, or at least none of its perplexities can influence your decision.[76]

No record of Margaret's "calm and solemn opinion" have been found. If it was given, it probably expressed her fears both for the threats against her husband's life and the threat of war with Mexico. Many members of Congress favored an invasion of Mexico. Volunteers were organizing with talk of crossing the border. In the hopes of preventing a war, Houston called for a special session of Congress to meet in Houston City on June 27, 1842. The President used the opening meeting of the session to urge Congress to use its authority to remove the government records from the frontier capital of Austin to a point of safety and convenience. He did not suggest a location, but left the choice up to the legislators. No doubt Margaret was pleased that in his message Houston called for the Congress to support his views in securing peace.[77]

The legislators refused to listen to his views. In July, they passed a bill for an offensive war against Mexico, and sent a delegation urging Houston to sign the bill into law. The President did not comment, but began a campaign to make the public aware of the condition of the country.[78]

In a message to the House of Representatives on July 22, 1842, Houston acknowledged that he was aware that there was enthusiasm for war throughout Texas, but he pointed out that few Texans seemed willing to stop and ponder the situation calmly. He warned the congressmen:

In various parts of the Republic, the feeling was so great, that many were unwilling to await the action of the government, but without counting the cost, and in despite of the Executive or the sanction of any constitutional authority, were anxious to advance upon Mexico. . . . If Mexico is invaded, it must be by a force, whose term of service will not be less than one year and whose numbers should not be less than five thousand men. If volunteers for less . . . than one year, or during the war, should be employed they would not be able to achieve any object of importance. Six months would be necessary to perfect them in the manual exercise, the drill and duties of the camp.

He then went on to discuss the poor economy in Texas and the effect that war would have on the situation:

To invite an army of five thousand volunteers into service without means to subsist them, would be productive of incalculable injury to the nation. . . . It is an established fact that if subordination and discipline are not maintained, an armed force is more dangerous to the security of citizens and the liberties of a country than all the external enemies that could invade its rights.[79]

Margaret left Alabama the first week in July, but did not reach New Orleans in time to sail on the *New York*. She wrote her husband from New Orleans on July 5, 1842, that she was "almost frantic and maddened with disappointment."[80]

News had reached the United States of the strife within the Republic. Houston stood in the way of war with Mexico, and because of this Margaret feared that there might be angry threats made against his life by over-zealous patriots who wanted to fight. When she finally returned to Texas she heard rumors of assassins. It was further rumored that some of the cabinet members talked of resigning, and few of the President's friends dared to approach his house unless they came secretly under the cover of night. Houston remained calm and cheerful, and Margaret tried to match his courage. She asked what she could do to help. The President told his wife that he could not hide behind the safety of his home, nor would he station guards around the door. The best way she could help would be for her to continue their normal routine of life.[81]

Years later in his *Memoirs*, Houston, writing in the third person, described how the couple had faced this particular crisis:

He stationed no guard around his house . . . The blinds and the windows of his dwelling were wide open, and he was often seen walking across his parlour, conversing cheerfully with his family. His wife calmly and confidently sustained him by her placid and intellectual conversations. Long after the lights had been extinguished through the town, and sullen, desperate armed men were gathered in secret meetings to plot and counterplot, the gay voice of his wife, mingling with the tones of the harp and the piano, which she had carried with her to the wilderness was heard coming forth from the open windows of Houston's dwelling.[82]

About the same time, the editor of the *Fort Pickering Eagle*, a Tennessee newspaper, visited the Houstons. He wrote in a letter to his paper that—much to his surprise—the opinion he had formed of Houston based on the remarks of others, was quite changed after his first meeting with the general:

Instead of finding him a dissipated, testy debauche in appearance, nothing is farther from the truth. I found him a very dignified, affable, and courteous gentleman . . . He is a large, noble specimen of physical humanity, dresses very genteelly, and is most certainly a perfect gentleman, as well as in many respects a great man.

He reported that he found Houston to be a "new man," a gentleman completely "different in character to that which has been reputed to be his," and he gave much credit to Margaret's influence on her husband. The letter was reprinted in many Alabama newspapers, and it probably gave Margaret great pleasure to read:

How happy for his country, for himself, for his many friends, and his excellent lady that so glorious a reformation has been wrought and a noble mind and heart saved to his country and friends, whom the demon of destruction for a long while seemed to have doomed.[83]

Houston had still not made public his intentions concerning a war with Mexico. Reports were circulating that he would veto the war bill. Houston's supporters asked him not to, for they feared it would ruin him and his country. They reasoned that if Congress were to adjourn without his signature or veto, the bill would become a law, and Houston could save both his conscience and his political reputation. But when Margaret heard him say, "I would not venture anything fraught with so much peril to my country," she knew he had come to another decision.[84]

A day before Congress was due to adjourn, Houston vetoed the war bill, and Congress did not try to override it. Threats of assassination were renewed, but gradually the people came to the realization that Houston had saved them from costly folly. A few weeks later James Morgan wrote to Ashbel Smith: "There was some little excitement caused by that veto, which has pretty much died away, and 'Old Sam' is more popular that ever I believe."[85]

Margaret was probably greatly relieved that the "excitement" had died away and that her husband's life was no longer in danger. A more pleasant excitement was aroused when a letter supporting the veto arrived from his old friend, Andrew Jackson. He assured Houston:

> To make offensive war without ample means both in money and men would be the hight [sic] of folly and madness, and must result in defeat and disgrace . . . and lead to the destruction of the army attempting it, and the disgrace of the general leading it.[86]

---

[1] Sam Houston, *Writings*, vol. 3, 10, Houston to William G. Harding, July 17, 1841.
[2] Sam Houston, *Writings*, vol. 2, 369, Houston to Williams, July 28, 1841.
[3] *Houston Telegraph and Texas Register*, July 28, 1841.
[4] Franklin Williams, family story.
[5] Sam Houston, *Writings*, vol. 2, 371, Houston to Smith, August 4, 1841.
[6] Wall and Williams, 159.
[7] Madge W. Hearne, family story.
[8] Franklin Williams, family story.
[9] Wisehart, 376.

[10] Sam Houston, *Writings*, vol. 2, 387, Houston to John G. Berry and others, September 30, 1841 and Houston to John H. Holland, Henry Raguet and others, October 11, 1841.

[11] Friend, 101.

[12] *Red-Lander*, October 28, 1841.

[13] Harris County Historical Society, *Houston—A History and Guide*, American Guide Series, (Houston: Anson Jones Press, 1942), 57.

[14] Sam Houston, *Writings*, vol. 2, 392–94.

[15] Marie Phelps McAshan, *On the Corner of Main and Texas A Houston Legacy*, (Houston: Hutchins House, 1985), 42–43. See also M. K. Wisehart, 378-9, and Franklin Williams Collection of Houston Correspondence, December 1841 through February, 1842.

[16] Franklin Williams Collection, Huntsville, Margaret to Houston, January 5, 1842.

[17] C. Stanley Banks and Grace McMillan, *The Texas Reader*, (San Antonio: The Naylor Company, 1947), 225.

[18] Franklin Williams Collection, Huntsville, Houston to Margaret, November 30, 1841.

[19] Ibid.

[20] Franklin Williams Collection, Huntsville, Margaret to Houston, December 6, 1841.

[21] Ibid.

[22] Ibid., Houston to Margaret, January 12, 1842.

[23] Ibid., Houston to Margaret, December 10, 1841.

[24] Ibid., Houston to Margaret, December 12, 1841.

[25] Ibid., Margaret to Houston, December 11, 1841.

[26] Ibid., Margaret to Houston, December 12, 1841.

[27] Ibid.

[28] Ibid.

[29] Ibid., Houston to Margaret, December 13, 1841.

[30] Ibid., Houston to Margaret, December 21, 1841.

[31] Ibid., Houston to Margaret, December 24, 1841.

[32] Ibid., Houston to Margaret, December 12, 1841.

[33] Ibid., Houston to Margaret, December 15, 1841.

[34] Ibid., Houston to Margaret, December 22, 1841.

[35] Ibid., Houston to Margaret, December 24, 1841.

[36] Ibid., Houston to Margaret, December 29, 1841.

[37] Ibid., Margaret to Houston, January, 3, [1842]. This letter is misdated 1841.

[38] Ibid.

[39] Ibid., Houston to Margaret, January 1, 1842.

[40] Ibid., Houston to Margaret, January 13, 1842.

[41] Ibid., Houston to Margaret, January 10, 1842.

[42] Ibid., Houston to Margaret, January 25, 1842.

[43] Ibid., Houston to Margaret, January 21, 1842.

[44] Ibid., Houston to Margaret, January 1–24, 1842.

[45] Ibid., Margaret to Houston, January 20, 1842.

[46] Ibid., Margaret to Houston, January 7, 1842.

[47] Ibid.

[48] Ibid., Margaret to Houston, January 12, 1842.

[49] Ibid., Houston to Margaret, January 19, 1842.

[50] Ibid., Houston to Margaret, January 8, 1842.

[51] Ibid., Houston to Margaret, January 19, 1842.

[52] Ibid., Houston to Margaret, January 21, 1842.

[53] Ibid., Margaret to Houston, January 12, 1842.

[54] Ibid., Margaret to Houston, January 13, 1842.

[55] Ibid., Houston to Margaret, January 14, 1842.

[56] Ibid., Houston to Margaret, January 21, 1842.

[57] Ibid.

[58] Ibid.

[59] Ibid., Margaret to Houston, January 14, 1842.

[60] Ibid., Margaret to Houston, January 15, 1842.

[61] Ibid., Margaret to Houston, January 20, 1842.

[62] Ibid.

[63] Ibid., Margaret to Houston, January 29, 1842.

[64] Ibid., Margaret to Houston, February 7, 1842.

[65] Sam Houston, *Writings*, vol. 2, 484, Houston to Washington D. Miller, February 15, 1842.

[66] Sam Houston, *Writings*, vol. 3, 38, Houston to Daingerfield, April 27, 1842.

[67] Franklin Williams Collection, Huntsville, Houston to Margaret, May 5, 1842.

[68] Ibid., Margaret to Houston, May 5, 1842.

[69] Ibid., Margaret to Houston, May 6, 1842.

[70] Ibid., Margaret to Houston, May 13, 1842.

[71] Ibid., Houston to Margaret, May 12, 1842.

[72] Ibid., Margaret to Houston, May 21, 1842.

[73] "Prescription for Mrs. Houston, Dr. Nathaniel Fletcher, n.d." Franklin Williams Collection, Rice University.

[74] Franklin Williams Collection, Huntsville, Houston to Margaret, May 29, 1842.

[75] Franklin Williams Collection, Huntsville, Margaret to Houston, June 3, 1842.

[76] Ibid., Houston to Margaret, June 4, 1842.

[77] Sam Houston, *Writings*, vol. 3, 74–83, June 27, 1842, "President's Message" to the Texas Congress.

[78] Wisehart, 405–06.

[79] Sam Houston, *Writings*, vol 3, 116–24, July 22, 1842, "President's Message " to the House of Representatives.

[80] Franklin Williams Collection, Huntsville, Margaret to Houston, July 5, 1842.

[81] Madge W. Hearne and Franklin Williams, family story.

[82] Lester, *The Life of Sam Houston*, 209–10.

[83] "General Sam Houston," Jacksonville, Alabama, *Republican*, July 13, 1842, Houston Unpublished Correspondence, University of Texas.

[84] Ibid.

[85] Ashbel Smith Papers, James Morgan to Ashbel Smith, August 20, 1842.

[86] Sam Houston, *Writings*, vol. 3, 124, n. 2.

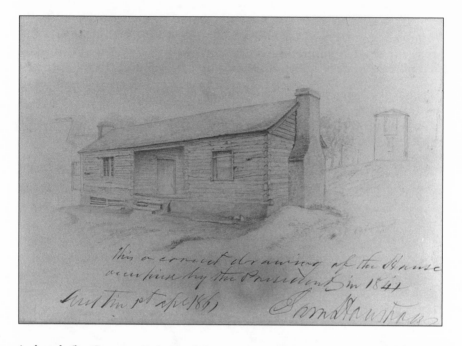

A sketch (by Gustave Behne) of Sam Houston's lodgings in Austin during his second term as President of the Republic of Texas. Across the bottom, Houston wrote: "This is a correct drawing of the House occupied by the President in 1841." Courtesy of Jean and Price Daniel Collection, Sam Houston Regional Library and Research Center, Liberty, Texas.

Chapter V

She would have graced the household of any man, be he president or prince.

John Lockhart,
Washington-on-the-Brazos, 1843

Houston now turned his attention to the next session of Congress and the relocation of the capital. Richardson Scurry wrote the President about the potential problems if Houston City was chosen for the capital. He suggested Washington-on-the-Brazos as a compromise.[1] Houston agreed with the suggestion, especially since the government was too poor to pay rent. At the beginning of the year he had reported to the Senate that proprietors in that city had offered to provide transportation for government properties and to furnish offices for the administration and suitable buildings for the Congress, all without cost, if the capital were relocated at Washington.[2]

The President sent Buck Pettus to confer with the citizens and to advise them of conditions in the government. Judge John Lockhart presided at a meeting in the old Independence Hall, where the citizens agreed to provide free use of all the buildings necessary for offices if their run-down condition could be repaired enough to make them suitable. They further agreed, since the town had only one small hotel, that each private family would take as many officials as they had room for.[3]

In the early fall of 1842 the capital of the Republic of Texas was once again moved. Margaret, with Eliza's help, packed the Houstons' belongings. On September 28, both the government property and the family's personal belongings left Houston City for Washington in a caravan of six wagons, each pulled by three oxen. Margaret rode in the wagon which carried her piano and harp. Houston made the trip on his mule, Bruin.[4]

The Brazos is the largest of the inland streams of Texas, and the little town of Washington was built on a bluff and could not be seen from the river. It had been named some years before by Dr. Asa Hoxie, who later became a close friend of the Houston family. It was a four-day trip from Houston City to Washington. The road ran up the eastern portion of the Brazos valley until it turned nearly at a right angle through the bottom lands within a few miles of the ferry, which was located at the foot of Main Street. Margaret's first glimpse of her new home came as the wagons ascended the second bluff. The residents lived in well-made log and clapboard houses which had been built on gently rising hills. About five hundred yards from the bluff stood Independence Hall on Main Street. There were some cross streets, with a few houses located on them, but the main business was confined to this one principal street.[5]

The Houstons and other government officials arrived at Washington on October 2, 1842. Judge Lockhart's son John described the scene as one of great rejoicing in the town. He was greatly impressed with the sight of Houston astride Bruin. John became a great admirer of the President, as well as of Margaret, whom he would later describe as:

> tall and of fine figure, handsome and intelligent, [she] had fine opportunities in her youth and had taken advantage of them. She was well educated and a good writer of verse. She would have graced the household of any man, be he president or prince.[6]

The Houstons were invited to stay with Judge and Mrs. Lockhart until suitable living quarters could be arranged. Margaret was delighted to discover that the Lockharts had come from Uniontown,

Alabama, which was in the same county as Marion. The Lockharts owned one of the largest homes in the new capital, so the chief executive and his lady were quite comfortable. They had at their disposal a comfortable bedroom with a small fireplace and large mahogany bed which Mrs. Lockhart had brought from her family home. The bed was equipped with a luxury for frontier Texas—a feather mattress. An outside door was cut into the room so that the president would not have to go in and out through the other rooms of the house.[7]

In 1842, the population of Washington was about two hundred fifty people, described by John Lockhart as "the usual proportion of gamblers, horse-racers and all-round sports—mostly floaters." The actual residents followed the customs of the time, for "however poor your host might be, he was the soul of hospitality."[8]

Margaret found Washington to be a city of fine people, generous, hospitable, and courteous to strangers. So honest were the townspeople that scarcely anything was ever stolen. When people left their homes, they of course closed the doors to keep varmints and wild beasts out, but the latch-string always hung outside so that a stranger might enter and make use of the house. This had not always been the case. In earlier days, before the revival meeting held by Judge R. E. Baylor and Reverend W. M. Tryon, Washington had been a rough place. Margaret was probably delighted to hear that during this meeting nearly all of the town joined the Baptist Church, and Washington was never as wild after this.[9]

For all its gracious people, Washington-on-the-Brazos was still a primitive, frontier town. The women spent much time in spinning and weaving, and most garments were homespun. The men often wore buckskin and moccasins. Margaret's poke bonnets from Alabama were probably brought out only for state occasions. The women used sunbonnets for common wear.[10] The President's favorite street clothes at this time were a hunting shirt, an ordinary cheap pair of trousers, and a very fine broad brimmed hat of a smoky color with fur nap half an inch long. However, on state occasions or when dealing with the Indians, he always discarded his frontier garb and wore his finest clothes.[11] According to John

Lockhart, Houston "would dress in the most gorgeous costume, with ruffles of the finest material around his wrists. . . . He was one of the most commanding looking men I ever saw: tall, large square frame, with no surplus flesh."[12]

It was no secret that Houston loved colorful, outrageous clothes, and it must have surprised the citizens of Washington when the President chose to dress in the mild manner of the common man. Houston's fame by this time had traveled to many distant lands. The Sultan of Turkey sent him a full set of Turkish clothing including the fez. Margaret thought the costume of flaming red silk quite pretty and urged her husband to put it on. He tried on the fez to satisfy her curiosity, and she thought it very funny. Houston, realizing how ridiculous he must have looked, never wore it again. Nor did he care for the baggy trousers with pointed shoes attached. He did, however, take a liking to the long robe which reached to his ankles, and frequently wore it in the privacy of his office.[13]

The time in Washington passed happily for Margaret. At the beginning of their stay her health was good and her husband was controlling his drinking problem. Houston wrote to a friend in Houston City, Tom Bagby, and asked him to save orange peels. Houston used them with bitters, an old Texas remedy for tapering off from hard drinking. As Houston explained, "The Doctors commend it. I don't drink hard, but what I do take, I wish to be palatable."[14]

There was another reason for Margaret's happiness. She was expecting a baby in the spring. The Houstons decided they should have a place of their own and made arrangements to rent a cottage on the outskirts of town. Houston wrote to Colonel William Bryan, who was the Texan Consul in New Orleans, and asked his old friend to order a double Barouch carriage and some furnishings for their new home. Among the items he requested were guitar strings, silk handkerchiefs, silk and cotton socks and fabric for upholstery and draperies. Margaret had vetoed some of the wilder prints that were appearing in Texas homes at that time. Houston warned his friend that none of the fabrics should exhibit "turkey gobblers, peacocks, bears, elephants, wild boars, or stud horses." He suggested "Vines, Flowers, or any figure of taste." One interesting item was underlined. It read: "1 do linnen diaper for Towels."[15] Houston's attempt at deception was for naught, for soon the secret was out that the President of Texas and his lady were expecting their first child.

He had also ordered some "Cambric Linnen" from Thomas Bagby, but it had not arrived. At Margaret's request Houston wrote to ask about the order. In the same letter he complained to his friend:

> I have in the discharge of my duties perplexities which no one can appreciate, unless they were to be with me all the time. From my uprising to my down lying at night, I have rarely one hour thro' the day to pass in company with Mrs. Houston. . . . Mrs. Houston is un- well [and] can see no company, so I would be happy to pass a portion of my time with her. Of that pleasure I have been almost wholly disbarred.[16]

Margaret was lonely and now experiencing some ill health due to her pregnancy, and since the Houstons' new home was not yet ready, it was decided that she should go for a short visit with her family. Vernal Lea had settled on the Trinity River near the Bledsoes at Grand Cane. Nancy came up from Galveston to visit as well. It was during Margaret's absence at this time that Houston strayed from his pledge of temperance.

One evening as he was passing by Hatfield's saloon the owner came into the street and waylaid him with a gift—a jug of fine Madeira wine. At first Houston declined to accept it, but finally agreed to take it to present to Mrs. Lockhart. Unfortunately, Mrs. Lockhart was not at home. Houston succumbed to temptation and disposed of a good portion of the gallon jug. Later in the night he was seized with the notion that one of the four posts on Mrs. Lockhart's fine old mahogany bed was interfering with his breathing. He went out to the lean-to where the servants slept, summoned his slave Frank, and ordered him to chop off the post at the foot of the bed. A trembling Frank followed his master's orders. Judge

Lockhart was awakened by the noise, and fearing that the president was being assassinated, rushed into the room. The Judge took the axe from the frightened Frank, sent him back to his quarters, and put the president to bed. The next morning, a very ashamed president was faced with the unhappy prospect of asking both his hostess and his wife for forgiveness.[17]

Most historians agree with family members that this was Houston's last binge. John Lockhart, who was eighteen years old at the time, later wrote that in his opinion Houston would not have succumbed if Margaret had been present. Dr. Lockhart advanced the theory that Houston had more or less controlled the habit, but the compulsion to drink had not left him. He suggested that Margaret, rather than Houston's own will power, was responsible for his ultimate victory over liquor. He wrote:

> She, by her great good sense and excellent management, had gained complete control over the general, and it is to her we owe as great a debt of gratitude as to the general himself, for it was owing to her wonderful influence over him that Texas received the benefaction of his great mind. After he married her he quit all of his old habits and dissipation and became a new man.[18]

Houston made a hasty trip to Grand Cane to confess what had happened and to ask Margaret's forgiveness. Her reply is lost to history, but it is obvious that she did forgive him, and he never disappointed her again in this manner. The Houstons returned to Washington together, bringing Nancy Lea with them. Mrs. Lea helped Margaret set up housekeeping in their rented cottage.

About this same time Margaret suffered a second shock. Word arrived from Major Townes that Martin Lea had died in March. Details were scarce, but Martin had been having severe financial difficulties, and suicide was rumored.[19] Margaret was desolate. Her grief was made worse by the mysterious circumstances. Houston wrote a letter marked "Private" to James Cocke asking for more information:

On the subject of the death of our departed brother, we hear no additional information to that furnished by you, except a short note from Major Townes, stating the fact without detailing the circumstances. Painful anxiety exists on our part to obtain minute information in relation to the occurrence. As you apprehend, the blow upon Mrs. Lea and Mrs. Houston was peculiarly [sic] distressing. Their grief, however, has become calm; and though it is impossible but that they should ever feel deep regrets, I hope their minds will gradually recover from sensations so trying and afflictive.[20]

The Lea family probably received more information eventually, but the facts were never publicly revealed, and not much is known today of the circumstances.

Margaret's general health improved, with the exception of a recurring problem. A few years past she had begun to have trouble with a small tumor in her breast. In 1843, Houston wrote a confidential letter to Dr. Cornelius McAnelly in Houston City with a request for the doctor to obtain some "Nipple guards" for Mrs. Houston. He explained, "She has indications of a 'sore breast' and expects soon, to have to 'Nurse.'"[21]

On May 25, 1843, a son was born. Houston had wanted to name him William Christy in honor of his old friend, but Margaret insisted that the baby be named for his father. Immediately his grandmother took charge of Sam Houston, Jr. Her first act was to purchase a milk cow so that Margaret could wean the baby. With the United States money she had brought with her, Nancy paid for other provisions for the presidential cupboard, to be brought on the stage which now ran between Washington and Houston City.

The President protested that he should be the one furnishing the family larder. To this Mrs. Lea replied firmly that it was all right for the President of the Republic to starve if patriotic motives compelled it, but her grandchild was not old enough to undergo the deprivations of Valley Forge. They finally compromised when she suggested that the President could reimburse her later if the bankrupt Republic got around to paying the President's salary. This became one of many occasions when Houston would bow to his mother-in-law's strong will. She often reminded him, "You may have conquered Santa Anna, but you will never conquer me!"[22]

Margaret was enjoying her role of motherhood to the fullest, and Houston was bursting with pride. When Sam, Jr., was three weeks old his father wrote to Charles Elliot expressing his hopes for his son's future: "He is stout, and I hope will be useful to his kind. May he be anything but a loafer, an agitator, or, in other words, a demagogue."[23] In later years Sam, Jr., lived up to all of his father's expectations. Exhibiting a mind of his own, not unlike his father, he served bravely with Texas troops during the Civil War, despite strong family objections. After that he became a doctor and gained fame as a writer.

The birth of a son into his happy home life had brought about a great change in Sam Houston. This was noted and recorded by Charles Elliot when he and his wife visited the Houstons in Washington and were entertained in their home. Captain Elliot wrote to H. U. Addington, who had socialized with Congressman Houston in Tennessee:

> His [Houston's] career during too large an interval between that time and this has been strange and wild. . . . Finally, however, a new connection with a young and gentle woman, brought up in fear of God, conquered, no doubt as women have been from the beginning and will be to the end, by a glowing tongue, but in good revenge making conquest of his habits of tremendous cursing and passionate love of drink . . . whatever General Houston has been, it is plain that he is the fittest man in this country for his present station.[24]

By the time baby Sam was a few months old, the Houston cottage was full. Margaret's older sister, Varilla Royston, had sent her daughter Sarah Ann, or "Sallie" as she was called, to help out. About this time a more permanent newcomer arrived in the Houston household. She was seven-year-old Virginia Thorn, who had been adopted by Vernal and Mary Lea in Alabama. After Mary's death Vernal had asked his mother to take charge of his ward for a while. Taking Virginia into the Houston family would later prove to be a big mistake.[25]

During the late summer it would be necessary for Houston to travel in order to meet with several of the Indian tribes. He had planned to take Margaret to visit the family at Grand Cane, but the baby became seriously ill. On July 14, 1843, Houston wrote to George Hockley:

> It has been my intention to visit Houston on my way to the Trinity where I expect to leave Mrs. Houston and the boy until my return from the Treaty. He has been too unwell for some days past to venture on a journey, and I fear he will not be able to travel.[26]

The next day he wrote to Charles Elliot on the same subject: "We ourselves had nigh lost our babe. He had quite a severe attack, but we entertain hopes of his recovery."[27]

Sam did recover, and by the end of July Margaret and the baby traveled to Grand Cane, leaving a lonesome husband and father behind. The first day he was back in Washington, Houston wrote to her of his loneliness:

> Dearest, I will not pretend to say to you what my feelings were as the shades of evening were closing around me on yesterday. The hour when I have usually left my offices, and returned from business of the day to meet you and inquire for Sam. Indeed I felt, as tho the earth was a desert, and I stood alone, in the midst of its waste.[28]

A few days later Houston traveled to Crockett for a meeting with a large number of important Texans. He was pleased with the changes that his administration was making in the affairs of his country and wrote Margaret to tell her of the progress:

> I am pleased to witness the glow of happiness, which I see diffused over many faces at the prospects of peace and the

manifestations of abundance which is every where seen. The cordiality with which I am received, and treated by all . . . seems equal to the change that has taken place in our political condition. . . . [b]ut I can assure you that I would truly exchange the expressions which may be offered to me for the pleasure which greeted me at home, when I returned care worn from my office, embraced you, and took a look at Sam.[29]

He mentioned that a barbecue was being planned, and perhaps remembering his slide from temperance during their last separation he assured her, "I will try and acquit myself so that you will hear a good report of me."[30]

In the same letter Houston began what would be a lifetime habit of advising Margaret on the skills of parenting while he was away. In speaking of Sam he advised:

I do trust that his mother's care and instructions will teach him to make his temper submissive to his reason! It is one of the great faults of early education that Parents are amused at the fits of temper which sprightly children are very apt to display. A look of disapprobation from a mother to infancy [sic] or an admonition in childhood, doubtless wou'd often have an influence on the future character and destiny of the child. . . . You will hear from me I know, for no being can more seriously deplore my infirmity in these matters than myself.

Houston went on to speak of the example he hoped to set for his son:

I would much rather that I could leave my off-spring the benefit and my friends the pleasure of referring to my character as the model of every thing that is amiable, virtuous, & truly pious, without guilt, than that they should only have it to say of my memory that "Your Father was the ablest of Generals, the wisest of Statesmen, and the most illustrious of mankind."

He confided in Margaret that no matter how gratifying such worldly compliments might be, he was well aware that "in the closing of life's drama it can yield no pleasure in the anticipated presence of that Being who is infinite in all His attributes as the very Author of Eternity." He promised Margaret that he would endeavor to act in a way that would give her peace here and eternal happiness.[31]

By the end of the month he was begging Margaret to end her trip and meet him in Houston or Galveston. He extended an invitation to Mrs. Lea to come also if it would "add to her comfort." To Margaret he wrote: "'tis said, my dear, that you rule me. This is all well enough ... were you here. I have two natures and you must be here to make me what I ought to be." He spoke to her of his pride in Sam and his hopes for his son in the future:

> I thought when I left him, that he was daily developing traits which bespoke some strong character. This may be all fancy, for parents will always think their progeny is in possession of Genius. As for our boy, my dear, I hope those who live to see him in manhood will find that he is capable in the Department of life in which he may be thrown. I have seen in him much which I admire, and hope that some day it will yield fruit.

He also showed his concern for her by urging her to hire a housekeeper:

> ... it would be well to do so. Or any one who will relieve you from the cares which would devolve upon you while Master Sam claims your maternal care. He is ours, and with the blessings of Heaven, he must be cherished under a mother's eye![32]

Margaret wrote that Sam was indeed "a wonderful boy." The time had passed pleasantly with her relations. They had also been visited by some of Houston's Indian friends. Full of compassion for their sad plight, Margaret wrote of an encounter with the chief:

Old Coleta and his family have been camping near us several days. . . . He took Sam in his arms, and his [Coleta's] dim eyes sparkled with delight. Oh how I wish I could speak thier [sic] language! . . . It pains my heart to know . . . they are passing away, and soon the lone forests they inhabit will know them no more.[33]

Both Houston and Margaret were weary of being separated, but in fact it would be another month before the roads to Washington would become passable enough for Margaret to return. When she did so, the Houstons fell into a regular routine of family life. The President was delighted that Sam remained healthy, and described him as "a hearty brat, robust and hearty as a Berkshire pig."[34]

The same day Margaret was writing her mother and describing Sam as the greatest baby she had ever seen. She wrote that she was well, but the combination of nursing and being up at night had kept her in such a weakened condition that both Houston and the doctor were urging her to wean the baby. She informed her mother how pleased she was with her husband's character:

If I should tell you how much his temper has improved, you would not believe me, so I would merely say that the change is astonishing. Indeed my dear Mother, I must think that it is the work of God and that his heart is under the influence of the Holy Spirit. His walk is certainly that of a pure Christian.[35]

Houston was hoping all the family's health would remain good so he could take them to Tennessee to meet Andrew Jackson. Houston wrote telling Jackson of the plan: "It is our ardent desire to see the day when you can lay your hand on our little boy's head and bestow upon him your benediction."[36] In the same letter Houston told his friend that the timing of the trip would depend on how speedily certain events of the business of the Republic took place. In fact, the trip would be delayed for over a year. The year of 1844 began with the President and the Congress on opposite sides. The lawmakers opposed him on nearly every issue. Margaret was to find her husband spending many hours doing diplomatic foot-work.[37]

On the question of Texas being annexed to the United States, Houston's diplomatic ploy was silence. The family members, as well as Houston's secretary, Washington Miller, were aware how much the President desired to bring it about, but he made no public announcement. Confidential letters on the subject were traveling between Jackson and Houston. In January, Jackson had written with a feeble hand, "I tell you in sincerity & friendship, if you will achieve this annexation your name & fame will be enrolled amongst the greatest chieftains of the age."[38]

When the legislative session was over, the Houstons traveled to Houston City. Here they stayed for several weeks before going on to Grand Cane for a visit with the Leas. They were delayed by heavy rain, so Houston wrote a long letter to his mother-in-law with news of her grandchild. He included the information that many had said the baby resembled Nancy Lea, and that his disposition would do for either side of the family. He added some opinions typical of a proud father:

> He is a clever child, and Margaret really thinks him handsome. He is truly good looking, but not pretty. We think him smart of course, and as his Mother is popular, people like to add to her happiness and . . . praise him very much. . . . Every day his mother & myself fancy that he does some smart thing, that "he did not do yesterday." He is quite as smart as any child that I have seen of his age.

In the same letter he chided Mrs. Lea for not writing more often. He pointed out that he and Margaret wrote all of the family frequently, as well as sending papers containing "Messages and other Documents to let you know that I was not beaten down by the assembly of our Great-ones." He explained that he was awaiting the arrival of the steamer *Neptune* which would bring dispatches from the United States on the status of an annexation treaty. He gave her his goals for the last few months of his presidency: "I hope before my term of office expires to be placed on some secure footing and leave the Government as well as the people in the enjoyment of prosperity, & happiness."[39]

Within a few weeks they had reached Grand Cane. Margaret remained with her family, while Houston attended to business in east Texas. He planned to attend the Treaty meeting with the Indians, but he also had some personal business. He had located a plantation fourteen miles from Huntsville and was in the process of buying it. Because he had observed that among the wildlife on the farm were ravens, he wanted the place to be called "Raven Hill."[40] Houston had chosen the name in part because of the name given him by the Cherokees, but there may have been another reason too. Earlier he had confided to Major Goree, his Alabama friend, of the raven's influence when he came to Texas. When Houston had lived among the Cherokees he had observed that whenever he saw a raven, the bird would fly in the direction of Texas, and he had at last determined to follow the course of its flight.[41]

Years later Houston's great-nephew, Sam Penland, commenting on Houston's love of nature, wrote:

It was his habit, as long as he lived, when he would leave the house in the morning[,] to observe the direction in which the first bird that he saw was flying, and also the first noise that was made by any animal when he first woke up in the morning. . . . These are the things that made a great impression upon the general.

Penland went on to say that, in his opinion, Houston was not superstitious, but rather believed that there was a link between nature and Christianity. Houston took "lessons from nature and the voice of nature was his guide in all spiritual things."[42] This may have been the reason why Margaret did not object to the name "Raven Hill" for her new home.

During the last few months of Houston's term in 1844, he and Margaret returned to Washington to pack for the move to Raven Hill. In one of his last letters as president, he wrote to Jackson of his plans:

When retiring from the cares of Office, I cannot forego the pleasure of making you one more communication. . . . It is the intention of Mrs. Houston and myself to visit you during the coming spring, if possible, at the Hermitage, as well as to embrace our relatives in the United States. We do not expect to remain long out of Texas as our desire is to settle down and improve a comfortable home.[43]

The Houstons traveled to Grand Cane, where they would remain with the Bledsoes and Leas until a suitable house could be built at Raven Hill. Both were looking forward to having a real home for the first time in their marriage. Margaret had anxiously awaited the conclusion of her husband's term in the hopes that she and the baby could spend more time with him. Houston wrote of his own feelings in his first letter to Texas' new president, Anson Jones:

On the 19th I had the pleasure to reach home and found all well,. . . . It was indeed a joyous meeting, and strange to say, I found my mind falling back into a channel, where the current flows in domestic peace and quiet, without one care about the affairs of Government, and only intent upon domestic happiness and prosperity.[44]

On that same day Houston found on his desk a poem of ten stanzas which Margaret had written to express her feelings. It was entitled "To My Husband" and it began:

Dearest, the cloud has left thy brow,
   The shade of thoughtfulness, of care
And deep anxiety; and now
   The sunshine of content is there.

Its sweet return with joy I hail;
   And never may thy country's woes
Again that hallow's light dispel,
   And mar thy bosom's calm repose.

Thy task is done! Another eye
   Than thine must guard thy country's weal;
And oh, may wisdom from on high
   To him the one true path reveal.

The poem went on to describe how Houston, with the help of God, had put to flight their country's foes and built a young nation. It concluded:

Thy task is done. The holy shade
   Of Calm retirement waits thee now,
The lamp of hope relit hath shed
   Its sweet refulgence o'er thy brow.[45]

Margaret may have known that this was wishful thinking on her part. She knew her husband well, and retirement was not Sam Houston's lot; he had only begun his long service to Texas.

---

[1] Madge W. Hearne Collection, Texas State Archives, Austin, Richardson Scurry to Houston, September 7, 1842.
[2] Sam Houston, *Writings*, vol. 2, 430.
[3] Jonnie Wallis and Laurence Hill, *Sixty Years on the Brazos*, (Waco: Texian Press Reprint, 1967), 95–96.
[4] Wisehart, 414.
[5] Wallis and Hill, 40.
[6] Ibid., 25.
[7] Wisehart, 417.
[8] Wallis and Hill, 13–14.
[9] Ibid., 15, 34.
[10] Ibid., 15.
[11] Ibid., 26.
[12] Ibid., 211.
[13] Franklin Williams, family story.
[14] Sam Houston, *Writings*, vol. 3, 236, Houston to Bagby, December 18, 1842.
[15] Ibid., 304–05, Houston to Bryan, January 24, 1843.
[16] Ibid., 323–24, Houston to Bagby, February 20, 1843.
[17] Franklin Williams, family story, and Wallis and Hill, 119–20.

[18] Wallis and Hill, 119.
[19] Hearne Papers, San Antonio, "Notes on the Lea Family," n.d.
[20] Sam Houston, *Writings*, vol. 4, 190, Houston to Cocke, April 22, 1843.
[21] Ibid., 193, Houston to McAnelly, April 24th, 1843.
[22] Madge W. Hearne, family story.
[23] Sam Houston, *Writings*, vol. 4, 211.
[24] Ellis, 73.
[25] Franklin Williams Collection, Huntsville, Houston to Margaret, August 3, 1843.
[26] Sam Houston, *Writings*, vol. 4, 216–17.
[27] Ibid., 219.
[28] Franklin Williams Collection, Huntsville, Houston to Margaret, July 30, 1843.
[29] Ibid., Houston to Margaret, August 3, 1843.
[30] Ibid.
[31] Ibid.
[32] Ibid., Houston to Margaret, September 1, 1843.
[33] Ibid., Margaret to Houston, October 6, 1843.
[34] Sam Houston, *Writings*, vol. 4, 233, Houston to William Murphy, January 23, 1844.
[35] Franklin Williams Collection, Huntsville, Margaret to Nancy Lea, January 23, 1844.
[36] Sam Houston, *Writings*, vol. 4, 265, Houston to Jackson, February 16, 1844.
[37] Sue Flanagan, *Sam Houston's Texas*, (Austin: University of Texas Press, 1964), 73.
[38] Madge W. Hearne Collection, Texas State Archives, Austin, Jackson to Houston, January 23,1844.
[39] Franklin Williams Collection, Huntsville, Houston to Nancy Lea, April 19, 1844.
[40] Madge W. Hearne, family story. This would be the only Houston home where ravens were found.
[41] A. W. Terrell, "Recollections of General Sam Houston," *Southwestern Historical Quarterly*, 16 (October, 1912):133.
[42] Sam Houston Papers, Barker History Center, University of Texas, Sam Penland to Maggie Houston Williams, January 7, 1915.
[43] Sam Houston, *Writings*, vol. 4, 407, Houston to Jackson, December 13, 1844.
[44] Ibid., 408–09, Houston to Anson Jones, December 21, 1844.
[45] Madge W. Hearne Papers, San Antonio, "To My Husband," a poem by Margaret Houston. December 13, 1844.

Chapter VI

Alas, what has always been my decision when my own happiness or the good of the country was to be sacrificed? . . . I wish you to be governed entirely by your own judgment, and though the decision may bring misery upon me beyond description, I will try to bear it without a murmur.

Margaret Houston
Raven Hill, June 20, 1846

The year of 1845 began with the Houstons planning their new home. The former president's mind was also on the Republic and the question of annexation. Houston went to Raven Hill to supervise the progress there, while Margaret remained with her family at Grand Cane. She was worried about her brother and did what she could to help. She was also worried about her husband's state of mind when he left. Realizing her anxiety, he wrote her at the first opportunity:

Before I left home I was pressed and oppressed by many causes. On reflection, I have concluded to assure you that you need be under no anxiety for my intention is not to drink any thing during my absence. . . . you may rest assured that under no circumstances will I indulge in taking one drop . . . I wish you to be happy![1]

Houston had drawn some simple plans for the house to be built on the highest of the gently rolling hills. He showed the plans to his servant Joshua, who had become an excellent carpenter. Joshua took over the project, and the two calculated that the house would be ready by October of that year. It would be along the lines of the Cedar Point house, only larger. There would be an open passage twelve feet wide in the center, with rooms on either side. Houston described to Margaret his plans for "galleries the whole length of the building 12 feet wide" and that they would be "neatly bannistered on." Set away from the house would be "a neat kitchen with pealed logs." He reported to Margaret that the workers had set out berry plants, quinces, plums, and plenty of figs.² In the same letter he indicated that the costs of the new home were running higher than anticipated. He would need to spend the next few months earning legal fees to meet expenses.

Houston visited briefly in Grand Cane, but by early spring he was back checking on Raven Hill. He reported that the shrubs and flowers he had set out were doing well, and the roses had bloomed. He hoped this was a good omen, which he seemed to feel they would soon need. He sent Margaret a message about Vernal's ward Virginia Thorn, "Watch with double vigilance. Virginia is a fearful child."³

Houston then set out to earn some money, and he wrote to Margaret from Montgomery, Texas. "I have much business affairs to do at this court and I think my dear that I will be able to secure at least one thousand dollars in fees." He had gone by to check on progress at Raven Hill and reported: "It looked changed and improved. It will be beautiful." He ended this letter too with a prophetic statement about Virginia Thorn which they no doubt would later remember: "Beware of Virginia. There is no telling what the little monster may do!" ⁴

In between court cases Houston traveled back and forth to Grand Cane, and he made several trips to Washington to get the furniture and clothing that they had left behind. He was still keeping a closed mouth on the political front. He was being pressed on all sides for a statement, but as he wrote Margaret:

> I have found much excitement on the subject of annexation, but have foreborn the expression of any opinion. All wish to know how I look upon or in what fashion of thought I entertain about

the matter and my reply is "I do not know what action has taken place or what may be necessary to be done. Therefore I can give no satisfactory opinion in the case."[5]

However, in a confidential letter to Andrew Jackson Donelson just a few days later, Houston made his opinion quite clear: "I am in favor of annexation, if it can take place on terms mutually beneficial to both countries. I have, on all occasions . . . withheld no means in my power towards its completion."[6]

His letters that spring indicated that Houston was still planning the trip to Tennessee. He had hoped to be home by late April to get Margaret and Sam and take them with him to Houston, where he would take care of some business before boarding a steamer for the United States. Because of the heavy spring rains it would be late May before he reached home.

Unfavorable newspaper reports denouncing Houston as a traitor began appearing. He finally agreed to make his stand known and accepted a speaking engagement in Houston City. On May 16, he spoke to a large group at the Methodist Church: "I can truly rejoice with you, my fellow citizens, . . . that our annexation to the mother country is assured. . . . I consider the benefit to be derived . . . great beyond the power of language to describe."[7]

While Houston was winding up his business affairs, Margaret was busy with her own project. Antoinette, Margaret, and their mother, along with Joseph and Benjamin Ellis, helped Reverend John B. Brown organize the Concord Baptist Church at Grand Cane. The first person uniting with the new church was Vernal Lea. Houston did not become a member of the church, but he gave his cooperation and joined with the others in erecting a large log house in which to hold services. He later attended the church regularly.[8]

In late May the Houstons and Sam, Jr., reached Galveston and boarded a steamer for New Orleans. Here they visited with William Christy, and Houston made a speech strongly favoring annexation. It was here that word was received that Andrew Jackson was seriously ill and near death. The Houstons hastily boarded a steamer for Nashville. They were delayed for two days when the ship ran aground in the Mississippi River.

The Houstons finally reached Tennessee, and on June 8, they were in a coach en route to the Hermitage when they were hailed by Dr. Esselman, who told them of Jackson's death a few hours before. Soberly they completed their journey up the banjo-shaped driveway to the mansion. With Margaret following, Houston carried Sam, Jr., into the room where Jackson's body lay on a couch. He knelt and laid his head on his old friend's breast. Taking Sam's hand he said, "My son, try to remember that you have looked on the face of this great man."[9]

The Houstons stayed on at the Hermitage. Late that night Houston wrote to President James K. Polk telling him of the circumstances of Jackson's death and expressing his grief that the delay on the river had "denied [him] the satisfaction of seeing [Jackson] in his last moments" and prevented him from administering "if I could, some comfort in the closing scene of his eventful life."[10]

In the same letter Houston described to the President the last few hours of Jackson's life as related by the physician: "He departed with perfect serenity and with full faith in the promises of salvation through the Redeemer." It must have been a painful blow to Margaret that she came so close, but now could never know the one person, besides herself, who was so close to her husband. Yet she would find that even in death, Jackson was her ally in trying to bring Houston into the church. The son of Benjamin Ellis later expressed his opinion of the subject:

> It is doubtful if ever the love of two unrelated men could be greater than the love of Jackson and Houston for each other. . . .
> It is probable that the death of such a faithful friend as Andrew Jackson turned Houston's thoughts more and more to things eternal.[11]

Jackson was buried in the rose garden of the Hermitage beside his wife Rachel, and Houston was a pallbearer. Later, the Houstons were the guests of Emily Donelson, Jackson's niece. Despite the mourning, there were many events honoring the Houstons. For several weeks they visited friends and relatives in Tennessee, including Eliza Moore, who was Houston's sister, and her husband S. A. Moore. Houston was delighted with the news that the Moores intended to relocate in Texas. The Houstons then left to visit Margaret's family in Alabama. Margaret stayed at Henry Lea's home, and her mother joined her there. Houston traveled around the South making speeches while keeping as close an eye as possible on Texas politics. A convention was set to meet at Austin on July 4, 1845, to vote on the American offer for annexation and prepare a state constitution for popular vote. Houston had been elected a delegate from Montgomery County, but he did not cut his trip short to return.[12]

Houston wrote to Margaret from each stop on his speaking tour, sending her the news that he had been welcomed and warmly entertained and pouring out his love for her:

> My Love, I can only say that you are the spring of my joys and the object of my hopes. In short, you are the companion of my heart, and the only star that sheds a light upon my affections. How painful it is to be separated from you.[13]

On a more serious note he warned her of a yellow fever epidemic reported in New Orleans and expressed the fear that for safety's sake, it would probably be necessary for her to stay in Alabama longer than he had hoped. He expected to be back at Raven Hill by the first week in October. However, he instructed her not to leave until she was sure that she could do so in perfect safety.[14] A few days later Houston wrote that he was particularly pleased by the trip to Rodney, Mississippi:

> I met there some men who had been with me at the "Horse Shoe" and one who played the drum at the time that I enlisted! I never have experienced so much feeling and generous enthusiasm in my life, as what was evinced in Mississippi.[15]

115

Margaret, too was feeling the pangs of separation, but found that little Sam was a great comfort to her. She described him as "more interesting than you ever saw him. His ideas and language would astonish you. We have many sweet conversations about dear papa far away." Of her own thoughts she wrote:

> Oh, how I long to see you! . . . It is of course highly gratifying to me to hear that my busy husband receives all honors due to him. . . . I am rejoiced, Love, to hear that you read your bible regularly! Oh continue . . . and purchance [sic] your eyes may soon be opened and you enabled to behold wondrous things out of his law![16]

Houston reached Texas in early October, and there he learned of the death of William Bledsoe. He immediately wrote to Vernal expressing his sorrow and the regret that it was "not in his power" to go to Grand Cane at this time. Things had not progressed satisfactorily at Raven Hill during his long absence and had to be remedied. He also had to make a trip to Washington to bring back the remainder of their furniture before going to Galveston to meet Margaret and Sam. On a happier note, he congratulated Vernal on his marriage to Katherine Davis, the daughter of their Raven Hill neighbor, General Davis.[17]

The following week Margaret read in a Mobile newspaper the notice of William's death. She was anxious for news and wrote to Houston: "We know not how to evaluate the truth of it, yet it seems strange that we have no letters concerning it. Mother is almost frantic, and I am deeply grieved. I long for our time of departure to come."[18] She regretted that this would probably not be until the last week in November. Bledsoe's death had renewed her thoughts about saving Houston's soul and she wrote, "how intensely I feel for your eternal welfare! Why do you hesitate? . . . Oh that the Lord would enlighten your darkness!"

She had written a poem expressing her feelings about this, entitled "To My Husband":

My own one we have said "farewell,"
And I am far far from thee now.
Nor can earth's highest wisdom tell
That we shall meet again below.

Then while thy distant footsteps roam,
Oh I would whisper in thine ear,
This earth is not our lasting home,
We've no abiding mansion here.

Beyond the grave and chilly tomb,
And all life's toil and care
There is a land of endless bloom,
Say dearest, will thou meet me there?

Ah, let me point thy restless eye
Unto the Saviour's bleeding side!
Hear, hear his cry of agony!
My Husband, t'was for thee he died!

And now may peace within thy breast
From Him descend and there remain!
Each night, oh mayst thou sweetly rest
And feel thou hast not "lived in vain!"[19]

Houston had not received her letter concerning the delay in departure and was waiting in Galveston when the ship docked on November 10. Instead of Margaret herself, the ship brought him three letters from her. He was so anxious to see her that he was tempted, "in spite of economy," to take the boat and meet her in New Orleans. Only the fear that she might have already sailed and he would miss her there prevented him from going. Instead he wrote her a long letter and sent her a newspaper clipping. He was still being accused of being against annexation, but he shared his delight with her that one of his old letters, written previous to the battle of San Jacinto, had turned up. In it, he had suggested

117

annexation. He told Margaret, "You will see that I have put the subject . . . pretty much to rest!" He also assured her, "I have not drank even cider since we parted, nor will I ever forget myself so far as to drink any thing which can intoxicate any one."[20]

A few weeks later the Houston family had a joyous reunion and traveled on to Raven Hill. Margaret was probably looking forward to the lazy pace of plantation life with her husband practicing law only a few miles away. However, Houston's inability to turn his back on the needs of Texas was to interfere with such plans. The state constitution had been accepted, but there remained many questions such as boundary limits, debts, etc. to be agreed upon. Many felt that Houston, because of his executive and legal experience, as well as his prestige and influence, was the only one to lead the Texas delegation to the United States Senate. At Raven Hill no doubt the sweet promise of family life crossed Houston's mind, but his friends, led by Ashbel Smith, consulted him about his willingness to serve in the Senate. Houston reflected briefly upon his and Margaret's dream of building their own home and enjoying plantation life, but the long habit of public service was too great.[21] Finally on December 9, 1845, Houston announced his intentions and wrote to Andrew Donelson:

> My friends have urged me to permit my name to run for the Senate, and I have consented on certain conditions, and they are that should my friends and the true friends of the country be satisfied that my services are of the paramount importance in the Senate to all others, and really necessary, I have agreed to serve.[22]

Houston arranged his business affairs so that he could be away and left Margaret and their son at home while he went to Austin. During the short campaign Margaret went to Grand Cane to console her newly widowed sister. Vernal and Katherine Lea had moved in with Antoinette. The plantation was now called "Council Hill" because it had been a favorite meeting place for Houston and the Indian chiefs during the days of the Republic. The house sat in the center of a carefully tended garden and was shaded by dogwood, wild peach, oak, and pine trees.[23]

It is highly improbable that, even in the beautiful surroundings of her sister's home, Margaret was happy at this time. All of her plans for a happy home life seemed to be slipping out of her hands. On December 29, 1845, the Texas state constitution was approved by the United States Congress. The Republic of Texas entered the Union as a state. The newly elected first governor, J. P. Henderson, predicted that "Houston will surely be elected to the U. S. Senate if he will take the place and so it is with Gen'l Rusk."[24]

On February 21, 1846, Houston and Thomas Jefferson Rusk were elected by a large majority to represent Texas in the United States Senate. About the same time Margaret discovered she was expecting their second child. She was determined to accompany her husband to the nation's capital, but Houston was apprehensive about her making so tedious a journey in the early stages of pregnancy. His sister, Eliza Moore, and her family were already en route to visit, and Margaret finally relented and agreed to make the trip later. She was very unhappy about the decision, however, as she expressed in a letter to him a week after he left:

> I was very gloomy during the last few days that you were with me, but I was merely in anticipation of the trial which I had to endure of parting from you. I did feel at one time as if I could not live through it.[25]

The Leas were urging Margaret to come to visit them while Houston was gone. Before he left, Houston wrote Vernal that "taking every thing into view, I doubt much if it would not be best for Margaret to stay here during my absence." He further suggested that it would be best if her mother came to stay with her at Raven Hill.[26]

The next day Houston left Margaret behind and began his journey to Washington. His letters written during the trip clearly indicate that he had mixed emotions about leaving Raven Hill and about the wisdom of his new pursuit. His first letter to Margaret

came from Huntsville and he described his feelings "of my departure from home today " when he had only traveled four miles:

> I had no foreboding of ill, and yet my heart was wrung with
> extreme sorrow and regret. No matter what may await me in the
> character of success or earthly fame, they will be poor requitals
> for what I felt. . . . Had my present attitude been of my own
> choosing, or from feelings of selfishness or ambition, my bitter
> feelings would weigh me down. I would believe that I was
> neglecting the best of wives, & the dearest of companions.[27]

Three days later he was in Houston City where he described
seeing the United States flag flying in the breeze: "We do really form
part, and parcel, of the American Union." He sent Margaret the news
he received that the Moore family had arrived in Galveston, and
that his nephew Houston Moore was already on the way to Raven
Hill. He was hopeful that Margaret would remain at Raven Hill for
a while and that her mother could come to be with her. He
concluded:

> Oh Dearest, you can have no idea, of my love, and my regrets at
> leaving home. . . . My thoughts fly to and embrace you, while sad
> & painful reality tells me that I am distant in sense from all that
> I most love on earth.[28]

In Galveston Bay the Senator boarded the *Alabama* for New
Orleans. Before he left, Houston sent Margaret various supplies
including bacon, apples, and pork, as well as silk and articles of
clothing. Along with them went a letter:

> Dearest, the task which I have to perform, if spared, is a toil, or
> burden which bears heavily upon me. Cou'd I have realized what
> I have done in my desire to return, I believe that I could not have
> consented to have left you & Sam. . . . I hope to write you from
> every point from this to the city, and from there, occurrences of
> every day.[29]

Everywhere Houston stopped the people asked why Margaret was not with him. He reported this to her along with his explanation: "My reply is, 'She is not, or soon will not be in first rate traveling trim. I regret the want of her society; but we do not quarrel about the course.'" From New Orleans he sought to reassure her about any anxieties she might have about his conduct while they were apart:

Were I again at home I could not consent to leave you or Sam. I declare to you my love, that I have no anticipations of pleasure or Glory, from what I may be, nor what I may do in the Senate. My only delightful anticipations arise from the hope which I cherish of again meeting you and Sam. . . . So far as God may enable me to do, I will not, in word, action, or thought indulge in aught that would distress you.[30]

About the same time Margaret was sitting down to write her husband of her feelings:

Many a long, long mile will be between us when you read this letter and it is with feelings the most painful that I think of it. . . . [e]re it reaches you many a prayer from your distant home will have arisen for your safety. . . . All is peace and quiet on Raven Hill. The balmy breeze murmurs so sweetly among the lofty pines and the spring flowers look up so cheerfully that I sometimes almost forget my grief and fancy that you are at my side. . . . Every thing grows finely that you have planted. The grape vines, rose bushes, and bois-d-arcs have all put forth their leaves and your favourite ash is covered with green leaves.[31]

In the same letter Margaret expressed how much comfort it was to have their nephew Houston Moore with her. She had found him "quite a business fellow and very useful." She was looking forward to the rest of the Moore family arriving and hoped they would stay until her husband's return. She had become convinced that she should remain at home instead of going to Grand Cane. She was worried about Houston receiving her letters and assured him: "If you do not get letters from me regularly, you may charge it all to the irregularity of the mail from this place." She told him she would try to keep her spirits up and would look forward to a great deal of consolation from his letters.

Almost as if he could read her mind, Houston was writing to Margaret from Louisville, Kentucky: "You may be assured that I will write whenever I can, no matter what the press of business. . . . Whenever we stop, if but for an hour, I will write if only to say that I live and love you dearly."[32]

Margaret's spirits rose when the Moores and their three youngest children arrived. Before Houston's departure he had arranged for his brother-in-law to rent a nearby farm. Margaret wrote that she was delighted that Houston Moore had agreed to stay on at Raven Hill and help her run the place. The three older girls were also planning to stay with Margaret until the Senator returned. The Moores had also brought news of Antoinette. They had met her as they sailed up the Trinity, and Antoinette and her niece Sarah Ann Royston were on their way to Galveston.[33]

On March 28, 1846, Houston reached Washington. He quickly sized up the state of affairs and described it to Margaret:

> My colleague . . . presented my credentials to the Senate where I took the Oath, and my seat. So Texas is fully represented in the Senate, and persons say as ably as any State of the Union. Ably I say because we are the tallest gentlemen from any State, and in all respects as sizeable. . . . On the Oregon Subject there is a pretty equal division, and it may be that the vote of the Texian Senators will decide the question in favor of the notice.

He continued by describing a visit to the White House in which he was "most kindly received by both the President and his Lady." He was pleased by the reception he was receiving in the capital:

> Every person renders to me respect, so far as it is in their power, and nothing pleases me so much as the inquiries which are made

about you, and the character which they tell me they have heard of you. This is done by old familiars, who more than rejoiced to see me. You have at least as much popularity, if not more than I have.... My love, you can have no idea of the pain which I endure in absence from you and our dear boy.[34]

With this letter began a pattern that would continue for the next thirteen years. As a senator, Houston had access to an ample supply of paper and writing materials, and the mail went out regularly. He would write almost daily, and on some occasions twice a day, to describe his activities and national politics. He would even write while in the Senate Chamber, often hurriedly, with the notation "not read over," excusing his missing words or repetitions. On Sundays he would describe his visits to church and report on the sermons, in letters often written while his rooms were filled with visitors attempting to talk to him. With the exception of the days when his shoulder wound was bothering him, his handwriting would be large and bold, and all letters would be full of devotion and the desire to be at home.

Margaret, on the other hand, was faced with a different situation. Her letters were written in quiet solitude or sometimes with the children at her side. Even when regular, the mail service was only once a week, and often it was held up by high water or bad weather. Sometimes it was almost a month before she could get a letter out. Paper was scarce. She wrote once a week in a neat, but small and cramped handwriting. If she came to the end of the paper before she had said everything, she would turn the paper sideways and write over the other parts. She made an attempt to be cheerful, and when problems arose she usually put off writing about them until after they had been solved. Her letters were full of family business, news of the children and her devotion to her husband. As Margaret described them:

> These are homely details (love for a senator at Washington) and would not bear repetition at a "President's Levee" but you must remember that our little world is a very contracted one and we know little there is occurring beyond it.[35]

Houston had only been in the capital for a week when he began making plans for Margaret to join him:

> Without your presence, I do declare to you, if earth contains a joy or happiness for me, I do not know it. The idea of being detained here until July is awful to me. How I can live without you, is to me an enigma. If you are satisfied that you can travel without danger to your situation . . . do not for once think of the expense! . . . Your health is my happiness. Do as you think well.[36]

By the next day he was already worrying for her safety on the long tedious journey he had just suggested:

> In coming on by the usual mode of conveyance from Texas here, the traveling is bad as far as stages are concerned, as you are compelled to travel day and night, from the Ohio river, to the rail cars. There is no stopping the stage when it might be highly necessary. . . . On yesterday I wrote to you to come on, if you could do so with perfect safety. Nothing on earth could render me more happy than to see you here, if it can be so without risk of your precious health and safety. If either is to be endangered, do not come, I beseech you.[37]

At Raven Hill Margaret was facing the same dilemma. Her ultimate decision to stay may have been influenced by the fact that war was brewing with Mexico and that it was the middle of May before she received any letters that her husband had written from Washington. She was packing for the trip when Eliza Moore arrived. Having just finished a trip herself, Eliza was strongly against Margaret's plan to travel. Reluctantly Margaret agreed and sat down to write Houston the news:

> You can imagine my state of mind for a few weeks past. It amounted almost to desperation. . . . Never have I been so strongly tempted to act in opposition to the dictates of my judgment, as by your proposal to join you in Washington. I felt

willing at first, to risk my life in the attempt rather than be longer without you, but our dear sister Eliza's cooler judgement prevailed against it, and I agreed the more readily to be governed by her, because I knew that with me, feeling had so much to do in the matter that it would really be unwise to decide for myself. . . . Oh my love, if you could only look into my heart this moment, I know you would never leave me again.[38]

While Margaret was making her decision she was also struggling with a family problem. She had heard that Mr. Charles Power, a wealthy English merchant in Galveston, intended to court Antoinette as soon "as she la[id] off her mourning." Margaret wrote to Houston that she thought it would be a useless attempt and that she presumed that Antoinette had not "received an intimation of it yet."[39] Margaret was wrong on both counts. When the Moore family had seen Antoinette on the Trinity River, she was on her way to see Charles Power. On April 16, 1846, less than a year after the death of her first husband, Antoinette Lea Bledsoe was married to Charles Power in Galveston. Once again Nancy Lea was unable to prevent a daughter's marriage, and a rift developed between Margaret and Antoinette. In Washington, Houston received the news and he, too, was not pleased:

So soon to marry and from home too, distresses me. . . . I fear that Antoinette will receive little aid from her companion in affairs of religious character!

He continued with a bit of advice to his wife in the hopes of healing the rift between the sisters:

If she and the family are satisfied, we ought not to object, and further more it is too late to express regrets. . . . My love, it may be that Mr. Power and Antoinette may visit you, and if they should, treat them with all the kindness in your power! Forget all that has passed. She is our Sister. I know your great affection for her, and that it wrings your heart to say or do anything that would wound her feelings.[40]

A few days later Houston received a letter from Charles Power. He sent the letter on to Margaret with the promise that he would write a kind letter in return. He assured her, "I will not for the world do aught that could mar your intercourse with your Sister." He added a P. S. as an afterthought: "Dear, I have just thought of It! We married to please ourselves, and Antoinette and Mr. Power have only done the same thing!"[41]

Margaret wrote that Vernal had received a letter from Antoinette in which she "considered herself the happiest being on earth." Mr. Power had presented Antoinette with two necklaces, one diamonds and the other emeralds. Margaret feared that the inducements of wealth and fashion would engross all her sister's time.[42]

Houston sent her his advice on the subject:

> . . . about our dear Sister Antoinette. I was distressed and some what irritated at first, but upon reflection I am perfectly satisfied with the match. I hope they will do well, live long, and be happy! Don't think of it again. Be satisfied, and not distressed. We do not know the reasons, or the motives, which caused her apparently hasty action.[43]

Eventually all would be forgiven and the couple would come into favor with all family members. The family ties would be further strengthened a few months later when Varilla's daughter, Sarah Ann Royston, married Thomas, the brother of Charles Power.[44] When Houston heard of this coming marriage he could not help comparing it to his own wedding and making a few "tongue in cheek" complaints:

> Will she make him go to Alabama for her? Or marry at the Island? Our relations are more cheap, I fear, than when you would not marry me or come to Texas, but required me to go after you to Alabama, and indeed, my Love, tho' I might not be willing to go as far again for any other Lady, I certainly would for you![45]

In the same letter Houston wrote his wife some news that would cheer her. He had been attending the Presbyterian Church every Sunday, where he always contributed for some purpose which was not announced by the minister. He had decided that he would now attend the E Street Baptist Church. He gave her his reasons: "If I do contribute, my Love, I would rather do it to that church, because it may be a means of enabling that society to send a missionary to our neighbourhood, and add to your happiness."

Houston continued to assure Margaret of his proper behavior. He described a dinner at the White House:

> I sat on the right hand of Madam President. . . . To be candid, my ever dear wife, I would rather have sat on your right hand in our Log Cabin, than to have been in the "White House." The Madam excused me from taking a Glass of even "white wine." They all know what my imputed failing has been, and all ascribe my reformation to your benign influence over me. This I do not disclaim. So you see my dear the position which you occupy in the esteem of the circles here.[46]

The next night he described to Margaret what he had worn to the White House. His clothing was much more conservative than in his previous visits to Washington: "You will wish to know how I dress, and I will tell you. A neat black hat, black vest and cravat, grey coat (frock) and pantaloons, with Boots."[47]

He wrote that he had received many invitations, but had been so busy that he had not returned any visits. One visit, however, would soon be made. Dolley Madison had requested that he call. "I have to visit Mrs. Madison. . . . She expects it of all men, whom she thinks distinguished."[48]

Margaret had already received favorable news from a friend. She informed her husband what she had heard:

> [y]ou were winning golden opinions from all classes of persons by the strictness of your habits and the sincerity of your manners. These things are very cheering to me, love, but not as you may suppose on account of the bearing they have upon your political advancement. We know that you may have a slight

influence with me, I admit, but the principal cause of my rejoicing is the hope that it may be the "promise of better things . . . even things pertaining to life everlasting" and that the calmness and serenity for which you are so much esteemed may be the dawning of that change which I have so earnestly sought for you at the throne of grace.[49]

Houston continued to praise Margaret by telling her what his colleagues were saying about her:

Indeed all whom I see and become intimate with express the greatest anxiety to see Mrs. Houston. . . . They have heard that you have done so much for me that they regard you as a very extraordinary personage. To tame, and regulate a man who has hereto been deemed untamable and now so sage and regulated is rather novel with all their . . . curiosity.[50]

He also continued to stress his unhappiness over their separation:

My Dear, I feel sad and melancholy. Sad because I will be detained here, Melancholy because you are far from me. . . . I am not enjoying an hour's happiness since we parted! . . . The sun here does not shine so bright, nor does the earth look so lovely here as it does in Texas. You my Love, are there![51]

A few days later he promised: "About my returning to the Senate will depend on you. I am cured of all love of office, or station when it interferes with my love for you and the sweets of home!"[52]

It was during this session of Congress that the first book about Sam Houston was begun. Ashbel Smith had long urged Houston to publish an autobiography. Houston was introduced to Charles Edwards Lester, a fluent young writer who wanted to take on the task. Houston, as custodian of the archives of the Republic of Texas, made these records available to Lester. For three months the two men spent many hours together in Houston's room at the National Hotel, with Houston dictating and amending the manuscript. When published it was titled *Sam Houston and His Republic.* It was written in the third person and included a preface which stated: "This book will lose me some friends, but if it lost me all and gained me none, in God's name as I am a free man I would publish it."[53]

It was rumored that this book was part of a campaign by Houston supporters to send him to the White House. Houston wrote Margaret that every day calls were made upon him and allusions to the subject of the next presidency. His opinion on the subject was that the office "will be a thorny path to those who are confined to it!" He reassured Margaret:

> If I could command the station, (if I know my own heart) I would not be willing to accept the Situation. Thus you see, my dear, I am more in love with your Dear Society and presence than with earthly honors. They have no charms for me, when they would call my time off from you & Sam.[54]

During this stay in Washington, D.C., Houston began a pattern of purchasing for his family things they could not get at home. He asked Margaret if she would like to have a locket with a daguerreotype of his likeness and a new velvet dress.[55] When Margaret received his letter she answered that she would be delighted with the likeness. As to the dress, she would wear it to make him happy, but if it was of no consequence to him, she would rather that he send her some books.[56] Later when the likeness arrived, she wrote delightedly that she could almost fancy that he had been thinking of her when it was taken, and that she had pressed it fondly to her lips and heart, wishing that he could have been as close at the moment.[57]

Margaret also wrote that her mother was coming for a visit and, since she might still be there upon his return, offered him some advice on how to get along with the headstrong Nancy Lea:

> If you find her here on your return, My Love, I hope you will endeavor to yield as much as possible to her prejudices. She is

high spirited and a little overbearing, I admit, but she has one of
the most gentle and affectionate hearts that ever beat, and the
surest way of gaining her acquiescence in matters of importance
is by yielding to her in trifles.[58]

When he answered her letter, Houston calmed her fears:

My Love, you may rely upon this assurance. Let what may take
place, my pledge is given. . . .I love the old Lady as a Mother, and
have resolved to defer to her age and her disposition. Her blood
is much like my own.

He also warned Margaret again about Vernal's ward, Virginia Thorn,
then living with Nancy Lea, and expressed the hope that when his
mother-in-law visited she would not bring with her "that little
sinner, Virginia."[59]

In Washington Senator Houston was dealing with a problem of
increasing national importance. The previous year when the Republic of Texas had been deciding the annexation question, Mexico
had threatened to go to war if Texas joined the United States.
General Zachary Taylor had been sent with a United States Army to
camp on the Texas side of the Rio Grande, and in the spring of 1846
several skirmishes broke out between the Mexican and the American soldiers. In Texas, Ashbel Smith wrote to Houston that if a
Texas company was to be taken into Mexico, the Texans were
looking to Houston to lead them into victory.[60]

Houston wrote Margaret of his visit with the President until
midnight to "discourse about the unpleasant news from the Rio
Grande." The House, he informed her, had that day passed an act
declaring war against Mexico and he expected the Senate to do the
same tomorrow. Houston expressed the hope that neither his
brother-in-law S. A. Moore nor his nephew Houston Moore would go
into the army, since they were both "new-comers to Texas."[61]

Margaret wrote him of the situation at home in regard to the
anticipated war:

We have great excitement through our county about the war. A large number of volunteers are preparing to set off, and as usual on such occasions, a perfect mania is abroad on the subject. [Houston Moore] is almost crazy to go, but I have no apprehension of his doing so before your return. Nothing however, but the care of us could keep him. Col. Woods expects to set off with his company on Thursday. He sent up today to request my presence at his house on next Monday to direct the making of his flag. Perhaps he thinks my connection with you may give it some charm.[62]

Houston was being pressed from all sides to accept a military commission and take part in the war. He hedged, wanting to discuss it with Margaret before deciding. During the next few weeks he wrote to her several times on the matter:

I wrote to you by last night's mail and assured you that I would not consent to accept any Military or civil appointment, unless by your free voluntary consent! I love you and home more than all the honors of the world.[63]

If I could be with you but one hour, I could tell you strange things which would convince you that I am not ambitious of Glory, or I could be in the field at once, and with high command. To all who speak to me, I reply that "I will not again accept of any station which will separate me from my dear family." This much only have I promised, that I will "write to Mrs. Houston, and see if she will freely consent for me to take a command or go to war." So you see my Love, I will not commit myself without your free consent. Dearest, I have no wish but yours.[64]

By early June things were coming to a head and Houston felt even more pressure to commit one way or the other. He dictated a letter which his secretary Washington Miller sent to Margaret. It gave her the news that in contemplation of a war with Mexico, there was "a very general feeling" that Houston should control one of the armies of invasion. He was totally uncommitted, and though strongly urged, he had not changed his "original resolve not to adopt any cause" that in the slightest degree violated any pledges he had made to her. The letter assured her:

> . . . if you decide against my entering the service, you will not inflict upon me the slightest pain, nor under any circumstances, will you ever incur from me a single reproach; for I will only regard it as an evidence of strong affection. . . . I know the decision will be painful.[65]

Later the same night when Miller had retired, Houston wrote a second letter, explaining that he had not felt comfortable dictating a letter which would discuss the bearing that Margaret's pregnancy might have on her decision. He was aware that no one could "judge of that and the feelings incident to it" but Margaret herself, and he truly desired her to consult her own wishes. He made it plain that it would be her decision and he would abide by it:

> I feel assured that you will know my unutterable devotion to you, and can appreciate my feelings about entering the army. You will regard the whole matter, placing your feelings and happiness and my love for you above all & every earthly consideration, and in view of these matters, you will decide.

The letter asked for her decision as soon as possible. He had given no encouragement to "solicitations from all quarters of the country," but he would soon have to give an answer. A strange postscript concluded his letter: "My love, what do your dreams indicate? You know they are famous for making great men!!"[66] Margaret's reply to this part of the letter would be that her dreams "partake so much of the melancholy of the day that I would dislike to trust them implicitly."[67]

While Houston was waiting for Margaret's letter, he made a decision which would ultimately bring her much happiness. He went to the E Street Baptist Church to hear a new young preacher, the Reverend Mr. George Samson, who he described as "one of the most able divines that I have any where heard."[68] As time went on, Dr. Samson would become one of Margaret's greatest allies in helping bring her husband into the Baptist Church.

It took over a month for Houston to receive Margaret's answer concerning a military appointment. Before her letter arrived in Washington, he wrote to her again:

> Long since, you have received my letter on the subject of my entering the army, and I doubt not my Love, but what you gave your negative to the proposition. If you have done so, you may rely upon my faith that I will be satisfied, for I could not give up the society of your dear self & Sam for all the honors of this vast world! Each day I live only endears to me more tenderly our woodland home, and disaffects me more & more to the world at large. I may truly say the days are wild, & I have no pleasure in them! I can not be happy, nor can I have pleasure where you are not![69]

Houston was wrong about her decision. As soon as she received her husband's letters Margaret returned her answer. First she expressed the hope that he would be home before her letter could reach him:

> . . . consequently, when my letter returns, as of course it will do so, you may have some curiosity to know what I said to you when you were far away. . . . I most sincerely hope, that when you read it, I shall be sitting, as in bye gone days, on your lap, with my arms around your neck.

Then, following the path she had long ago chosen concerning her part in determining Houston's career, she stated absolutely that she would not stand in the way of his joining the army. However, she could not resist a tug at his heartstrings by mentioning little Sam:

Dearest, you tell me that I should decide whether or not you are to go out with the army. Alas, what has always been my decision when my own happiness or the good of the country was to be sacrificed? Have I not invariably ascertained your views and then coincided with them, let my own sacrifices be what they might? And even now, though your personal danger will be far greater than it has been on any previous occasion, since our marriage, I will not express one word of opposition, but I cannot . . . hear my poor boy's plaintive cry, "What makes pa stay so long?" and then tell you that I am willing for you to go. . . . I wish you to be governed entirely by your own judgment, and though the decision may bring misery upon me beyond description, I will try to bear it without a murmur. [70]

Margaret followed that letter with another in case the first one did not reach him:

. . . you will be anxious to know what I have to say in relation to your going into the army. You call upon me, dearest, to decide the case as a mark of affection & confidence. . . . I assure you that I would not oppose your going [torn] single word and even now I will say nothing against it, but I cannot give you a "cheerful consent" as you require. There are too many reasons why I could not.

I shall now resign myself to the belief that you are going so that you need have no apprehension of the sudden effects of a surprise upon me when I hear that you have taken the command. [71]

Margaret was as wrong in her assumption as Houston had been in his. Houston made the decision to turn down the commission, and answered her immediately:

Your decision was right about army matters. I am not committed, and nothing but an emergency of great need will induce me to renew the toils of camp, and then not until we have talked it over face to face. . . . I assure you that your request shall be complied with, and carried out to the letter.

Houston went on to comment on her mention of Sam, Jr., acknowledging that while he most truly sympathized with her, he knew that she must have been feeling "great depression & melancholy, or [she] would not make the request which you have done in relation to our dear Boy." He confessed that he blamed himself "necessary as it seemed to be," that he had ever left her in her present situation:

> It was not without pain of heart. It seemed like tearing me from all the ties of tenderness and life. No one could have felt more truly or more tenderly. It was the only time in my life that I yielded so reluctantly to what I thought a duty to you and all of us![72]

Margaret had often written that there were many things she wanted to say to him that she could not put in a letter. Houston mentioned the same problem and declared that if it were possible, he would be willing for her to know his every thought and action that had transpired "since Sam had pointed to the tear on my cheek, and said 'Pa what is that?'" He wrote of his anxiety to be home: "I have a thousand reasons to wish to be at home, and not one to be absent!"[73]

A few days later he wrote Margaret that he hoped to be on his way before this letter would reach her, and he described his feelings at the time:

> Never did a poor exile sigh for the home of his birth or the companions of his youth, as I do for our woodland home. The sweet breezes of the south, and their music in the tall pines of Raven Hill visit me only in fancy, while my heart is with you and the inmates of our quiet home. . . . I am as much, if not more in love with you than I have ever been in my whole life.[74]

At the end of the Congressional Session Houston hurried back to Raven Hill. Perhaps as he began his trip to Texas with the hope of reaching home before the birth of his second child he was thinking of one of Margaret's last letters, which had expressed her expectations for the future: "Bright days and cloudless skies may be in store for us, brighter from the laughing faces that may gather around us."[75]

---

[1] Franklin Williams Collection, Huntsville, Houston to Margaret, January 24, 1845.

[2] Ibid., Houston to Margaret, January 27, 1845.

[3] Ibid., Houston to Margaret, March 25, 1845.

[4] Ibid., Houston to Margaret, April 1, 1845.

[5] Ibid.

[6] Sam Houston, *Writings*, vol. 4, Houston to Donelson, April 9, 1845.

[7] Ibid., vol. 4, 12–13. The Texas newspapers were all greatly opposed to Houston at this time and did not publish the speech. However, a shorthand reporter was in the audience and took down the entire speech. It was some years later before it was published.

[8] Ellis, 51–52.

[9] Andrew Jackson Houston, family story.

[10] Sam Houston, *Writings*, vol. 4, 424, Houston to Polk, June 8, 1845.

[11] Ellis, 79.

[12] Friend, 159.

[13] Franklin Williams Collection, Huntsville, Houston to Margaret, September 17, 1845.

[14] Ibid., Houston to Margaret, September 26, 1845.

[15] Ibid., September 28, 1845.

[16] Ibid., Margaret to Houston, October 13, 1845.

[17] Ibid., Houston to Vernal Lea, October 14, 1845.

[18] Ibid., Margaret to Houston, October 20, 1845.

[19] Ibid., Margaret to Houston, n.d.

[20] Ibid., Houston to Margaret, November 10, 1845.

[21] Wisehart, 487.

[22] Sam Houston, *Writings*, vol. 7, 15–16.

[23] Rosa Brown, *Texas Scrapbook,* (Houston: Concord Press, 1945), n.p.

[24] Ashbel Smith Papers, Henderson to Smith, January 10, 1846.

[25] Franklin Williams Collection, Huntsville, Margaret to Houston, March 19, 1846.

[26] Jean and Price Daniel Collection, Houston to Vernal Lea, March 6, 1846.

[27] Franklin Williams Collection, Huntsville, Houston to Margaret, March 7, 1846.

[28] Ibid., March 10, 1846.

[29] Ibid., March 14, 1846.

[30] Ibid., March 16, 1846.

[31] Ibid., Margaret to Houston, March 19, 1846.

[32] Ibid., Houston to Margaret, March 23, 1846.

[33] Ibid., Margaret to Houston, March 24, 1846.

[34] Ibid., Houston to Margaret, March 31, 1846.

[35] Ibid., Margaret to Houston, April 14, 1846.

[36] Ibid., Houston to Margaret, April 4, 1846.

[37] Ibid., Houston to Margaret, April 5, 1846.

[38] Sam Houston Papers, Barker History Center, University of Texas, Margaret to Houston, May 16, 1846.

[39] Franklin Williams Collection, Margaret to Houston, April 6, 1846.

[40] Ibid., Houston to Margaret, April 27, 1846.

[41] Ibid., Houston to Margaret, April 30, 1846.

[42] Ibid., Margaret to Houston, May 28, 1846.

[43] Ibid., Houston to Margaret, May 25, 1846.

[44] Madge W. Hearne Papers, San Antonio, "Notes on the Lea Family," n.d.

[45] Franklin Williams Collection, Huntsville, Houston to Margaret, May 10, 1846.

[46] Ibid., Houston to Margaret, April 8, 1846.

[47] Ibid., Houston to Margaret, April 9, 1846.

[48] Ibid., Houston to Margaret, April 17, 1846.

[49] Ibid., Margaret to Houston, May 28, 1846.

[50] Ibid., Houston to Margaret, May 30, 1846.

[51] Ibid., Houston to Margaret, May 2, 1846.

[52] Ibid., Houston to Margaret, May 7, 1846.

[53] Charles Edwards Lester, *Sam Houston and His Republic* (New York: Burgess, Stringer, and Co., 1846), n.p.

[54] Franklin Williams Collection, Huntsville, Houston to Margaret, May 22, 1846.

[55] Ibid., Houston to Margaret, April 23, 1846.

[56] Ibid., Margaret to Houston, May 28, 1846.

[57] Ibid., Margaret to Houston, n.d. (circa June, 1846).

[58] Ibid., Margaret to Houston, May 28, 1846.

[59] Ibid., Houston to Margaret, June 25, 1846.

[60] Ashbel Smith Papers, Barker History Center, University of Texas, Smith to Houston, May 13, 1846.

[61] Franklin Williams Collection, Huntsville, Houston to Margaret, May 10, 1846.

[62] Sam Houston Papers, Barker History Center, University of Texas Library, Margaret to Houston, May 16, 1846.

[63] Franklin Williams Collection, Huntsville, Houston to Margaret, May 21, 1846.

[64] Ibid., Houston to Margaret, May 25, 1846.

[65] Ibid., Houston to Margaret, June 1, 1846 (in the handwriting of W. D. Miller).

[66] Ibid., Houston to Margaret, June 1, 1846.

[67] Ibid., Margaret to Houston, n.d., circa June, 1846.

[68] Ibid., Houston to Margaret, July 12, 1846.

[69] Ibid., Houston to Margaret, June 28, 1846.

[70] Sam Houston Papers, Barker History Center, University of Texas, Margaret to Houston, June 20, 1846.

[71] Franklin Williams Collection, Huntsville, Margaret to Houston, fragmented, n.d.

[72] Ibid., Houston to Margaret, July 17, 1846.

[73] Ibid., Houston to Margaret, July 21, 1846.

[74] Ibid., Houston to Margaret, July 24, 1846.

[75] Ibid., Margaret to Houston, n.d., circa June, 1846.

Photograph of an engraving of Sam Houston about age 53 by J. C. Buttre. Courtesy of Sam Houston Regional Library and Research Center, Liberty, Texas.

In June of 1846, Margaret wrote Houston that his picture had arrived safely: "Would that my beloved were as near me as it is at this moment. I almost fancy, my dearest, you were thinking of me when it was taken."

Chapter VII

I have suffered two or three mails to pass without writing to you for the reason that my breast was in such condition that I could not write without detriment to myself. It has risen three times and the last time presented such an angry appearance that Brother Charles prevailed upon us to send for Dr. Smith. . . . He has decided it must be operated on. . . . With the help of God I hope to sit down to it like a soldier.

Margaret Houston, February 10, 1847

Congress closed late on August 10, 1846, and Houston wrote letters until early the next morning. To one friend he wrote, "I am most painfully anxious to see my dear Wife, and my young Pioneer. I was always fond of home, but I now place something like a true estimate upon the source of true happiness—Home."[1] Margaret would be happy with the news that he had declined an army appointment. The next day he left Washington and arrived at Raven Hill in time for the birth of his first daughter. Nancy Elizabeth Houston was born on September 6, 1846. She was named for both grandmothers and would be called Nannie.

When Houston returned to Texas he found the Raven Hill plantation greatly improved. The main house was finished and now was a comfortable home. A large kitchen stood apart from the house connected by a covered runway. Nearby was the smokehouse. Rows of slave cabins had replaced the primitive lean-to structures. Across the road from the cabins were the black-smith shop, barns, and pens for the horses and cattle. A large vegetable garden provided most of the food for the family and all the workers.[2]

While he was home during the summer Houston supervised the start of a new project. Joshua was building him a small boxlike cabin which he would use for an office. In this room Houston would store his trunks of documents and papers. He spent the remainder of his time tending to family business and making a few political speeches.

No doubt his time with Margaret and the children was all too short to suit her. For some time Margaret had been having problems with a small tumor in her breast, and now it was increasing in size and beginning to give her pain. It was decided that she would go with the children and Virginia Thorn to visit the Leas at Grand Cane as soon as she was able to make the trip. By late November Houston had left her and was reluctantly on his way back to the nation's capital.

Margaret sent a letter by Mr. Holliman, a friend who was to see Houston before he sailed from Galveston. Knowing that the friend would repeat to Houston the family's concerns for her health, Margaret wrote in detail about her situation. Her breast had been lanced and the tumor seemed smaller. However, if this treatment did not prove successful she would "proceed directly to Memphis and have an operation performed by Dr. Thomas." Katherine Lea would accompany her and the children would stay with Margaret's mother. Margaret was hopeful that this would not be necessary and felt that she would soon be well.[3]

After reaching the capital, Houston and the other Texas officials left Washington and spent a week in New York. He wrote Margaret that never had he "seen persons more kindly treated than was the Texas Delegation." He himself received "nine cheers" from the audience at a "horse theatre." He sent her the accounts of the visit as reported by the newspapers with the comment, "All seemed pleased and gratified that we turned out not to be savages."[4]

On the night of New Year's Eve Houston made a speech to the temperance society. He wrote Margaret that while he would have rather spent Christmas and New Year's with her than "in the hurly burly of New York" he was pleased with the success of his speech:

> I was taken by a committee, introduced, and made a speech which
> was received with great enthusiasm. . . . My love, I could well

make a temperance speech because during the tremendous festivities of the season, I did not take even a glass of Egg[nog] or any thing else stronger than pure water.[5]

Houston's name was still being mentioned as a commander in the army. Unbeknownst to him, a few weeks earlier President Polk had written in his diary that he was committed to Houston if another major general was to be appointed.[6] Houston sent Margaret some of the newspaper clippings mentioning his name with the comments:

> You need not be alarmed my Love, about any impression which may be made upon me by such things for I assure you that my affection for you has not been clouded for one moment nor would I exchange even a woodland with you surrounded by our babes and friends for any earthly situation. . . . I seek no station higher than the possession [of] your affections for I esteem that the hight [sic] of mortal bliss.[7]

A few days later pressure was being put on him and he wrote to Margaret:

> Altho the President, Genl. Rusk, and many friends are anxious that I should go, I nevertheless decline all solicitations solely because I love my Dear Wife and little ones more that than I favor the honors of this world. To fame and to the world, I have generously dedicated a great portion of my life in the hope that I was promoting human happiness. . . . The only hours of pleasure which have cast sunshine upon my heart in manhood (where no cloud could dim its brightness) are those which I have passed with you, and I would not exchange my hopes of future joys and happiness anticipated for the triumphs of a Hero who had dictated peace to a conquered nation, even in the "Halls of Montezuma." Were it your request I would freely, tho' not willingly . . . do it.[8]

When Margaret received this letter, she replied:

> I would give you my opinion on the war question in this, but it is
> not necessary as I have already written at length upon it.
> However, lest my letter should have missed you, I will merely
> mention that I left it entirely to your own discretion. How much
> my happiness depends upon your society, I need not repeat, but
> if the path of duty is plain before you, I would not dare to place
> an obstacle in your way.[9]

Houston had made the decision to decline the appointment
even before her answer reached him. It must have been a great relief
to her when he sent her an editorial from a large Pennsylvania paper
with the message:

> Where I resist much more and direct influences to accept such
> place, you will be able to some extent to judge of my affection for
> home and yourself.... I see ... proud men, daily panting for such
> and humbler stations, yet I wish for none. I sigh for no place but
> home!! ... I have no wish to be engaged in any excitement but to
> spend the balance of the Session as usefully and quietly as
> possible.[10]

From Grand Cane Margaret wrote to her husband some of the
problems she was having with Virginia. There had been an earlier
incident at home which Margaret referred to as "the poisoning."
Although she did not discuss it in front of little Sam, he still
remembered it and seemed to be afraid of Virginia. Margaret
described the situation: "That he identifies her I can not doubt, for
he never speaks to her, but I perceive him occasionally at a distance
casting a cautious glance toward her."[11]

Houston replied and described his son as "the most cautious
and wary of all human beings" and commented that Sam's conduct
with Virginia "demonstrates a wonderful degree of wisdom &
prudence."[12] He did not tell Margaret then that when he read her

letter he was seized with a feeling of anxiety which he did not understand at the time. Later her would tell her of his feelings:

> Why it was so I can't tell, but I felt or I thought something like a cold sensation of feeling come over my heart when I read your letter. This is no fiction, I assure you. It was a painful sense, but why the emotion was, I can not yet resolve![13]

At the same time Houston was dealing with another personal problem. His sister, Mary Wallace, had suffered what was first thought to be a mental breakdown. Now she was not expected to survive. He poured out his sorrow to Margaret:

> Her afflictions are the most distressing and melancholy that can exist. She is not in an asylum now, but in the vicinity of Lexington. Her disease arises from an enlargement and pressure of the bone upon the brain. There is no possibility of her recovery. No circumstance so fearfully distressing has ever befallen me as to think that a sister is to leave this world with a mind shattered and not capable of reflection nor placing any estimate upon the awful transaction from time to Eternity.[14]

A few days later his mind was still on Eternity, although this time his thoughts had turned to his children:

> Life is at best a fleeting show, and we can only render it profitable and our latter end happy by virtue and active piety. I pray God to enable me to impress this conviction upon the minds of our dear offspring! I feel more and more each day anxious to imbue their young minds with lessons of such character. If spared, I will draft a code for our son, and hope he will read it at an age when he will imbibe such feelings and sentiments as will guide him in after life. . . . We cannot be too careful of our charge, and I feel assured that I will never forget my duty to them, and their dear mother.[15]

Houston had been in Washington for six weeks and had only received two letters from Margaret. He was sad and lonely and homesick for Texas. The weather did not improve his mood. "When I look out of the window, the air and earth looks gloomy to me. I think of the sunny south, my wife, my young barbarians, and our friends, and sigh for our rustic home."[16] He also had received no further word on the condition of his sister and was deeply concerned over her fate. He described to Margaret how slowly the time seemed to be passing: "...I know the sand of life is wasting by hours and days and years, and when once exhausted, it can never run again."[17] He was counting the days until the session of Congress was over and he would be released from what he described as "this prison."

> I will fly with all speed to meet and greet my Love and embrace our little ones. You are continually clustering around my heart & mingling with my best affections. My whole heart is thine and every day the desires of preferment which I ever had are diminished or swallowed up in my rustic love of home! I will write every leisure moment and I will constantly think of and love you all.[18]

Houston had been keeping a low key in the Senate, listening more than speaking. When the senators were engaged in a debate on finance, he wrote Margaret commenting on his own weaknesses in that area: "This you know my dear, is not suited to my capacity, so you will not expect me to speak upon it."[19]

The army bill was a different matter, and he reported that he "took a pretty active part in the discussion":

> I will not gratify grown children in mischievous fancies. So I have been obedient to a sense of duty. Too much was required of the party. A sacrifice of principles was I thought demanded of me so I dissented from the wishes of the administration in its desire to raise a Regular and standing army.[20]

A few days later he was supporting the administration in asking Congress to give the president three million dollars to negotiate a peace treaty with Mexico. Houston wrote of his friends as being extremely gratified by the speech and described it to Margaret:

> I furnished the world much new matter and information relative to Texas. The audience was immense and perhaps the best evidence which was rendered in favor of the speech was that none left, tho' I spoke for more than two hours. I was not personal to any one, but treated the subject as a Texian and as an American Senator.[21]

While things were going well politically for the Senator, his mind was on Margaret. It had been weeks since he had received a letter from her and he had begun to sense that there were serious problems at home. During the first week of February he began to mention his fears:

> Weeks have now elapsed since I have heard from you or home. . . . I am left sad and melancholy. I am not complaining my Love, of neglect, but of disappointed hope! Vernal . . . could have written to me a single line if you were sick or could not write.[22]

> I am painfully apprehensive that you are ill or that our dear little ones are suffering. Unless I get letters in a few days, I will despair of hearing again until I reach home. . . . I thought when I was at home that I loved you all tenderly. I did so, but I find that absence has changed the character of my affections from tenderness to wildness.[23]

He began to search for reasons for the missing mail:

> It may be that they have been purloined as statesmen are in some instances jealous of me and may suppose that I am writing treason to you, and that your letters would render a key to my

designs. That they should think so is reasonable when we reflect that the idea is afloat that you are really my "confidential adviser."[24]

A few days later he wrote that his mind was filled with a "foreboding," and his anxiety was increasing hourly. He now felt certain that sickness was the cause of his not receiving any letters.[25] Houston was even more apprehensive when he received a letter from a Galveston friend and learned that no one had heard from Margaret in some time. On Februrary 12, he wrote to Margaret of his "tortured" mind,[26] and by February 16, he was even more frantic:

> You can have but little idea of my state of mind at this moment. Only think that I have not heard a word from home since the 27th of December. I have so often written in hopes that I would get responses from home or at least hear some thing that I am almost in a state of despondency. I must have written at least some fifty letters. Indeed I have on one or more occasions written to you two letters in one day.
>
> Never before have I so forcibly felt the solitude of heart as I have done for the few last [sic] weeks. When a mail is handed to me, my heart sickens. So often have I been disappointed in seizing and looking over my letters that now I am unprepared to sustain it longer. Oh my Love! I declare to you that if I had flown from guilt of crime, I shou'd deem that my punishment would be replete in the suffering which I endure.[27]

Finally, on February 19, two letters from Margaret reached him. The first one held no unusual news, but the second letter informed Houston that, although he was now fully recovered, Sam had been seriously ill. Margaret described her anxiety at being aroused by Sam's deep groans and finding their son cold and stiff. This was soon followed by a scorching fever, and Margaret described his skin as assuming "a dead purple hue." She had been sure that Sam was dying, and described for her husband the joyful gratitude that filled her soul for the restoration of their child: "What shall we render unto the Lord, for his goodness and mercy towards us? Oh let us dedicate ourselves and our children unto his service, and let us never, never wander from him."[28]

Houston, too, was gratified with Sam's recovery, but he also was worried over the cause of Sam's illness and quickly wrote to warn Margaret of his suspicions:

> . . . may it not be possible that Virginia <u>may have given him something</u> that caused his sickness? Can she not be separated from our dear <u>jewels</u>? . . . It may be that she was not the cause, but as it has doubt and mystery about it, I am willing to suspect her from past events! Judge ye!![29]

A few days later Houston wrote a second warning to his wife:

> I fear Virginia! If she had not burnt the letters and cut the Bible, I might entertain hope of reformation, but as it is, I have no hope of her, or any thing which could be expected of other children! If you should deem my suggestions of any value, I pray you that you take some measures to guard the dear little loves from her dreadful disposition. I pray you my love, to watch with increasing vigilance our treasures![30]

In the same letter he voiced his concerns for Margaret's health, as he was well aware of Margaret's habit of not writing to him of serious problems until after they had been solved.

> My dear Love, I was sorry that you did not let me hear all, all particulars about your breast. If you had known how anxious I was to know the exact prospect of your entire recovery, you would have been minute in your details. . . . You my dearest, are the subject of meditation with which my mind sinks to repose and the first which bursts upon my waking imagination.

Houston's fears for Margaret were well founded. The tumor had swelled and she was in great pain. When the Powers had arrived after the first of the year, Charles decided the situation was so serious that he wrote Ashbel Smith and asked the doctor to come immediately:

> She wishes much to see you to consult about the best means of having an operation performed and the tumor extracted, and I believe if you would put your instruments in your pocket and come up here, she would submit herself to you, having confidence only in you in the performance of such a surgical operation.[31]

Dr. Smith came immediately and quickly made the decision that Margaret was in no condition to travel to Memphis. It would be necessary for him to operate within a few weeks. Margaret wrote to Houston for the first time in nearly a month:

> I have suffered two or three mails to pass without writing to you for the reason that my breast was in such condition that I could not write without detriment to myself. It has risen three times and the last time presented such an angry appearance that Brother Charles prevailed on us to send for Dr. Smith. . . . He has decided that it must be operated on so soon as I can dry up the breast. With the help of God I hope to sit down to it like a soldier. . . . Now my precious Love, let me entreat you not to be anxious about me, for the Dr. assures me that the operation will be a mere trifle and easily performed in two minutes.[32]

She told Houston that she had not planned to tell him this news until after the operation was completed, but she feared he might hear it from other sources. The surgery was set for a day early in March, and Margaret reported that "every one is so kind and affectionate to me in my illness that my heart is not troubled by it."[33]

Vernal Lea, however, was troubled, and on February 24, 1847, he wrote to Dr. Smith urging him to come sooner as "we think the cancer is advancing more rapidly than usual."[34] Dr. Smith, with Dr.

Beauers to assist him, hurried back and brought with him whiskey to use as an anesthetic during the operation. Margaret refused the whiskey, although Antoinette protested that the surgery could not proceed without some kind of painkiller. Margaret took a silver coin, clenched it between her teeth and the operation was completed.[35]

Houston had written earlier that as soon as the senate adjourned, he would "let no grass grow to his heels" in reaching Margaret and home.[36] When he received Margaret's letter he decided to leave for home immediately even though a special session of Congress had been called and would last for a few more weeks. A letter from Dr. Smith was waiting at home for him. The doctor expressed his hope that his old friend would be satisfied with the state of Margaret's health:

> It was with some anxiety that I undertook so serious an operation in your absence, but an operation offered the only possible cure and its necessity was urgent. It is useless to mention to you that Mrs. H. bore the pain with great fortitude.[37]

Houston found Margaret improving and wrote Dr. Smith to express their thanks: "I will not attempt to express to you my pleasure at finding her on the recovery on my return, nor my deep, and abiding sense of obligation to you for you[r] skill & kindness to Mrs. Houston."[38] Perhaps his anxiety over Margaret's health prompted Houston to write in the same letter: "As to my future position, I have but one desire, and that is for home & peaceful retirement, with . . . social quiet."

Two weeks later Margaret's condition worsened and Houston was again writing to Dr. Smith asking him to come or to send Dr. Beauers as soon as possible:

> Mrs. Houston has more anxiety than is agreeable about the condition of her breast. The ligature remains in the wound. In addition to this, from immediately below the wound, there is diagonally across the stomach, bearing to the left side, some-

thing like a cord or tendon, which is quite sore, and she is fearful that it may be a root of the Cancer."[39]

Dr. Beauers returned to Grand Cane and treated Margaret. She was soon recovering and the family was able to return to Raven Hill. Houston's first term in the Senate would soon expire, and he was not campaigning to be reelected. Margaret had hopes that he would remain at home, so this was a happy time for her. Houston took over the duties of supervising the farm work, and Margaret had more time to be with the children. In the late summer she discovered that she was once again pregnant.

The combination of Margaret's last illness and her continued loneliness at Raven Hill convinced Houston that the plantation home was too remote a place to leave her if he should return to Washington. He found a beautiful piece of land on the outskirts of Huntsville, complete with its own spring, and made a trade with the owner, Frank Hatch, who had been managing Raven Hill during the family's absence. Houston wrote to Joseph Ellis, the agent for the Alabama and Coushatta Indians, that it was a "bang up place."[40] He supervised plans for expanding the existing cabin into a house big enough to accommodate his expanding family. This home would be known as the "Woodland Home" and would become Houston's favorite residence.

In the fall Houston resumed his law practice. The windows of the new home were being fitted and new fireplaces were being added. Houston deposited Margaret, her mother, and the children in Huntsville to stay with friends while he traveled to Nacogdoches and San Augustine for some court trials. While he was gone, Margaret received word that Vernal was seriously ill at Grand Cane. Leaving the children with Nancy Lea, Margaret went to spend some time with Vernal and Kate. She wrote to Houston at San Augustine when she returned that she found her mother had been seriously ill with an inflamed leg. During their grandmother's illness the children had become "almost wild" and Margaret found that her presence was "much needed." Her trip had taken her past their old home, and she was concerned about their possessions which were still there:

> We came by Raven [H]ill and took our lunch in the old house. The family were gone and the scene was desolate indeed. I hope I shall be able in a short time to send a waggon [sic] for our furniture for I do not like to let it remain there without protection.[41]

The brief return to nearly-normal family life came to an end on December 20, 1847, when Houston received the news from Austin that he had been re-elected to the Senate. He quickly made plans to travel to Washington on the inland route through Natchitoches.[42] Once again Margaret was left behind. She was now twenty-eight years old, the mother of two children with another one on the way. For only about half of the seven years of their marriage had she and her husband been together. She would spend much of her time alone supervising the construction of their new home, determined to make it a place in which Houston would want to remain.

---

[1] Sam Houston papers, Barker History Center, University of Texas, Houston to Nathaniel Leven, August 11, 1846. See also Llerena Friend, 179.

[2] Lenoir Hunt, *My Master*, (Dallas: Manfried, Van Nort, and Co., 1940), 13–15.

[3] Houston Family Correspondence, Texas State Archives, Austin, Margaret to Houston, November 27, 1846.

[4] Franklin Williams Collection, Huntsville, Houston to Margaret, January 5, 1847.

[5] Ibid.

[6] Friend, 181.

[7] Franklin Williams Collection, Huntsville, Houston to Margaret, January 5, 1847.

[8] Ibid., Houston to Margaret, January 10, 1847.

[9] Ibid., Margaret to Houston, February 10, 1847.

[10] Ibid., Houston to Margaret, January 17, 1847.

[11] Ibid., Margaret to Houston, December 5, 1846.

[12] Ibid., Houston to Margaret, January 5, 1847.

[13] Ibid., Houston to Margaret, February 11, 1847.
[14] Ibid., Houston to Margaret, January 5, 1847.
[15] Ibid., Houston to Margaret, January 10, 1847.
[16] Ibid., Houston to Margaret, January 25, 1847.
[17] Ibid.
[18] Ibid., Houston to Margaret, January 19, 1847.
[19] Ibid., Houston to Margaret, January 26, 1847.
[20] Ibid., Houston to Margaret, January 24, 1847.
[21] Ibid., Houston to Margaret, February 20, 1847.
[22] Ibid., Houston to Margaret, February 3, 1847.
[23] Ibid., Houston to Margaret, February 5, 1847.
[24] Ibid.
[25] Ibid., Houston to Margaret, February 9, 1847.
[26] Ibid., Houston to Margaret, February 12, 1847.
[27] Ibid., Houston to Margaret, February 16, 1847.
[28] Ibid., Margaret to Houston, January 20, 1847.
[29] Ibid., Houston to Margaret, February 19, 1847.
[30] Ibid., Houston to Margaret, February 22, 1847.
[31] Ashbel Smith Papers, Barker History Center, University of Texas, Charles Power to Ashbel Smith, February 3, 1847.
[32] Franklin Williams Collection, Huntsville, Margaret to Houston, February 10, 1847.
[33] Ibid.
[34] Ashbel Smith Papers, Barker History Center, University of Texas, Vernal Lea to Ashbel Smith, February 24, 1847.
[35] Peggy Decker Everitt, family story.
[36] Franklin Williams Collection, Huntsville, Houston to Margaret, February 22, 1847.
[37] Ashbel Smith Papers, Barker History Center, University of Texas, Smith to Houston, April 4, 1847.
[38] Sam Houston, *Writings*, vol. 5, 10–11, Houston to Smith, April 12, 1847.
[39] Ibid., 11, Houston to Smith, April 27, 1847.
[40] Sam Houston, *Writings*, vol. 5, 13–14, Houston to Ellis, June 12, 1847.
[41] Franklin Williams Collection, Huntsville, Margaret to Houston, October 3, 1847.
[42] Sam Houston, *Writings*, vol. 5, 27–28, Houston to Ebenezer Allen, December 21, 1847.

Chapter VIII

How strange it seems when I compare my feelings now enjoyed, and those I possessed when I was here [Washington] some twenty years ago. One thought is now worth all the feelings of years gone by. My wife and the children are to me everything that can charm or delight my heart. . . . Oh my Love, I do assure you that I feel more anxious in my present exile than I did when in the wilds of Arkansas. I am where it is said the world is, and yet I am far from all that constitutes my world on earth.

Houston to Margaret, May 12, 1848
Washington, D. C.

Houston's trip back to the nation's capital in January was a strenuous one. The first stretch was by stage, and he wrote Margaret from San Augustine that they traveled day and night and that he had only been able to sleep for a few hours. At times the horses could not see the road and the stage would stop and remain until daylight. He was already missing her and making plans for her to join him in Washington as soon as she recovered from the birth of the baby expected in April.[1]

The trip became more bearable in the town of Milam, where Houston chanced to meet up with an old friend, Colonel Gaines, whom he induced to travel with him to Sabine. Houston wrote to Margaret that he had stayed up all night talking with Gaines:

He has been here for 36 years—was here at the commencement of the Revolution when Mexico declared her Independence, and has been here ever since. He knows more about the History of Texas and its boundary than any man now living. I have been taking notes of his knowledge of facts, as they may be of use to me in Washington.[2]

Houston continued his journey by stage to New Orleans. From there to Mobile he traveled by steamboat, stopping in Alabama for a short visit with Robert and Varilla Royston, their children, and the Lea cousins. From an unknown point farther east he finished the journey by railroad. Upon reaching his destination, he wrote to Margaret that his health was good despite the fact that he had not lain down until he reached Washington. As soon as he took his Senatorial Oath he was called on to chair a group of Democratic senators who were meeting to decide a convention date. He described the capital as filled with a vast crowd:

Our Presidential aspirants are on their tiptoes. If I were one, I would desire things to be as they are. . . . [I]t is the general opinion [that] Gov. Cass is now managed to pass me up, but many changes will take place before matters will take a final direction.[3]

Houston was lonesome for Margaret and the children, and in the same letter he expressed to her that if not for his expectations of seeing her in June, he would not be able to bear the long absence. The next day he advised her:

Don't regard the expense or cash, if you can come. If you do not come, I will [be] miserable, miserable because where you are not, I can not be happy. No society, no charms, no pleasures, nor any thing on earth can supply your presence.[4]

Once again, Houston began to worry that something was seriously wrong at home. The entire month of January passed with only one short note from his wife. Finally, in February, he heard from Henderson Yoakum, their neighbor and good friend, that Margaret had been seriously ill with a near-fatal case of pneumonia. Houston immediately wrote to her:

Before I heard, I had been painfully anxious to hear some news from you, and when I did hear that you had been dangerously ill, for I know it was so, I only had my fears realised. . . . I pray that we may meet again and never be doomed to part while we are spared on earth. I drag a miserable existence. It must be so my Beloved, while I am absent from you. I feel that I am but half myself, and every day seems only to protract my misery and multiply my cares and anxieties.[5]

No doubt Houston was greatly relieved when a long letter from Margaret arrived several days after the one from Yoakum. In it she justified her three-week silence:

I have suffered minor anxiety—lest you should be distrest [sic] at my silence, but I knew it would not do for any one to write for me, as I apprehended it would give you more concern than my silence so I determined just to let you charge the mail with it all. . . . Col. Birdwell and his dear wife and Dr. Evans and Mrs. Evans have been such untiring friends during my illness that I can never forget them, and I feel that the Lord has blessed me particularly with friends.[6]

Houston was probably also relieved to hear that Margaret had been relieved of the responsibility of Virginia Thorn. Katherine Lea had come up to visit Margaret when she was ill, and had taken Virginia back with her to Grand Cane. When he received Margaret's letter he replied:

You were right in suffering that I had "charged it to the mails" in part but not entirely. I was fearful that you were too unwell to write, and that my friends did not wish to distress me until the result of your illness shou'd be known.[7]

The letter also expressed his gratitude over the help the Birdwells were giving Margaret. As well, he made known his unhappiness over a rift in the family between the Moores and the Houstons, and the fact that his sister Eliza had not come to Margaret's aid during her recent illness.

Others in the family also had been ill with the same disease, and one of the servants had not been as fortunate as Margaret, who wrote in her next letter:

> When I last wrote to you, Mother's negro woman Vina was expected to die of the disease, but I did not mention it to you. . . . She only survived a short time, and I can say with safety that her death was one of the greatest trials I ever endured . . . because I knew she had died from the want of medicine.[8]

On a happier note, Margaret informed him in the same letter that four-year-old Sam was becoming very helpful to her, doing such chores as going to the post office for letters. She bragged: "I have never seen such a boy for business and he sees every thing about the place that is not just right."

Margaret and the children were now in their new home. It seems that Sam, in particular, was impressed by the brick chimneys and glass windows. And Margaret was herself pleased with the results:

> Our home is looking cheerful and pleasant. The rubbish is cleared from the yard, and every thing looks neat and comfortable. The woods too are glowing with the first smile of spring. How I wish you were with us at this balmy season! But it can not be and I will not sadden you with my regrets.[9]

Margaret was still planning on going to Washington. She felt it would be impossible to make definite plans until after the baby arrived, but did not want to leave all her planning until the last minute:

> I hardly feel that it were right to say much about it [the trip] at present, but I am perfectly aware that if all the arrangements are not made before the great trial is over, it will then be too late in the season to begin them. So I will just say that it is my present calculation to set off the latter part of May or first of June. If I go

I must take Sam. His character is developing so rapidly that I think
nothing ought to induce me to leave him. . . . [10]

Margaret was aware that bringing Sam might be seen as favoritism
for him over his sister, so she explained: "A mother, like a good
Gen'l, ought to watch that part of her little force which is most
exposed to the fire. And it is this which causes me to feel more
concern about our dear boy than [Nannie]."

Although Houston was anxious to see Margaret, he began to
worry about his family's safety on so long a trip. He wrote her that
he was overwhelmed at the idea of her traveling alone with a new
baby and Sam. He was fearful of what might happen if one of them
were to become ill traveling among strangers so he suggested that
perhaps Margaret might want to go to the Cane Brake in Alabama
and wait for him there instead.[11] A week later he was even more
adamant that she should not attempt the trip:

When I reflect on the certainty of your being sick in crossing the
Gulf and again in crossing from Charleston to Washington if you
come by sea, or traveling in stages, if you come by land, for 230
miles, and this in two nights and a day, I would expect it to be
done at infinite hazard of your own or at least the life of your
Babe. . . . you would be wheeled along at the rate of six miles an
hour and only stay fifteen minutes at any one place.

He assured her that his hesitancy in no way implied a reluctance to
see her, and promised that if she would wait until fall to make the
trip by way of Alabama, he would hire a private carriage from there.
He felt that "for a Lady and two or three children to travel by public
conveyance and be subjected to the coarseness of stage drivers and
car conductors is too painful to contemplate."[12]

Margaret was also having second thoughts about making the
trip, especially about leaving Nannie, whom she described to her
father as "one of those little charmers that endanger a parent's
heart." Although Margaret desperately wanted to join her husband,
she had come to a painful conclusion:

I have tried to lay plans for the journey merely that I might have something on which to rest my thoughts and not allow them the dreary range of six or seven months absence from you, but when the subject is brought closely to view, there are so many things in the way that I do not think it will be possible.... I think the best plan will be for me to remain quietly at home until you return.[13]

When Houston received her letter, he had to agree with her decision:

You my Love, have come to a proper conclusion. To travel with Master Sam, and I hope a [baby] would be at the imminent risk of your safeties, if not your lives. I am aware of the pain of absence, and this I feel in the most acute manner. Not one night of my life do I sink to sleep but what you are present in my thoughts.[14]

Now that Margaret had made the decision to remain at home, she turned her energies toward the many problems involved with managing a farm. The overseer had run off to get married and had not returned, but her good friend Colonel Thomas Birdwell was of great help to her. Despite the problems, Margaret remained cheerful, and frequently had a house full of company. Minerva and Eliza Davis were staying with her while they attended school in Huntsville, and their sister Carry was expected for a visit soon. Margaret also spent much time with Tercey Birdwell and Frances Creath, who lived close by, and on improving the appearance of the Woodland home:

Mr. King is very anxious to go on with our galleries and rooms, but his calculation is that the lumber will amount to five hundred dollars, independent of the work, so that I have concluded to let it alone for the present. I am improving our yard very neatly. I have set out a great many shrubs and they are budding beautifully. I have not lost any of it. I expect I should get a little scolding if you were at home, for I can not keep away from my flowers.

Toward the end of the long letter was some news about his first wife Eliza Allen Houston (now Mrs. Douglas) which no doubt surprised Houston. Vernal Lea had been in Gallatin, Tennessee, and had reported to Margaret that he had seen the former Mrs. Houston. Margaret passed the news on to her husband: "By the bye, I must tell you that [Vernal] had curiosity enough while in Gallatin to take a good look at Mrs. D. He stopped at the same hotel and saw her at the table. He thinks she is very fine looking."[15]

Although Margaret was writing regularly, Houston was not receiving the mail. Just before he left for a tour of speaking engagements in New York and other eastern states, he wrote her of his anxiety: "If you have not time or can not by any means write to me at length, just write me three words, 'all are well,' and I will be happy compared to what I now am."[16]

In Margaret's opinion, Houston had used a poor choice of words. When she received the letter, she promptly took him to task:

I am so nervous and agitated by learning that you have rec'd no letters from me. . . . I have written to you once every week since I recovered from my tedious attack of neumonia [sic], but my heart sinks within me when I find that they (my letters) have not reached you. Why it is, I can not tell you. There must be something wrong in some quarter. My Love, you ought not to have said, "If you have not had time to write." I never felt more pained by an expression. Can you believe for a moment that I would put off writing to you for any other occupation? I know you can not, and let me here remind you that we are too far apart for home explanations. We have often made friends over a slighter affair than that cruel expression of yours, and I do not know that the wound will ever be healed until we meet. . . . [Even] if you get no more letters from me, you may rest assured that if I am living and can use a pen, it is my regular business to write to you once every week.[17]

Houston would later find that her letters had been delayed because the mail boats had been employed in returning troops from Vera Cruz, Mexico. He quickly sent his apologies:

My Love, I am as much pained as you could be at my expression "to write if you had time." . . . When Sam or Nannie are sick you know they are always in your arms. . . . So my Love, I really did fear as they had been ill that you might not have time to write unless you taxed your constitution beyond your strength. . . . I hope, my dear Love, when you receive this letter . . . you will forgive my indiscreet expression to which you took exception. Could I have anticipated the effect of the expression, it certainly would not have been used. I would not have caused you pain for the world. I do hope my Dearest, that your mind will be at ease, and if you do not excuse me, that you will pardon me. The distance—your situation, and my anxieties for your welfare & that of our dear family had almost run me crazy. If I did wrong it arose from the excess of love![18]

Houston's northern speaking tour had been quite a success. He had made nine speeches in thirteen days, traveling thousands of miles by steamboats, railroad, and carriages. He informed Margaret in a way that would give all the credit to her:

Since I have been to the North, successive assurances have arrived bringing conclusive evidences that my trip there has [had] the effect of convincing the people there that Texas is a fine country—the inhabitants are clever people, and that I am a first class and well behaved gentleman, and that my wife must be very amiable and excellent, as she has been mainly instrumental in making me so.

There is evidence that this tour was made to improve Houston's chances of becoming the Democrat's candidate for president in the next election. Houston himself alludes to the fact in a letter written to Margaret on March 30:

Matters here are moving on rather briskly in the political world. Who will be the nominee of the Convention at Baltimore no one can say, but many suppose that a southern man may be the individual. Matters are now gliding to that point unless an eddy should take place in the current. You will hear as the subject progresses. I will send you news papers occasionally. I assure [you] it is of much less interest to me than the anxiety which I feel at home.[19]

Much of Houston's home worries centered around the problems in running a farm, particularly as Margaret's pregnancy progressed. He wrote often of his frustrations in not being able to be with her, and attempted to assure her of his affections.

Daily, nightly, and hourly, I think of you and our dear little ones, and I reflect upon what you have to pass through in a short time and beseech our Creator to be with & sustain you and preserve you. I sicken and become sad when I feel that I can not be near you to sustain and comfort or cheer you. I can only say my Love, that every hour of existence renders you more dear to me and increases my affection and my love.[20]

He also sought to relieve her fears that he might find fault with her management of the farm. For instance, he assured her that he had no regrets over the drowning of some sheep and goats which had occurred in March.

So long as Providence mercifully preserved my Love and our little Lambs, I will make no complaints about our Lambs out of doors. . . . Long ere this letter can reach you, you will have been confined, and I will pray as I have done each night upon my bended knees that our God may sustain and preserve you and make you the mother of a perfect Babe.[21]

Houston did not know it at the time, but owing to the fact that he had not written daily while on his northern tour and to the delay of regular mail, Margaret would have to pass through this crucial time without hearing from him. She tried to keep up her spirits as the time for giving birth drew near:

No letter from you by today's mail, and I am sad indeed. . . . I can imagine many reasons for your silence, (or rather the non-arrival of your letters, for I know that you have written) but they can not entirely console me. But I must not distress you with my melancholy.[22]

Margaret attempted to continue her letter on a more cheerful note by describing their woodland home:

You can not imagine how beautiful our forest here appears. The hillside is loaded with the loveliest verdure I ever beheld, and our little prairie is dotted with flowers of every hue. Oh shall we ever sit together under these sweet shades, and look around upon the lovely gift of our Heavenly Father![23]

As the next mail still did not bring word from her husband, Margaret's next letter made no pretence of being cheerful:

No letter from you on yesterday! My fortitude is failing. I must either hear from you regularly, or you must come home. I know I ought to conceal every feeling of distress from you, but I am so disappointed that my heart sickens. . . . If I could get your letters, I should be cheerful.[24]

Margaret enclosed a note marked "confidential" in one of her letters during this time. She was concerned over what to name the new baby, and did not want to make the decision by herself:

What do you think of Temple Lea for a boy? If a girl's name should be required, how would you like your Mother's maiden name? We could substitute Lea or Moffette in Nannie's you know. Do not say you leave it to me. You must be frank about it.[25]

On April 12, Margaret sat down to write again. She began, "I can only write you a few lines, but I must write a—" As she was interrupted by labor pains, it was ten days later before she again took up her pen:

164

There is no doubt about it, my dearest Love, she is one of the loveliest little creatures you ever beheld. I mean our second daughter, for we are now the parents of three children. . . . You must look upon the unfinished paragraph of this letter as a great proof of my devotion to you, for I had endured much suffering, for a day and night, and in about 8 hours, the little one was added to our circle, but I thought I would make out a letter, as the mail was to go out the next day.[26]

Margaret asked his advice again about what name to give the little one. What she did not tell her husband was that one of her fondest dreams had been to present him with a child on April 21, the anniversary of the Battle of San Jacinto, so she was somewhat disappointed that the young lady had arrived a few days too soon.[27]

In the meantime, Houston was sending a letter with his preferences for names, although he was careful not to make them sound like demands.

About the names, my Dear . . . I thought . . . the expected would (if a daughter) be called Margaret, and if a son, Temple Lea. . . . My Love, these suggestions are made for your reflection and not by way of objections to any arrangements which you may make. I confess that I have some superstition about changing children's names. . . . [28]

A few days later he was dwelling on the fact that the baby had probably already arrived. He wrote Margaret he hoped that she had passed through her "troubles" safely. He had felt all along that the baby would be another son, but assured her:

If it should be otherwise, I will not be in the least mortified, for I declare to you that I have no choice unless it were that we might have a dear little Maggy. I have often regretted that I did not call Nannie Margaret. . . . If a Maggy should be in the family, I only hope that she may be all that her dear Mother is in excellency and many amiable qualities.[29]

Before the announcement from Margaret arrived, Houston received the news from a neighbor and wrote to Margaret of his joy:

> You have no idea of my extreme happiness when I received Mrs. Creath's letter of the 15th of April. I had been desponding for days as you will see from my letters, and was truly miserable. . . . The first thing, my Love, upon which I felicitated myself was your good turn and the prospect of your doing well. The next thing was that the Babe was a precise resemblance to you, and lastly that it was a daughter. . . . I feel very truly obliged to our Sister Creath for her very acceptable letter. I would rather have received it than a mine of Gold.[30]

When Margaret's letter arrived Houston expressed his joy that she was well enough to write. He was still apologizing about his previous use of the expression "if you have time to write":

> My love, I hope we will pass through our lives without any intention to hurt each others feelings. I feel that we have had much happiness and I regret that I have not been more sedulous to make you perfectly happy. . . . To you I may say that nothing on this earth could give me so much pleasure as to see and embrace you and the little flock. Yes, my love, I would like to chat of the past, and smile upon the present.

He also reminded her of how his values had changed since the time when he had first come to Washington as a young congressman from Tennessee:

> How strange it seems when I compare my feelings now enjoyed and those I possessed when I was here some twenty years ago. One thought now is worth all the feelings of years gone by. My wife and children are to me everything that can charm or delight my heart. . . . Oh my Love, I do assure you that I feel more anxious in my present exile than I did when in the wilds of Arkansas. I am where it is said the world is, and yet I am far from all that constitutes my world on earth.[31]

Two weeks after her announcement letter, Margaret again wrote Houston assuring him that the baby was in fine health and beginning to look like her father. She obviously had not received the letter with his name preferences, because she again admonished him to suggest a name as the baby "is becoming quite a young lady to have no name."[32] It was finally agreed that she would be named Margaret Lea Houston for her mother and would be called Maggie.

As Houston's anxiety for Margaret and the new baby passed, his letters turned to less serious matters. He inquired about the welfare of Margaret's mother and her comfort in the Houstons' new home. He had written her earlier that he was happy to hear that Nancy Lea was "satisfied or more so than you anticipated at any house but her own." He promised Margaret that when he returned he would try "to submit to the old Lady, and let her manage all matters in the yard & garden."[33] Three weeks later, he sent more specific instructions:

My dearest, I want you to draw on me for any money that you may want for any purpose, either for yourself or the family. In that I especially include our Mother. Her peculiarity of disposition or temper is not to be considered only with filial regard. I often regret that I ever felt the least irritation. I ought not to have done so. Her kindness of heart, and not her manner, ought to be noticed and esteemed. The interest which she feels in our welfare can not be questioned, and for this we ought to be grateful, as well as dutiful.[34]

Margaret's thoughts turned to the fact that her husband did not seem to be attending church as regularly as he had in the previous session of congress. She expressed her worries in a letter on May 8, 1848:

My dear Love, I fear that you are suffering your mind to be drawn off from the subject of religion by the political excitement of the day. . . . Oh when I think of the allurements that surround you, I tremble lest they should steal your heart from God. . . . There is something so bewitching in the voice of fame.[35]

167

Margaret was alluding to the coming presidential election. It was time for the Democrats to select a candidate, and Houston's name was still being mentioned. Ashbel Smith had made note of his friend's work in the Senate and enscribed in his diary: "Gen Rusk said Houston has behaved very well, and if he continues as he has done he will 'rent the White House.'"[36]

Before he left for the convention at Baltimore, Houston expressed to Margaret his own feelings on the subject:

> I learn that all the candidates are on their feet. Some of them must must be disappointed. For my part, so far as my name has been used in [connection] with the high office of the Executive chief of the nation, I have not, nor will I ever set my heart upon it. So let the result be what it may. I pray you to believe that it will not diminish my happiness, but were it possible, it would give new charms to home.[37]

The next day he wrote again:

> The confusion of the Delegates increases as their numbers increase in the city. For my own part my Love, I have nothing to say in the matter. If it comes, it is well, and I will be prepared to meet the occasion, but I declare to you, I will not truckle nor degrade my feelings for any station on this earth![38]

When the Convention met, Lewis Cass was selected as the candidate, but he immediately asked Houston to embark on a speaking tour to New York on behalf of the Democratic party. Houston wrote Margaret to assure her he was not unhappy with the results:

> ... that I was not the nominee of the convention is truly gratifying to me. . . . Had I been selected, it would not have increased my reputation. As it is, my name is used with good effect, and there will not be the same cause or reason to assail me. . . . My name will insinuate itself among the people & there will settle down to a decided bias in my favor, and should I at some future day be

brought before the nation, it can be done successfully. The feeling in all parts, even beyond the strength of the Democracy is in favor of my name being used in 1851. I had to refuse the Vice Presidency most positively. I hope my Love, that you will no[t] chagrin at the result of matters.[39]

When she heard that he had not been nominated, Margaret admitted to feelings of selfishness:

We have heard that Cass was the nominee for the presidency, and I think from what I can learn that there is great disappointment among the democrats. My first thought was that your family would have more of your society than if you had been nominated and therefore I felt gratified.[40]

She reminded her husband of the personal sacrifices he was making in order to have a life of public service:

Tomorrow our precious babe will be two months old. . . . Oh shall I ever place the little cherub in your arms? The charms of early infancy are passing away and you will never see them. That sweet expression which seems to see more of Heaven than earth is almost gone, and her bright eyes now gaze with delight on earthly things.[41]

Margaret had caught a cold after the baby's birth and was desperately afraid of catching pneumonia again. Her June 12th letter mentioned that the Leas were anxious for her to go to Sour Lake to try the virtues of the mud baths there. Mrs. Birdwell had offered to go with her and take care of her, but Margaret had decided she would put it off until Houston's return. She told her husband she thought her health would then improve immediately, since she was sure that her depression over his long absence had a great deal to do with her physical health.

No doubt Margaret's spirits began to improve when she finally received several letters from her husband reassuring her that his mind was still on religion. She expressed her delight:

I perceived in your feelings an increased seriousness and a greater concern than ever for the salvation of your soul. At this I rejoice greatly for I do believe that you "are not far from the Kingdom of Heaven" and the Lord will soon reveal the blessed Jesus to your soul. . . . To see my husband enjoying the comforts of religion, and to have his aid in bringing up our children for the Lord would be greater blessings than I can ever deserve. . . . [42]

These letters also reveal Houston's preoccupation with the condition of his sister, Mary Wallace. He was worried that she was not receiving the proper care.

I have heard from General Wallace and the news is truly distressing. There is no investigation of her mental malady, tho [sic] her health is considerably improved. . . . I can only hope and pray for Sister's recovery, but I can not expect it. It is a fearful calamity! I will write to Genl Wallace soon and advise him to try electricity.[43]

Dr. Ashbel Smith was visiting in Hartford, Connecticut. Knowing that Smith had been trained in the treatment of the mentally ill,[44] Houston wrote urging him to go home by way of Tennessee so he could see Mary. He assured his friend, "I believe if you can see her that you can restore her to health, of Body and Mind."[45]

Margaret received the news with great sorrow:

My love, I can not describe to you my feelings while I read your account of our dear sister Wallace. My heart is cheered by the last hope of returning reason and I humbly trust that the Lord will banish her night of gloom and darkness. I determined once to write to her today, but on reflection concluded as you would be at home so soon, it would be better to wait until we could consult about the language and determine what would be the most suitable things to say to her.[46]

Margaret was also worrying about the health problems of her servant Eliza, who was suffering from scrofula. Margaret described her as "a pitiful object," so disfigured that her husband "would not recognize her." Margaret had sent Eliza to Dr. Evans in the hopes of finding a cure. The children, however, were all doing well:

> She [Nannie] is the most amusing little creature I ever saw. She has none of Sam's gravity but evidently a great deal of genius. . . . The baby enjoys fine health, but is not a large child. I could say a great deal about her beauty, but as she is said to be so much like me, I will leave that for you to do.

Margaret's letter also reported favorably about her neighbors:

> Indeed I have so many more friends in the place, that I hardly know which to tell you about. They seem to feel so much for me on account of your absence that they have endeared themselves to me in a peculiar manner.[47]

In another letter she had written of her pride in her flowers:

> Our yard looks beautiful. I wish you could see my circle in the front yard bordered with pinks and chrysanthemums. It is lovely indeed. . . . Time will move slowly until I am with you again.[48]

Houston was indeed anxious to see his home and family. The Democratic Party had pressured him to remain after Congress adjourned to help with campaigning, but he flatly refused, as he reported to Margaret:

> . . . the party wished me to go to all the important cities & towns in New York. Would you believe it possible for me to desire to pass the whole summer in the North & speak to the people on Political topics? Yes, my Dearest, and not to see you, nor our dear little ones. It is all that I can do to keep my temper at such suggestions. I assure you that no station or earth could induce me to forego my instant return to my home so soon as Congress adjourns![49]

During his last two months in Washington, Houston's letters indicate that his mind was clearly on Margaret, the children, and going home, rather than on politics. On June 22, he reported:

> I am almost crazy to see you and be with you and never again to be seperated [sic] in life. . . . Nay my Love, if you could only look into my heart, I feel assured (as my brightest hope is in Heaven) you would never believe for one moment that my <u>affections</u> or my <u>passions</u> could attach to any earthly object but your dear self. . . . so long as I hope to be with you again on earth and to unite with you in preparing ourselves and our children for a happy eternity, so long may you rely upon my <u>constancy</u> and my affection.[50]

On June 28, he emphasized again his anticipations of being with his family:

> I sit down at times to listen to speeches in the senate intending not to lose a word. The first thing I know is that I have lost all note of it, and find that my mind has wandered to my woodland home and I fancy myself enjoying some scenes which you have so prettily described.[51]

A few weeks later he was telling her that he was "sure there is not any man in the Senate who thinks about home as I do or is so anxious to see his family as myself, ergo there is no man who loves his wife & children as much as I do."[52]

Houston continued to advise Margaret on some of the specific problems that she faced at home. Upon hearing of Eliza's bout with scrofula, for instance, he wrote:

> I am truly distressed at the situation of poor Eliza. I hope that she can be cured, and if not otherwise, I have no doubt but the sour lake would cure her and if needful, or you think well of it, contrive

to get some of the oil from the lake & give it to her. At this distance all that I can do is to make suggestions.[53]

He also commented on her complaint that the field hands, with the exception of Joshua and Prince, had become extremely lazy and stubborn: "Tell the servants that I yet hope they will all behave well, I trust pride of character will make them do right. They know how and ought to be ashamed not to do well."[54] In his next letter Houston suggested that Margaret imply to them that she was expecting him home at any minute: "I would be willing that the servants shou'd expect me constantly and soon. It will make them more careful and industrious."[55]

As the summer dragged on, he continued to fret over Margaret's health. With Eliza ill, he was afraid that his wife was taking on too much work. He offered a solution:

Why have you not hired a nurse? I do not my Love, care what price you give. Have one and do not my dearest, permit yourself to be worried. I wish you to be happy and comfortable, if earth has means within my command to make you so![56]

He had already begun to pack up his papers in the hopes that he might leave the moment Congress adjourned. On August 2, he wrote of his continuing impatience:

I have often said if it were possible I [would] send myself home by the electric Telegraph or by an air Balloon. But this can not be done. . . . If ever a heart glowed with and love and hope on earth, my own seems to realise a double portion. I feel at times that I must be an unpleasant companion to those with whom I am associated on account of my absence of mind. Upon this subject, you have some experience from the times of 1842 & 3 in Washington, Texas. One thing is certain, if we are spared, I intend never again to visit this place without you as my companion & friend. I am too solitary and my anxiety is so boundless to see you and the little Brood.[57]

173

In the waning days of the session, Congress was meeting long hours to debate the question of admitting Oregon as a free territory. Houston felt some of his colleagues were delaying the vote for the sake of publicity. He described the scene:

> The evening sessions bring large audiences, and hard as we are pressed for time, there are members who wish to make displays before a wondering crowd. My Love, I am not among the members! It is scandalous to see grave Senators thus play the fool.[58]

However, the very next day he was on his feet explaining to the Senate why he was supporting the Oregon Bill even though such a vote would make him unpopular with other southern senators. He pointed out that thirteen northern senators had voted for the admission of Texas as a slave state. As for himself, he was from the South and was ready to defend it; but "he was for the Union" because "The Union was his guiding star, and he would fix his eyes on that star to direct his course."[59]

The Bill passed and Congress adjourned on August 14, 1848. Houston wasted no time in getting to Huntsville to meet his new daughter. He was delighted with both little Maggie and the little cabin which had been expanded into a two-story house. There were double chimneys on either end of it, and a big open breezeway dividing it in half both upstairs and down. One room served as a parlour and the other was their bedroom. The children slept in the upstairs rooms.

To this house Margaret brought her best furnishings from all the places they had lived. She covered the parlour floor with an elegant hand woven rug of rose and gold. Into this room went her piano and the marble top table Houston had used for a desk when he was President of the Republic. She added a serpentine sofa of richly carved rosewood. Above the sofa, on the wall, was a Seth Thomas clock, one of the first of its kind in Texas. Across the breezeway in the bedroom stood the big four-poster bed which had been brought from the East. Nearby was the baby's cradle. In bad weather much of the family living took place in front of the big fireplace in this cheerful room. The two bedrooms upstairs also had fireplaces. They opened out onto a central porch. The outside wall of the porch was covered with thin bars of wood to let in the breeze and to keep the small children from falling out. On warm afternoons the children spread pallets and took their naps on this porch.[60]

Spacious grounds with walnut and pecan trees surrounded the house. Along the fence Margaret planted beds of lilacs, roses, and iris. On either side of the front walk she had a profusion of lilacs, syringas, narcissus, jonquils, and Easter lilies. At the corner of each flower bed grew a Crepe Myrtle tree, sixteen in all, and in spring the entire yard was full of their fragrance. The kitchen stood apart from the house to safeguard the home from the fire hazard and the constant heat of the fire in the open fireplace. Here huge iron and copper pots gleamed, and the slaves busied themselves feeding the growing Houston family. The back yard surrounding the kitchen was filled with fruit trees—quince, apple, peach, and fig.[61]

Houston spent the early fall supervising the construction of a log cabin to serve as his law office. He seems not to have known how little time he would spend at home. It is doubtful that he did much actual practice in the small building which would serve mainly as a place to keep his growing collection of books and important papers. Joshua was the only one allowed in the office to make even a pretence of cleaning it, and Margaret rarely entered the room.

Beyond the main house were the slave cabins and the carriage house. The latter housed a buggy for trips into town. Large vegetable gardens which supplied food for the family and servants completed the grounds of the family's favorite home.[62]

---

[1] Franklin Williams Collection, Huntsville, Houston to Margaret, January 3, 1848.
[2] Ibid., Houston to Margaret, January 4, 1848.
[3] Ibid., Houston to Margaret, January 24, 1848.
[4] Ibid., Houston to Margaret, January 25, 1848.
[5] Ibid., Houston to Margaret, February 9, 1848.
[6] Ibid., Margaret to Houston, January 29, 1848.

[7] Ibid., Houston to Margaret, February 17, 1848.
[8] Ibid., Margaret to Houston, February 14, 1848.
[9] Ibid., Margaret to Houston, February 28, 1848.
[10] Ibid., Margaret to Houston, March 9, 1848.
[11] Ibid., Houston to Margaret, April 3, 1848.
[12] Ibid. Houston to Margaret, April 11, 1848.
[13] Ibid., Margaret to Houston, March 21, 1848.
[14] Ibid., Houston to Margaret, April 26, 1848.
[15] Ibid., Margaret to Houston, March 21, 1848.
[16] Ibid., Houston to Margaret, March 4, 1848.
[17] Ibid., Margaret to Houston, March 30, 1848.
[18] Ibid., Houston to Margaret, April 20, 1848.
[19] Ibid., Houston to Margaret, March 30, 1848.
[20] Ibid., Houston to Margaret, April 14, 1848.
[21] Ibid., Houston to Margaret, April 20, 1848.
[22] Ibid., Margaret to Houston, April 5, 1848.
[23] Ibid.
[24] Ibid., Margaret to Houston, April 9, 1849.
[25] Ibid., Margaret to Houston, n.d.
[26] James, *The Raven*, 367–68.
[27] Family source, Marian Williams Whittemore quoting Maggie Houston Williams.
[28] Franklin Williams Collection, Huntsville, Houston to Margaret, April 27 1848.
[29] Ibid., Houston to Margaret, May 2, 1848.
[30] Ibid., Houston to Margaret, May 7, 1848.
[31] Ibid., Houston to Margaret, May 12, 1848.
[32] Sam Houston Papers, Barker History Center, University of Texas, Margaret to Houston, May 8, 1848.
[33] Franklin Williams Collection, Huntsville, Houston to Margaret, April 6, 1848.
[34] Ibid., Houston to Margaret, April 26, 1848.
[35] Sam Houston Papers, Barker History Center, University of Texas, Margaret to Houston, May 8, 1848.
[36] Journal of Ashbel Smith, August 20, 1846, Barker History Center, University of Texas.
[37] Franklin Williams Collection, Huntsville, Houston to Margaret, May 16, 1848.
[38] Ibid., Houston to Margaret, May 17, 1848.
[39] Ibid., Houston to Margaret, June 20, 1848.
[40] Ibid., Margaret to Houston, June 12, 1848.
[41] Ibid.

[42] Ibid., Margaret to Houston, May 24, 1848.

[43] Ibid., Houston to Margaret, May 7, 1848.

[44] Elizabeth Silverthorne, *Ashbel Smith of Texas*, (College Station: Texas A & M University Press, 1982), 13.

[45] Sam Houston. *Writings*, vol. 5, 57, Houston to Smith, July 21, 1848.

[46] Franklin Williams Collection, Huntsville, Margaret to Houston, June 28, 1848.

[47] Ibid.

[48] Ibid., Margaret to Houston, May 30, 1848.

[49] Ibid., Houston to Margaret, June 20, 1848.

[50] Ibid., Houston to Margaret, June 22, 1848.

[51] Ibid., Houston to Margaret, June 28, 1848.

[52] Ibid., Houston to Margaret, July 21, 1848.

[53] Ibid., Houston to Margaret, July 16, 1848.

[54] Ibid.

[55] Ibid., July 26, 1848.

[56] Ibid., July 30, 1848.

[57] Ibid., August 2, 1848.

[58] Ibid., August 11, 1848.

[59] Sam Houston. *Writings*, vol. 5, 58–60.

[60] This home is a part of the Sam Houston Memorial Museum, and much of the original Houston furniture is displayed.

[61] Williams, 171–72. Also Hearne Papers, San Antonio, a copy of a map drawn by Mrs. W. A. Leigh. Original in the Sam Houston Memorial Museum, Huntsville, Texas.

[62] Sam Houston Memorial Museum.

Sam Houston, age 55, from lithograph by F. Davignon, 1848. Courtesy of Sam Houston Regional Library and Research Center, Liberty, Texas.

On July 2, 1848, Houston wrote to Margaret, "I send to Master Sam a Lithograph of myself. All here say it looks too old for me. I think so indeed."

The kitchen of the Woodland Home. Courtesy of Sam Houston memorial Museum, Huntsville, Texas.

Here Eliza presided, and on November 28, 1851, Margaret wrote Houston describing her day: "We arise with the sun and so soon as we are dressed assemble for worship. . . .When that is over we proceed to breakfast which Eliza is getting ready."

Chapter IX

My Love! The time seems <u>so long</u> . . . the days pass by and are gone <u>forever</u>, yet I do not wish them to linger until I am with you & our treasures. I need not tell you my Love, how devotedly I do love you. I feel all the frenzy of other days, for last night, as I came home, . . . I saw our 'Star.' If you can fancy what my thoughts once were, and hopes, and then add to them the realities which we have since enjoyed with the addition of our circle, you can partially determine my anxiety to be with you again.

Houston to Margaret, February 11, 1849
Washington, D. C.

Houston was home for only four weeks during the fall of 1848. He spent his brief time making speeches, tending to family business, and getting to know his new daughter. All too soon the recess from Congress ended, and it was time for him to return to Washington. Because the next session was expected to be a short one, Margaret reluctantly decided to remain at home. She was in charge of Sam's schooling now and felt that she needed to stay with the children. A new resident overseer, Thomas Gott, had been hired, and Margaret's presence was also needed to handle the problems with the farm. Furthermore, Virginia Thorn had returned from Grand Cane.

Houston began his trip back to Washington in November. The letters he wrote along the way contain instructions for the hands on planting the crops and caring for the carriage and buggies. On November 22, 1848, he wrote Margaret, "I do hope Mr. Gott has had the roof patched and the seams to the north lathed." He sent Margaret seeds, along with instructions of how and where they should be planted. Among them were magnolia, locust, bois d'arc, crepe myrtle, tobacco seed, and clover and grass for the yard. As usual, when he passed through New Orleans, he purchased food such as sugar, coffee, syrup, lard, pork, hams, apples, and preserves, and had them sent to Margaret. One letter asked her to search for some important missing papers and instructed her to take care of his "Big Book," or as it was officially called, "Journal of my Administration."[1] Margaret would later reply that she had not been able to find his papers.[2]

Houston was back in the capital by the first week in December. He immediately sent Margaret a draft,[3] but warned her not to let anyone but her mother know she had received it. He also described for her his difficult journey, saying that for seven days he never took his clothes off and he was able to lie down only once. Consequently, he arrived with a bad headache.[4]

In Huntsville things were off to a good start. Margaret was optimistic about Thomas Gott's abilities as resident farm manager. She wrote her husband that it had rained for a week, and the children had been confined as "noisy prisoners." She had decided the house would be more pleasant if she added two "shed rooms" to the south side of the house, with an entry between. One would be used as a dining room and the other would be a bedroom for Nancy Lea. As cheerful as the letter was, it still expressed her feelings about the separation:

> When I think of the waste of months between us, I feel as if I had a dreary pilgrimage to perform, but when I compare it with our last seperation [sic], the time seems to diminish, and I feel as if we would soon meet.[5]

When the next letter she received from Houston was cheerful, she felt guilty for even that little bit of melancholy. The next day she apologized:

> . . . there are times my Love, when I write under such great depression of spirits owing to my separation from you, that I can not say any thing cheerful and the very effort to conceal my feelings seems to chill every thing I write. So if I should be so unfortunate again as to write in a melancholy mood, you must

just take it for what it is worth, and I will try to be cheerful dearest, for I have much to make me so, although I am deprived of my greatest source of earthly happiness, my husband's society.[6]

In an effort to make future letters more optimistic, Margaret would write of the comfort given her by friends such as Virginia Maxy, Tercy Birdwell, Frances Creath and Mrs. Evans, who all came to call regularly. Other friends sometimes came to spend the night. She also wrote of her activities involving both the church and the Temperance Society. On one rare occasion she even wrote of politics, although she admitted that any argument from her would probably seem "like the prattle of a babe" to Houston: "I hope you will not be greatly distrest [sic] if Taylor should really be elected. If Lamar had not skill enough to ruin poor little Texas, have no fears of what Taylor can do." She went on to remind him of the time she had dreamed of a fragmented map showing the United States being put back together, and commented:

I believe that will yet be realized. One thing is certain. There is a great and wise Being, who holds the nation in his hands, and directs their councils to the ultimate promotion of His own glory. This is my politics, and I want no better.[7]

Houston's mind was also on politics, but at the same time he was relieved not to be any more involved than he was. He had been in Washington just three days when he wrote Margaret:

The Democrats are very quiet and say, "If we had only run Houston, we would not have been beaten." Such are the speculations and even these my dear, do not create in me a single regret. Nor will I ever desire the place, if it can by any means diminish the prospects of my domestic happiness or impair your health.[8]

A letter written ten days later seems to corroborate his disinterested stance towards politics. Responding to Anson Jones's San

Antonio newspaper article attempting to discredit Houston's role in Texas's annexation to the United States, Houston tried to reassure his wife.

> No doubt you have seen "my friend Anson Jones' late develop-
> ments." I pray you not, my Dear to think any thing of them or of
> his course. It does not injure me, but it will ruin him. For myself,
> I am glad that it has come out at this time, as it will be of use to
> Texas in adjusting her boundary. . . . I think . . . it is probable that
> he was displeased with me because I did not unite in his favor to
> beat Genl Rusk for the Senate. If this is not the cause, I can assign
> none other. I will dismiss this subject for I declare to you, it has
> not even provoked me to anger.[9]

Contrary to the Houstons' established pattern of not discuss-ing politics in front of their children, in this case Houston asked Margaret to tell Sam in simple words the matter of the Jones affair and report back to him what Sam had said. This she did, explaining to Sam that his father had helped Jones to become President of Texas and that now Jones had turned against him and was writing letters about him trying, as she put it, "to make it appear that he is a greater man than your pa." She asked young Sam's opinions, and he replied, "Is that envy?" Margaret reported this to Houston with the comment that she had thought of many other adjectives, but Sam's seemed to be the right one. She also reminded her husband of a dream she had told him about many years before. Probably in reference to Houston's inclination to consider her dreams as predictions, she wrote:

> You were very close to the truth when you supposed that I might
> be excited by the Dr.'s letters. It has been a long while since I felt
> so much inconvenienced by my Irish blood. I apprehended no
> injury to your reputation (on the contrary I felt a little malicious
> pleasure to see how quietly he was laying himself on the shelf for
> the rest of his days) but I felt indigence at myself for dreaming
> such a creature into existence, for indeed dearest, he is the

184

offspring of your superstition. I will try to dream to better purpose next time if you intend to convert my phantoms into realities.[10]

In the same letter, Margaret wrote of the birth of a son to their friends, B. L. and Jane Wilson. She informed her husband that the baby had been named for him and offered to give the baby her share of presents Houston was sending. She also mentioned hearing that Dr. Samson had returned to Washington from the Holy Land. She hinted that it would be nice if Houston's public duties allowed him time to converse with the Reverend, and asked if her husband could hint to Dr. Samson "as delicately as possible" how delighted she would be to receive something from the Holy Land, "though it be but a withered leaf or flower."[11] She would be overjoyed a few weeks later when Houston wrote that Dr. Samson was sending her two phials, one containing waters from the Dead Sea, the other from the Red Sea. Also coming was a piece of the mosaic from the floor of the Temple of Jerusalem and cedar from Bethlehem.[12]

December brought a winter storm. Margaret wrote that the trees were hung with icicles, and although it was snowing and sleeting, the sun occasionally peeped out and promised better times. On a cold, rainy day she told Houston of her feelings:

I imagine that every kind of weather would be delightful if you were here to share it. Sitting together by our own fireside, we could draw something interesting, even from the cold dark clouds and the deep toned thunder whose distant mutterings are heard occasionally through the pattering rain.[13]

But the weather had its good points too. This was young Sam's first sight of snow, and Margaret shared his experience with her husband: "He had heard you talk about running in the snow when you were a boy, and I think he had taken up an idea that he could never be a man until he had done the same."[14]

Margaret's sympathies were with her husband while he was away. She wrote that she was thinking of him and knew he had "arduous duties" and was faced with a "tiresome routine," and that she knew he would be happier at home with his family. Still, she had to wonder if she would ever be able to enjoy her husband's society "without the painful consciousness that it must be but for a few days!"[15]

For Christmas, Houston sent home apple, orange and grape seeds, along with walnuts and almonds and instructions on how to plant them.[16] But Margaret probably appreciated even more his letter about the Christmas party in the parlour of the house where he was residing. He had been pressed upon to take an "egg nog or apple toddy" but had refused. He assured her that his resolve was so strong and his purpose so firm that he would "as soon take arsenic as anything containing alcohol!"[17]

Another indication that Houston's drinking was no longer a problem was his ability to joke about it. In January, he had a bad cold or influenza. In the hopes of helping his ailments, he took a bath in whiskey. His letter to Margaret said: "As I do not take anything that contains alcohol inwardly, I can afford to use it outwardly." He had also promised to make a temperance speech, and assured his wife:

> I have become more pleased with temperance than I have ever been previously. I witness so many souls sinking to perdition from the vice of intemperance that it teaches a fearful lesson to the wise or reflecting.[18]

While Margaret no longer needed to worry about Houston's drinking, she was faced with other concerns. Cholera was epidemic all over the eastern United States, and Margaret was worried about her husband's health. She was also worried about the health of their good friend and neighbor Colonel Birdwell, who had been seriously ill. Margaret felt that if the colonel should die, she had scarcely a hope that Mrs. Birdwell would survive him long. This situation, of course, reminded her of her own situation, and she worried:

> I need not tell you how deeply I am grieved on her account for you know that her sorrows are to me the sorrows of a sister. . . . I do hope dearest that you will never leave me again, for I find that my fortitude decreases with my years, and I feel that I cannot endure much longer the anxiety that your absence entails upon me. It is true that the care of our little flock is an absorbing thing with me, but even their merry prattle can not banish my loneliness and gloom.[19]

She wished that he could be there to share with her "the delightful task of instructing our noble boy," a process which "expanded" her feelings and "elevated" her thoughts more than anything she had done before. She described Sam sitting by her side sketching on a sheet of paper, and praised his drawings even while admitting he was not "a young Raphael."[20]

The mails were detained by high waters for several weeks after the first of the year, and Margaret's spirits were seriously affected by not hearing from Houston. By January 16, she was quite desperate, and again questioned the wisdom of Houston's choice of careers:

> I long to see you cast off the weight of political cares and turn away from the unhallowed influences about you that in our quiet home you may be enabled to seek with your whole heart the only thing worthy of our affections. . . . I endeavor to rejoice with my little ones, but with me, it is but a semblance of joy. And must it be ever thus? Are your duties always to call you away from your family? If so, mine must be a lonely destiny. My advice to you would be to take leave of Washington now and forever, but there is much selfishness in it I admit.[21]

Margaret's low spirits were raised on the last day of January when she received six of Houston's letters all at once. She took pleasure in arranging them chronologically before she allowed herself to read them. She realized, however, that they did not really compensate for her weeks of misery. She immediately began to worry about her husband again: "When I calculate the days and weeks that have passed since the last was written, I fancy many things that may have happened, and my heart sinks within me."[22]

Apparently the mails came regularly after January, for the following week Margaret was delighted to receive some treasures from the Holy Land. A Miss Watson had sent her a flower and some cedar from Jerusalem. She had also received books, a trunk, and a new cloak as gifts from her husband.[23]

In January, while Margaret had been worrying, Houston had spent his time in the Senate trying to improve transportation in the state.[24] He introduced bills to create both a national road and a transcontinental railroad through Texas. In his spare time, he and Senator Rusk were attending a series of lectures and experiments on mesmerism, clairvoyance, and the relationship of these sciences to religion. He wrote Margaret that Rusk was a believer, but as for himself, he would make up his mind later.[25] A few weeks later Houston relayed to Margaret his conclusions on the matter:

> . . . with Gen'l Rusk and some other Gentlemen, I make a class of students to a teacher on mesmerism. We are all greatly interested in the science. I have not a shadow of doubt on it nor in Clairvoyance. I have seen such experiments since I commenced attending the Lectures that it entertains with confidence. One thing, my Dear that will delight you much is that it throws or casts light upon many parts of the old as well as the new Testament. I know you will be gratified at this assurance.[26]

Houston went on to describe some of the events he had witnessed. A youth "in a Clairvoyant state," who had never been out of Washington, perfectly described the town of Nacogdoches, although Rusk and Houston were the only persons present who knew anything about Texas; and he also described homes and families to members present. Houston was afraid to ask for a description of his home lest "something unhappy might be presented to my mind that I might not wish to believe and yet could not disbelieve it!" So he asked for a description of Sam's donkey, and the youth "described his color and appearance as accurately as if he had been standing present." Perhaps remembering some of Margaret's unexplained experiences he entreated her: "... please don't think I am crazy, and so sure as we live to meet, I will satisfy you on the art, if I can not give you the reason for it. You once had a disposition to believe in it when I had none."[27]

Margaret would answer that she had had strange feelings ever since she read his remarks about clairvoyance. This was despite her own experiences and the fact that she believed what she had heard and read on the subject. She added that Houston's evidence was "like the evidence of my own senses, and it is [really] awful to think of an influence so spirit-like unless you have some objective which I do not understand."[28]

Feeling that perhaps he had not been explicit enough about the experiments he had seen, Houston wrote Margaret that if at any time he had discovered that the lectures were at war with Christianity, he would have abandoned them as an "enemy to his peace." On the contrary, he found that the subject of mesmerism increased "the wonder of the power of an Almighty God." He further reported, "It is indeed wonderful, and its curative powers great."[29]

The next series of lectures was on the science of phrenology. Houston and some of his colleagues arranged to have their heads "charted" by a blind phrenologist. Houston's sense of humor was quite evident when he wrote Margaret of the trick that had been played on the poor man. Houston had obtained a "chart" of his head without giving his name. During the reading someone spoke of the Senator as if he were not present, and the blind man launched into a tirade, giving his opinion that Houston was one of the most perfect reprobates and rowdies that he had ever heard of. The man then returned to reading Houston's head, saying that this man had very high moral points and constancy and comparing him to Daniel Webster and Horace Greeley. Much to Houston's amusement, the poor man was aghast when he learned the identity of his famous client. Later they became great friends, and Houston joked with Margaret :

I am happy to learn that I improve upon acquaintance. Do you really think so? If you do, my Dear, perhaps it is because you are blind too, as the poor phrenologist, only yours is the blindness of partiality.[30]

Margaret's letters began to show concern for farm matters. She wrote that although Mr. Gott was "industrious, pious, and attentive to his duties," he was having difficulty controlling the servants. She asked her husband to write and tell Gott what should be done, "particularly your regulations about the conduct of the servants."[31] Houston complied, tactfully omitting the information that Margaret had mentioned the problems.[32]

On the subject of politics, Houston wrote Margaret that he pitied those who had hopes resting on the "firmness or sagacity" of president-elect Taylor. He compared them to the followers of the Pharaoh at the Red Sea: "They will find two shores, but can reach neither." He had attended a reception at the White House, and had walked Mrs. Polk around the East Room. He used that experience to remind his wife how much he preferred to have Margaret on his arm, and further described his feelings on being at the White House and so far from her:

I would rather have you there . . . than any one on earth, and if we had to assume other relations to the public than those which we now do, I would infinitely prefer to have you than any one on earth. I suppose that not less than one hundred persons of both sexes spoke to me on the subject of bringing you to the White House & living there! It may be so![33]

As the congressional session wore on, Houston's loneliness increased. He wrote Margaret that the time seemed to be passing too slowly, and again revealed the comfort he took in gazing at the heavens as they had so often done together.

I need not tell you, my Love, how devotedly I do love you. I feel all the frenzy of other days, for last night, as I came home . . . I saw our "Star." If you can fancy what my thoughts once were, and hopes, and then add to them the realities, which we have since enjoyed with the addition[s] to our circle, you can partially determine my anxiety to be with you again.[34]

A few days later he wrote that his mind was so "troubled about getting home" that he had decided "that it is the last time that I will come alone, or remain here without my Dear Wife, and family."[35] History shows that this promise was simply a reflection of Houston's desperation at the moment. In fact, he would be absent from her for the larger part of the next ten years.

He wrote Margaret that he intended to be home from this session by the first of April, and that he was looking forward to having his children around him again, but added, in acknowledgement of her situation: "The noise which I endure here from the grown children is ten times more annoying to me than all that I know you hear at home from the children."[36]

Margaret was disappointed when she later received word that Houston would be delayed with a stop in San Augustine for a court case on his way home. She had "measured her fortitude" to the first of April and did not want to endure a longer separation. She had told Sam that his pa would be home when the flowers bloomed and now that was not possible:

> The sweet spring is indeed here and the air is redolent with the breath of flowers, but he is far away without whom the brightest and sweetest objects of nature lose their charms. Do not fear dearest that I am forgetting myself and writing from other days. Indeed no! What time should be sweeter than the present![37]

She had taken Sam to Mr. Davis, the daguerreotypist, to have his likeness made for his father. She had planned to have one made of herself, but before she could have it done, Mr. Davis was arrested for the murder of Edwin Banton. Margaret also wrote Houston that she needed to warn him against the fascinations of a certain person in Huntsville:

Her name is Maggie Lea Houston and she reigns as a queen in our family. The grave and philosophic Sam, the sprightly and self-willed Nannie and even Mother herself, all bow to her gentle sway, and unless you guard yourself carefully, I fear that you will soon think more of her than any of us. Beware of her bright eyes, rosy lips, and merry laugh.[38]

Houston was back in Huntsville by the end of April, 1849, renewing his affections with Maggie Lea and all the family. Here he learned that one of the domestic problems that Margaret had been dealing with was the growing attraction that fourteen-year-old Virginia Thorn had developed toward Thomas Gott. Margaret was sending Virginia for visits with the Reverend and Mrs. Creath in the hopes of forestalling more serious problems.[39]

Houston spent the summer in a way which would become typical of his activities for Senate recesses. He renewed his legal practice with cases in San Augustine and Nacogdoches. He spent time with his family and entertained friends in his woodland home. He wrote to Ashbel Smith and invited him to come for a long visit. He wrote political letters and made speeches, including one for the July 4th celebration of the Temperance Order.[40]

One of his activities in late summer was spurred no doubt by the lectures he had attended earlier in Washington. Dr. D. C. Bellows appeared in Huntsville and advertised that he was a "Practical Phrenologist." Houston decided to take Sam in for a reading. Dr. Bellows described Sam as "naturally cheerful, hopeful, and confident," and he warned that parents and teachers must avoid pressing Sam's mind with anything supernatural. He also reported that Sam had a tendency to believe everything he saw or heard and predicted that Sam would excel more easily as a linguist than a mathematician.[41]

As the beginning of November approached, and it was discovered that a fourth baby was on the way, Houston and Margaret each faced a difficult personal decision. Both wanted to remain together. Margaret had to weigh family responsibilities and her health against personal happiness. Houston also had to make a similiar decision and choose between remaining at home with his family or assuming his political duties with the hope that he could somehow hold the Union together. Together, they each reached a decision. Houston left her behind and returned to the capital. Although Margaret's going to Washington would continue to be discussed through the years, the trip never became a reality, and, although Houston frequently wrote about retiring from public life, that too was not to be.

Margaret wrote immediately after Houston left, in the hopes that her letter would be in Washington before his arrival. Their home looked desolate to her after his departure, but she was attempting to remain in "constant occupation to keep myself from indulging in useless regrets." She also filled her time with participating in the Bible school class which had just been organized.[42]

On the very same day, Houston was writing to Margaret. He was still concerned over his missing papers and, reflecting on the time when Virginia had cut up Margaret's Bible, he suspected that she was connected with this new incident. He wrote Margaret to warn her of his fears:

> I want my "Big Book" or journal "laid" under the head of mother's bed and the slat so that it may be safe. Those papers that were lost I can only account for as one principle. You recollect how your Tennessee Bible was used. The same persons are with us that were there. Do not by any means allude to this matter, but think of it my Dearest.[43]

When Houston reached Washington he wrote Margaret that this time he felt "a thousand times more anxious to see and be with you and our dear children than I have been before." He felt deep cares and anxieties about having to leave her, but his decision arose from a sense of duty. He assured her that "I am and ever will be for the Union, yes and for our Union![44] A few days later he made a speech and reported its contents to Margaret: "I only intended to say that my presence is wanted here as a southern man to meet and to rebuke southern fanatics. The Union will be preserved, and I must act out your dream about the 'Map'."[45]

Before he left Huntsville, Houston had realized that Margaret was having a more difficult time with this pregnancy than she had with the previous ones. He had promised her that since this was expected to be a very long session, he would make every attempt to return in the spring for a short visit when the new baby was expected. She reminded him of this promise in a letter, and he responded:

> You wish my Love, for me to say whether I intend to see you in the spring. It is not only my intention, but it is my ardent desire as well as my hope! It will depend upon the pressing of business in which my presence will be imperatively required.[46]

As the year 1850 began Margaret was struggling to be cheerful. She started her first letter with her wishes for the new year: "Another year has commenced. May it be the last that shall find us this far apart." She continued with the message that she was more attracted to their home and neighbors than ever before, and felt that if she could only get him to love this place as she did, she would be perfectly satisfied. She had one request to make. She asked if it would not be possible for her husband to obtain the office of Marshal of the State of Texas for Colonel Birdwell, as she knew that their friend much desired it. And of the political problems facing Houston she expressed an opinion: "I fear it will be late in the session before . . . Oregon and 'the Texas boundary line' will be settled. I am selfish enough to hope that they will make the boundary line of your sabbatical life."[47]

Houston was facing an old political problem that he needed to discuss. He wrote a long letter on the subject of his running for president, but he broached the subject tentatively: "Now my dear, I am about [to] present a matter to your attention. Many persons and those in high position in the Democratic Party are anxious that I should yield my attention to the succession. . . . " He informed her that these persons thought his chance was quite good, if not better, than that of any one who could be brought forward by either party. He reminded her that it had always been his intention to defer to her wishes if she was opposed to his remaining in public life or if she really believed that it would be safer for their happiness if he spent the remainder of his life "in private station." He then assured her:

> I declare to you, if I know my self that my heart is not set on the Presidency, and I will hear your suggestions and wishes with paramount consideration.... I assure you that it would not be the splendour of the station that would induce me, if it were at my disposition to accept it, nor any other consideration short of a conviction that I cou'd benefit my country more than another upon whom it wou'd otherwise fall to act for the country.[48]

Turning to family matters, he responded to her questions about having family portraits made. The famous artist George Allen had come to Huntsville. Margaret had decided against having Sam's and Nannie's portraits done, both because of the expense and the fact that she thought it would be hard to get accurate likenesses of the children. Margaret was having hers done and Houston wrote her not to worry about the expense if she wanted the children's made. He had one other suggestion: "by no means fail to have Mother's taken for us. I want our Mag to have it, to look at when she becomes old. . . . She will surely see a likeness."[49]

Houston enjoyed buying clothing for Margaret which she could not get in Huntsville. He admitted to her that he really knew little about women's fashions, but that he had seen some dresses that he would like to get for her. He was disappointed because she never asked for anything and he was not sure what was needed.[50]

A week later, he sent small pox vaccine so that the children and the servants could be vaccinated, but he worried that it would not reach Huntsville before the disease did. Of the matters in Washington, he wrote that there was a great opposition to his resigning his Senate seat, but thus far it had produced no change upon his determination.[51]

The next day he presented the Senate with a Resolution proposing terms of compromise between the North and South in the hopes of taking "the wind out of the sails of Nullification and abolition." He wrote Margaret that he would be sending her a copy of it:

> I hope that you are statesman enough to see that it is the only feasible plan by which such matters can be reconciled! I think you will perhaps recur to the dream of the "map." It is not, I assure my Love, either vanity or ambition or the love of fame which have induced me to take the course that I have, but mostly a sincere desire to serve the best interests of my country, and to leave to my posterity all the blessings of Freedom which I have enjoyed in life.[52]

When he reported this to Margaret, he mentioned being reminded of a year earlier when he had written that he saw something of her dream of the map "beginning to shadow forth its interpretation" and he hoped that there would be "enough good men and true to save the Union!"[53]

As to family matters, Houston had decided to reward Sam with a sword if he demonstrated "good and kind feelings to all the family." He asked Margaret to inquire as to whether Sam would prefer to have a new sword with his own name on it or his father's San Jacinto sword.[54]

The mails from Huntsville were delayed once again, and by mid-January it had been many weeks since Houston had received a letter from Margaret. He continued to write of his devotion and his plans for a visit home in the spring. He wrote that he had worked out a plan:

> I can get some one of the Whigs to pair off with me on important Party questions, and that will enable me to return and see you, and my absence will neither incur censure nor render me obnoxious to the charge of neglecting my duty either to the country or to my Party.

He went on to confess that he was sure that in the past he had made greater sacrifices for his county than he would ever be able to make for her, but at the present if his duty to her required him to neglect the country's interests, he "would not hesitate as to the course he would pursue."[55]

While Houston was pondering his political and personal problems, Margaret was dealing with serious ones of her own, and as usual, did not tell him about them. A persistent cough was sapping her strength. She feared it was consumption and could not throw off the feeling that she would not survive the birth of her next child. She frightened Eliza when she begged the trusted servant to promise that if Margaret did not survive that she would never leave the Houston children and see to it that they were properly raised.[56] Margaret also suffered a fall during this time which seriously injured both ankles.

In addition, she was trying to deal with the problem of a growing mutual attraction between Virginia Thorn and Thomas Gott. Unknown to Margaret at the time, fourteen-year-old Virginia had told Gott that she was nineteen. Virginia was following Gott around at every opportunity. The two were spending late hours together on the front porch. When Margaret attempted to correct her, the girl became insolent and ungovernable. Since Virginia was a member of the Baptist Church, Margaret sought the advice of Mrs. Birdwell and Mrs. Evans as to whether the matter should be brought before the church council. Her friends advised Margaret not to do this, but to correct Virginia privately. Margaret attempted this and thought the problem somewhat solved. In fact, the situation became worse, and unbeknownst to Margaret, Virginia complained to Gott that Margaret had mistreated her.[57]

Margaret finally wrote to her husband about it when the affair came to a head:

> You may prepare yourself for an astounding piece of news. On last night Virginia eloped with Gott, as I supposed to marry him, but today I learn he has taken her to Cincinatti to go to school to Miss Rankin['s] one session and then they are to marry. You may

form some idea of my astonishment by your own, for I was totally unprepared for it.

She went on to say that since Virginia had seemed happier and more cheerful than ever before, Margaret had thought they were getting along fine. Now, she heard from several sources that she had been "nursing a viper." She felt that she had done all she could for the girl, who now seemed to have "rushed upon her own ruin." She even tried to look on the brighter side of the surprising events: "You will remember dearest that in my great perplexity, I told you I would carry it to a throne of grace, well truly the Lord has delivered me out of my great troubles, but in a way which I looked not for."[58] This was one time when Margaret's predictions would be wrong. Her troubles were not over, and Virginia would return to cause the Houstons a great deal more difficulty.

Even before Houston received the letter about Virginia he had begun to worry about Margaret's health and frame of mind. He wrote her:

> I don't intend to trifle with your feelings, but my Love, I am in hopes your apprehensions are groundless. So far as I can with delicacy, I have inquired and I find that Ladies are more distressed with the **fourth child** than at any previous birth, and that the longer they have children, or the more they have, the more they are distressed in spirits.

He added that he would be almost crazy if he could not be there in her "hour of trial." He assured her that as soon as he could leave he would telegraph to William Christy in New Orleans, who would immediately inform Margaret of her husband's departure.[59]

Their letters were crossing in the mails. When Margaret received news of his expected visit in the spring she wrote to express her delight. She suggested that he come for their tenth wedding anniversary, May 9. She also wrote that she was uncommonly helpless due to the sprained ankles and she feared it would be a great while before she recovered entirely from the accident.

Anthony Hatch had been hired as manager for the farm, and Margaret described him as "naturally obscene and illnatured and [someone who] must have an object on which to vent his spleen." This object turned out to be her mother, whom Hatch disliked intensely.[60]

The next week Margaret wrote about a strange visit from Mrs. Birdwell and Mrs. Wilson that would puzzle her for some time. Her friends seemed very anxious to know if she had urged Houston to come home in the spring. She reported that Mrs. Birdwell felt that Margaret was wrong in urging Houston to leave his post:

> I am perplexed and know not what to say about it. She says I must tell you to have no uneasiness on my account, for I shall have every consolation that friendship can supply and on no account to leave your post at this unfortunate crisis. Remember the words are not my own and that I merely repeat theirs that you may know how much consideration your friends feel for your reputation. [61]

Houston, however, had already made up his mind before he received Margaret's letter. He wrote her that he hoped by March to be "in the sunny south and enjoy your smiles and the children's which are far brighter to me than all the glare of fashion or the splendour of place." He told her that he would not exchange one day at home for all the pleasures that he could enjoy in Washington. He expressed his ambition:

> To be a good man, an affectionate husband, a kind parent, a generous master, a true patriot, and to leave my family and the world a spotless reputation comprise all the objects of my earthly ambition! No one of these objects will be disserved by my being here, while others will be advanced and my country's good promoted as I fervently hope![62]

In this same letter, Houston begged Margaret to arrange for a doctor to be with her during the birth, although she had never had one before. He tried to assure her that he did not think her situation any more dangerous than usual for ladies in that situation, but that he was acting on the principle that it would be prudent to have somone standing by just in case there were complications. He concluded: "My suggestions arise from the confident hope that all will be well with you and that your forebodings have arisen from some physical cause of which now will be entirely relieved before your time may arrive."[63]

At home, Margaret was struggling to cope with her depression. The late winter had brought storms with hail, thunder and lightning. Sunny days were rare and "the bleak and cheerless days" were affecting her spirits. She wrote again that she was hoping he would be there in a few weeks. She felt that she might have done wrong to insist that he come, but she was hoping for the best. She elaborated on the conditions under which she had previously written:

> When I did so it was under the melancholy impression that I should not survive the spring, and even now I am not free from apprehension but my health is much improved, and my cough has almost left me altogether.[64]

In Washington, for the first time in his career, the Senator put politics aside. His anxiety was too great. Following the plans of which he had earlier written Margaret, he telegraphed William Christy to write Margaret that he was on the way home.[65]

---

[1] Franklin Williams Collection, Huntsville, Houston to Margaret, November 10, 18, and 22, 1848. This "Big Book" probably refers to the large volume "Private Executive Records of the Second Term of Houston's Administration as President of the Republic of Texas." It may be viewed at the Sam Houston Regional Library and Research Center, Liberty, Texas, a gift of Charlotte Williams Darby.

[2] Ibid., Margaret to Houston, December 12, 1848.

[3] To the best of the author's knowledge, a "draft" was like an IOU among friends and merchants—a way of borrowing small amounts of money without interest for a short time. The author has several of these drafts in

her grandmother's collection, along with letters from Houston to different people asking that Margaret be allowed to borrow money. Most of the drafts have "Paid" written across the top of them.

[4] Sam Houston, *Writings*, vol. 5, 62–63, Houston to Margaret, December 3, 1848.

[5] Franklin Williams Collection, Huntsville, Margaret to Houston, November 16, 1848.

[6] Ibid., Margaret to Houston, November 18, 1848.

[7] Ibid., Margaret to Houston, November 28, 1848.

[8] Ibid., Houston to Margaret, December 6, 1848.

[9] Ibid., Houston to Margaret, December 16, 1848.

[10] Ibid., Margaret to Houston, January 9, 1849.

[11] Ibid., Margaret to Houston, December 5, 1848.

[12] Madge W. Hearne Collection of Houston Letters, San Antonio, Houston to Margaret, February 15, 1849. The whereabouts of these items is unknown.

[13] Franklin Williams Collection, Huntsville, Margaret to Houston, December 5, 1848.

[14] Ibid., Margaret to Houston, December 12, 1848.

[15] Ibid., Margaret to Houston, December 19, 1848.

[16] Ibid., Houston to Margaret, December 6, 1848 and December 26, 1848.

[17] Ibid., Houston to Margaret, December 25, 1848.

[18] Ibid., Houston to Margaret, January 30, 1849.

[19] Ibid., Margaret to Houston, January 3, 1849.

[20] Ibid.

[21] Ibid., Margaret to Houston, January 16, 1849.

[22] Ibid., Margaret to Houston, January 30, 1849.

[23] Ibid., Margaret to Houston, February 6, 1849.

[24] Houston's personal map with the route drawn in red is in the San Jacinto Museum of History, La Porte, Texas, a gift of Charlotte Williams Darby.

[25] Franklin Williams Collection, Huntsville, Houston to Margaret, January 1, 1849.

[26] Ibid., Houston to Margaret, January 20, 1849.

[27] Ibid.

[28] Ibid., Margaret to Houston, February, 6, 1849.

[29] Madge W. Hearne Collection of Houston Letters, San Antonio, Houston to Margaret, February 25, 1849.

[30] Ibid., Houston to Margaret, February 15, 1849.

[31] Franklin Williams Collection, Huntsville, Margaret to Houston, January 3, 1849.

[32] Ibid., Houston to Margaret, February 1, 1849.

[33] Ibid., Houston to Margaret, February 8, 1849.

[34] Madge W. Hearne Collection of Houston Letters, San Antonio, Houston to Margaret, February 11, 1849.

[35] Ibid., Houston to Margaret, February 15, 1849.
[36] Franklin Williams Collection, Huntsville, Houston to Margaret, March 3, 1849.
[37] Ibid., Margaret to Houston, March 29, 1849.
[38] Ibid.
[39] Henderson Yoakum Diary, Texas State Archives, November 8, 1850.
[40] Sam Houston, *Writings*, vol 5, 94, Houston to Ashbel Smith, May 31, 1849.
[41] Sam Houston Hearne Collection, Barker History Center, University of Texas, Phrenological Chart of Sam Houston, Jr., September, 1849.
[42] Franklin Williams Collection, Huntsville, Margaret to Houston, November 24, 1849.
[43] Ibid., Houston to Margaret, November 24, 1849.
[44] Ibid., Houston to Margaret, December 18, 1849.
[45] Ibid., Houston to Margaret, December 23, 1849.
[46] Ibid., Houston to Margaret, December 31, 1849.
[47] Ibid., Margaret to Houston, January 1, 1850.
[48] Ibid., Houston to Margaret, January 2, 1850.
[49] Ibid.
[50] Ibid., Houston to Margaret, January 6, 1850.
[51] Ibid., Houston to Margaret, January 12, 1850.
[52] Ibid., Houston to Margaret, January 13, 1850.
[53] Ibid., Houston to Margaret, December 26, 1849.
[54] Ibid., Houston to Margaret, January 13, 1850.
[55] Ibid., Houston to Margaret, January 15, 1850.
[56] Family story told by Madge W. Hearne quoting "Aunt Liza."
[57] Henderson Yoakum Diary, Texas State Archives, November 8, 1850.
[58] Sam Houston papers, Barker History Center, University of Texas, Margaret to Houston, January 28, 1850.
[59] Franklin Williams Collection, Huntsville, Houston to Margaret, January 24, 1850.
[60] Ibid., Margaret to Houston, February 6, 1850.
[61] Ibid., Margaret to Houston, February 12, 1850.
[62] Ibid., Houston to Margaret, January 29, 1850.
[63] Ibid., Houston to Margaret, not dated, 1850.
[64] Ibid., Margaret to Houston, February 18, 1850.
[65] Ibid., Houston to Margaret, January 24, 1850.

Chapter X

I must acknowledge to you that I am gratified to see that you are homesick and weary of public life. I extract no promise from you, but, oh my love, do not leave me again.

Margaret to Houston,
July 23, 1850, Huntsville

Houston's trip back to Texas was hurried, and the only explanation he gave his colleagues in Washington was that he was needed at home because of illness in the family. To those at home who questioned his deserting his post, he answered that nothing of importance would transpire in Washington until he returned.[1] During the few days of his visit home, he hired another overseer, Daniel Johnson, to replace Thomas Gott, and checked on the farm matters. He sought to bolster Margaret's low spirits and saw to it she would get proper medical care during her confinement. Within thirty days he was back on the road to Washington, and he wrote from Sabine Town advising Margaret to take care of herself after the baby arrived:

Do my Love, I beseech you, be greatly prudent, as to the matter of too early exposure! You cant be too careful. My belief is that your general health is greatly dependent upon the care which you take of yourself after confinement. If you are very well, you have only to take the more care of yourself to keep so.[2]

203

A few weeks later, not having received news of the baby's birth yet, he wrote to Margaret from the capital:

> I have from some cause felt confident that you wou'd do well and soon recover. Why this is, I can't say. My anxiety has been as great as you can imagine, but my fears have been less than before I went home. . . . I will tear many letters open with painful anxiety until I can know the result.[3]

The Powers were visiting with Margaret, and it was Antoinette who wrote Houston the news of the birth of his third daughter on April 9, 1850. It had already been decided that, if a girl, the baby would be named Mary for Houston's sister. He immediately wrote Margaret that he was happy to hear that it was a daughter. Margaret's mother had been of the opinion that he would be disappointed that the baby was not a boy. Houston asked Margaret to give her a message: "Give her my love and tell her that I thought more about your safety than any thing else on earth, and if I had any other wish it was subordinate to that." He also mentioned that several letters from Margaret had arrived before he reached the city and they all reassured him that his visit home had been beneficial to her. He hoped that she was in a more comfortable situation now and would have peace and more happiness than she otherwise could have enjoyed.[4]

At the same time Houston received word of the birth of his daughter, he got Margaret's letter containing the news that his sister, Eliza Moore, had died shortly after he left Huntsville. She had died very suddenly of "an inflammation of the brain," and Margaret had not known she was ill until she was gone.[5] Houston expressed his shock and acknowledged that the joys he experienced over the birth of a daughter were blemished with the sorrow of his sister's death.[6]

Their tenth wedding anniversary was May 9, 1850, and Houston wrote Margaret on that day that he could not let it pass without the pleasure of reminiscing about their happiness:

I could tell you very truthfully that each passing day only increases my affection for you and my anxiety to see you and to be so situated that we will not part again. I consider my absence an exile of the most painful character! Not one moment am I, nor can I, be happy where you are not.[7]

At home, Margaret was recovering slowly. As soon as she was strong enough she wrote her husband:

I have had a long and wearisome confinement and although the baby is five weeks old today, I am just able to walk about my room. I have not exposed myself at all, but it seems impossible for me to recover my strength.

She mentioned that Mr. Johnson was having trouble managing the field hands because he was "too good natured," but that Eliza was the one servant who had been "kind and faithful during [her] sufferings."[8] When Houston received this letter he immediately wrote Margaret to tell Eliza that he was bringing her a special present because she had been so devoted to her mistress.[9]

A few weeks later Margaret expressed her relief that Houston was not disappointed with the fact that the baby was a daughter. She reported that Sam had not complained to her, but she had overheard him telling someone else that "he believed he was never to have a little brother." The same letter told Houston that some strange things had happened since he left home. Virginia Thorn had returned to Huntsville and was boarding with their friends the Wilsons while she went to school. Stories were beginning to circulate that Margaret had mistreated Virginia while she was living in the Houston home. Margaret informed him:

Wilson has taken up the cause of Gott and Virginia. . . . I begin to suspect that he is the grand instigator of the whole plot, but God forbid that I should judge too harshly. The World is busy with the affair, but from my quiet home, I try to look calmly on the storm as it passes by, and await with humility whatever my Heavenly Father designs for me.[10]

A week later Margaret was sorry she had told Houston about the Wilsons taking Virginia in. She wrote, "Mrs. Wilson seems so distrest [sic] lest I should be hurt with them that I now wish I had not told you about it."[11] When Houston received this news he replied:

> The only effect which the notice of Wilson's conduct had upon me was to send him more papers than before. . . . I never intend to know any thing about what Wilson has done until he tells me himself, and then not notice it.[12]

A few days later Houston sent Margaret advice on how to handle the unpleasant situation. He suggested that she just act as though she did not know the fact, and that the matter would cure itself in time. He reminded her that "patience will work wonders!" He was of the opinion that the other matter with Gott and Wilson would blow over because Gott had neither influences nor money enough to satisfy Wilson. And as a final suggestion he advised her, "Be calm and trust in God."[13]

One might wonder if perhaps, at this time, Houston's mind went back a few years to something he had told Margaret. He had confided in her that there was only one way that his enemies could really hurt him, and that was through his family.

> The object of my enemies will now be to assail me in domestic relations. They know that [my family] are dearer to me than any other thing on earth! Their assaults will be, I apprehend, against the females of my family. This they think would render me desperate, and thereby, they would gain the only advantage which they now hope to obtain.[14]

Whatever reasons had brought the matter about, this would be a trying time for Margaret. Friends were coming to her support, but she could see that they were troubled by the situation. Margaret had made up her mind to trust in the Lord. She felt that if only she could "be resigned to His blessed will, it will all be for my good."[15]

She attempted to follow Houston's advice. She wrote him that the Birdwells had been over to visit and had brought with them a letter from Houston which had given them great pleasure. Margaret reported that Mrs. Wilson had also been out and "seems more attached to me than ever. I trust the storm is past."[16]

When Houston first reached Washington this time he had promptly ordered a new wardrobe sent to Margaret. When she discovered this she immediately wrote Houston of her concern about the expense:

> I can not account for the fit of extravagance which has come upon you, but trust it has passed off before this. I will not quarrel with my dear husband, but just think of four costly dresses for the mother of three daughters. . . yet to be reared, fed, clothed, and educated.[17]

Houston's reply assured her that he could afford the gifts and he gave his reason why he did not ordinarily discuss finances with her:

> I have not talked to you about money matters so much as I would have done, had it not been that I do not recollect that I ever alluded to any expense but what I thought you became somewhat excited, and at last I resolved never to name it again.[18]

He had also sent mourning dresses and bonnets to Margaret and Nancy when he learned of his sister's death. Margaret did not put them on, and she wrote him her reasons with the hope that he would not be hurt. Her father had been opposed to the the practice. In consequence, Margaret wrote, "I have had scruples about it myself." She reminded Houston that she had not worn the garments for her father or for her brother Martin. She no doubt felt that Houston would support her in this decision as he always did when she stood up for her beliefs.[19]

Houston's reply must have reassured her:

You have done right in this matter because we ought never to sacrifice a principle to any power or custom no matter what it may be or who its advocates are![20]

Margaret's future letters turned to a far less serious problem and once more her husband would support her decision. They had not yet decided on the baby's middle name. Resisting the forces of societal opinion, Margaret chose a boy's name for her daughter. She suggested William in honor of Houston's brother. This was finally agreed upon and the name was shortened to Mary Willie and she would sometimes be called "Mollie." Margaret also mentioned her own sister. Before Mary's birth, the Houstons had planned to name the next daughter for Antoinette, and Houston was concerned that there be no hurt feelings. Margaret assured him that although her sister would have been gratified to have a namesake, Antoinette agreed that it was their duty to call the baby Mary. "My dear kind sis seemed perfectly willing to await her turn, and I really believe she looks upon it as a mere postponement of courtesy."[21]

Houston noted that he was receiving adverse publicity in eastern newspapers, as well as those in Texas. Knowing that these reports would upset Margaret, he told her of his confidence that public sentiment would fully sustain him in the course which he had pursued for years:

The people are now satisfied that others intended Disunion, and that my course was to prevent it. I, as you know, have been honest in my course, and I have at times, felt for you, fearful that you would doubt my judgment because I was so much opposed and abused. It will be all right and honest![22]

He wrote to her that his good conduct in the capital was surprising to many persons who "from the carefully exaggerated slanders against me formerly . . . were prepared to see me any thing but a decent man." When they sought a plausible reason for his reform, he told her, she was receiving the credit.[23]

Senator Houston was also struggling with problems concerning the settlement of the Texas boundary line and the reaching of a compromise between the northern and southern states. He felt that if he could help accomplish these two things he would be ready to leave Washington, and he wrote Margaret of this feeling:

My Love, the wish to be with you and to be with you under the Stars & Stripes of the double union will cause me to exert all my energies in the settlement of all discord that I may retire and be at rest if a kind Providence should spare me longer days. Surely a wise man should not desire to waste all his days in turmoil and anxiety.[24]

The next week Houston was writing Margaret to describe that inner turmoil.

You have but little idea of my varied feelings since I left you my Love, and at this very moment I feel not only all the affection that is possible for you and our dear little ones, but I feel for my country with a painful interest. . . . The Union is too strong to be destroyed by Fanatics. Honest men and good patriots are misled by them. . . . [25]

Once again, Houston was beginning to weary of public life. His letters all summer evince his increased homesickness, and, as he wrote on June 6, 1850, "in the same ratio of that increase does my fondness for public life decrease." He again made Margaret a promise:

Should we live to meet, I assure you that you will find me the most kind, constant, and affectionate husband & tender parent in Texas. . . . When I look back on the days which I have spent in vain and insanely, I condemn myself more than the world is disposed to condemn me![26]

Three days later, he reassured her of his continued love for her even at the expense of his own reputation:

> So far as my affection will delight you, my Love, you ought to be happy, for I am sure no one was ever so much delighted with, or devoted to a wife as I am to you. I grant you that is not the fashion altogether, but I am willing to have it thought that I am peculiar. . . .[27]

In Huntsville, Margaret was becoming weary of being a politician's wife. She was sure that many of her physical ailments arose from what she called her "continual anxiety of mind." She wrote her husband that although she was trying to be composed and patient, she saw no possibility of it until he was with her again.

> I have heretofore been guarded on the subject of your return lest I might say something that would make you unhappy, but I begin to think that "honesty is the best policy" and I will now tell you that if you knew how anxious I am to see you, I think you would almost come home right away. Ah no, I can not hope to accomplish that much, I do really hope that the remembrance of our present distress will have some bearing on your future course.[28]

Perhaps mental telepathy was at work, for on the very same day Houston was writing to Margaret of his thoughts on his "future course":

> If I ever had ambition, I am now cured of it entirely. Fame may suit the young and those who have not passed through so many various scenes as I have done! If spared to pass down a lengthened vale of years, I hope to enjoy a tranquil evening and be prepared for the setting sun of life and the dawn of a happy immortality.[29]

A few days later he was even more specific about his wishes for the future:

210

If spared, my Dearest, it is my fixed purpose to retire from the scenes of public life and return to the bosom of my family. . . . I know how very imperfect all my efforts must be to accomplish any good work. Yet I will endeavor to do as little harm and as much good with God's helping as may be in the compass of my power. Each day but renders me more dissatisfied here & more anxious to be with you. I feel that there is a crisis in our natural affairs that demands of me as a Patriot to stand by our country, and if in my power to aid her in her struggles.[30]

He added just two days later:

I am pained that a sense of duty to our country compels me to remain for the present position. . . . Nothing but the crises could keep me from you, My Love, and our children.[31]

When Margaret received these letters she had to admit they made her happy. She was "gratified" that he was "homesick and weary of public life." She stopped short of extracting from him a promise of retirement, but begged: "Oh my love, do not leave me again. . . . I will tell you no more of my troubles if I can possibly avoid it and merely say, Oh never never leave me again." She went on to say that she could not agree with the ambitious schemes of his friends. If she could be fully satisfied that the Lord had work for him to do at the helm of government, she would feel that he were honored indeed, but, she added: "Were my own feelings alone to be consulted, I would say let our home be amid the quiet shades of rural life, but I need not tell you this, for on this subject, I know that we think and feel alike."[32]

There occurred one problem of which Margaret would write Houston. It involved little Sam who seemed to be feeling less important since the birth of his third sister. Margaret described some of the problems she was having with him: "Sam is making some improvement in reading and writing, but he is more fond of oral instruction than of reading for himself. He is rather irritable and self-willed and it is a great grief to me. . . ."[33]

211

Upon receiving this letter, Houston did two things. He wrote to Margaret, telling her he would try to "improve [Sam's] disposition" when he got home,[34] and he wrote directly to his son, beginning a regular correspondence with him that would continue throughout the years that Houston was in the Senate. He would send messages for Sam to give the rest of the family and the servants, and he would instruct Sam to do certain jobs around the farm. Each letter was full of love and advice such as: "Boys should always be kind and generous to their Sisters. No man is either good or great who is unkind to women! . . . You will early learn . . . that no man can be great who is not good!"[35] Houston always pointed out that he was writing to Sam because he loved him and wanted to make him happy. He felt that the key to happiness was in serving others:

> I want you to make [your sisters] happy as well as your Grand Ma and your own dear Ma! It is by making people happy by acts of kindness that they will learn to love us and then they will try to make us happy. In this way we are made good & kind. . . . You ought to be kind to all good people and not injure the bad ones, but let them pass in peace![36]

Houston may have feared that his son was hearing some of the slander about Margaret that was being circulated through Huntsville when he wrote Sam in late September:

> Bad men and bad women are the only beings that will not return good for good and kindness for kindness. . . . [They] cannot be happy & they wish to see other people unhappy like them. . . . Learn to be good while you are young, and if you live to be old, you will be happy.[37]

As the summer progressed, so did Houston's inner conflicts between his civic duty and his love for Margaret. In July he wrote that his anxiety to be with her was most painful, but to leave before Congress adjourned or while the rights of Texas and the preservation of the Union were subjects of discussion "would be a desertion of the highest duty of a man and a Patriot." These were the only subjects which could keep him away from her. He assured her:

> I have not one ray of happiness before me here for I declare to you my Love, that I would not forego your society as I have done for years, nor for the Presidency of the U. States if that would secure it. My Wife, my children and my home are more dear to me with my friends than all the honors of this World![38]

As August began, the Compromise Bill was defeated and the Senators began to work on the parts of it that might be passed. By mid-August Houston had made the decision that he was going to leave for home "so soon as the Bills concerning Texas have passed Congress whether it should adjourn or not." He wrote:

> I do believe that no human being was ever more anxious to retire from public cares than I am. So long as I am compelled to remain, I must do my duty. . . . I would resign [the Senate seat] with more pleasure than I accepted it. My situation, tho [sic] is one of peculiar delicacy. Texas is not on her legs fairly, and I wish to see . . . a good work finished which I saw commenced.[39]

Houston was not sure when Congress would adjourn. He wrote Margaret that he could not advise her to be patient, for he had no patience himself. But, he consoled her, "All that I can say and hope is that the longer we are separated, the more we will love each other."[40]

By the end of August, Washington was experiencing autumn-like weather. He described the rays of the sun as growing pale and reminding him of October at home. Houston was even more homesick. He wrote Margaret that home to him had charms which office never had power to impart. The joys of home, he said, were pure and rational, while the excitement of public life brought no sweet solace. He went on to compare the two:

The consciousness of having done well in the harvest of public life will afford gratification to the patriot, but it seldom reaches to the tender affection of the heart. "Wife, children & friends" are the green spot to which memory recurs from distance and where the tenderest affections of the heart are blooming and are rendered more charming by time.[41]

Shortly before Congress adjourned and Houston left for home, he wrote Margaret that nothing but the "urgent & critical condition of our country at this moment" could induce him to remain absent from her. Furthermore, he said he was "sick of the cares incident to [his] place & position."[42]

While Houston was waiting for Congress to adjourn, Margaret was dealing with one of the most unpleasant experiences of her life. Thomas Gott had managed to have the court appoint him as Virginia Thorn's guardian, and in that capacity he had filed assault and battery charges against Margaret on behalf of Virginia. On September 25, 1850, Gott brought Virginia to testify before the grand jury of Walker County. The result was that Margaret was indicted and a trial was set for the following year.[43]

When Houston returned home and found out what had happened, he immediately asked Henderson Yoakum to be his wife's attorney. On November 8, 1850, Yoakum made notes in his diary: "Gen. Houston returned home from the long session of Congress a few days since. He is somewhat troubled about some domestic matters." Yoakum went on to record the complete sequence of events as Houston had described them, beginning when Virginia was seven years old and Vernal had become her guardian, and concluding when Gott had brought Virginia to the court and "procured Mrs. H. to be indicted before the grand jury."[44] Yoakum agreed to defend Margaret, and Houston was sure this was the best representation that could be secured.

No doubt the attack against Margaret greatly affected Houston and made him want to remain home all the more. It would appear from his letters of the summer that he and Margaret were at last to have a life together. And, on November 25, 1850, the Texas

Legislature voted to accept the proposition passed in Congress for the Texas boundary. Yoakum relayed the news to Houston and recorded in his journal that Houston replied, "I may now retire then, for it is consummation of what I have struggled to attain for eighteen years past."[45]

However, in January, 1851, Houston was on his way back to Washington to answer the call of public life. It would prove to be a long, tedious trip. While he was en route, Margaret wrote him in a tone which must have seemed familiar by then:

> I shall look with great anxiety for a letter from Washington, and shall be so happy when I know that you are safely over the fatigue and dangers of the journey. If this can make me happy, how much greater will be my happiness, when we meet again with the hope of being together till death shall part us.

She told him she was being cheered by the company of "Miss Goree and Miss Kittrell" who were visiting her for several weeks. Despite her court troubles, her spirits were good, and she was "more pleasantly situated" than she had ever been during his absences. She expressed her gratitude for being relieved of the responsibilities of the farm. That had made her feel as if she "had thrown off a little world."[46]

When he reached Washington in January, Houston wrote Margaret that he had counted up the days he must spend there and they amounted to fifty-five. It seemed short compared to the long previous session. Houston's name was still being mentioned as a candidate for the presidency, although he was not actively seeking candidacy.[47] On this subject Houston wrote:

> To me it seems strange that men who are much older than myself should engage with passion in the pursuit of Fame when it seems to me that they would be more wise were they to enjoy the reputation they have acquired in the bosom of their families. . . .[48]

Houston's mind was still on the troubles that Margaret was undergoing at home, and he gave her this advice: "I will hope, my dearest, that you will not be annoyed by vile enemies and the wicked who have sought to harass you and persecute you."[49]

Margaret wrote that she was attempting to be cheerful during their "painful separation." She did not expect him to resign his seat as he had implied he would during the previous session. She had, however, made a decision which indicates the two had discussed her moving to Washington to be near him.

> I would like for you to select a pleasant boarding house for us about 8 or 10 miles from the city. There are many arguments in favour of a country home, one which would weigh greatly with me, is that at night I would have your company, without being so much interrupted by visitors. Many other arguments will suggest themselves to your mind.[50]

Their minds were in tune, for on this same day Houston was writing Margaret on the same subject:

> I surely will never again come here to spend a long session without you . . . and you will not come without our little ones. You say I may look out for a place here near the city for you and the children. . . . This I have thought on and inquired about. That may be done. I will not resign until I go home. . . . My purpose is to let you make an unbiased decision.[51]

Houston wrote several times a week and always attempted to keep Margaret's spirits up. He sent messages of affection: "My greatest happiness of this earth is to assure you of whatever will promote your happiness. For indeed, My Love, I am willing to confess that I love you more than I ever did."[52] He sent her some advice on the coming trial, warning her not to let anyone know of his plans:

You need not fear my Love, if I live, that the whole earth can keep me from court. You must not intimate that I intend to be home, but say that I may return by Galveston. It is true that I may do so, but it is not my intention now to do so. You can say that I have spoken of that route![53]

By the next day he was sending her important evidence for her case that had come into his hands. With it came the sad news that her friends Jane Wilson and Tercy Birdwell and their husbands had been involved with Gott and seemed to be siding with him. Houston was concerned that she "not let these things trouble" her or her mother.[54]

Houston wrote Yoakum that he would be home as soon as he could, but that if something unforeseen should happen, he wanted the trial put off until he arrived. He told his friend he "would not fail to be present for millions."[55] Fearing that he might have been misunderstood, he wrote again a few days later: "I have entire confidence in my Counsel, but her [Margaret's] alarm and feelings would subject her to pain if I were not present."[56]

Within a few days he was packing to go home. He wrote Margaret that several dresses had been made for her. He was also bringing bonnets and parasols. He hoped to bring her "finery enough to have [her] trousseaued trimmer than for [their] wedding." It was his wish "not only to see [her] smile, but to keep [her] smiling."[57]

Houston was back in Huntsville by late March, 1851, long before Margaret's trial date in September. He spent the summer renewing ties with his children, entertaining friends, and supervising the farm. One day as he was out riding he discovered that he needed a saddle switch. He reached down to pull up a pecan sapling. It came up complete with roots, and when Houston returned from his ride, he planted the sapling in the ground in back of the house. Here it grew into a tree approximately one hundred feet tall which shaded the house for many years.[58]

Through a friend, Nicholas Dean, Houston had managed to secure a nurse for the children. Margaret was delighted when

Isabella arrived. Houston wrote his friend to express his thanks. He reported that the children were "all bewitched by her," and since Isabella's arrival there had been much improvement in their manners and disposition. Houston mentioned their friendship of thirty-five years and commented that his own life had been "one of strange vicissitudes and dark clouds [which] have often shrouded my horizon in deep gloom." But, he told his friend,

> I assure you, when I am at home, in my woodland residence, with my wife and brats, I feel no disposition to return again to scenes of official conflict. . . . Nevertheless, I have yielded so far to my friends [as] to agree to a return . . . and serve part of next session of Congress. . . .[59]

Houston went on to tell his friend that he did not plan to serve for the entire session, for this would entail an absence of eight to ten months, and this was far too long for a man who loved his family.

During the summer the family visited in Houston City and Galveston, and much to the delight of the children, spent a few weeks at the Cedar Point home. Houston enjoyed the summer with his family, and his letters to friends reflected his pride in his children. He wrote to Colonel John Burke that he was "anxious to get out of public life, and remain in quiet the residue of my days." Burke, he said, would be astonished to see "my pretty little flock of girls." Sam was described as "a tall, long . . . lad, fairly smart in some things," and his father hoped he would make a good man, if not a great one. In the same letter Houston invited his friend to take a trip with him and gave evidence of the influence Margaret had wielded over him:

> I can not promise to take any liquor on the road, but I will try to supply a full share of "good spirits," for the trip! . . . For years past, I have been a whole souled teetoteller [sic] and so intend to be as long as I live. It suits me!!![60]

All too soon the happy summer ended, and Margaret's trial began on September 30, 1851.[61] Colonel Yoakum was assisted by A. P. Wiley, and J. D. Hay was the district attorney for the State. Yoakum recorded the events in his diary under the heading of "The State vs. Margaret Houston."[62]

The first witness was Virginia, who testified to an incident of the previous year. She was upstairs at the Houston home dressing Nannie and the child was crying. After she tried to bring the child to her mother, Virginia said, Mrs. Houston came upstairs and accused her of hurting Nannie. Mrs. Houston then knocked her against the bed post and struck Virginia perhaps twenty times with a cowhide whip.

Under cross examination by Yoakum, Virginia stated that after the incident she had only two bruises, one on the wrist, and one on the elbow. She denied discussing the incident with Mrs. Baines or Mrs. Creath, both of whom would be witnesses for Margaret. She admitted that it was Gott who had taken her before the grand jury. Although records proved she was now sixteen, Virginia claimed that she did not know her age.

Thomas Gott was the next witness and he testified that on the morning after the incident Virginia showed him a bruise on her wrist. Afterwards, he stated, Mrs. Houston in his presence warned Virginia to be careful how she behaved and reminded her to remember what she got last night. According to Gott, Mrs. Houston was supposed to have said, "That cowhide is still here." Although Virginia had told him she did not know her age, Gott testified that he thought she was about nineteen. He admitted to Yoakum that the Houstons had treated him kindly, and that he took Virginia to the town of Cincinnatti in Walker County. The judge would not allow him to testify as to whether Mrs. Houston objected to his sitting up late with Virginia.

Vernal Lea was Margaret's first witness. He testified that he was still Virginia's legal guardian as far as he knew. He described Virginia's character as "hard to manage" like all children not raised under the eye of parents. A neighbor of Vernal's, Mr. Holliman, testified that he lived near the Leas and had known Virginia since

1842. He knew her disposition and characterized her as hard to govern and requiring strong discipline. Margaret did not testify at the trial, but she had plenty of character witnesses who came to her defense. Among them were Frances Creath, Melicia Baines, Mrs. Evans, Martha Ransom, and Thomas Parmer. The jury was unable to agree, and a mistrial was declared. The matter was then turned over to the Baptist Church, and Yoakum recorded that the Church "after a lengthy investigation of all the facts fully acquitted Mrs. H. of all blame in regard to Virginia."[63]

Yoakum also recorded Houston's opinions on the matter: "General H. . . understood that the matter had been urged on & brought to court at the instance of some of his enemies for the purpose of affecting him."[64]

The ordeal was now over for Margaret, although perhaps the hardest part of the entire affair for her was the loss of two close friends.

---

[1] Friend, 203.
[2] Franklin Williams Collection, Huntsville, Houston to Margaret, March 22, 1850.
[3] Ibid., Houston to Margaret, April 22, 1850.
[4] Sam Houston, *Writings*, vol. 5, 145–47, Houston to Margaret, April 30, 1850.
[5] Franklin Williams Collection, Huntsville, Margaret to Houston, March 26, 1850.
[6] Sam Houston, *Writings*, vol. 5, 147, Houston to Margaret, April 30, 1850.
[7] Franklin Williams Collection, Huntsville, Houston to Margaret, May 9, 1850.
[8] Mrs. R. E. McDonald Collection, Dallas, Margaret to Houston, May 8, 1850.
[9] Franklin Williams Collection, Huntsville, Houston to Margaret, May 19, 1850.
[10] McDonald Collection, Dallas, Margaret to Houston, May 21, 1850.
[11] Franklin Williams Collection, Huntsville, Margaret to Houston, May 28, 1850.
[12] Ibid., Houston to Margaret, June 6, 1850.
[13] Ibid., Houston to Margaret, June 9, 1850.
[14] Ibid., Houston to Margaret, April 29, 1846.
[15] McDonald Collection, Dallas, Margaret to Houston, May 8, 1850.

[16] Franklin Williams Collection, Huntsville, Margaret to Houston, July 29, 1850.

[17] Ibid., Margaret to Houston, May 28, 1850.

[18] Ibid., Houston to Margaret, June 6, 1850.

[19] Ibid., Margaret to Houston, May 28, 1850.

[20] Ibid., Houston to Margaret, June 18, 1850.

[21] Ibid., Margaret to Houston, June 4, 1850.

[22] Ibid., Houston to Margaret, May 11, 1850.

[23] Ibid., Houston to Margaret, May 19, 1850.

[24] Ibid., Houston to Margaret, May 13, 1850.

[25] Ibid., Houston to Margaret, May 20, 1850.

[26] Ibid., Houston to Margaret, June 6, 1850.

[27] Ibid., Houston to Margaret, June 9, 1850.

[28] Ibid., Margaret to Houston, June 18, 1850.

[29] Ibid., Houston to Margaret, June 18, 1850.

[30] Ibid., Houston to Margaret, June 28, 1850.

[31] Ibid., Houston to Margaret, June 30, 1850.

[32] Ibid., Margaret to Houston, July 23, 1850.

[33] Ibid., Margaret to Houston, July 29, 1850.

[34] Ibid., Houston to Margaret, August 19, 1850.

[35] Sam Houston, *Writings*, vol. 5, 236, Houston to Sam Houston, Jr., August 23, 1850.

[36] Franklin Williams Collection, Huntsville, Houston to Sam Houston, Jr., August 26, 1850.

[37] Sam Houston, *Writings*, vol. 5, 258, Houston to Sam Houston, Jr., September 23, 1850.

[38] Franklin Williams Collection, Huntsville, Houston to Margaret, July 21, 1850.

[39] Ibid., Houston to Margaret, August 14, 1850.

[40] Ibid., Houston to Margaret, August 22, 1850.

[41] Ibid., Houston to Margaret, August 28, 1850.

[42] Ibid.

[43] Walker County Minutes, Book A, 274, September 25, 1850.

[44] Henderson Yoakum Diary, Texas State Archives, November 8, 1850.

[45] Ibid., November 26, 1850.

[46] Franklin Williams Collection, Huntsville, Margaret to Houston, January 10, 1851.

[47] Ibid., Houston to Margaret, January 8, 1851.

[48] Ibid., Houston to Margaret, January 18, 1851.

[49] Ibid., Houston to Margaret, January 26, 1851.

[50] Sam Houston Papers, Barker History Center, University of Texas Library, Margaret to Houston, February 8, 1851.

[51] Franklin Williams Collection, Huntsville, Houston to Margaret, February 8, 1851.

[52] Ibid., Houston to Margaret, February 15, 1851.

[53] Ibid., Houston to Margaret, February 18, 1851.

[54] Ibid., Houston to Margaret, February 19, 1851.

[55] Sam Houston, *Writings*, vol. 5, 287, Houston to Yoakum, March 1, 1851.

[56] Ibid., 292.

[57] Franklin Williams Collection, Huntsville, Houston to Margaret, March 6, 1851.

[58] C. C. Springfield, "Sam Houston's Home at Huntsville," *Texas Parade Magazine*, 12 (January, 1951): 8–9.

[59] Sam Houston, *Writings*, vol. 5, 297–98, Houston to Nicholas Dean, May 8, 1851.

[60] Ibid., 303, Houston to Colonel John R. Burke, July 19, 1851.

[61] Walker County Minutes, Book A, 368, September 30, 1851.

[62] Henderson Yoakum Diary, Texas State Archives, September 30, 1850. (Note: The entry is mistakenly dated 1850 instead of 1851. It would appear that the court record books for Walker County are correct.)

[63] Henderson Yoakum Diary, University of Texas Archives, September 30, 1850.

[64] Ibid.

Nancy Lea, in a painting by George R. Allen. Original in possession of the Houston Historical Society, Houston, Texas. Courtesy of Sam Houston Regional Library and Research Center, Liberty, Texas.

On January 2, 1850, Houston wrote Margaret: " . . . by no means fail to have Mother's [likeness painted] for us. I want our Mag to have it, to look at when she becomes old. . . .She will surely see a likeness."

223

A contemporary photograph of the Woodland Home. You can see the roof of the small kitchen building to the left. Courtesy of Sam Houston Memorial Museum, Huntsville, Texas.

On the first day of 1850 Margaret wrote to Houston, who was in the nation's capital, telling him of her love for their home in Huntsville: "Another year has commenced. May it be the last one that shall find us this far apart. . . . I am more attracted to our home and neighbors than ever. If I could only get you to love this place as I do, I would be perfectly satisfied."

Chapter XI

Dearest, I must tell you that sometimes a dark thought presents itself to my mind "if his affection had been equal to mine, could he have left me?" But it is a mere phantom, and soon vanishes leaving but a shadowy trace. . . . I do not know why I have written thus unless it is to show you how important it is that we should always be together.

Margaret to Houston
Independence, May 24, 1854

Margaret's dream of returning to Washington with her husband was shattered when she once again discovered she was pregnant. By the middle of November Houston was on the way to the capital without her. After only a few days' absence he was already homesick. From Louisiana, Houston wrote that he was kindly received and "at times almost caressed," but he considered that a poor requital for "the sacrifice of conjugal and domestic happiness." He described his feelings: "At meal times I get no kisses, nor do I see any bright eyes or pretty curls displayed. I feel that there is but one house in this world for me and that is where you are present."[1]

Houston stopped in New Orleans to purchase supplies for the family larder. He visited with friends and relatives on the trip, and from Mobile he wrote Margaret that he could say with sincerity that he had "seen no children that will compare with ours." He was sure that the reason for this was that he had not seen "any mother who will compare with theirs!"[2]

At home Margaret resigned herself to the separation and made every attempt to be cheerful. She wrote that the household matters were moving more smoothly and harmoniously than they had ever done since she became a housekeeper. She was astonished at her own success and wished her husband were there to admire it. She gave him an insight on how the family spent their time:

> We all arise with the sun, and so soon as we are dressed, assemble for worship, an exercise in which the children engage heartily. When that is over, we proceed to breakfast which Eliza is getting ready. . . . Soon after breakfast, Isabella and myself sit down to our sewing while the children are engaged with their lessons. We do not confine them long to their books, but allow them an abundance of time for exercise. Thus one duty after another is taken in regular succession and all confusion is avoided.[3]

As was her custom, Margaret wrote descriptions of the children. Sam was improving in reading. Nannie was a "great girl," but one that Margaret feared would have a bad temper. Maggie was "as incorrigible a romp as ever." And of the baby Mary Willie she wrote: "We are no longer at a loss to know whom she resembles, for her features are growing singularly like a certain fancy face [a painting of Sam Houston] that hangs in our parlour, about 21 years of age."[4]

As the Christmas holiday approached Margaret felt the need to get out of the house. She borrowed Colonel Yoakum's horse and buggy to go to the church meeting. She wrote Houston not to be alarmed. She had wrapped up well in the cloak he had sent her. Her mother drove her, and Joshua walked before the horse into town.[5]

The baby was due in January and Houston wrote that he was feeling "inexpressible anxiety" about Margaret and the "crisis" which awaited her in the coming month. He had arranged for Henderson Yoakum to send word to Colonel Christy in New Orleans when the baby arrived. Christy would then telegraph Houston, whereby he would hear the news in only four days. Margaret was hoping for a boy, but he cautioned her not to be disappointed if it were another girl. He would be gratified with either result. In all of his December letters, he admitted his mistake in agreeing to go back to Washington. On December 4, he wrote: "When I . . . [think of] . . . all the associations of home & family, my heart is sad and I am pained that I did not adhere to my resolution to remain where I was happy."[6] Ten days later, he wrote again: "At times when alone, I think of you and home until my heart seems to sink in me with a leaden weight. I am truly sorrowful that my fate [separates] us for a moment."[7] And only five days after that: "What would I not give to be at home surrounded by my domestic circle? It would be to me more precious and delightful than all and every thing which can result to me here."[8]

Many of Houston's letters reflect that he was aware of the burden that his absence placed on Margaret with regards to raising their growing brood. He wrote long letters to the children as soon as he felt they were old enough to understand specific instructions on behavior and advice. He often gave them a little chore to do or a message to convey to someone, in the hopes of developing a sense of responsibility. He regularly sent chests of clothing, gifts, and books for them. He also sent "pieces" and comics from newspapers for them to paste into scrapbooks. For her part, Margaret devoted a part of her daily discussions with them to the subject of their father. Many years later, Maggie would remark in a letter that her father was with the family so little of the time that his visits home stood out as "pictures on Memory's wall." She added that when her father came home, each one in the family was remembered with some gift, and that the servants were never forgotten by "Master."[9]

When Houston reached the capital he had found that his name was still being mentioned as a presidential candidate. He wrote Margaret that every day brought him some new paper with his name "up as the Democratic candidate!" Margaret probably had mixed emotions when he described the situation to her:

> The people are for me. The politicians or a majority of them are not with me, and the only question is "Can the minority rule and control the majority?" I think not. The people are speaking out and will be heard.[10]

He further described his situation as similar to when Andrew Jackson was first brought forward as a candidate. "He had the politicians against him, and the people for him."[11] Houston, too, had mixed feelings about being a candidate. He assured Margaret that he would rather his children say, "My Father was a wise man & patriot" than that "he was President of the United States."[12]

Houston's original plan was to resign his seat in March, but Margaret had begun to doubt if this could really make her husband happy. The Democratic State Convention met on January 8, 1852, and adopted a resolution presenting Houston's name to the national party as a "patriot, chieftain, and statesman eminently worthy to be the standard bearer of the party in the approaching canvass for the Presidency."[13] Margaret wrote her husband that the hope of seeing him soon would make the time pass more pleasantly, but she wanted him to "weigh the matter well and not do any thing that [could] possibly militate against [his] interest or take any step that [he might] here after regret."[14]

Margaret again stood by her decision not to stand in Houston's way, and in her letter the next week she elaborated on the subject:

> I still say to you that I do not wish you to do any thing that you will afterwards regret. It is an important year with you, and if you think it will be more favorable to your prospects to remain at your post, distressing as the loss of your society would be, I will try to summon fortitude and take care of our little ones at home.[15]

When Houston received this letter he replied to Margaret:

> You wish me, my Love[,] to do nothing which might cause me regret hereafter. My notions are all set on political matters, and in them you know I am a predestinarian, and above that, I will not for any high and national office descend to the petty employment of a Grog-shop electioneerer.[16]

On January 20, 1852, the fifth Houston, another daughter, was born. Margaret wrote that quite frankly, for his sake she had wanted a boy, but that "from the moment of her birth I was reconciled, and now I am very happy." Margaret's sister had her namesake. The baby would be called Antoinette Power, which would be shortened to "Nettie."[17]

Houston journeyed home in late February to meet the new arrival. He stayed for a month and then returned to Washington to find that not much had transpired during his absence. Congress was absorbed in the politics of the presidential election. On this subject Margaret wrote him that based on what she could infer from the newspapers she did not think he would get the nomination. She confessed that she would not be very sorry: "If you should be nominated and elected it would only carry me into scenes for which I had no relish and surround me with people whom I could not love."[18] Houston, however, told his wife that both his opponents and his friends were of the impression that: "if I am nominated that I will be elected." He did not feel that the nomination was certain, though, and he would not "stake [his] happiness upon the issue of the election."[19]

Houston had rented out Raven Hill when he moved the family to Huntsville, but Margaret wrote that she had a great inclination to go there if he found that he was "to have the privilege of withdrawing from politics." She was desiring more and more the quiet rural life. Her health was good and she was enjoying attending to her household affairs. She reported that "truly every thing does much better with my constant attention."[20] She had settled into a quiet domestic life. She wrote that she was so occupied with the children's lessons and other duties that she had little time and even less inclination to go out. When their twelfth wedding anniversary arrived she noted her feelings: "Oh how changed are my feelings towards you! Then I loved you much, but now, alas, I love you so much more that I am not happy when you are absent from me!!"[21] Houston's thoughts were also on the anniversary, and on the same day he wrote her:

> Twelve years have been this day completed since you were pronounced to be my dear Wife, & I am free to confess that I love you more than I did at that hour. I thought I loved you then. I know I love you now!!![22]

A few weeks later the Democrats met in Baltimore to nominate their candidate. Houston wrote Margaret that he had no anxiety about the results. He felt it was in the hands of Providence, and all his anxiety "could not reverse His purpose." He was happy for another reason:

> One thing I may say to you without egotism. My standing with the people at large and the nation, I would not exchange for that of any man who may be selected by the Convention. I am regarded as above intrigue or corruption, and this I know you would vastly prefer to my getting the Presidency![23]

He wrote that "in view of the influences . . . at work" he did not see how he could be nominated. He urged her not to be upset over the results: "I will myself feel no regret, and I will have the more time to love you and our children than if I were nominated and elected. I write to prepare your mind and fortify your feelings for the events."[24] When he did not receive the nomination, Houston seemed relieved, but worried that Margaret might feel hurt:

> I have not felt one pang of disappointment. Had it been an election by the people, and I had not been elected, I would have been mortified, but when a new man was selected that no one knew, as a candidate, I felt that I had lost nothing. He is a clever man, and I will support him and the party in all good faith! . . . I fear you will be chagrined at the result—be as I am and let it pass.[25]

Five days later he wrote again:

> I have forgotten politics, my Love, and find that I knew myself in part, at least! Had I been nominated I would have been miserable about your dream, which had caused me some unhappiness, as you know I am superstitious.[26]

When Margaret heard from Houston she "rejoice[d] to see" that he was unmoved by "the recent affair at Baltimore." She added: "Strange and wonderful are the ways of Providence, and I humbly pray that it may be for our mutual spiritual good." She was not the only relieved family member: "Sam was opposed to your nomination, lest it might keep you from home."[27] She took his defeat as a "promise of better things," and an "assurance . . . that [he was] now taking leave of politics."[28]

Margaret wrote that as far as she could learn the results had "astonished the Democratic party" in Texas. In a rare comment on politics, Margaret expressed her views that the convention delegates were chosen from among the most active politicians in each state and consequently were men aspiring to office who would vote for the candidate who could best help them.[29]

As Congress would soon be adjourning, Margaret asked her husband to do one thing before he came home. She needed him to purchase "a neat, comfortable carriage that would carry a lady, gentleman, and five children."[30] This he did, and soon a large yellow coach was brought to Huntsville. It would make many a trip carrying the growing Houston family to the various homes they would own in Texas.

Back in Texas, Houston made several speeches in favor of Franklin Pierce. In December, he handled some law business in east Texas, but soon afterward he was back on the road to the capital. The new yellow coach did not take Margaret and the children back to Washington with him. He left alone by stage. He described to Margaret his feelings at the sad parting, especially his feelings at little Mary Willie's good-bye:

> I think that my time spent at home is as profitable and far more pleasant than that passed from home. . . . And to reflect that a child of more than three years old should say, when leaving home & family that "Pa is going home" does not sound pleasant in my ears! nor rest agreeable on my heart.[31]

He had only been gone a few days when Margaret received word that Vernal had died of "lung disease." This renewed Margaret's fears that her chronic cough was also consumption. She wrote that her mother was "completely crushed in spirit, and I think will never be the same." Her letter also contained the news that Jane Wilson had suffered a mental breakdown and was calling for her:

> It is one of the most melancholy cases of insanity I have ever heard of. I suppose several causes combined have produced it. I am almost afraid to breathe my own impressions of the subject for the dispensations of Providence are too solemn to be lightly spoken of.[32]

Houston replied with many words of consolation. He, too, was worried about Nancy Lea, and his thoughts went back to the bereavements of his own "aged and pious Mother when successive blows fell upon her." He was thankful for the consolation that Vernal "was prepared for the judgment." He also had some advice for Margaret. He felt that she should not go to see Mrs. Wilson unless Margaret felt some good would come of it, and if she did go, she should take Mrs. Evans or Mrs. Creath with her.[33]

Houston's term in the Senate expired on March 4, 1853, but two months earlier, on January 15, 1853, he had been re-elected senator and once more accepted the office. Margaret resumed her schedule of household duties, including that of educating the older children. The couple's letters frequently discussed Sam's education in particular. Houston was concerned about the development of his son's character and was afraid they had spoiled him:

> His wants have always been anticipated, and he has wanted nothing. . . . I will spare no pains so far as it may be in my power to aid in making him a good and useful man. . . . Honor has much to do with this. We can let him understand what constitutes honor & truth! No man can be truly great without both of these high and noble qualities. Without them, no man can be happy.[34]

In March, Houston received a letter from Margaret's cousin, Columbus Lea, informing him that Varilla's husband Robert Royston was not expected to survive. He shared the sad news with Margaret: "Death is making inroads in our family, and I pray Heaven that we may all be ready for the summons when it shall come. Sure it is, we can not be [too] well prepared for the dread event."[35] Houston was correct in his assessment. Royston soon passed away, and in the following year, Henry, the last surviving Lea son, would also die.[36]

During these sad times Houston's thoughts remained on religion. He had a plan for helping Margaret's church in Huntsville to purchase a bell they had long desired. He frequently made lectures for the Baptist Churches surrounding Washington. He never accepted a fee, not even for his expenses of travel. He had now decided to accept enough in fees to pay for the bell. He felt that "if I could help the church or congregation at home, it seems to me quite reasonable and just." He had talked to the Reverend Mr. Samson, who agreed and made the arrangements.[37] Margaret was overjoyed by the news.

An early spring had arrived, but it was a bittersweet delight to Margaret:

> The spring has stolen upon us with a noiseless and spirit-like step. Already many of my flowers have come forth to greet its welcome arrival. . . . Even the solemn evergreens look sad and seem to say "although we can not blush with the wood-bine and rose, or smile with the hyacinth, lily and jonquil, yet we love the spring too." How hard it seems that at this sweet season, I should be seperated [sic] from the only being that could ever really sympathise with me in my love of nature.[38]

Houston had similar responses to the spring season:

> When I look out of the windows and see the flowers & foliage, I am delighted until I recall the thought of home, and then my feelings are painfully excited. I pine, as the caged bird does, for freedom, and my affections beat against the bars of their cage in the quickened pulsations of the heart.[39]

233

Margaret worried that her love for him "approached too near idolatry." She reasoned that it might be that "the Lord takes from me the companionship so absorbing to every thought and wish, that I may have more time to think of the immortal soul."[40] The family was counting the days until the short congressional session would be over and Houston would return. Margaret wrote that Sam had expressed the wish that he "could keep from dreaming that pa had come because in the morning I feel so disappointed."[41]

Houston also was reflecting on their current separation and on his life. He expressed his thoughts to Margaret:

> Look at my sacrifices for the last twenty years and you will readily discover the [secret] of my life. Before we were united, and I may even go back to my dawn of manhood, and you will find that I was governed by a feeling of emulation to confer upon humanity great benefit and extend my sphere of usefulness[,] for it was not ambition.

He went on to reflect that when they were united in marriage, he felt his life took on a "double nature":

> To you I gave all my love, and to secure your confidence, I could not prove faithless to my country or disregard my position in the world. My love for you, my own reputation, the regard for our offspring, united with the peculiar circumstances of our country, all united have caused me to endure a painful exile from you, and the dear pledges of our love. Not one hour of unallayed happiness have I ever enjoyed in this place or absent from you since we were united.[42]

About the same time Margaret was writing to an old friend. She described herself as a mother of five with "an abundance of employment." She wrote that General Houston was "absent much of his time," and of course "the household cares devolve upon me." She went on to voice the hope that her husband would soon quit politics, for "it is a dreary life without him." She praised her husband as "much changed" and a good Baptist: "His disposition is now as gentle as a lamb, and if religion has not wrought the change, I can not tell what has."[43]

When Houston returned in late spring he had made a decision. It may have been based on a desire to remove Margaret to another location where she would not be constantly reminded of her unpleasant experience in court, or it may have been influenced by his concern about his children's education. Earlier, Nancy Lea had purchased a home in the town of Independence some seventy miles away. It was here that some of the best schools in the state were located, among them the Baptists' Baylor colleges, for both male and female. Each college had an associated school for young children. The surrounding farming prospects were good, and according to Nancy the countryside was some of the most beautiful in that part of Texas. Antoinette and Charles Power now had a home there, and Varilla had finally left Alabama after her husband's death and settled nearby.

Houston went to Independence in June, and while he was there he made arrangements to buy the Hines place which was located on a hill directly across the road from Baylor. The pleasant farmhouse was surrounded by three hundred sixty-five acres of land, some cultivated, some in timber. Houston wrote his former secretary Washington D. Miller that he did not think that "Austin or anywhere else presented the same advantages in a[n] Educational point of view that Independence does." He and Margaret, along with Sam and Nannie, planned a preliminary visit, after which he intended to move the family there in the fall.[44]

The house which Houston took Margaret and the children to see was a sturdily-built log house which had been erected in 1837 by the first owner, Thomas Baron. A lovely grove of oak trees surrounded it, and nearby was a clear spring which trickled over limestone rock.[45] The house was later covered with clapboard. It was built in an L-shape with one room extending out toward the front. From this room across the other part of the house was a covered porch supported by four posts. There were three chimneys, one on the side and two on the back.[46]

The house was simple and could not compare with their home in Huntsville, but the location was what pleased the Houstons. Their land was adjacent to the Baylor preparatory schools in which they would enroll Sam and Nannie, now aged ten and seven respectively. Directly across the road was the home of the Baylor University president. Many of the presidents through the years would be old friends of the couple.

The Houstons now owned four homes which they kept furnished and in good order. Whenever Houston became restless, he would put Margaret, Eliza, and the small children into the big yellow coach, and they would head for a different house. He would ride ahead, either on the mule Bruin or his horse, or sometimes in a buggy with one of the older children. The movings did not work a great hardship on Margaret since all the homes were equally equipped. They often carried nothing with them but clothing.[47]

And so it was that Houston moved his family to Independence on October 25, 1853. Sam and Nannie were placed in the schools in town, and Margaret continued to educate the younger girls at home. The Baptist Church was just down the road across from Nancy Lea's steep-roofed cottage. Margaret joined the church in which her mother was an active member. Their friend Rufus Burleson was the pastor, as well as being the president of Baylor. The Houstons established themselves in the community and contributed $330 toward the education of young ministers at the University.[48]

Houston had planned to be back in Washington by early November, but his return was delayed by the difficulty he was having in getting the new home furnished. He had ordered new furniture to be sent from Houston City, and Margaret was greatly upset when it arrived in a disreputable state. Houston promptly wrote the merchant a not-so-friendly letter describing what they had received:

> I have received a small cooking stove without any pipe, one large Bed-stead without Tiester [sic], . . . one of the bed-posts split—no side rails. . . . The Bureau came also, and the locks all off it. The "scratchings" of the key holes are handsomely fixed with wax or

236

putty . . . and taking it all in, it surpasses anything that I have ever seen, except, the sideboard—that is infamous beyond all things else. . . . The looking glass was broken before it left Houston, and hardly a splinter reached here. . . . I have not told you all, nor is it worth the trouble. . . . The furniture, I assure you, I would not accept as a gift in your city, nor would I give it house room here any longer than I could get rid of it.[49]

While he was attempting to straighten out his domestic problems, Houston had many serious talks with Dr. Burleson, whom he deeply respected. No doubt Margaret was enlisting the minister's help in her foremost project—that of getting her husband to join the Church. She was probably hoping that with the combined urging of Brother Baines in Huntsville, Dr. Burleson in Independence, Dr. Samson in Washington, and herself, she would ultimately succeed. When Houston returned to Washington in December he continued to attend Dr. Samson's church, and frequently he would send Margaret the texts of the sermons.

On New Year's Day, Houston wrote that he had no gift to send Margaret except "to remit the gift long since made—my heart." He sent her, along with "boundless affection," hopes and wishes for her to enjoy very many happy New Years.[50]

Margaret was pregnant for the sixth time, and although her letters were filled with news of friends' and family's visits, her spirits were low. She was still clinging to the hope that Houston would resign and return home before the baby's birth in June. She wrote him that her dreams were so vivid that when she awoke she "almost imagined [she] could feel [his] breath upon [her] lips."[51]

Living in Independence proved to be more expensive than it had been in Huntsville. Margaret mentioned this to Houston: "What has become of your copper mine? I am not jesting now, for I assure you we will need a mine of some kind if we live in Independence." Her letter went on to offer a solution if they could not afford to continue living there: "I sometimes think if you would urge Cedar Point now, I would not be very obstinate." She then promised, "Oh my love, if you will just come home, I will do anything on earth you ask of me."[52]

Concerning farm matters, she wrote that her mother sent word that Margaret was "worth fifty dollars more for the experience of the last few months." Margaret had given the overseer a serious talk about what was expected of him. She urged him to exert himself a little more, and the result was that "he got sick of work in a week" and quit. She employed a Mr. Sprott, who was quite industrious. Best of all was the fact that he was keeping Sam busy. She had decided that if Houston thought well of it, she would put Sam to work on the farm instead of sending him to school. She feared Sam would never have another such an opportunity of learning to work. She mentioned he had already improved in just a few days.[53]

Concerning the expenses, Houston gently reminded her that there was nothing that he "could go at" to earn a steady amount comparable to his Senate salary of two hundred and forty dollars a month. Even with his expenses in Washington, he was currently managing to save one hundred fifty dollars of it each month.[54] Houston also wrote that he planned to come home for a visit in the early spring, and no doubt some of his savings would be spent then. Margaret was overjoyed. She quickly replied:

> My soul springs from its dreariness and overleaps the interven-
> ing weeks as the hare bounds over the wild hills. . . . Do try to fix
> on some plan, rather than the terrible one of leaving me again. I
> would live on bread and water, or make any sacrifice of comfort
> rather than give you up again.[55]

While Margaret was dealing with problems of the farm and expenses, Houston was wrestling with the most serious question of his senatorial career, one which would have to be faced before he could leave for home. The Kansas-Nebraska Bill was before Congress. Because it would repeal the Missouri Compromise of 1820 and reopen the slavery extension issue which lawmakers had sought to settle with the Oregon Compromise of 1850, it had created a bitter debate between northern and southern factions. Houston warned Margaret not to be upset if he were abused because of his stand. He reminded her that he was the only southerner who voted for the Oregon Bill but he would vote alone again "if it is my conviction of right."[56] Houston described the situation in Washington as a "fearful storm . . . gathering in the political sky," one which would "break upon the south."[57] Senators from the South stood in a solid block for passage of the Bill, with the exception of Houston. He could not be in favor it, for he feared it would destroy the Union. He must have known that this stand would be a serious blow to his political career. Houston voted against it, but the Bill passed by nearly three to one.[58]

A few weeks later Houston returned to Independence for a short visit, where he made a few speeches defending his vote. He confided to Rufus Burleson his feelings about what had transpired in the capital. He told the pastor, "while that is the most unpopular vote I ever gave, it was the wisest and most patriotic."[59] Some old friends were not speaking to him, and several newspapers called for his resignation, branding him a traitor to the South. One of the few favorable reports appeared in the *Texas State Gazette* which urged him not to resign:

> Notwithstanding our objections to his course on the Nebraska bill, we should regret to see him leave the Senate at this time. Texas has large interests in many questions likely to arise in Congress during the present session, and his great abilities and enlarged experience would materially aid in securing them. We hope that he intends only a short visit to his family, and does not design permanently vacating his seat in the Senate.[60]

Margaret was greatly disappointed when Houston took the *Gazette's* advice and returned to Washington in May. He wrote her from Washington-on-the-Brazos that after he had started back he had a strange inclination "to turn my horse and retrace my steps home again, and wait for another stage." He had controlled the urge, as it would only mean parting again, and he feared it would be seen as a childish action.[61] As it turned out, his premonition had been valid. Shortly after he left, the baby contracted a serious case of scarlet fever. Nancy was also ill, and Margaret nursed them both.

239

The resulting anxiety and fatigue, combined with her advanced stage of pregnancy, caused her spirits to sink. She wrote her husband that she was trying not to think of the night he left, when "the whole earth seemed to me enshrouded in darkness...." Instead she tried to concentrate on "the recollection of the sweet, sweet hour we have passed together and the hope that the future hath many such in store for us." But she confessed to still being depressed:

> Dearest, I must tell you that sometimes a dark thought presents itself to my mind "if his affection had been equal to mine, could he have left me?" But it is a mere phantom, and soon vanishes, leaving but a shadowy trace.... I do not know why I have written thus unless it is to show you how important it is that we should always be together.[62]

As often happened, their letters crossed in the mails. At about the same time, Houston was writing her:

> A work has begun, and if spared, I must go on to its completion. It is not vanity I hope, my Dearest, but this very crisis, I do believe, and our country at this moment requires my aid.... To this end I will act, and I am as anxious my Love, to be and stay with you as you are to have me.[63]

A week later she was writing that although she had received no mail from him, she had read in the newspapers that there was still a great excitement in Washington. She expressed the wish that Houston could be released from "those harassing subjects" and mentioned in a not-too-subtle way what a joyful surprise it would be if, on reaching Washington, he would just hand in his resignation and set off for home. This, she said, would more than repay her for the anguish of spirit which she had endured lately. She was longing for the "quiet shades of Cedar Point" and wondered if she would ever enjoy those sweet scenes again with him: "I know the country needs your services, but when we calculate the the sacrifices which must be made at home, is it not a question, which has the strongest claims upon you, your country or your family?" In addition to her own unnamed sacrifices, she mentioned one that had even more importance. She urged him to think of "the influence that [his] society would have upon Sam." She felt incapable of continuing to raise him on her own, and reminded her husband that their son had "attained an age that requires the most delicate and judicious management, and I tremble lest I should err in this all important matter."[64]

Sam had just started school, but remained for only two weeks. Margaret reported that she was teaching him at home, and added mysteriously: "I will not annoy you with the various reasons which I had for taking him home."[65]

As time drew near for her confinement, Margaret's spirits continued to sag. She wrote that she knew it was wrong to complain of anything, but without him everything seemed so dreary and desolate.

> Indeed if you were with me, I am sure I could be quite cheerful. . . . As usual I have serious presentiments with regard to my situation, but I am striving hard to attain a perfect resignation to the will of God.[66]

Margaret's spirits probably rose when on June 21, 1854, the Houston's second son was born. On the very day of his birth Houston was writing Margaret:

> As the time of your confinement approaches, my prayers & hopes for your safety are incessant. For you alone I feel, and for the issue of our Love, I only care that it may be a perfect child, for indeed, I have not been so daring as to desire or wish that it should be a son. Thinking as I do, that our Father in Heaven knows what is best for us in his gifts & that he will order what is proper for us.[67]

241

A few days later he wrote again, this time more adamant in his concern for her welfare:

> I will be in pain of heart until I can hear from you and of your safety. . . . For you are my wife, my friend, the mother of my children, and the repository of my honor. . . . You can not know, can not realise the deep and abiding attachments which I feel towards you.[68]

When Houston received the news, he was overjoyed. The baby's name had already been chosen. He would be called Andrew Jackson Houston. Family legend is that since he had long been praying for another son, Andrew's birth strengthened Houston's religious convictions. Whatever his reason, soon after the baby's birth he discussed joining the Baptist Church with Dr. Samson, but decided to wait until he returned to Independence to make his final decision.[69]

---

[1] Franklin Williams Collection, Huntsville, Houston to Margaret, November 16, 1851.

[2] Ibid., Houston to Margaret, November 25, 1851.

[3] Ibid., Margaret to Houston, November 28, 1851.

[4] Ibid., Margaret to Houston, December 23, 1851.

[5] Ibid.

[6] Ibid., Houston to Margaret, December 4, 1851.

[7] Ibid., Houston to Margaret, December 14, 1851.

[8] Ibid., Houston to Margaret, December 19, 1851.

[9] Madge W. Hearne Papers, San Antonio, "A Short Biography of Sam Houston," by Maggie Houston Williams, n.d.

[10] Franklin Williams Collection, Huntsville, Houston to Margaret, December 16, 1851.

[11] Ibid., Houston to Margaret, January 7, 1852.

[12] Ibid., Houston to Margaret, January 9, 1852.

[13] Friend, 218.

[14] Franklin Williams Collection, Huntsville, Margaret to Houston, January 7, 1852.

[15] Ibid., Margaret to Houston, January 14, 1852.

[16] Ibid., Houston to Margaret, February 13, 1852.

[17] Ibid., Margaret to Houston, January 28, 1852.

[18] Ibid., Margaret to Houston, April 22, 1852.

[19] Ibid., Houston to Margaret, May 1, 1852.

[20] Ibid., Margaret to Houston, April 29, 1852.

[21] Ibid., Margaret to Houston, May 9, 1852.

[22] Ibid., Houston to Margaret, May 9, 1852.

[23] Ibid., Houston to Margaret, May 14, 1852.

[24] Ibid., Houston to Margaret, June 4, 1852.

[25] Ibid., Houston to Margaret, June 15, 1852.

[26] Ibid., Houston to Margaret, June 20, 1852.

[27] Ibid., Margaret to Houston, June 25, 1852.

[28] Ibid., Margaret to Houston, July 2, 1852.

[29] Ibid., Margaret to Houston, July 17, 1852.

[30] Ibid., Margaret to Houston, July 9, 1852.

[31] Ibid., Houston to Margaret, January 5, 1853.

[32] Ibid., Margaret to Houston, December 20, 1852.

[33] Ibid., Houston to Margaret, January 7, 1853.

[34] Ibid., Houston to Margaret, February 4, 1853.

[35] Ibid., Houston to Margaret, March 9, 1853.

[36] Madge W. Hearne Papers, San Antonio, "Notes on the Lea Family," n.d. See also Stake Genealogy Library, San Antonio, Computer Records on the Lea Family. Robert Royston died May 11, 1853. Henry Clinton Lea died November 7, 1854.

[37] Ibid., Houston to Margaret, February 20, 1853.

[38] Ibid., Margaret to Houston, March 8, 1853.

[39] Ibid., Houston to Margaret, April 8, 1853.

[40] Ibid., Margaret to Houston, March 8, 1853.

[41] Ibid., Margaret to Houston, March 23, 1853.

[42] Ibid., Houston to Margaret, March 27, 1853.

[43] Llerena Friend File, Sam Houston Memorial Museum, Margaret to an unidentified "My dear friend," April 18, 1853.

[44] Sam Houston, *Writings*, vol. 5, 456–57, Houston to Washington D. Miller, September 13, 1853.

[45] Wilfred O. Dietrich, *The Blazing Story of Washington County*, (Brenham, Texas: Banner Press, 1950), 95.

[46] Madge W. Hearne Papers, San Antonio, photograph of the home on the day it was torn down.

[47] Williams, 213, and Madge W. Hearne, family story.

[48] Friend, 224.

[49] Sam Houston, *Writings*, vol. 5, 463–64, Houston to Mr. Sarla, November 28, 1853.

[50] Franklin Williams Collection, Huntsville, Houston to Margaret, January 1, 1854.

[51] Ibid., Margaret to Houston, January 3, 1854.

[52] Ibid., Margaret to Houston, January 10, 1854.

[53] Ibid., Margaret to Houston, January 30, 1854.

[54] Ibid., Houston to Margaret, January 23, 1854.

[55] Ibid., Margaret to Houston, February 7, 1854.

[56] Ibid., Houston to Margaret, January 6, 1854.

[57] Ibid., Houston to Margaret, February 26, 1854.

[58] Ibid., Houston to Margaret, March 5, 1854.

[59] Georgia J. Burleson, ed., *The Life and Sam Houston Writings of Rufus C. Burleson*, (Waco: Georgia J. Burleson, 1901), 579.

[60] *Texas State Gazette,* April 4, 1854.

[61] Franklin Williams Collection, Huntsville, Houston to Margaret, May 13, 1854.

[62] Ibid., Margaret to Houston, May 24, 1854.

[63] Ibid., Houston to Margaret, May 13, 1854.

[64] Ibid., Margaret to Houston, May 31, 1854.

[65] Sam Houston Papers, Barker History Center, University of Texas, Margaret to Houston, June 14, 1854.

[66] Ibid.

[67] Franklin Williams Collection, Huntsville, Houston to Margaret, June 21, 1854.

[68] Ibid., Houston to Margaret, June 25, 1854.

[69] Madge W. Hearne, family story.

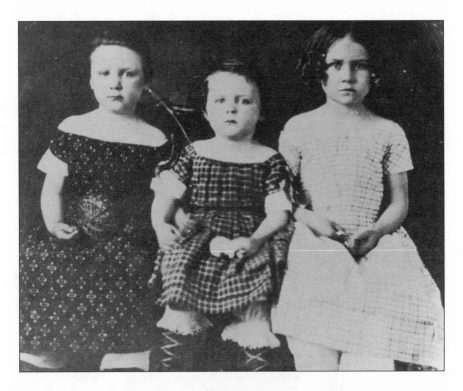

Maggie Houston, age 4; Mary Willie Houston, age 2; Nannie Houston, age 6; circa 1852. Courtesy of Sam Houston Regional Library and Research Center, Liberty, Texas.

Sam Houston by J. Wood, 1826. This is a painting done on ivory which is now in the San Jacinto Museum of History. Photograph courtesy of Sam Houston Regional Library and Research Center, Liberty, Texas.

Margaret may have been referring to this painting on December 23, 1851, when she wrote to her husband that "We are no longer at a loss to know whom she [Mary Willie] resembles, for her features are growing singularly like a certain fancy face that hangs in our parlour, about 21 years of age."

Margaret at age 34. On January 29, 1853, she wrote to Houston, "I have had fine daguerreotypes taken of them [the children] and myself."

Sam Houston from a daguerreotype made when he was a U.S. Senator. Courtesy of Sam Houston Regional Library and Research center, Liberty, Texas.

Margaret wrote to Houston: "We were all delighted to see your picture. Mary Willie recognized it at a glimpse and Sam exclaimed after looking at it thoughtfully, 'It looks so much like pa it makes me feel strange!'"

Independence farmhouse of the Houston family. The picture was taken the day before the house was torn down, circa 1890, and the people standing on the porch are probably the owners of the house at that time. The Houstons lived here from 1854–56, and Andrew was born here. Original in possession of the author, copy in the Daughters of the Republic of Texas Library, San Antonio, Texas.

Photograph of a portrait of Sam Houston in his twenties painted by Thomas Sully. In the Library of Congress Collection. Courtesy of Sam Houston Regional Library and Research Center, Liberty, Texas.

This portrait, along with the one by J. Wood, hung in the parlor.

Chapter XII

There is everywhere a void which nothing can fill, but the presence of my darling husband. It is well for me that my time is so occupied, else I should be miserable indeed, but I am cheered by the bright hope of seeing you in the spring. Oh do not disappoint me, if you love me. And yet, what a journey I am requiring of you. Well it is selfish I confess, for I would cheerfully perform it to get to you my Love.

Margaret to Houston
February 5, 1856

Before Houston left the capital to see his new son, he received his pension for his service in the United States Army during the War of 1812. It was paid in silver dollars, and he decided to use it for a gift for Margaret and the children. He sent the silver to Gault Jewelers in New York with instructions that it be melted down. He wrote Margaret that he had sent for "seven handsome silver cups for my Dear Wife, and her little brood." He had ordered that "suitable engravings" be put on them. These would become known in the family as the "pension cups." He also ordered for Margaret a beautiful silver tea service.[1]

It was October before Houston reached Texas and saw Andrew for the first time. Margaret was overjoyed by the news of Houston's desire for baptism, but there was still a problem to overcome. Houston hesitated to join the church because he felt he might not be worthy of taking communion. Long ago as a child he had attended a Presbyterian service and heard a sermon taken from Paul's letters to the Corinthians that warned that the taking of communion by someone who was not truly saved was a road to eternal damnation.

Dr. George Baines stopped by the gate one day when Margaret was in the yard and she asked for his help. She explained the problem and said, "I want you to talk to him about it for I know he has the greatest confidence in your knowledge of such things." The next morning Houston rode to Brenham with Brother Baines. During the long ride, Houston verified what Margaret had said and added:

> I enjoy a sweet peace of mind in believing in the Lord Jesus as my saviour, yet I know it is possible that I may be mistaken. . . . And if I should be, then should I join the church and commune unworthily, there would be no possibility ever to correct the sad and awful mistake.

Dr. Baines explained the passage to which Houston had referred and suggested another scripture for him to read. Houston returned home, read the scriptures mentioned, and made a definite decision to join the church.[2]

A revival meeting was being held the next month, and the baptism was set for November 19, 1854. Nancy Lea was present, and the sermon was preached by the Reverend Mr. Morrell, who had known Houston's mother in Tennessee.[3] The baptismal pool was a very unusual one. Located behind the church, it was carved out of the limestone in the shape of a coffin. The night before the ceremony was scheduled some mischievous boys filled the pool with sticks and mud, so it could not be used. It was deemed necessary to use the chilly waters of Rocky Creek about a mile from the church. Here Houston was baptized during a Texas "blue norther" in which both he and the pastor almost froze to death. Houston later remarked that his pocketbook had also been baptized, for he had agreed to pay half of the pastor's salary.[4] Family lore has it that at the close of the baptismal service, Burleson told Houston, "Well, General, all your sins have been washed away." Houston replied, "If that be the case, God help the fish down below!"[5]

Margaret felt that she had succeeded in saving Houston's soul. Only one last task remained. Her husband still did not feel ready to take communion, but no doubt Margaret felt that this also was within her grasp. Her boundless joy was probably marred only by the news that her husband was returning to Washington. Before he left, Houston made a contribution to Baylor University of several valuable public documents, and offered what was described by university officials as his "large and well-selected library" for the use of the university students.[6]

Houston was still being criticized for his stand on the Nebraska Bill, and Margaret constantly worried about his being challenged to a duel. From Nashville he wrote hoping to soothe her fears. "You know my rule is 'not to fight down hill,' and being an Ex-President, my rule would exclude all men but Mr. Pierce." He added that he hoped that "moral restraints as well as religious . . . would govern" him if he were challenged.[7]

As usual, Margaret worried about his safety on the trip. Her first letter said that she would feel much easier when she got a letter from him in Washington and knew that he had once more been "preserved through the perils of steamboats and rail cars." She informed him that the family was well, but that one of the servants was ill with mumps and winter fever. She did not feel that she could afford another doctor's bill, so she was nursing him at home.[8] A few weeks later Houston was shocked to receive a telegram from Charles Power informing him that Margaret had been so ill that at one time she had not been expected to live, and that Andrew was being cared for by Mrs. Horace Clark. Houston immediately wrote Margaret of the distress he felt upon receiving the telegram.[9]

For the next few days Houston was so worried that another telegram might come that he scarcely left his room.[10] He finally decided that his family had deemed another telegram unnecessary because Margaret was recovering.[11] He wrote her that his feelings were "overwhelming" and he could not even begin to describe his anguish. All he could do was to pray for her recovery. He sent her some news which he knew would make her happy: "This morning, Dearest I went to church, and in the evening the Communion took place, in which I joined." Margaret had at last reached her goal.[12]

Finally a letter arrived from Dr. Graves with the news that Margaret was doing well and had every prospect for a speedy recovery. Houston wrote to Margaret of his relief in receiving the news.[13]

Houston was now able to continue his regular routine of writing Margaret from his seat in the Senate then returning to his room to attend to business and meet with the many callers who visited him there. Sundays he attended Brother Samson's church and usually wrote Margaret a summary of the sermon. He continued to lecture in various Baptist churches in the eastern cities. On one of his lecture tours he made a special trip just to please Margaret. He stopped in Hartford, Connecticut, to pay his respects to Mrs. Lydia Sigourney, who was one of the most famous poetesses of the time, as well as a particular favorite of Margaret's. He told her that Margaret also wrote poems and that she had published several in the *Mother's Journal* of Philadelphia and the *New York Recorder*. He obtained a book of Mrs. Sigourney's poems to take to his wife. Back in Washington, Houston wrote to thank her:

> The acknowledgment of your beautiful present has been deferred for some days owing to the press of business of Congress. . . . I will not indulge in the luxury of its perusal until Mrs. Houston and myself can unite in the pleasure. Your Poems, Lady, afford her the purest delight and form with her a theme of frequent commendation. Had I failed to make my visit to "Mrs. Sigourney" while in Hartford, it would have been a cause of regret on her part, and justified a "Curtain Lecture."[14]

While Houston was visiting the famous poetess, back in Independence, Margaret was also entertaining a writer of some merit: John Henry Brown, who later wrote a history of Texas. He took tea with Margaret, and three decades later wrote Maggie (who was present at the time) that her mother had been a charming hostess, and he still held her in high regard.[15]

When Houston returned to Independence in the summer of 1855, he found that the Gorees, who had rented the Woodland

Home in Huntsville, were leaving. He decided to take his family back to their old home. Margaret had come to love Independence, and when they left she wrote a poem. It was called "Farewell to Independence." Two of its verses in particular show how attached she had become to her home there:

Sweet village!
Thou loveliest spot on earth to me;
Oh, I shall think of thee and weep,
As oft at day's decline I see
The lengthening shadows as they creep
From out thy clustering oaks and glide
So soft, so spirit-like along
The quiet prairie and gentle hill-side
And hear the wild bird's low sweet song
From every grove.

.   .   .   .   .   .

'Tis past! 'Tis past!
These hallowed scenes are far removed,
And I have mingled once again,
With Friends of other days long loved,
But never shall the precious chain
That binds my heart to thee, sweet spot,
One gem of recollection lose!
Where e'er on earth be cast my lot,
Bright as thy glorious sunset hues,
Shall be my dream of thee.[16]

The big yellow coach was once more loaded up for the trip to Huntsville. This time another relative went with them: Martin Lea, Margaret's cousin. He was going not only to help Margaret run the farm, but also to study law in Houston's office.[17] Houston himself went back to Washington at the first of the year, and arrived during a severe winter storm which covered most of the country. He wrote

Margaret that he wore his vest made of leopard skin which was "most comfortable in this weather."[18]

Margaret had just settled back into her life at Huntsville and renewed old friendships when a calamity occurred. Her dearest friend, Frances Creath, became seriously ill. Margaret was sent for, but could only hold her hand until the end. Margaret wrote that the Reverend Creath seemed to be "crushed beneath the mighty blow." She added a personal thought for her husband: "Oh how often have I thought his condition would be yours, but here I am, still spared . . . while the good, the great and the useful are taken."[19]

Texas too was suffering under a severe winter. Margaret wrote on a day that was too cold for the children to go out that she was "shivering over the fire in the midst of play-blocks, doll clothes, etc." Before the storm hit she had gone in to town and had a daguerreotype taken of herself and one of Nannie and Antoinette. Andrew's would have to wait for another time because he had just "fallen and made a scar over his left eye." She reported that she was busy, but added that if her husband thought she could "find no time to pine" for him he was mistaken:

> There is every where a void which nothing can fill, but the presence of my darling husband. It is well for me that my time is so occupied, else I should be miserable indeed, but am cheered by the bright hope of seeing you in the spring. Oh do not disappoint me, if you love me. And yet, what a journey I am requiring of you! Well, it is selfish I confess, for I would cheerfully perform it to get to you my love.[20]

Just a few days later she was struggling to care for Andrew, who had come down with pneumonia. She felt his illness had been brought on by his constant exposure to the elements during the severe winter, and wrote Houston of her difficulties in dealing with their youngest child: "I felt anxious about him all the time, but it seemed like chaining a young tiger to keep him within doors. Indeed it would require an artificial woods and sky within the house to keep him contented."[21]

Houston was delighted when he received the daguerreotype of Margaret. He had heard of a new method called photography which would allow him to have several copies made of her likeness. He intended to give several to friends in Washington and was sending the others to Margaret to distribute as she desired. He also wrote that he had obtained "the finest dog in America," a very large "half San Bernard and & New Foundland." Houston bragged that the dog was the "noblest animal of the Dog Kind," large enough to carry Andrew, and able to "protect [the children] against any animal in our forests or fields." He would be bringing the dog with him on his trip in the spring.[22]

Margaret continued to remind her husband that it was wrong for them to be separated as much as they were, and she warned him light-heartedly of her intent to "preach him a perfect sermon" on the subject:

I feel as if I could be quite eloquent with such a theme, but as my audience will not be very numerous (consisting only of my dear husband) it will hardly be a test of my orational powers. However, if I can bring my sole audience round to my way of thinking, I shall be abundantly satisfied.

She ended her letter with the request to be presented affectionately to Brother Samson: "If I never see him in this world, I do believe I shall see him and know him in Heaven."[23]

Even before receiving her letter, Houston was doing more than that. He presented Brother Samson with a framed photograph of Margaret. He also allowed the pastor to see some poetry Margaret had sent him to be sent on to the *Mother's Journal*.[24] After reading the poetry the pastor sent Houston a note: "Please assure Mrs. Houston of my appreciation & admiration of her letters & poetry. She should not remain unknown as an authoress."[25]

One of the poems Margaret had not sent to Washington was written while she was waiting for Houston's return in the spring. It was a tribute to their four daughters. Of Nannie she wrote:

STAR OF DESTINY

The eldest is an Autumn bloom,
Just as the Summer rose grew pale
She smiled on our woodland home
The brightest flower in all the vale.

Then she described Maggie:

The second—April—Came with the showers
The buds to ope'—the vines to wreathe
And left the sweetest of its flowers
Upon my joyous heart to breathe.

She next told of Mary Willie's arrival:

Sweet month! but two short years had past
And lo, with smiles again she came
And left a bloom fair as the last
A strange bright flower for me to name.

She went on to tell about Nettie:

Almost two years had passed away
And winter looked upon my flowers,
With meaning smile that seemed to say,
I bring no vine-wreath for your bowers.

No Spring bird's song nor summer breeze
Nor leaves of Autumn's glowing hue
To throw around my love bare trees,
But winter had its offering too.

And, oh, the brightest rose there lay
Upon his hand! "It is thine own"
He whispered as he passed away
"Oh guard it well, the fragile one."

258

The poem concluded with a prayer for all her daughters:

> May buds of innocence in time
> Be formed to bloom beyond the skies,
> Within the cloudless spirits clime,
> Unfading flowers of Paradise.[26]

Houston arrived home in late spring. A family story is told that whenever Houston was ready to leave Washington, he would send word to his Indian friends at Livingston as to the time he would reach home and ask them to visit. By this time, Margaret had long since overcome her fear of the Indians and would lay in supplies of all kinds. In the pasture lot was an old gray mule which had served his day. At least an hour before the Indians would arrive, if the wind was from the north, the old gray mule would begin to snort and jump. Margaret would instruct Eliza and the other servants to start cooking. The Indians would come riding up in single file. Houston would greet them and they would sit in a circle on the lawn and feast on beef ribs from a large washtub.[27] Neighbors reported that this would happen at least once a year, and that the Indians would bring trinkets and gifts. Houston would sometimes dress in Indian garb and smoke the peace pipe with them.[28]

About this time, Houston arranged for another activity in the yard. In the spring which ran through the meadow north of the home, he had the servants spade out the sand to the proper depth for a baptismal pool. It was used by the Baptist Church for many baptisms, including those of Eliza and other servants.[29]

Houston often came into town and visited at the post office or Gibbs Store, sometimes sitting on a barrel and whittling as he told stories to the village children. On one occasion Margaret was expecting dinner guests and had asked her husband to send home a barrel of flour in time to make bread. Houston forgot the request, and when the guests were seated Margaret explained why she was serving corn pudding instead of bread. Houston offered to return to town for the flour. Amid the laughter which followed Margaret gently explained the time required for preparing biscuits.[30]

Once again, their pleasant time together was over all too soon. Margaret "preached her sermon" about it being wrong for them to be apart, but her audience was back in Washington before the summer of 1856 was over. Houston continued his practice of sending Margaret the latest fashions. He wrote her that hoops and whale bone were now in great demand, and sent a hoop that he was anxious to see her in. He wondered if hers would be the first in Huntsville so that she could "be ahead of the fashions." He also had a critique for the new style: "The way they move on the pavement would astonish one of Texas moderation."[31] He also had some "beautiful mementos and ornaments" made for the females of his family. There was a broach made with strands of hair from Margaret, Antoinette, and Varilla to be presented to Nancy Lea, and a bracelet with hairs from all their daughters for Margaret.[32] For his son Sam, he sent some good, if oft-repeated, advice:

> It is a matter of great satisfaction to me to hope that my children will be in circumstances to receive a good education. Mine was defective and I feel the inconvenience, if not the misfortune of not receiving a classical education. Knowledge is the food of genius, and my Son, let no opportunity escape you to treasure up knowledge.[33]

Houston continued to attend Brother Samson's church and to participate in the Communion Service.[34] His mother-in-law Nancy devised a more tangible way of showing her religious dedication. She decided, some thought in celebration over Houston's conversion, to provide a long-needed bell for the Rocky Creek Baptist Church at Independence. The Lea family silver was sacrificed in order to pay for it. The bell was ordered by Dr. Burleson from the McNeeley Bell Foundry of Watervliet, New York. A legend persisted for many years that the Lea silver was actually melted down and added to the materials in the bell to insure a sweeter tone.[35] As repeated by a granddaughter of Antoinette Power: "It was the Lea silver that made the bell that still rings at the little Baptist Church at Independence. Nancy Lea sent a man north with the silver to be sure that it was actually melted and used in the bell."[36]

Meanwhile, repairs were being made to the Huntsville home. While Margaret was struggling with workmen and finances, Houston was struggling with his conscience. He wrote her that she would be hearing "a great press about members raising their pay & going back with the law to last Session." Houston voted against the law, and when it passed he did not take the money. He stated his reasons to Margaret for his actions despite the status of their finances, and Margaret probably had mixed emotions when she read his explanation:

> It was not that I thought the law wou'd be unpopular that caused me to vote against it, but because I thought it was wrong, and it being wrong, I did not touch the money. It stands to my credit, and is mine by law. The amount is said to be some $2,000 and upwards.[37]

Houston was becoming weary of the politicians who did not have the nation's welfare at heart. He described the situation to Margaret:

> I feel as tho there was no head of the Government, and that we were kept together only by the collusive power of habit. . . . Our great lights of the Senate are extinguished, and I fear a day of gloom approaches. I hope it may not end in the darkness of night.[38]

Houston often spoke of Margaret's "not being interested in politics," but in fact, when the politics concerned him she was vitally interested. He never failed to send her copies of his speeches and often asked her opinion. In letters he expressed the wish to talk with her before he made his speeches.[39]

Houston had made up his mind to leave after the presidential inauguration rather than stay for the called session of the Senate. He wrote Margaret that when he reflected on the distance from Washington to where she was, he felt that he was indeed an exile.

He admitted:

> I have felt exiled in other lands and from other homes, but then
> I was an exile that combined no wish or hope of return. In my
> present case there is blended both desire and hope. Desire to be
> with you and hope that the day is not distant that it will be the
> case.

He also reminded Margaret that she had around her many of the
pleasures that he so much desired:

> Sam with his mannish conceits. Nannie with determination to do
> all that will with genius can accomplish. Miss Maggie with her
> quiet brooding mischief. Mary Willie with her sparkling temper.
> Antoinette relying on the truth of her conclusions and the justice
> of her perceptions. Andrew doubting nothing in achievements,
> and believing that which he can not accomplish he ought to do by
> some means. And you, my Dear, a kind Mother looking on . . . I
> hope . . . to find them all that a fond Father can wish them to be
> and their Dear Mother happy.[40]

When Houston returned to Texas a few weeks later, he immediately plunged into state politics. In August a governor was to be
elected. Houston let it be known that he desired the office. The state
democratic convention seemed divided almost equally between
those for and against Houston, but when the votes were counted,
it was Hardin Runnels, a disciple of Calhoun, who was nominated
for governor.

Houston approached Margaret with the question of whether he
should run for governor as an independent. Evidence of Margaret's
answer has not survived, but no doubt she followed her pattern of
not standing in his way. Houston's mind was made up. While in
Washington, Houston had heard many Jackson Democrats say that
they could never vote for Runnels. While he was trying to decide,
Houston received word that an opponent had declared that Houston dared not run for governor because he would be met at every

crossroad and would eventually be killed off. He wrote to Rusk that he had declared himself a candidate:

> You will be surprised, as I believe, for you know it was my intention to retire from the Senate to private life. They make the issue as they declare "Houston and anti-Houston." So now the whip cracks and the longest pole will bring down the persimmon.[41]

Some time earlier on a trip into town, Houston had found a crowd gathered in front of Gibbs Store, and soon discovered that a slave auction was in progress. Standing on the slave block, being teased by some white children, was a little black boy. He was crying and it was obvious that he was hot, thirsty, and tired. Houston had plenty of servants and farm hands, and he really did not need another slave, but he looked at the pitiful little boy and on the spot made an offer of $450 for him. The boy was Jeff, who became his personal buggy driver and devoted servant. It would be Jeff who would now accompany Houston on his campaign tour around the state of Texas.[42]

When it came time to leave on his speaking tour, he found anti-Houston factions at work even in his hometown. He could neither get a seat on the stage nor hire a buggy at the livery stable. There was in town on that day a plow salesman named Ed Sharp. He rode in a bright crimson buggy with the words, "Warwick's Patent Plow" painted in huge gilt letters on either side. Foreseeing a golden opportunity to attract attention to his wares, Sharp offered the buggy as transportation to the Senator.

With some misgivings for her husband's health and safety, Margaret saw Houston off on a speaking tour that would last two months. Jeff later described the trip as one where Houston met sixty-seven speaking engagements. He had no campaign manager, preferring to rely on old friends to arrange the details of his speaking and the barbecues that followed. He usually spoke from a stand made by placing two wagons side by side and putting boards on the seats in the wagons. Jeff described Houston's deep voice as both firm and pleasing. He talked slowly and distinctly, with a voice that carried through the largest crowds. On many occasions he was forced to limp because his San Jacinto wound was bothering him. They traveled from Montgomery to San Antonio, many nights camping out on blankets under the stars.[43]

Houston closed his campaign in San Antonio in late July and returned to Huntsville, where tragic news awaited him. His close friend, Senator Rusk, had committed suicide. More unhappy news awaited him after August 3, election day. There were no telegraph lines in Texas at that time, and it took two weeks to get the results: Runnels had won by a margin of almost ten thousand votes. Houston and Margaret were sitting on the porch of their Huntsville home when a messenger brought the news. Houston was carving an Indian head out of soft pine. He went on with the carving for a few minutes, and then said softly to his wife, "Margaret, wait until 1859."[44]

---

[1] Franklin Williams Collection, Huntsville, Houston to Margaret, August 5, 1854; Marian W. Whittemore, family story. Maggie's cup is on display with some of the silver service pieces in the Sam Houston Memorial Museum. Margaret's silver coffee pot is in the San Jacinto Museum of History, La Porte, Texas. Other pieces are in possession of various family members.

[2] Crane, *Life and Select Literary Remains of Sam Houston of Texas*, 244–45.

[3] Hunt, *My Master*, 29.

[4] James, *The Raven*, 385.

[5] Madge W. Hearne, family story.

[6] Lois Smith Murray, *Baylor at Independence*, (Waco: Baylor University Press, 1972), 125.

[7] Franklin Williams Collection, Huntsville, Houston to Margaret, January 1, 1855.

[8] Ibid., Margaret to Houston, January 6, 1855.

[9] Ibid., Houston to Margaret, January 30, 1855.

[10] Ibid., Houston to Margaret, February 4, 1855.

[11] Ibid., Houston to Margaret, February 6, 1855.

[12] Ibid., Houston to Margaret, February 4, 1855.

[13] Ibid.

[14] Sam Houston, *Writings*, vol. 6, 179, Houston to Mrs. Sigourney, March 5, 1855. The book may be seen at the Sam Houston Memorial Museum, Huntsville.

[15] Madge W. Hearne Papers, San Antonio, Brown to Maggie Houston Williams, August 29, 1889.

[16] Madge W. Hearne Papers, San Antonio, "Farewell to Independence" by Margaret Houston, November 10, 1855.

[17] Franklin Williams Collection, Huntsville, Houston to Margaret, January 7, 1856.

[18] Ibid., Houston to Margaret, February 17, 1856.

[19] Ibid., Margaret to Houston, January 19, 1856.

[20] Ibid., Margaret to Houston, February 5, 1856.

[21] Ibid., Margaret to Houston, February 19, 1856.

[22] Ibid., Houston to Margaret, March 4, 1856.

[23] Sam Houston Papers, Barker History Center, University of Texas, Margaret to Houston, March 11, 1856.

[24] Franklin Williams Collection, Huntsville, Houston to Margaret, March 12, 1856.

[25] Madge W. Hearne Papers, San Antonio, Dr. Samson to Houston, March 12, 1856.

[26] Ibid., "Our Daughters" by Margaret Houston, April 14, 1856.

[27] Sam Houston Memorial Museum, Temple Houston Morrow in a letter to Grace Longino, January 17, 1957.

[28] Ludie Anders Binney, "Personal Recollections of Sam Houston," The Alcalde, (Sam Houston State University Yearbook), 1925, n. p.

[29] Sam Houston Memorial Museum, Temple Houston Morrow to Grace Longino, January 17, 1957.

[30] Binney, "Personal Recollections," n. p.

[31] Franklin Williams Collection, Huntsville, Houston to Margaret, August 2, 1856.

[32] Ibid., Houston to Margaret, August 25, 1856. The jewelry is on display at the Sam Houston Memorial Museum, Huntsville.

[33] Sam Houston, Writings, vol. 6, 373, Houston to Sam Houston, Jr., August 15, 1856.

[34] Franklin Williams Collection, Huntsville, Houston to Margaret, August 3, 1856.

[35] Madge W. Hearne Papers, "The Church," n.d. A typescript copy of a speech made by Mrs. Hearne for an unidentified homecoming celebration at Independence, Texas.

[36] Mrs. John Little, The Sunday Enterprise, March 24, 1946. Experts today deny that the bell has any silver content. It was described in 1931 by a foundry official as weighing 502 pounds, and made of 78 parts copper and 22 parts tin. (Sam Houston Papers, Barker History Center, University of Texas, A. C. McNeely to Temple Houston Morrow, July 16, 1931.) Regardless of which story is true, the bell was housed in a belfry made of the stones from the buildings of Baylor University for many years, until it fell

and was cracked. Today it is preserved in the Baptist Museum in Independence.

[37] Franklin Williams Collection, Huntsville, Houston to Margaret, August 21, 1856.

[38] Ibid., Houston to Margaret, August 27, 1856.

[39] Ibid., Houston to Margaret, January 6, 1857.

[40] Sam Houston, *Writings*, vol. 6, 434, Houston to Margaret, March 1, 1857.

[41] Sam Houston, *Writings*, vol. 6, 444, Houston to Rusk, May 12, 1857.

[42] Hunt, 14, 31. See also: Walker County Deed Records, vol. D, 669, September 23, 1856.

[43] Ibid., 31.

[44] Ibid., 34.

Sam Houston wearing his leopard skin vest. Photograph of an engraving made by Bernhardt Wall for his book, *Following General Sam Houston,* 1935. Courtesy of the San Jacinto Museum of History, Houston, Texas.

On February 17, 1856, Houston wrote to Margaret, "I wear my leopard skin vest which is most comfortable in this weather." Another time he mentioned he "had chosen to wear [the leopard skin] next to [his] bosom because the scripture says 'a leopard cannot change his spots.'"

267

Margaret Houston, age 36 in 1856.
Courtesy of Sam Houston Regional Library and Research Center, Liberty, Texas.

On February 5, 1856, Margaret wrote her husband: ". . . we were in to have our daguerreotype taken, as we heard Mr. Bailey would leave soon. I had a fine picture taken of myself."

Chapter XIII

I do hope you will hurry back, for the truth is—I can not bear you out of my sight. Do you know I am more in love with you than I ever was in my life? It is true, I assure you. . . . Oh, do hurry back, my Love.

Margaret to Houston
May 4, 1859, Independence

Margaret was fearful of the effects that Houston's first defeat at the hands of the people of Texas might have on him, but he took it calmly. He wrote Ashbel Smith that the "fuss is over, and the sun yet shines as ever." He would return to Washington and have "some fish to fry."[1]

Houston was probably far more concerned over the debts his unsuccessful campaign had incurred than he was over the defeat itself. In order to meet his bills he would later have to sell the Huntsville home. He was also concerned about the finances of his pastor, George Washington Baines. Before he left for the nation's capital, Houston renewed a note for the pastor without interest, commenting that Brother Baines had the luck "to minister to congregations who think that you can afford to preach to them gratis." He cautioned that if the minister did not devise some plan to change this practice, the congregation would "think that [he] ought to pay them a good salary for attending church."[2]

Editorials were again appearing in the newspapers clamoring for Houston's resignation, but again he ignored them and returned to the Senate. When he reached Washington he wrote to assure Margaret that he was "easy in mind & body." He told her not to have any fears about his position on the question of the Kansas Constitution when it was presented to Congress. He reminded her that he could not be "read out of the Democratic party as an Heretic," as that had already been done.[3] He also sought to calm Margaret's fears about his feelings in regard to the defeat:

> I suppose it would be natural for you to think that my situation, since I was beaten in Texas, would not be very enviable or rather disconsolate. It is quite the contrary. . . . At no period of my service in Congress have I been more sought after than at this very time, and tho I take pains to impress people with the idea that I have no influence with the President, I cant succeed.

He continued by mentioning the many persons from all sections of the Union who were anxious to be introduced and to shake his hand. In order that she not interpret his words as boasting, he assured her that he had written these facts only to make her feel at rest as to his situation. He deemed them proper to write a "Dear Wife and family, and to no one else."[4]

Referring to his defeat, Houston told his colleagues in a speech to the Senate that the people of Texas "had not disowned me in beating me—they have only preferred another."[5] He apparently harbored no animosity toward his enemies, and his mind was beginning to wander toward the following year when his Senate term would expire. Once again Margaret was expecting, and there was a prospect of another child in late spring. Houston wrote Nat Young, an old friend from Tennessee, that "the grapes were not sour" and that he was delighted with the "prospect of retirement." He spoke of his six children and the one on the way, and his desire to "be at home and render them all aid in my power."[6]

Houston continued his practice of rendering aid to Margaret by sending advice to the children. He wrote Nannie advising her that above all things she should "discard envy" and never "indulge bad temper." He expressed a hope that:

. . . my Dear Daughters will strive to keep down anger & never permit themselves to wrangle or quarrel with each other. . . . Would to kind Heaven that I could have had some one to admonish me in my boyhood, I would not now have felt the many regrets that I experience.[7]

Margaret was more concerned about Sam, whom she felt had never reached his potential in his experiences at school. She had finally come to the conclusion that he should be sent away to school. Houston investigated different schools in the east, but arrived at the theory that it was best "to educate people in the Country in which they are to reside—for instance, a Yankee in the North & a Southerner in the South." He gently chided Margaret for worrying about "every little trifle." There was another reason why he felt it would be best for Sam to be educated in Texas. He knew Margaret would not be happy with her son so far away, and doubted that she would consent to his being away from home until time of graduation. He felt that they should discuss it in full when he returned home, but in the meantime he had a suggestion for her:

You will have to take a mild course with him, and not abrade him for every little trifle, but let him know how kindly, how deeply, and tenderly you feel for him, and how much of your happiness depends on his conduct, as well as how far the well being of his sisters and little brother is dependent on him and the course he may take in life. Indeed how much of parental happiness is dependent on his conduct in life. . . . Dont get provoked at me my Dear, for I assure you my intention is only to express my admiration for your maternal kindness applied to practical matters of which you have only looked at one side.[8]

Margaret was not sure when the baby was due, and Houston was waiting for more information before he planned his trip home. He wrote that he hoped to be "advised by you, so as to be at home 'in time'" and reminded her, "tis the motto, you know, of the family. 'In time!'"[9] But Houston was not receiving letters from Margaret. The six previous pregnancies and the constant attacks of asthma and respiratory infections had finally taken their toll. She was dangerously close to losing the baby. Dr. Rawlings was sent for. On April 3, 1858, Houston wrote Margaret that he had spent a sleepless night after receiving a letter from Dr. Rawlings giving him this news. Houston reported the doctor's analysis that while the situation had been alarming, Margaret and the baby were now thought to be out of danger.[10]

Houston longed to go home now, but he faced a dilemma concerning "the necessities of [his] situation, as well as the painful state of [his] feelings." He wrote Margaret that if he went home now, it would only be for a short time, and he would have to return before the baby's birth. Furthermore he would be accused of "having dodged a vote on the Kansas Bill" which would soon be before the Senate.[11] It took him five days to decide, but on April 8, he wrote Margaret: "I felt satisfied that you wou'd rather I should forego my purpose of seeing you in March provided I would be with you when my presence would be more useful & when I would not have to leave you again!"[12]

To make up for his not being there, he wrote to Margaret daily, attempting to raise her spirits and keep her advised of his political situation:

> I do feel all that I say, of anxiety and a desire to see you, to be with you, and to stay with you, and let the world wag; for I can not control the destiny of this country. Were I its ruler, I could rule it well. . . . To govern well is a great science, but no country is ever improved by too much governing. Govern wisely and as little as possible![13]

He was greatly worried about Margaret's asthma and wrote that he was considering moving the family to the Red Lands of East Texas. He had not only heard that the climate there was beneficial in preventing asthmatic attacks, but also that it was "the most healthy portion of our State." However, he would not take any steps in relation to the move without "a full conference" with her. He wrote that he reflected more about her present situation than he did about politics. It preyed on him that he was "absent and ought to be at home."[14]

In this instance, Houston did not live up to the family motto, for he did not arrive home "in time" for the birth of his third son on Sam's fifteenth birthday, May 25, 1858. The name had already been chosen, William Rogers, for Margaret's cousin who lived in Independence and was a favorite of Houston's. The Rogers family had named their baby for Margaret, so the Houstons returned the favor. When he heard the news, Houston wrote his wife: "I am more anxious to be with you than I was to go to our nuptials."[15]

The other Houston babies had been born hale and hearty, but Willie was pale and sickly. When Houston reached home in late June, he also found Margaret to be suffering from almost daily attacks of asthma. Houston decided that the two might benefit from the salt water and sea breezes of Cedar Point, and the family set off for the coast. Houston remembered an earlier conversation he had with Dr. B. F. Sharp, a San Augustine physician, on the effect of the Red Lands of East Texas upon asthmatic patients. He wrote to the doctor for the facts and asked him to express an opinion as to whether Margaret could "recover her health if she were to reside in the Red Lands."[16]

If the doctor replied that letter has not been preserved. In any event, Houston left in the fall for his last trip to Washington without deciding whether or not to move his family. He had barely reached the capital when Margaret began to receive letters telling her how anxious he was to return to her: "Not only to see you, but to be with you, and stay with you for the residue of my days. If it were possible, I wou'd fly to you with the fleetness of an Eagle, to the defense of its erie."[17] The next day he wrote that when the Huntsville home was sold, he hoped to find a cottage for temporary shelter. He joked with her that he was going to try to get one with nine rooms so that they might "sometimes be alone."[18] The next week he wrote her again that he was truly happy his public life was "drawing to a close," and he would rejoice when he could devote his life to God and his family. As for his feelings towards his enemies, he assured her: "I have no regrets to harbor, no unkind thoughts towards those who have caused my release. They will be the sufferers, and not me."[19]

Houston planned one last trip to New York City during the Senate recess at the end of the year. His purpose was two-fold. He had business with an architect to design a new house for Cedar Point, and he wanted to bid farewell to his many friends there. Some of these friends, Houston wrote Margaret, were saying that he would never be content at home to live a "retired" life. Houston replied with long descriptions of Margaret's charms and the "excellencies of character as well as the smartness and beauty" of their children.[20]

Margaret wrote of her pride in Maggie, now ten years old, who was writing her father regularly to keep him posted about home affairs. Margaret pointed out that she did not correct Maggie's letters because she was sure their daughter's child-like expressions would please Houston "more than the most polished style." Although Sam and Nannie had promised to write, Margaret explained that with both "procrastination" was a "besetting sin." Mollie, who always wanted to copy Maggie, would never be happy until she had learned to write.[21]

Houston was more than ready to come home. He wrote of his longing to "throw off the harness" and submit to "petticoat Government," for as he expressed it:

Of the future. . . I anticipate in our rude home (for rude it must be for a while) more pleasure in one month than we have experienced for years since our union. I can . . . and will throw off the care of politics, for I can not control them![22]

The next day he wrote of going to dinner at the White House. As for his choice of dinner companions, he assured Margaret that he "would freely live on bread and water for a month" if he could have the pleasure of taking one quick meal with her.[23] He assured her that leaving his good friends in Washington would cause him only slight regrets because he would "meet dearer objects at home." On their part, his friends expressed regret at Houston's "determination to retire forever from public life," but they did "not know how much . . . love" he had for his family, "or they could account for it!"[24]

The next day Houston was writing Margaret that he loved her "more each day than the day which is fled." Like a shy school boy, he reflected on his difficulty in expressing his feelings when they were together. He wrote that when he was away from her he could "say so many things of a pleasant character," but when they met he could not recall what he wanted to say.

> . . . I feel like a Booby when I reflect. I suppose it arises from that embarrassment, which all persons feel, who are truly in love. This is my apology for not saying a thousand pleasant things which I hope I have yet to say to you on meeting![25]

It would appear that Margaret's dream of a stable family life with her husband might finally be coming to pass. Houston was writing daily of his disillusionment with public life and his desire to return to her. Although he had often stated that Margaret had no interest in politics, he frequently sent her the current newspapers and sought her advice. At the end of his Senate term he wrote that he now needed her "society and advice" more than he had ever done. He longed to be with her and the children at Cedar Point: "I am sick, weary, and I may add disgusted, with all the developments around me. Family, flocks, and honest thrift are all I am now interested in. I feel that my views are in perfect accordance with your own."[26] The next day he wrote that he was sick of the place, the customs, and his employment:

> I wish my Dear, you could really appreciate, not my resignation only, but my extreme gratification that I am so soon to throw off the harness which I have worn so long. I hope you may again feel as you did when you wrote the beautiful piece of Poetry when I went out of office in 1844 in Texas.[27]

Houston had one more task "yet to finish" before he could start for home. Old enemies were once more circulating stories of his unfavorable conduct during the Battle of San Jacinto. He was going to make a speech on the Senate floor, as he told Margaret, "to repel the slanders." He explained:

> The vindication of my reputation against slanderous conspirators is a sacred duty, and God willing and with His aid, I will do it. It will close all acts of my political life, and I hope will be a land mark to our dear children.[28]

Houston worked on the speech for several days, and on February 28, 1859, rose to make what he described to Margaret as "the last I ever expect to make of an official character." The galleries were crowded with over two thousand people, and he was told that many more wanted to hear who could not get in. It appeared that the audience was delighted. When he sat down, he told Margaret, "there was considerable applause in the Galleries, and no call to order was made."[29]

He began a letter to Margaret as soon as he sat down from speaking. In it he expressed his great relief that the speech was over. He told her that he felt a burden had fallen from him, and he hoped when she saw the speech she would be pleased with it. He regarded his departure from Washington as "an act of emancipation from toil" and assured her that he had no regrets:

> I have, my Dear, borne myself in such sort at this session, that I believe there will be a universal regret at my leaving the Senate, as that which can be felt for the departure of any other member of the national councils. This will be gratifying to me, and the extenuation of the world will become a matter of course gratifying to you & may stimulate our children & cause them to love and estimate characters properly. All this causes me no regret that I am to leave here, and retire to my family.[30]

Houston had a few more matters to settle before he could leave for home. He purchased gifts for all the Houston children and sent a "magnificent" silver cup "handsomely engraved" to Margaret's namesake, Maggie Houston Rogers. He had dresses made for Margaret and her mother, and picked out calico and gingham for dresses to be made for his daughters at home. He made the rounds to say good-bye to old friends and reported to Margaret that there seemed to be a "universal feeling of regret" among them. This, he said, should be soothing, if he "needed any balm," but he assured her he required none:

> The hope of seeing you my Love, has superseded all other feelings, and changed regrets into joy. I will not attempt to describe the pleasure I feel in the hope that we may meet & be happy, and while we live, to remain so. I am most happy that I have no wish to gratify, apart from my God, and the happiness & well being of my family.[31]

One of his last letters told of his weariness and desire to come home:

> 'Tis true that each day I become more and more disgusted with public life. . . . I am content to retire to my home . . . and pass the residue of my existence. . . . Indeed I have not a plan or a wish to pass the limits of Texas.[32]

Perhaps as an apology for all their years of separation he wrote:

> I know my imperfections are great and many, and yet the great study of my life has been since our Union how to make you happy. All my life has been devoted to that purpose. . . . You are aware that even in my excuses, I cou'd not allow my love of you to be for a moment diverted from you, nor to suffer an act to be done that could seem for a moment to withdraw my allegiance from you, or the ties which unite us.[33]

Margaret, while reading these lovely sentiments, was probably reflecting on all the other times he had promised to retire. She had been disappointed many times when he had once again "yielded" to duty and left her. Houston wrote that he had "thrown all other ambition to the Dogs," but surely she must have had some apprehension when he wrote:

> I learn from Texas that there is a general wish that I should again enter into the Arena of Texas politics. I am poor, but Texas cant buy my services. I would not, as I have said, give one smile of yours for all the domain of Texas, but what I already own! Cedar Point!!![34]

A few days later, Houston left the nation's capital for the last time. On March 11, 1859, the editorial writer of the Washington *Evening Star* gave him a final tribute:

> This distinguished man left Washington yesterday afternoon for his home in Texas. Up to the hour of his departure, his rooms were crowded by his friends calling to take leave of him. No other public man ever made more . . . sincere friends here, nor was severance of a gentleman's connection with American public affairs ever more seriously regretted than in his case.[35]

And so Houston returned to Texas, never to leave it again. He had a joyous reunion with Margaret, Mollie, and the younger boys. Sam, Nannie, Maggie, and Nettie were living in Independence with their grandmother while the three oldest children attended school there. Houston relocated the family to the Independence farm, then returned to Huntsville to make arrangements to sell the property there. A new chapter was beginning in Margaret's life, and no doubt she approached it with mixed feelings. Her piano and guitar were on the way to Independence with other household goods. She asked her husband to be sure to get their church letters, as well as Eliza's. Never again would they reside at her beloved Woodland Home where four of her children had been born, and where she had so lovingly tended her beautiful gardens. But on the other hand, she would not be faced with the problems of running a farm by herself or struggling to keep the hands in line. Her husband would be with her, and she had often said that she would live anywhere happily as long as he was by her side. Houston had only been in Huntsville for a few days when Margaret wrote him:

> My health is improving constantly, no doubt from your treatments. . . . I do hope you will hurry back, for the truth is—I can not bear you out of my sight. Do you know I am more in love with you than I ever was in my life? It is true, I assure you. . . . Oh, do hurry back, my Love.[36]

The Houstons spent much of the summer at Cedar Point. While there they were visited by a reporter from a Galveston newspaper, who later reported that the old chief seemed to be satisfied in his retirement and had no thought of running for governor. However, another writer published an editorial admonishing the people to wake up and remedy the injustice done General Houston. And in Waco a citizen urged Texans to put the General back to work where he could stay the tide of disunion and expose corruption in high places.[37]

The Democrats met in a Convention on May 2, 1859, and again nominated Hardin Runnels, who was a strong advocate for slavery and secession. Houston had remained quiet, but Margaret probably became apprehensive as her husband began to waver. George W. Paschal, editor of the pro-union *Southern Intellingencer* in Austin decided to come out in favor of Houston as an independent candidate. First he wrote to Ashbel Smith for help:

> This is . . . a time to serve your old and devoted friend, Genl. Houston. The Constitution, the Union, the frontier, state reforms, and a large debt of gratitude demand his services. . . . I therefore beg you . . . to advise Genl. Houston to run. Let us redeem the Democracy. . . . Help us Ashbel. The people will elect Houston. . . .[38]

It is not known what Smith said to his old friend, but Houston discussed the situation with Margaret, and the next week he wrote Paschal:

> On yesterday I yielded my own inclinations to the inclinations of my friends, and concluded, if elected, to serve the people as the Executive of the State. The Constitution and the Union embrace the principles by which I will be governed.[39]

Houston had no party, organization, or campaign funds. He only made one speech, which was at Nacogdoches on July 9, 1859. Margaret was probably preparing herself for another defeat, but in August she again became the first lady of Texas when her husband was elected by almost the same number of votes that had defeated him previously.

The Houston family was in Independence when they received the news and began to make preparations for the move to Austin. While Margaret was dubious about the future and somewhat unhappy about removing the children from the Independence schools, Houston was like a country boy getting ready to make his first trip to town. All the family belongings, including Margaret's piano, were packed into wagons and sent ahead, with Joshua along to supervise. When the family was ready, Margaret and Eliza herded the children into the big yellow coach. Jeff drove Houston in the buggy. Houston was in such a hurry that often the coach was left behind, and the buggy would have to halt and wait for it to catch up.[40]

The open hostility of the new Texas legislature probably did not add to Margaret's happiness. The beautiful Governor's Mansion was only a few years old, and the legislature promptly blocked an appropriation for furnishings needed for the executive mansion. One member had even gone so far as to suggest that a man who had lived in a wigwam was not entitled to the luxuries of public expense.[41] Margaret would have to make do with what was already there and the pieces she could take with her.

[1] Sam Houston, *Writings,* vol. 6, 447, Houston to Ashbel Smith, August 22, 1857.

[2] Sam Houston, *Writings,* vol. 7, 32, Houston to G. W. Baines, November 23, 1857.

[3] Franklin Williams Collection, Huntsville, Houston to Margaret, December 25, 1857.

[4] Ibid., Houston to Margaret, January 24, 1858.

[5] Sam Houston, *Writings,* vol. 7, 41, March 19, 1858.

[6] Friend, *Sam Houston,* 261.

[7] Franklin Williams Collection, Huntsville, Houston to Nannie Houston, January 10, 1858.

[8] Ibid., Houston to Margaret, February 28, 1858.

[9] Ibid., Houston to Margaret, March 31, 1858.

[10] Ibid., Houston to Margaret, April 3, 1858.

[11] Ibid.

[12] Ibid., Houston to Margaret, April 8, 1858.

[13] Sam Houston, *Writings,* vol. 7, 100, Houston to Margaret, April 22, 1858.

[14] Ibid., 113, Houston to Margaret, May 19, 1858.

[15] Franklin Williams Collection, Huntsville, Houston to Margaret, June 7, 1858.

[16] Sam Houston, *Writings,* vol. 7, 183, Houston to Dr. B. F. Sharp, September 7, 1858.

[17] Franklin Williams Collection, Huntsville, Houston to Margaret, December 19, 1858.

[18] Ibid., Houston to Margaret, December 20, 1858.

[19] Ibid., Houston to Margaret, December 28, 1858.

[20] Ibid., Houston to Margaret, December 30, 1858.

[21] Ibid., Margaret to Houston, January 11, 1859.

[22] Sam Houston, *Writings,* vol 7, 218–19, Houston to Margaret, January 20, 1859.

[23] Ibid., 219–20, Houston to Margaret, January 21, 1859.

[24] Franklin Williams Collection, Huntsville, Houston to Margaret, January 23, 1859.

[25] Ibid., Houston to Margaret, January 24, 1859.

[26] Sam Houston, *Writings,* vol. 7, 224–25, Houston to Margaret, January 29, 1859.

[27] Franklin Williams Collection, Huntsville, Houston to Margaret, February 1, 1859. Houston is referring to the poem "To My Husband" written by Margaret on December 13, 1844.

[28] Ibid., Houston to Margaret, February 14, 1859.

[29] Ibid., Houston to Margaret, February 28, 1859.
[30] Ibid.
[31] Ibid., Houston to Margaret, March 5, 1859.
[32] Ibid., Houston to Margaret, n.d.
[33] Ibid., Houston to Margaret, March 1, 1859.
[34] Ibid., Houston to Margaret, March 5, 1859.
[35] Wisehart, 576.
[36] Houston Correspondence, Texas State Archives, Margaret to Houston, May 4, 1859.
[37] Wisehart, 579.
[38] Ashbel Smith Papers, Barker History Center, University of Texas, George W. Paschal to Smith, May 27, 1859.
[39] Sam Houston, *Writings,* vol. 7, 339, Houston to George Paschal, June 3, 1859.
[40] Hunt, 43–44.
[41] Wisehart, 583.

Sam Houston, about age 66, while visiting his friends in New York in 1859. Original photograph by Matthew Brady. Courtesy of Sam Houston Regional Library and Research Center, Liberty, Texas.

The night before he left Washington for New York, he wrote to Margaret: ". . . I will not regret my visit, for I look upon it as my last visit, and I have many warm friends to whom I am much attached."

Chapter XIV

General Houston seems cheerful and hopeful through the day, but in the still watches of the night, I hear him agonizing in prayer for our distracted country. . . . I cannot shut my eyes to the dangers that threaten us . . . but, oh, I have such a sweet assurance in my heart that the presence of the Lord will go with us wherever we may go.

Margaret Houston to Nancy Lea
January 21, 1861, Austin

It was no doubt with a twinge of sorrow that Margaret turned her back on Independence and the promise of happiness that life there, as well as at Cedar Point, would have brought. The dry fall weather made the trip a dusty nightmare for her. She was choked with asthma and was gasping for breath when they finally arrived in Austin. Her first night as mistress of the Governor's Mansion was spent sitting up in a chair. She did not dare to lie down for fear of strangulation. Jeff gathered autumn leaves from in front of the mansion and put them into big tubs. He and Eliza took turns all night long burning the leaves in the bedroom in an effort to help Margaret breathe easier.[1]

Houston immediately attacked his problems with the State Legislature. When the House debated the use of its chamber for the inaugural ceremonies, Houston promptly made his own arrangements. He announced that he believed the Legislature did not represent the will of the people. On December 21, 1859, Margaret sat in front of the capitol within view of her new home. She watched as her husband became the only man in American history to ever serve as governor of two states. While the legislature was against Houston, it would seem that the people were for him. Margaret could not have been anything but proud and pleased with the response. A newspaper reporter described him as the "eagle-eyed, lion hearted patriot" and the crowd as immense and enthusiastic:

> Then burst forth the mighty heart of the people with a great throb, all former applause was weak with that which now made the old capitol building shake to its center. Long and continued was the spontaneous outburst of feeling, while the hero of San Jacinto—the People's choice for Governor stood like a mighty Hercules in their midst.[2]

A few days before the inauguration Houston had been visited by the famous painter, Gustave Behne, in Austin on behalf of Houston's friends who wanted his portrait made to hang in the capitol. Houston accepted with pleasure, but was often too busy thereafter to keep his appointments with the painter. Behne made several sketches but did not finish the full length portrait until after Houston was out of office. When he finally saw the portrait Houston "declared it the only portrait—oil or photograph—with which he was completely satisfied."[3]

The Governor's Mansion, adjacent to the capitol, was by far the most elegant home Margaret had lived in during her married life. It had been finished in 1855 with money received from the United States government on settling the boundary dispute with Texas under the 1855 compromise law. When the state legislature refused to give Houston money to furnish the mansion, they apparently forgot that Houston, himself, had been instrumental just ten years before in getting the money to build the mansion. It is still in use today and has changed very little in the years since the Houstons lived there. It is a magnificent home with a beautiful grassy yard and fine trees. Wide porches extend across the front of both the upper and lower stories, and six tall, graceful columns support the roof. Beyond the reception hall at the front door is a winding stairway which is so nearly perfect that it has been inspected, described, and copied by architects for years. At the top of the stairway is the bedroom which is still referred to as the "Sam

Houston" room because Houston chose the furnishings for this master bedroom. On his campaign tour of 1857, he had visited the home of Colonel Hollamon in Seguin. Here he slept in a magnificent oversized four-poster bed which he now asked if he might have copied for the governor's mansion. The mahogany copy, made by the same Seguin cabinetmaker who had made the original, is a beautiful piece of furniture with extra length to accommodate those over six feet tall.[4] When the Houstons left the mansion the bed remained, and today it furnishes the guest room in the mansion.

On the ground floor, the wide entrance hall extends through the center of the house. To the right of the hall is the big parlor which was used for formal state occasions. To the left is the smaller family parlor and dining hall. In the family parlor hangs a chandelier which was used in Houston's day. During that time, the lamps were filled with kerosene. The fixture was later changed to a gas light, and then wired for electricity.

Never before or since has the Texas Governor's Mansion been filled with such a large and lively family. At the beginning of the new year Sam was entered in the Allen Academy in nearby Bastrop, but the six other children were all at home. The older girls had been taken out of Baylor to attend public school in Austin, while Margaret instructed them in Latin at home. The children's friends were always welcome in the mansion, and young men were beginning to call on Nannie and Maggie.

In writing of the Houston family, biographer Pearl Jackson described the lively Houston children as "no better than the average children of [the early 1900's]." In fact, Margaret often had her hands full with her brood, and some visitors to the mansion were dismayed at all the disorder. It was reported that when Margaret had company, the smaller children's battles would sadly interfere with the conversation of their elders. Andrew was particularly mischievous, and on one occasion he crawled under a table and pinned together the skirts of Nettie and her friend, Ellen Graham.[5] On another occasion Houston was standing at the doorway bidding good-bye to Jeff Caldwell, an old friend from Walker

County. They were interrupted by Andrew, who came sliding down the stair railing and landed at their feet.[6]

On one occasion while Margaret was resting upstairs, the young people gathered in the living room under the watchful eyes of the Governor. One of the young ladies, Adele Atwood, offered to show the crowd the latest dance step, the "pigeon's wing." Everyone, including Governor Houston, was enjoying himself to the utmost when Margaret, who was opposed to dancing in any form, appeared at the door, and with a stern frown put an end to the proceedings.[7]

Margaret tried to divert Houston's mind from the gathering political troubles with rounds of social functions and family gatherings. Antoinette was a frequent visitor at the mansion, as was their mother. But in the spring of 1860 social activities were curtailed because the Houstons were again expecting a baby. A carriage accident added to Margaret's already failing health and forced her to withdraw from many of the social activities.

Back in Independence, Nancy Lea was worried that Margaret and the children were not getting the proper food, since the pinch of pre-Civil War shortages was already beginning to be felt in Texas. She persisted in sending her family parcels of food including fresh sausages and fruits, which were in abundance at Independence. Much of the food spoiled in transit, and by the time Houston paid the high transportation charges the goods cost him much more than if he had purchased them in Austin. He tried time and time again to prevent his mother-in-law from sending the parcels. Finally, in desperation, he sent her the message, "For the Lord's sake, send no more food. Thy dutiful son, Sam."[8]

Even with her husband living at home, Margaret found that he was so busy that she rarely saw him. Despite the mansion being only a short distance from the capitol, Houston often did not come home for meals. When this happened, Margaret would send Jeff over to the governor's office with a tray of hot food.[9]

Houston did take time to write long letters to Sam. As often as possible he went to visit his son, taking Jeff with him to drive the buggy. Houston would stay at the old Nicholson Hotel in Bastrop.

Although Margaret had been responsible for most of Sam's earlier education, she now deferred to her husband's desires on the subject. Houston wanted Sam well taught in grammar and history, but felt that Greek and Latin were a waste of time. It was his plan to take Sam from school before he was twenty and place him in a clerk's office or store. While he wanted all his children to receive the best education possible, he wanted Sam to be educated in human nature too, instead of becoming what he called an "educated fool."[10]

As he had during his senate years, Houston continued to write letters of advice to Sam, but now they also contained news of the family. He told Sam about being compelled by the press of business to eat dinner in his office, about Margaret being pleased with a drawing of the mansion which Sam had sent her, and about Andrew's bringing dogs into the mansion. The Governor had been forced one night to "take off [Andrew's] flannels, turn them inside out and whip them in the Hall, as I think the Fleas would have nearly eaten him up otherwise."[11] In another letter he wrote that he wished all his sons "to love and revere the Union." He urged Sam: "Mingle it in your heart with filial love."[12]

The Houstons were also concerned with Sam's health. Margaret had heard that there was an epidemic of scarlet fever in Bastrop. Houston wrote warning Sam not to go into town, and asked him to "write every day until your Ma's alarm is over."[13] The next day Houston again wrote his son with some instructions from Margaret on preventive medicine:

> I would advise, if it is there, that you get a small piece of camphor with a piece of asafoetida [sic] and put them in a piece of buckskin around your neck. Suspend it by a string or tape in your bosom. This will, in my opinion, do good in keeping off the disease, and if they are moistened with turpentine, so much the better.[14]

Houston later wrote Sam that although he and Margaret missed having Sam at home, they felt it was to their son's advantage to be at school, for a week "well employed" was worth years in later life. He advised:

Now is your seed time of life, and the harvest must follow. If the seed is well planted, the harvest will be in proportion to it. Oh, if I had only enjoyed an education of one year, I would have been happy.[15]

During this period Margaret probably was also concerned about her husband's future. On April 21, 1860, a group of enthusiastic supporters meeting at San Jacinto had passed a resolution to nominate Houston for president of the United States in the coming election. Houston thanked the men for their regard, and reminded them of what he had said a few weeks before: "If my name should be used in connection with the Presidency, the movement must originate with the people themselves, as well as end with them.[16]

Although Houston had not authorized his nomination, it was presented to the National Union Convention on May 9, 1860 in Baltimore. He received a large number of votes, but John Bell held the majority. Concerned over the effects that this event might have on his sixteen-year-old son, Houston immediately wrote to Sam, Jr., with the advice: "[i]f you are taunted, take it kindly" and say 'My Father said his name should not be used nor would he accept any platform'." He also expressed his personal feelings to his eldest son:

If I really desired the Presidency I would not consider the action at Baltimore as any hindrance to my chances. I will recognize no action of a caucus or convention. The people only are sovreign in such matters. I write you this to put your mind and feelings at rest on this subject. So my son, by all means think no more of the affair.[17]

While much of the Governor's mind was on his oldest child, he was also wrestling with his state legislature. The lawmaking body was against Houston's legislative program and for secession, and both were very much in the news. However, one day Andrew Houston stole the political spotlight from both the Governor and the Legislature.

Andy frequently visited the office of Secretary of State Major E. W. Cave. Here he was a great favorite and was allowed to sit up to a big desk with paper and pen and "write" official letters. On one occasion the Major was busy, or perhaps in a bad humor. At any event, he reproved the boy sternly, and Andy ran off in a fit of temper. He climbed the stairway to the Senate Chamber, where a key caught his eye. Andy pushed the door shut, locked it, and gleefully hid the key across the street. In a few hours the senators discovered their predicament and began to call out the window to a passer-by. A crowd gathered in the street, and soon the Governor was made aware of the situation. When someone mentioned that Andrew had been seen in the vicinity earlier, Houston immediately suspected what had happened. Jeff was dispatched to fetch the boy, who was threatened into a tearful admission of the key's whereabouts. A hungry senate retired to lunch, and Houston jokingly reported to Margaret that their son had shown more generalship in handling the members of the Legislature than he himself had shown with all his power as Governor.[18] To Andrew's older brother, Houston wrote: "I have had to keep Andrew at the office some days, as they can't manage him at home."[19]

In the spring of 1860, more serious family problems arose. Martin Lea, who had been looking after the farming and business interests at Cedar Point, was now planning to join the army. Houston wrote to Sam that although he was opposed to it, he had allowed Martin to have his horse, Bull. Since Martin was leaving, Houston would have to go to Cedar Point to attend to family business.[20]

The Houstons were having financial problems also, and when Sam wrote and asked for a new coat his father asked: "Will not the coat you have do to wear in company?" In one of the few instances that finances were discussed with his children, Houston went on to explain to his son that he was being so "particular" because his expenses were so heavy. It was costing a thousand dollars per year to educate all the children. Nevertheless, he told Sam to write him all the reasons why a new coat was required and if it was "necessary to your becoming appearance and to place you on an equality with other cadets, it must be done."[21]

Another problem was Margaret's health, which deteriorated as the time approached for the birth of the baby. The fact that there was talk of nominating her husband for the presidency of the United States probably added to her anxiety at this time. Because of the carriage accident, Margaret worried constantly that her child might be born deformed.[22] Both parents were delighted when a healthy boy arrived on August 12, 1860. He was named Temple Lea for Margaret's father. The Houstons now had four boys and four girls. Their family had come full circle. The first child had been born when Margaret was first lady of the Republic of Texas; the last child was born when she was first lady of the state of Texas.

Margaret was in very weak condition after Temple's birth, and Houston was greatly alarmed. He wrote a friend that she had been so ill that for ten nights he had been up with her and had not even undressed.[23] When she was beginning to recover, Houston wrote another friend of his joy at having eight children, "all healthy, smart, and lively. How grateful parents ought to be for these gifts. . . ."[24]

It must have been a great relief to Margaret that her husband was not unhappy over his failure to be nominated for president. Houston described his situation as being "out of the scrape for President." He told one friend he had his "arms folded" and would "stay so unless some malice is squinted [sic] at me."[25] To another friend he confided his opinions on those who had been nominated: "Lincoln under no circumstances, would I vote for. Douglas, Bell, or Breckinridge, I could not support, unless to save my Country—and Mr. Bell, I could not vote for."[26]

Political problems were never aired in front of the Houston children. They were not aware that their father was laboring under a terrible burden. With the possible exception of Maggie, who sometimes served as her father's private secretary and wrote letters for him, the children did not suspect anything was wrong. However, in private, Houston always discussed everything with his wife and often asked her advice. Margaret must have known that he was heading for disaster, and yet there was nothing she could do to stop him. She agreed that everything must be risked for the sake of his basic principle—"To be honest and fear not is the right path."[27] She could not help but fear for the future of her family.

During this unsettled time, Margaret was also agonizing specifically over the future of Andrew, who was seriously ill. He had been bitten by a dog, and the inflammation was so great that the doctors were considering amputating his leg in an effort to save the boy's life. Margaret blamed herself for his condition, since the wound had not been serious at first, and probably would have healed normally if Margaret could have kept Andy quiet in bed and out of the cold. Fortunately, after a long illness, he finally recovered without having the leg amputated.[28]

Margaret was also fearful for her husband's life at this time, due to events which probably brought back memories of earlier times in Houston City when he was President of the Republic. Once again there were rumors that Houston was marked for assassination, this time by men reported to belong to a secret political club called the Knights of the Golden Circle. Two men, Cook and Montgomery, were thought to be the ringleaders of this club. They hung around the capitol building late into the night, and on one occasion peeked into a window and actually pulled a pistol. Houston's secretary, Mr. Penland, stood in the way and witnessed the attempt. He immediately tried to persuade Houston to carry a gun. Houston replied that he was not afraid of any man that ever lived, and it would not look right for the governor to go around with a big pistol buckled to his side. Mr. Penland suggested that Houston's life was more important to his country than the dignity of the office and asked to be allowed to order him a pair of derringers. After much persuasion, which included the suggestion that Houston have two pockets sewn on to the back of his pants so than he could conceal the guns, Houston finally agreed, but when they arrived he carried them for only a few days and then put them away.[29]

Now sixty-seven years old, Houston was aging fast. His old wounds were paining him, especially during the cold and damp Austin winter. He was forced to use a cane constantly and sometimes a crutch. During the weeks that preceded the presidential election, he suffered from a bad cold, and Margaret insisted that he go to bed. He did for a few days, but got up against her wishes to make a speech at a rally for Bell. He felt that if Bell should be elected there was less chance that the Union would be dissolved. He had confided to Margaret that if Lincoln were elected, the south would probably secede, and that he hoped then to find some way to save Texas for the Union.[30]

Election day dawned with an damp and chilling rainstorm, as if the weather were giving a hint of the trouble to come. Houston refused to make public for whom he voted, but paused long enough to comment that slavery was a damnable thing at best, and that he hoped that God in some way might perform a miracle to save the country from destruction.[31] With Lincoln's election, the cry for secession became louder and louder throughout all of Texas. Houston called for a special session of the legislature. On January 21, 1861, in an emotional speech, he pleaded that whatever the course of Texas might be, "she should take no step except after calm deliberation."[32]

Years later Jeff would tell of hearing a speech during this time in which Houston warned of the dangers of secession. Jeff remembered his master speaking of taking an oath to support both the constitutions and flags of Texas and the United States. Houston reminded his audience that he had almost died fighting for both the flags. He also warned:

> To secede from the Union and set up another government would cause war. If you go to war with the United States, you will never conquer her, as she has the money and the men. If she does not whip you by guns, powder, and steel, she will starve you to death. . . . it will take the flower of the country—the young men.[33]

While Houston was speaking to the legislature, Margaret was writing to her mother about their troubles. She wrote that the present appearance of things was gloomy, but she hoped that the Lord would bring "lights out of darkness and beauty out of chaos." She described their situation:

Gen'l Houston seems cheerful and hopeful through the day, but in the still watches of the night I see him agonizing in prayers for our distracted country. . . . I can not shut my eyes to the dangers that threaten us. I know that it is even probable that we may soon be reduced to poverty, but oh I have such a sweet assurance in my heart that the presence of the Lord will go with us wherever we may go. . . . [34]

Houston had confided to Margaret that the reason he had agreed to be governor in the first place was to help the state get back on its feet, but now everybody seemed to be getting along nicely without him. He did not feel that he could ever give up his loyalty to the Constitution. It would appear that he was trying to prepare Margaret for his deposition when he said, "I have a home and livestock and can live without the office."[35]

During these turbulent times, a soldier stationed at Camp Verde near San Antonio visited the Governor's Mansion. His name was Robert E. Lee. It is a strange coincidence of history that a friendship could develop between Lee and the Houstons, as it was common knowledge that many years before he met Margaret, Houston had once courted Mary Custis. She turned down his proposal of marriage, telling him that her heart belonged to a young West Point student by the name of Lee. Margaret enjoyed the visits of this southern gentleman. There was a branch of her family which spelled its name "Lee" and Margaret and Robert called each other "cousin." A nephew of Robert E. Lee later claimed that they actually were related, but no proof of a relationship exists today.[36]

As the Secessionist crisis in Texas worsened, Lee and Houston had similar thoughts. Just before Lee left Texas, he rode over to Austin from San Antonio to say good-bye. He and Houston talked until three in the morning, both very unhappy. Houston told Lee that he would never sign the order for Texas to secede, and Lee said, "If war comes, I will go with Virginia." Maggie Houston was fifteen at the time, and later wrote about this last visit. The governor of Virginia at the time was John Letcher, a cousin of Houston's. It was at Governor Letcher's request that Lee boarded a train to Richmond to accept a command in the service of Virginia which ultimately brought him to the command of the Confederate armies. When Lee left, he carried with him a letter from Houston to Letcher. Lee and Houston were never to meet again.[37]

The election was held on a secession referendum, and on March 3, 1861, the results were announced. The Houstons were sitting on the porch of the mansion when loud cheering was heard from the capitol. This was followed by the firing of cannons and ringing of bells. A short time later a messenger arrived to announce that Texas had voted to secede. Houston's face turned ashen. His head dropped to his chest and his whole being shook with emotion.[38] Maggie remembered hearing her father tell Margaret, "Texas is lost. My heart is broken." The couple could no longer protect their children from becoming engulfed in politics, and the thought that his wife and children might have to suffer greatly grieved Houston. His political career was now over, and he never recovered from this blow. His children later told of how soon after this event their father became an old man and failed in health.[39]

Sam Houston was not a man to give up gracefully, and much to Margaret's dismay, he made one last attempt to save Texas from the Confederate War. The referendum question put to the people had been whether Texas should secede from the Union. Joining the Confederacy had not actually been part of the question. Houston's plan was now to persuade Texas to resume her nationality and once more form a Republic instead of joining the Confederacy.

Both Margaret and her brother-in-law, Charles Power, tried to stop Houston, but he made several trips in a final effort to stop the secessionists. On one of these trips Houston spent the night in Georgetown at the home of his friend, Elias Talbot. During the visit a messenger brought Houston a confidential message from Abraham Lincoln that gave him a new opportunity. The message said that when Lincoln became president in about two weeks, he would make Houston a major general in the United States Army, and send to Texas a fleet with five hundred thousand federal soldiers so that Houston might put down secession in Texas. Houston considered this idea very seriously. He returned immediately to Austin and showed the letter to Margaret. She remained silent, but Houston knew that she was filled with a dread that he would bring the war to her very doorstep.[40]

Houston then called in four of his loyal friends whom he knew to be strong Unionists—Benjamin Epperson, James W. Throckmorton, David Culberson, and George Paschal. The five men conferred in the front parlor of the mansion in what is now called the Green Room. Houston told his friends of the offer and asked their advice. Epperson favored accepting it; the others were against it. Houston listened carefully and then said, "Gentlemen, I have asked your advice and will take it, but if I were twenty years younger, I would take Mr. Lincoln's proposal and endeavor to keep Texas in the Union." He then went to the fireplace of the green room and burned Lincoln's letter. He had made his decision, and he never mentioned the matter again.[41]

Houston returned to his original plan of re-establishing the Republic of Texas, but the legislature refused to support him and further added salt to the wound by voting that all state officers must take an oath of allegiance to the Confederate Government by March 16, 1861. On the evening of March 15, 1861, the Houston family followed their usual rituals. After supper the servants cleared away the dishes. Margaret brought the family Bible to her husband. The children sat at the table, and the servants brought in cane bottom chairs and sat along the wall. As was his custom, Houston read a chapter from the Bible and translated its meaning into simple English for the benefit of the servants. Then they all knelt together in prayer.

About eight o'clock George W. Chilton arrived with the order from the legislature for Houston to take the Confederate oath. The children were sent from the parlor, but Margaret remained. Chilton asked for an immediate answer as to whether the Governor would appear at noon the next day to take the oath. Houston replied that he could not make such a serious decision immediately; he must have time to think it over. Chilton gave him until the next day. After Chilton left Houston told Margaret that what happened to him personally mattered little to him, but that he wanted to give careful thought to the consequences that the refusal might place upon his family. As usual, Margaret told him to ask the Lord's help as guidance, and that she would abide by his decision.

Houston retired to an upstairs bedroom. Margaret heard the floor creaking as he knelt in prayer. Later he removed his shoes so that he would not disturb the household while he walked the floor for most of the night. He wrestled with the problem of whether or not to take an oath to support a government that was opposed to everything he believed in. He was tortured by the fact that his wife and children would suffer if he did not. Margaret could not sleep and waited downstairs for him until near dawn. When he came down, he told her, "Margaret, I will never do it."[42]

No doubt Margaret knew from past experience that this was the only decision he could ever have made, and she tried to reassure him. She told him that she would stand beside him, and she had faith in God to help them in their time of trouble. They probably reflected on the many difficult times they had passed through together. Perhaps the worst of their misfortunes would be his removal from office, which they both knew would follow.[43]

Together they slowly climbed the winding stairs of the mansion—Margaret to retire and Houston to work on a message to the people of Texas explaining why he could not take the oath. It would be published in *The Southern Intelligencer* on March 20, 1861. It would be a long message which began by Houston's reminding the people that he had become governor when "worn out with the cares of office," having retired to "the bosom of [his] family to spend the remnant of [his] days in peace." He had come out of retirement only when the people "urged [him] to forget the peace of home and duties [he] owed to [his] children." He detailed the past events of his administration and presented his personal feelings to the public:

> I have declared my determination to stand by Texas in whatever position she assumes. Her people have declared in favor of a separation from the Union. . . . I go out from the Union with them; and though I see only gloom before me I shall follow the 'Lone Star' with the same devotion as of yore.[44]

Knowing that the office of governor would be declared vacant when he refused to take the oath, Houston's message went on to state his personal view of the matter:

> In the name of the Constitution of Texas, which has been trampled upon, I refuse to take this oath. I love Texas too well to bring civil strife and bloodshed upon her. To avert this calamity, I shall make no endeavor to maintain my authority as Chief Executive of this State, except by the peaceful exercise of my functions. When I can no longer do this, I shall calmly withdraw from the scene, leaving the Government in the hands of those who have usurped its authority; but still claiming that I am its chief Executive.[45]

The same morning a message arrived notifying Houston that he must be present at the capitol at noon to take the oath to the Confederacy. Instead of going to the room where the convention was being held, he entered by the entrance to the basement. He took out his knife and a piece of pine and began whittling. William Mumford Baker, who was present, described the scene:

> . . . the old governor sitting in his chair in the basement of the capitol . . . sorrowfully meditating what it were best to do. . . . The officer of the gathering up stairs summoned the old man three times . . . but the man sat silent, immovable, in his chair below, whittling steadily on.[46]

Lieutenant Governor Edward Clark was sworn in as the new chief executive, and Houston left the capitol for the last time. In the meantime, at the mansion, Margaret told her children what was taking place. She was beginning the task of packing their belongings so that they could vacate as quickly as possible. She and Houston had decided that they would return to Independence, at least for a short time.

Old friends appeared to give the Houstons moral support and to help Margaret with the packing. They worked several days, and on the evening of March 19, 1861, Houston and Margaret were sitting in the parlor with their friends when a knock was heard at the door. Houston opened it and discovered a large party of men outside.

Margaret's first thought was that the convention had sent a force to hasten their eviction. But it soon became apparent that these men were friends of Houston and that they were armed. Most of them stayed back in the shadows, but some came forward to tell the ex-governor that they were prepared to disperse the convention and reinstate him in office if he would only give the word. They believed that the people of Texas would support them. Houston was astonished at his friends' willingness to inaugurate a war that would be more horrible than the one proposed by secessionists "merely to keep one poor old man in a position for a few days longer." He made a short speech expressing his thanks:

> Go tell my deluded friends that I am proud of their friendship, of their love and loyalty, and I hope I may retain them to the end. But say to them that for the sake of humanity and justice to disperse, to go to their homes and to conceal from the world that they would have ever been guilty of such an act.[47]

Fearing for the future safety of their friends, the Houstons never revealed the names of their night visitors. The next morning Margaret loaded the children and Eliza into the big yellow coach. They turned their backs on Austin, where they had lived for just fourteen months, and headed down the road to Independence followed by wagons loaded with their belongings.

---

[1] Hunt, 45.
[2] *Daily Herald* (San Antonio), December 27, 1859.
[3] Jean and Price Daniel Collection, Sam Houston Regional Library, Liberty, Texas, Gustave Behne to Governor A. J. Hamilton, March 31, 1866.
[4] Flanagan, 153.
[5] Madge W. Hearne Papers, San Antonio, from a sketch by Pearl Jackson, n.d.

[6] Professor Joseph Clark, Sam Houston vertical file, Sam Houston State University, Huntsville, n.d.

[7] Madge W. Hearne Papers, San Antonio, Jackson.

[8] Mrs. S. L. Shipe, "Recollections of Mrs. Sam Houston," n.p. and Madge W. Hearne, family story.

[9] Madge W. Hearne, family story.

[10] Hunt, 45–46.

[11] Sam Houston, *Writings,* vol. 8, 8, Houston to Sam Houston, Jr., April 7, 1860.

[12] Sam Houston Hearne Collection, Barker History Center, University of Texas, Houston to Sam Houston, Jr., April 3, 1860.

[13] Sam Houston Papers, Barker History Center, University of Texas, Houston to Sam Houston, Jr., April 25, 1860.

[14] Ibid., Houston to Sam Houston, Jr., April 26, 1860.

[15] Sam Houston, *Writings,* vol. 8, 33–34, Houston to Sam Houston, Jr., April 30, 1860.

[16] Ibid., 60, Houston to John Manley, May 17, 1860.

[17] Sam Houston Papers, Barker History Center, University of Texas, Houston to Sam Houston, Jr., May 17, 1860.

[18] Hunt, 53–55, and Andrew Jackson Houston, family story.

[19] Sam Houston Papers, Barker History Center, University of Texas, Houston to Sam Houston, Jr., May 25, 1860.

[20] Franklin Williams Collection, Huntsville, Houston to Sam Houston, Jr., May 21, 1860.

[21] Sam Houston Papers, Barker History Center, University of Texas, Houston to Sam Houston, Jr., July 10, 1860.

[22] Madge W. Hearne, family story.

[23] Sam Houston, *Writings,* vol. 8, 126, Houston to Charles L. Mann, August 27, 1860.

[24] Ibid., 134, Houston to Samuel A. Blain, September 4, 1860.

[25] Ibid., 128, Houston to Ben McCulloch, August 28, 1860.

[26] Ibid., 120, Houston to A. Daly, August 14, 1860.

[27] Madge W. Hearne, family story quoting Maggie Houston Williams.

[28] Sam Houston Papers, Barker History Center, University of Texas, Margaret to Nancy Lea, January 21, 1861.

[29] Hunt, 59–61.

[30] Ibid., 63–64.

[31] Ibid., 69.

[32] Sam Houston, *Writings*, vol. 8, 250.

[33] Hunt, 72.

[34] Sam Houston Papers, Barker History Center, University of Texas, Austin, Margaret to Nancy Lea, January 21, 1861.

[35] Hunt, 74.

[36] Madge W. Hearne Papers, San Antonio, Texas, "Robert E. Lee in Texas," n.d. See also White, "Robert E. Lee in Texas," *Naylor's Epic Century Magazine*, February 1938, 12–14.

[37] Madge W. Hearne Papers, San Antonio, "An Account by Maggie Houston Williams," n.d.

[38] Jennie Morrow Decker, family story quoting Nannie Houston Morrow.

[39] Madge W. Hearne, family story quoting Maggie Houston Williams.

[40] Temple Houston Morrow to Grace Longino, January 17, 1957. Sam Houston Memorial Museum, Huntsville.

[41] Ibid., and Madge W. Hearne, family story quoting Maggie Houston Williams.

[42] Ibid.

[43] Ibid.

[44] Sam Houston, *Writings*, vol. 8, 271-78.

[45] Ibid., 277.

[46] Baker, "A Pivotal Point," *Lippincott's Magazine*, November 1880, 566.

[47] Sam Houston, *Writings*, vol. 8, 293, March 19, 1861.

A sketch of Sam Houston as Governor of Texas, age 67, sketched in his office by Gustave Behne while in the process of painting a portrait. Courtesy of Sam Houston Regional Library and Research Center, Liberty, Texas.

On March 31, 1866, Behne wrote Governor A. J. Hamilton and told him of meeting Houston in Austin around the time of his inauguration as governor: "The General expressed his willingness and pleasure to sit for me . . . he, himself declared it the only portrait—oil or photograph—with which he was completely satisfied."

303

Margaret Houston, age 41, in 1860, when Sam Houston was the governor of Texas. Courtesy of Sam Houston Regional Library and Research Center, Liberty, Texas.

A painting made from this photograph is at the Bayou Bend Collection of the Houston Museum of Fine Arts, Houston, Texas.

One of the first known photographs of the Texas Governor's Mansion. Courtesy of Barker History Center, University of Texas at Austin, Austin, Texas.

On January 21, 1861, Margaret wrote her mother from this house that in the still watches of the night she could hear her husband "agonizing in prayer for our distracted country" and that she could not "shut her eyes to the dangers" that threatened them.

Chapter XV

I have no spirit to write to any of you on account of my deep affliction from my dear boy being sent to Mississippi. My heart seems almost broken. . . . When I first heard the news, I thought I would lie down and die . . . I did not love him more than the rest of my children, but he absorbed all my anxiety, all my hopes and fears.

Margaret to Nancy Lea
April, 1862, Cedar Point

The Houstons still owned their farm across the road from Baylor in Independence, but the house, along with Houston's library, had been loaned to the University. Nancy Lea's little cottage was not large enough for the whole family. They went instead to the home of Dr. Asa Hoxey, a friend they had known since they lived in Washington-on-the-Brazos. It had been in this house that General Houston and his staff had stopped on the way to San Jacinto. While there, Houston had gathered in his arms the two-year-old daughter of Dr. Hoxey and said, "if this baby smiles, I shall win, but if she frowns, I will lose the battle." The baby smiled.[1] The Hoxeys were known for their hospitality and were well able to entertain the Houstons. Their home was one of the show places of early Texas. Located about two miles from the center of town, it was two stories high, and had many rooms. Long broad porches enclosed with glass surrounded the home. The drawing room was so large that it called for two complete sets of furniture.[2]

To this elegant setting, in the early spring of 1861, Houston took his family and tried to hide his grief. However, the people of Texas had dealt him a blow from which he would never recover. The family planned to visit only a short while, and then travel to Cedar

307

Point where a new home was being built. It would be the timber from the oak grove there, requested by Margaret so long ago, that would furnish most of the income for the Houston family in the years to come. The spring rains made the roads impassable to coaches and delayed the family's departure, forcing them to stay longer with the Hoxeys than they had planned. Houston, however, left almost immediately on a quick trip. He was anxious to reach Cedar Point because of a troublesome situation with Sam. His oldest son was an eager disciple of secession and anxious to join the army, and Margaret was frantic. Houston had given Sam instructions to go to the home at the bay and supervise the hands. He was probably in hopes that all the work to be done there would keep Sam too busy to think of war.

On his way to the bay, Houston stopped in Brenham. Here he was asked to make a speech. He first refused, but then in typical Houston fashion, he agreed after he heard that a threat had been made against his life if he were to speak out against the Confederacy. He began speaking to an unruly mob which overflowed the courthouse. He talked about preserving the Union and made predictions that the Civil War, which was near at hand, would be stubborn and of long duration. When he finished, no hisses broke the silence.[3] This speech was to be one of many, despite the pleadings from Margaret that he keep silent.

Houston continued his trip and wrote Margaret from Galveston that all was well at the Point. He sent her a newspaper with the news that there had been "an awful fuss" there and in Houston City about his deposition. His friends were glad to see him, and he had been asked to speak at the Battlegrounds on San Jacinto Day. He described their new house as "decent" for what they had planned to spend.[4]

He did not write Margaret that at Cedar Point he found Sam anxious to join the other youths who were volunteering for the Confederate Army. Sam feared the the impending conflict would be over before he could get into it. For the present, Houston convinced his son that he was too young and that he was needed at home. He put Sam in complete charge of the farm and timberland that surrounded the house on the Point. As soon as Houston returned to Independence, he sent instructions to Sam to "keep the hands busy." He urged Sam to "think for himself" and assured his son that he would be satisfied with whatever Sam did.[5]

He sought to calm Margaret's fears for their oldest child. The rains continued and Houston wrote Sam that he was "weary and distressed" to be thus detained. Furthermore he and Margaret did not like to "eat our friends out of House and home" on one visit. He spoke of how anxious they were to get to Cedar Point. He gave his son some more advice about joining the army:

> Do you, my son, not let anything disturb you; attend to business, and when it is proper, you shall go to war, if you really wish to do so. It is every man's duty to defend his Country; and I wish my offspring to do so at the proper time and in the proper way. We are not wanted or needed out of Texas, and we soon may be wanted and needed in Texas. Until then, my son, be content.[6]

Houston wrote Sam that his mother was ill and anxious to see him. As soon as the family could reach Cedar Point, perhaps as a ploy to keep Sam from joining the army, Houston planned to send him back to the farm to get the sheep and goats. The same letter told how in Sam's absence, Andrew was trying to help out. He was anxious to return with Sam from Cedar Point and assist his brother in driving the stock down from Independence.[7]

Finally, the spring rains ceased, and as soon as the roads were passable, the family left Independence for their home on Galveston Bay. When they reached the point, they found that their son was not there. Sam and his cousin Martin Royston were participating in drill practice across the bay with a company of Texas Infantry. It was called the Bayland Guards and was commanded by Ashbel Smith. Margaret was frantic that Sam would join the army, and Houston tried to console her. He was almost as opposed to Sam's joining the Confederate Army as was Margaret, but for different reasons. Houston's country was not the Confederacy; it was Texas, and he wanted it to be his son's country as well as his own. They both were hoping that when the drill was over, perhaps Sam would return to his job at home. Margaret begged Houston to do something. He sent Sam a letter expressing his views:

> In the events now transpiring, I think I perceive disasters to Texas. The men and arms are all leaving this quarter for the theatre in the great Drama which . . . is to be played. . . . Texas is in possession of the the Gulf. . . . If Texas is attacked she must be in her present isolated condition. She can look for no aid from the Confederacy and must either succumb or defend herself.

He assured Sam that if Texas did not require his service and he wished to go elsewhere, all would be well. However, he said, at the present this was not the case:

> . . . as she will need your aid, your first allegiance is due to her and let nothing . . . in a moment of ardor cause you to assume any obligation to any other power whatever, without my consent. If Texas demands your services or your life, in her cause, stand by her. Houston is not nor will be, a favorite name in the Confederacy. Thus you had best keep your duty and your hopes together, and when the Drill is over come home.[8]

A few days later Houston visited Houston City. He was sitting on the balcony of the City Hotel when a group of young recruits came by on their way to enlist in the Second Infantry. They paused and called out a respectful greeting to him. Perhaps remembering himself at their age when he first went off to war, he rose and spoke to them of things that only an old soldier would know. He honored them even if he did not approve of their cause. They would go off to battle with his blessings and his prayers "that they may be brave, trust in God, and fear not."[9]

When Houston reached home, Sam was already there. Houston found that he had blessed his own son. All of his pleas had fallen on deaf ears. Sam was now eighteen. He had joined the Confederate Army on August 13, 1861, without his parents' consent, and was now a private in Company C, 2nd Texas Infantry.[10] He had been one of the recruits who heard Houston speak. Houston tried to hide his pride from Margaret for he knew she was beyond consolation. Her grief was magnified when Andrew brandished his toy sword and begged for a uniform.[11] Soon Houston had to go to Huntsville on business, and from there he wrote Margaret in an attempt to console her:

> If war should come upon you before I return, don't keep Sam from going, my Love, but let him go. God can shield him as He has his father before him. He will take with him a Mother's and Father's hopes & prayers for his safety and his honor.[12]

Houston had made a prophecy that would late come true. Sam left to join his regiment, and his commander, Captain Ashbel Smith, called at Cedar Point to say farewell to his old friends. Houston and Smith talked less of the war than about the old days in Texas. Margaret took the opportunity to ask a favor. Sam had gone off to camp without the Bible which she had bought and inscribed for him. She asked Captain Smith to deliver it when he joined the regiment. This request brought about a strange coincidence which would later save her son's life on two different occasions.[13]

During these turbulent times an incident occurred which showed how successfully Margaret had protected her children from some of the unpleasant aspects of politics by refusing to discuss Houston's enemies in front of them. Nannie had been visiting friends a few miles away and met an old gentleman whom she reported to her parents had been both charming and entertaining. She told her father, "You certainly must remember him for he said that he knew you in the early days of Texas, and made such kind inquiries about you." Her father asked the gentleman's name and was told it was Judge David G. Burnett. Margaret and Houston exchanged glances and Houston laughed heartily. Some time later the children learned that this charming gentleman had been one of their father's worst enemies. Maggie later reported, "He must have felt very insignificant when my sister told him that she had never heard her father speak of him!"[14]

311

Sam's division was ordered to Mississippi, and Margaret received the news with utter desolation. She was sure he would never see her son again and wrote to her mother that although Houston left nothing unsaid that could give her "hope and consolation," she could not forget that her darling boy who was to be "the prop" of her old age was away from her "probably never to return." She wrote Nancy of her feelings:

> My heart seems almost broken, and yet I am astonished that I bear it at all. . . . I left nothing undone that was in my power to prevent his going, but my weakness gave him the opportunity of displaying traits of character that made his father's heart swell with pride. . . . When I first heard the news, I thought I would lie down and die.

Margaret spoke of Sam as if he were already dead. She wrote her mother that she did not love Sam more than the rest of her children, but that "he absorbed all my anxiety, all my hopes and fears." She was hopeful that her sister Varilla, whose son Martin was with Sam, could come for a visit so that they could "mingle [their] prayers and tears."[15]

Margaret received a letter from her cousin, Columbus Lea, who was in Mississippi with Sam. He assured her that Sam was "in robust health" and seemed as likely to bear "the fatigues of the campaign" as any soldier in it. However, he suggested to Margaret that she "tell the General to secure a lieutenancy for Sam" to save him from the rougher duties of the camp.[16]

Houston must have had mixed emotions at this time concerning the pride he felt for Sam, who had acted in the same manner which Houston probably would have done in a similar situation, and the genuine pity he felt for Margaret's suffering. He swallowed his pride and made a decision to seek help from an old enemy, William S. Oldham, who was now the Confederate Senator from Texas in Richmond, Virginia. He wrote to Oldham asking for a commission for Sam. He pointed out that Sam had been absent from home on business when the company was first organized, and all the offices were filled by the time he had returned. Furthermore, Sam had been offered a rank of lieutenant if he would consent to be transferred and stationed at Galveston, but the boy had turned it down to go into the immediate campaign. Houston described his son as a scholar with good habits who was "ardently devoted to the cause in which he is engaged, as well as to the life of a soldier." He assured Oldham that if the senator could secure a promotion for Sam, "I trust and believe he will never disgrace his patron."[17]

Houston would not know it for several months, but the day after he wrote his letter the battle of Shiloh near Corinth, Mississippi had begun. Here Ashbel Smith was wounded and Sam's life was saved by Margaret's Bible for the first time. In his knapsack, Sam carried the Bible into battle. He was struck by a minnie ball which is said to have stopped in the Bible at the 70th Psalm—"Oh God: thou art my help and my deliverer."[18]

The next day Sam was not as fortunate. He was struck in the groin by a ball and lay semi-conscious as the Confederates retreated and the Yankees swept over him. Later as a Union surgeon looked at him and passed on, Sam was awake enough to realize that the doctor had felt that he was beyond help and was leaving him for dead. All afternoon Sam lay in the field waiting to die. In the early evening a Yankee chaplain passed among the dead and saw a faint sign of life in Sam's body. He picked up the Bible from Sam's knapsack and opened it to the flyleaf. Although the Bible was torn, the chaplain could still read the inscription, "Sam Houston from his Mother, March 6, 1862." He asked if the boy was related to the General Houston of Texas who had served in the United States Senate.

Fate once again intervened, for this chaplain had been one of the ministers who petitioned the United States Senate not to repeal the Missouri Compromise. Houston had received the group and defended the right of the ministers to petition. The minister hurriedly secured a doctor to take another look at Sam, got a litter, and stayed with him until the wounded boy was carried off the field. Thus it was that Margaret's Bible had saved her son's life two times in as many days. Later the Houston family made many efforts to discover the identity of this chaplain, but they were never able to locate him.[19]

The news of the battle at Corinth reached Texas. Houston wrote to Maggie and Nannie, who were in school in Independence, that they had not learned the result. Margaret was in a painful anxiety, but both parents were praying that "God has shielded him from harm in battle's hour."[20] A few days later the southern newspapers listed Sam among the dead and missing and his name was struck from the rolls of his company. Unbeknownst to his family, Sam was sent to a prison at Camp Douglas, Illinois. He would later be exchanged for a northern prisoner before his family even learned that he was alive. But for now, Margaret was torn between grieving for him as dead and praying that if he were alive, he was not suffering from unattended wounds. She wrote to Maggie that she had mourned until she had "almost forgotten the feeling of joy." She had great hopes that he was a prisoner, but "all is veiled in mystery."[21]

Tom Armstrong had written his father, a Houston neighbor, that Sam was a prisoner. He said that Margaret's cousin, William Rogers, had been leading the charge, and Tom had witnessed Sam fall. Tom reported that Sam was not wounded, but had collapsed after eating "nothing for 48 hours and standing guard in a drenching rain." Margaret told her daughter:

> If the Yankees can treat him any worse than this, I hope I may have grace to forgive both. The truth is I am told that none but the Texians would drive the Yankees and therefore they were sadly imposed upon.[22]

A few days later they received another report that Sam had been seen during the retreat. Margaret summarized it in a letter to Maggie:

> . . . he got up and tried to follow his company, but his strength failed, and he was captured. Your papa says if Sam is alive, he is glad of one thing—that he was last in the retreat. That he was foremost in the fight seems to be universally admitted.[23]

314

The War had united many former enemies in sharing grief, including the Houstons and Anson Jones. Rumors had reached Houston that Sam was dead and Charles Jones was injured. Finally a letter from a mutual friend, Jim Hageman, to his mother, sent the news that Sam was a prisoner and that Charles' wound was not serious. Mrs. Hageman sent the letter to Mary Jones, who in turn forwarded it to Margaret. It was returned to Mrs. Jones with a note from Margaret: "I heard on yesterday that you had received a letter from your son, Charles. If it is true, I congratulate you and rejoice with you sincerely. My heart is still crushed with anguish and suspense."[24]

As usual Margaret put her faith in God, and while she was waiting for news of her eldest child's fate she wrote a poem called "A Mother's Prayer." It concluded:

Thy glorious Eye doth follow him
On toilsome march, mid prison gloom
On Southern soil, through Northern clime,
Or mid the cannon's dismal boom.

His life is safe beneath thy sight,
As though a mother's love could soothe,
And for the weary head each night,
With tender hand, his pillow smoothe!

But for the guardian care that kept
My patriot boy on Shiloh's plain,
His youthful form would now have slept,
With thousands of the noble slain,

And can I doubt thy power and love!
Oh Father, let me doubt no more!
Each cloud of unbelief remove
And hide me till the storm is o'er!

Into thy hands, Oh God, I yield
My first born treasure and my stay!
Be thou his guardian, guide and shield
And save him, in the last great day![25]

While Margaret was full of anguish in Texas, Sam was slowly struggling to recuperate in a northern prison. He had inherited his mother's literary talent, and perhaps imagining what his mother must be feeling, he wrote a poem called "The Southern Captive":

Softly comes the twilight stealing through my prison bars
While from out the vault of heaven gently glimmering come the stars.
Well I know my mother's weeping for her long lost wandering boy
Does she know that still I'm living—even that would give her joy.
No—they tell her that I'm sleeping 'neath the turf on Shiloh's plain
That she ne'er will see her wanderer—never on this earth again.
Oh my poor heart sinks within me as the months roll slowly by,
And it seems in this cold north land a lone captive I must die;
Yes, far away from friends and kindred, without a hand to mark my grave
And not upon a field of glory I'll sleep amid the southern brave.[26]

However, Sam did not die, and later he would give his mother the poem.

Back home in Texas, his parents were struggling with yet another problem. Martial law was declared in Texas in May of 1862, and Houston was still an object of suspicion and speculation. Citizens' rights everywhere were being violated. The Provost Marshal had even interrogated some of the Houston children about movements in their household. This was more than Houston could stand and he wrote a letter to Governor Francis Lubbock protesting the evils that were "annoying and vexatious" to patriots:

I murmur at no necessary contributions to crown our cause with success. In my only son, out of childhood, I have given to it the staff of my [old] age and the right arm of my strength. The unutterable anguish which I have witnessed in my domestic circle, as well in relation to the mystery which hangs around our son's fate . . . has not caused me . . . to think less of my rights as a free man and patriot than I have done in other days.[27]

The Houstons braved the dangers of the martial law and traveled to Huntsville. They stayed at Captain Sim's Hotel while Houston made an unsuccessful attempt to buy back the Woodland home. When this failed, he made arrangements to rent a house owned by Dr. Rufus Bailey of Austin College.[28] The house stood about a half-mile from the courthouse on the corner across the road from the village burial ground. It had been given the name of "Steamboat House" because of its strange resemblance to a sternwheeler. A piazza ran the entire length of the house on one side. The second floor was reached by a wide, steep stairway on the outside. A huge oak tree shaded the stairway and the yard.[29] The Houstons would divide their time between here, Independence, and Cedar Point.

By late summer they were back at Cedar Point. A bright spot in the war years occurred on Nannie's sixteenth birthday, September 6, 1862. Despite the dwindling Houston fortune, her father bought her a thousand dollar Steinway grand piano of delicately carved rosewood. It was shipped by water to Galveston, and from there to the home by wagon. The huge piano was not out of place in the Cedar Point home. The tiny summer cottage where Houston had brought his bride had grown to a large, roomy house. The fireplace in the living room was described as so large it made the uncut wood seem like kindling.[30]

About the same time, unknown to his family, Sam was freed from his northern prison when he was sent in an exchange of prisoners to Vicksburg, Mississippi on September 23, 1862. Though extremely frail, he was eager to return to service. He was appointed Instructor of Tactics with the rank of Lieutenant. Perhaps as a reward for his own valor or in respect for his father's earlier request, Sam's rank and pay were back-dated March 11, 1862. After only a few days, however, it became clear that Sam did not have the physical strength to serve, and on October 3, 1862, he was given a medical discharge.[31]

In early fall Margaret and Jeff were in the Cedar Point garden tending flowers when a crippled soldier appeared at the gate. Pale, wan, and dirty, he was supported on crutches made of saplings. Margaret left her work to speak to the stranger and see if she could help. The soldier said, "Why Ma, I don't believe you know me." It was Sam, and his mother had not recognized him.[32]

Margaret and Jeff carried Sam to a bedroom. They bathed the wearied boy and fed him soup. Shortly afterwards, Houston rode in from a neighbor's house, greatly excited. He told Margaret he had had a premonition of good news. He told his son, "Sam, all morning something seemed to tell me that you were alive and safe, and that you would come home to us."[33] Sam mended fast in the warm salt air of the seaside. He gave Margaret his battered Bible and told her its story.[34]

When Sam was strong enough he went to Independence to attend Baylor University. Margaret sent him a little book containing passages of scripture for every day of the year, and implored him to give his heart to God. Margaret wrote Sam that they were expecting an old friend: "We are expecting Col. Smith this evening . . . previous to his departure for the army . . . and I almost tremble when I think of meeting one who is so intimately associated . . . with the great trial of my life."[35]

Soon after that Houston became seriously ill, and it was feared he was dying. The doctor sent for a close friend, Hamilton Stewart, who later described the scene for one of Houston's biographers. Stewart related that he came immediately in a driving rain, and was asked to break the news to Houston that he was dying. This Stewart did. For a few moments Houston did not reply. Then he asked that all the family and servants be sent for. As they all gathered around his bed, Houston proceeded calmly to give each one of them instructions of things he wanted done. When he had finished, he asked Margaret to read a Psalm from the Bible. Then he asked Nannie and Maggie to sing a hymn. The girls began to sing, but broke down sobbing, and Houston finished it himself. He then told them all to go back to bed. Although he was very ill, he did not die. He astonished his family by getting up a few days later, and asking Stewart to send out the message, "Tell my enemies I am not dead yet."[36]

When Houston recovered, the family returned to Huntsville. A short time later they discovered that one of their slaves was missing. He was Tom Blue, a big mulatto that Houston had brought with him from Washington. Tom had been born in the West Indies and had a good education. He drove the big yellow coach and four for Margaret. Later the Houstons learned the story of how Tom had planned his escape to Mexico with Walter Hume, a young black boy. Tom was light enough to pass for white at the immigration office in Eagle Pass where he claimed to be Walter's "owner." As soon as they had crossed the border, Tom promptly sold the unsuspecting boy for eight hundred dollars and used the money to live on. When Tom's money was gone he finally returned to Texas and ended his life as a beggar on the streets of Houston City.[37]

If Tom had only waited a few more days, he would have been a free man anyway. Before Sam, Jr., had been discharged from the army, he had learned of Lincoln's Emancipation Proclamation which said that all slaves in the seceding states would be free on the following January first. When Margaret and Houston were informed of this they decided not to wait until then. One Sunday morning in October of 1862 Houston sent Joshua to gather all the servants at the front door. Margaret and all the children, with the exception of the absent Sam, stood by as Houston read the Proclamation from a newspaper. Then he slowly explained to his slaves what it meant.

He told them that he had decided not to wait until January to give his "people" their freedom. He told them that the laws of Texas, the Confederacy, and of the Almighty God gave him the right to free them whenever he wanted to, and that he was glad to be able to do it. He added that he would always be ready to help them whenever he could. If they wanted to stay and work for the family, he would pay them wages as long as he could. The entire family, with the exception of baby Temple, was in tears by the end of Houston's speech.

Joshua, who had already earned his freedom, was the first one to speak. He announced that he was going right on working just as he had always done. Several others expressed the same desire. Eliza somehow got the idea that emancipation meant that the soldiers would come and force her to leave. She grabbed up Temple, clung to him, and begged not to be "mancipated." Margaret had to remind her that she had promised Eliza that they would never be separated.[38]

The Houstons traveled to Independence in November of 1862 and visited with Nancy Lea. The old lady felt she was nearing the end of her life and was making plans of a practical nature. She had already selected her grave site across the street from the church where she could hear the sound of "her bell." On the edge of her property she had ordered a brick vault constructed and pointed out that it was large enough to include graves for Margaret and Antoinette. One of Nancy's main concerns was that, because of the War, she would have to be buried in a plain pine box. Earlier she had ordered a beautiful metallic coffin from the east, and stood it in her closet. It was during this visit that Houston put the coffin to a much less serious use than Nancy had intended.

Coffee was selling for seven dollars a pound. Nancy had noticed that it and the equally precious sugar were disappearing from the larder. Houston suspected two of the servants, but he called all of them together and expressed the opinion that "ghosts" were at the bottom of it. He then picked the two young girls under suspicion to help him find a safe place to store the food. Together, they made a complete tour of the house, with Houston eliminating each suggestion until they reached the closet where the coffin was stored. Houston open the door and suggested that they place the food inside the coffin. The girls dropped their packages and ran screaming from the house. Nancy continued to store her food there until her death, and no one ever bothered it again.[39]

Soon after the family returned to Huntsville, Houston's health began to fail. His shoulder wound was a running sore, and the pain in his ankle grew worse. Margaret watched him with great anxiety. She kept as many family problems from him as she possibly could.

She wrote to Sam in Independence about his leaving school without permission and the possibility that his father would scold him when he found out. She gave Sam some advice:

> I fear your pa will lecture you about leaving school without leave. If he does I do hope you will show no morbid sensibility about it. The time will come soon enough when you will have no one to admonish you when you do wrong. . . . Do let us be gentle and affectionate with each other the little while we have to live.[40]

Margaret had not told Houston about the store account Sam had run up in Independence, but she was not afraid to instruct her son concerning the problem: "As to your store account, I do not know what to say. I do not think your father has the remotest idea that you have made any bills. Do not get any thing more I beseech you."

Margaret had good reason to fear for her husband's health. At age seventy, he had a chronic bad cough and was losing weight. He rarely felt well enough to ride a horse. On the times he did he tied a crutch to the saddle horn to support him when he got down to walk. On April 2, 1863, Houston wrote out his will, making Margaret the Testamentary Guardian of their children during their minority.[41] Soon afterwards he took to his bed, but this bout of illness did not prove fatal either.

As soon as he was well enough he wrote Nannie at Independence to advise her on some problems with her latest beau. He suggested that she neither return the gentleman's letters nor ask for the return of hers, since he presumed that she had written nothing indiscreet. He gave advice on ending the romance:

> I would give as reasons that "it would cause me to withdraw a portion of my time from studies. It is a rule of Mr. Clark's school that no scholar of his school shall correspond with any gentleman unless he is a relative, & I do not wish to violate his rules."

In the same letter he imparted the news that Sam had been given leave to go to Mexico on business with Charles Power. Houston

321

wrote that he did not really feel that he could spare his son at that time, but he said he had yielded because it was something Sam wanted to do for himself. The next day, before he sent the letter, Houston wrote across the margin, "Today I am afraid I have taken a relapse."[42]

Houston's Indian friends heard that he was ill, and Chief Blount sent a delegation to visit him. Unable to venture too far from home, Houston received them on the porch of the house. The Indians sat in a circle around him and they conversed in Indian language. Houston asked them to sing some of his favorite Indian songs. This they did, and he was greatly touched by their visit.[43]

Margaret suggested to Houston that he go to the mineral springs at Sour Lake in Hardin County, in the hopes that the warm baths would improve his health. Sour Lake was a health resort where health seekers bathed in black, sticky mud in body-sized holes.[44] As soon as Houston was strong enough, Jeff drove him to the resort while Margaret remained at home. She wrote him there that they all missed him, but were getting along, and he was not to think of coming home until he was better: "It is my daily prayer that you may be benefited by the springs. . . . If you find that you are improving at Sour Lake, I would not . . . change it for any other place." Houston did not benefit from his trip. When he returned to Huntsville he had caught a cold. Margaret put Houston to bed and sent word for the girls to return from Independence. Houston did not tell his wife how bad he felt, but to Jeff, who helped take care of him, he confided that he felt he could not live two weeks more. Meanwhile, the news of the fall of Vicksburg had reached Texas. It dealt Houston a blow from which he did not seem to be able to recover.

The hot, dry weather of Texas in July added to Houston's difficulty in breathing. The doctor ordered that his bed be placed in the center of the room to give the sick man more breeze. Jeff put a pallet on the floor in order that he might take short naps, but most of his time was spent in giving his master medicines and fanning the air around his head. Once, Jeff fell asleep on his feet, and the fan he was holding fell down to Houston's face. Houston roused and said, "Margaret you and that boy go and get some rest. There is no use in both of you breaking yourselves down."[45]

When Houston's condition worsened, Margaret sent one of the servants to summon Dr. P. W. Kittrell. He and Dr. T. H. Markham told Margaret that Houston had a severe case of pneumonia. Dr. Markham offered him brandy as a stimulant. Houston refused with such emphasis that Dr. Markham would later report that even to the end of his life Houston's great will power yet abided.[46]

Word spread throughout Huntsville, and friends and neighbors appeared at the Steamboat House each night to help Margaret and sit up with their old friend. Joshua left his work to hold himself in readiness to act as a messenger wherever Margaret wished to send him.[47]

On July 25, Houston drifted in and out of a coma. Margaret sent Jeff to the penitentiary to summon the superintendent, Colonel Thomas Carothers, one of the trusted friends whom Houston had asked to help Margaret. With him came the Reverend Samuel McKinney, president of Austin College. When they reached Steamboat House, they found that Houston had roused from the coma and could speak coherently. They talked for a while about the War and slavery. When Colonel Carothers asked about Jeff, Houston replied that he had freed all of his slaves, and that he had instructed Sam, Jr., to see that Jeff was taken care of. The Reverend McKinney then asked Houston how things were between him and the Lord. Houston was slipping back into unconsciousness, but he understood the question. He opened his eyes and replied faintly, "All is well, all is well." The family gathered around the bedside, and the Reverend offered prayers.[48]

Houston slept through the night. It was Sunday, and perhaps Margaret was thinking of a letter he had written to her so long ago concerning death. He had expressed his feelings then: "My hope and prayer is that we may be enabled so to get on in life that when the summons shall come that we may be prepared for a mansion about the skies."[49]

By her husband's bedside, Margaret opened the Bible to the fourteenth chapter of John. She began to read: "In my Father's house are many mansions; if it were not so, I would have told you. I go to prepare a place for you." Maggie later wrote about that sad day:

> . . . we heard his voice in a tone of entreaty, and listening to the feeble sound, we caught the words "Texas! Texas!" Soon afterward my mother was sitting by his bedside with his hand in hers, and his lips moved again. "Margaret," he said, and the voice we loved was silent forever. As the sun sank below the horizon, his spirit left this earth for a better land.[50]

Houston's last thoughts were of the two things he loved the most in this world. Shortly before six on the afternoon of Sunday, July 26, 1863, Houston and his beloved Margaret were separated by death. Margaret prayed that God would make her children men and women worthy of their father. Perhaps she was remembering earlier in their marriage when Houston had told her: "If I leave no other legacy on earth but love and honor, they shall stand and remain pure and unsullied as the moon beams which play around our cottage home."[51] She removed the simple gold ring that Elizabeth Houston had placed on her son's finger more than fifty years before. Margaret held the ring so that her children might see and be inspired by the word that their father had carried with him throughout all his adult life. It was "Honor." [52]

---

[1] Madge W. Hearne Papers, San Antonio, "Homes of Independence," a typescript copy of a speech by Madge W. Hearne for an Independence Homecoming Celebration, n.d.
[2] Ibid.
[3] Sam Houston, *Writings,* vol. 8, 299-300, S. A. Hackworth's report of Sam Houston's speech of March 3, 1861. See also Mrs. James V. Carroll, "My Mother Saw Sam Houston," *Banner Press* (Brenham, Texas), March 2, 1936.
[4] Franklin Williams Collection, Huntsville, Houston to Margaret, April 18, 1861.
[5] Sam Houston, *Writings,* vol. 8, 305, Houston to Sam Houston, Jr., May 15, 1861.
[6] Ibid., 306, Houston to Sam Houston, Jr., May 22, 1861.

[7] Ibid.

[8] Ibid., 308–09, Houston to Sam Houston, Jr., July 23, 1861.

[9] James, *The Raven*, 414, from an account by recruit William Christian.

[10] Mae Wynne McFarland, "General Sam Houston and Young Sam's Confederate Record," an unidentified clipping in the Daughters of the Republic of Texas Library, San Antonio, Sam Houston Vertical File. From information furnished by Secretary of War George H. Dern, January 4, 1936.

[11] Jennie Morrow Decker, family story.

[12] Franklin Weston Williams Collection, Woodson Research Center, Rice University Archives, Houston to Margaret, August 16, 1861.

[13] Madge W. Hearne, family story.

[14] Ibid., and, Henry Bruce, *Life of General Houston*, (New York: Dodd, Mead and Co., 1891), 210.

[15] Sam Houston Papers, Barker History Center, University of Texas, Margaret to Nancy Lea, March 17, 1862.

[16] Sam Houston Papers, Barker History Center, University of Texas, Temple H. Morrow Collection, Columbus Lea to Margaret, April 2, 1862.

[17] Sam Houston, *Writings*, vol. 8, 315, Houston to Williamson S. Oldham, April 5, 1862.

[18] Madge W. Hearne, family story quoting Sam Houston, Jr. See also Temple Houston Morrow, "Bullet Marks Psalm in Bible," *Dallas Morning News*, March 5, 1939.

[19] Ibid.

[20] Sam Houston Hearne Collection, Barker History Center, University of Texas, Austin, Houston to Maggie Houston, April 16, 1862.

[21] Ibid., Margaret to Maggie Houston, May 10, 1862.

[22] Ibid.

[23] Ibid., Margaret to Maggie Houston, May 12, 1862.

[24] Anson Jones Papers, Barker History Center, University of Texas, Austin, Margaret Hageman to Mary Jones, May 1, 1862. Margaret Houston to Mary Jones, May 15, 1862.

[25] Margaret Houston Album, Cedar Point, July 30, 1862. In personal possession of Meredith Morrow Spangler.

[26] Mrs. E. A. Everitt Collection, Sam Houston Regional Library, Liberty, n.d.

[27] Sam Houston, *Writings*, vol. 8, 320, Houston to Francis R. Lubbock, August 9, 1862.

[28] The name of the college was later changed to Sam Houston University.

[29] Ed Kilman, "Steamboat House is Monument to Sam Houston," *Houston Post*, June 16, 1935. The house was later moved to the grounds of Sam Houston Park.

[30] Ellis, 88.

[31] Mae Wynne McFarland, "General Sam Houston and Young Sam's Confederate Record."

[32] Madge W. Hearne, family story quoting Sam Houston, Jr.

[33] Ibid., and Hunt, 108–09.

[34] This Bible may be seen in the Sam Houston Memorial Museum, Huntsville, Texas.

[35] James, *The Raven*, 422, Margaret to Sam Houston, Jr., September 21, 1862.

[36] Alfred Williams, 370–71.

[37] Hunt, 370–71.

[38] Madge W. Hearne, family story quoting Aunt Eliza, and Hunt, 101. Most of the servants remained, and were cared for until their deaths by Houston children and grandchildren.

[39] Hunt, 117.

[40] Sam Houston Papers, Barker History Center, University of Texas, Margaret to Sam Houston, Jr., February 6, 1863.

[41] Sam Houston, *Writings*, vol. 8, 339–40. Will of Sam Houston, April 2, 1863.

[42] Sam Houston, *Writings*, vol. 8, 344–45, Houston to Nannie Houston, April 14, 1863.

[43] Hunt, 114–15.

[44] Flanagan, 189.

[45] Hunt, 118.

[46] Brown, *Encyclopedia of the New West*, 35.

[47] Mrs. Ike Barton McFarland, "All Texas Mourned Death of General Sam Houston," *Houston Press*, August 1, 1935.

[48] Hunt, 119.

[49] Franklin Williams Collection, Huntsville, Houston to Margaret, January 12, 1847.

[50] Alfred Williams, 366; and Bruce, 217.

[51] Franklin Williams Collection, Huntsville, Houston to Margaret, December 9, 1841.

[52] Madge W. Hearne, family story quoting Maggie Houston Williams. This ring may be seen at the San Jacinto Museum of History, La Porte, Texas.

MADGE THORNALL ROBERTS

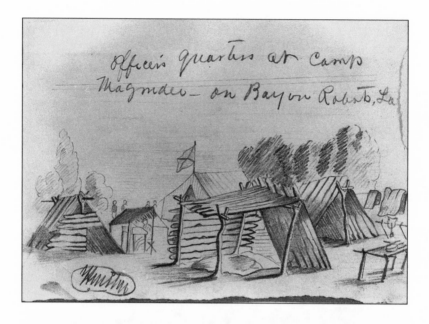

Drawings by Sam Houston, Jr., during the Civil War, 1863:
Officers' Quarters at Camp Magruder—on Bayou Roberts, La.
Night on the Battlefield—1863
Louisiana Swamp on Bayou Roberts, La.
Courtesy of Sam Houston Memorial Museum, Huntsville, Texas.

Sam demonstrated his talent as an artist at an early age. Houston wrote to Margaret on January 6, 1850, that he had shown Sam's drawings around Washington "with much pride" and for her to tell Sam to "send to me every fine specimen that he may make, and I will be gratified with it."

Chapter XVI

A few months ago when the great sorrow first fell upon me and crushed my spirit in loneliness and desolation, I could not see how I could ever guide my little flock through the dreary wilderness. But now I can truly say ... the Lord helped me. Not one of his precious promises has failed.

Margaret to Sam, Jr.
July 1, 1864, Independence

Perhaps in her sorrow Margaret remembered a letter written long ago in which Houston expressed the goals he had set for himself. He had written her from Washington:

To be a good man, an affectionate husband, a kind parent, a generous master, a true patriot, and to leave my family and the world a spotless reputation comprise all the objects of my earthly ambition![1]

Shortly after her husband's death, Margaret opened the big family Bible. Below the birth dates of all the Houston children she wrote, "General Sam Houston, the beloved and affectionate husband and father, the devoted patriot, the fearless soldier, the meek and lowly Christian died July 26, 1863."[2]

Friends quickly gathered at the Steamboat House when the news spread through Huntsville. Colonel A. P. Wiley and Colonel Bob Hayes offered to make the funeral arrangements, and Margaret gratefully accepted their help. It was decided that the funeral would be held at the house, since it was so close to the burial grounds, at 4:00 P.M. the next day. Funeral notices were quickly

331

printed on small black bordered cards and distributed on the streets.[3] The Masonic brethren of Huntsville, many of whom had seen Houston preside over the Grand Lodge of Texas, were in charge at the grave. The next day, the unbearable summer heat broke with a rain storm which descended upon the little village. The Baptist minister was not available, so Margaret chose Dr. John M. Cochran, a Presbyterian minister, to preach the funeral service. There were remarks by Judge J. H. Banton, a friend who had been an almost daily visitor during Houston's last illness. The procession moved across the road to the cemetery amid the storm, and Houston was laid to rest in a simple pine coffin which had been made during the night.[4] Despite the weather a large crowd was present. When the first part of the cortege reached the grave, the end of the procession had not yet left the Steamboat House.[5]

Dr. Kittrell wrote a letter to the newspapers to announce the death of his famous patient:

> He died after an illness of five weeks. At one time during his sickness hopes were entertained of his recovery, but his improvement was only apparent, and it soon became evident that the hand of death was upon him. To his numerous friends it will doubtless be a matter of great satisfaction to learn that in his last hours he was sustained by the Christian hope that he died the death of the righteous.[6]

Two days after his funeral the newspapers gave notice of Houston's death and traced his career. E. H. Cushing of the *Tri-Weekly Telegraph* wrote:

> He has not always been right, nor has he always been successful, but he has always kept the impress of his mind upon the times in which he has acted. . . . His noble qualities will ever stand out clear before the people. So let us shed tears that are due to one who has filled so much of our affections. Let the whole people bury with him whatever of unkindness they had for him. Let his monument be in the hearts of those who people the land to which

his later years were devoted. Let his fame be sacredly cherished by Texans. . . .[7]

Houston's Indian friends heard of his death and slipped quietly into Huntsville to pay their respects. They camped in the woods across from the cemetery and at night they celebrated at the grave the solemn rites that honored Houston as a great chief of their race.[8]

Margaret was left a forty-four-year-old widow with seven children still at home to support. She was helped in business and financial affairs by Thomas Gibbs, Thomas Carothers, J. C. Smith, and Anthony Branch, all of whom Houston had appointed as executors of his will. In this document, Houston had described the four as "My beloved friends, in whom I place my entire confidence to make such disposition of my personal effects and real estate as may seem to them best for the necessities and interest and welfare of my family."[9]

Houston's will asked that his debts be paid and that the remaining estate be bequeathed to "my beloved wife Margaret and our children." He specifically left his library, watch and jewelry to Margaret. After Houston disposed of his tangible effects, he left instructions of how he wanted his children raised:

My will is that my sons should receive solid and useful education[s] . . . they they may possess thorough knowledge of the English language, with a good knowledge of the Latin language. I also request that they be instructed in the knowledge of the Holy Scriptures, and . . . Geography and History. . . . I wish particular regard to be paid to their Morals, as well as the character and morals of those with whom they may be associated or by whom instructed.[10]

Sam was the only child mentioned by name. To his eldest son Houston left the "sword worn in the Battle of San Jacinto" with the instructions that it was "never to be drawn, only in defense of the Constitution, the Laws, and the Liberties of this Country. If any attempt should ever be made to assail one of these, I wish it to be used in its vindication."[11]

Sam wasted little time in putting his father's famous sword to use. On August 20, 1863, he traveled to Galveston and without mentioning his previous service or asking for a renewal of his commission as Lieutenant, he enlisted as a private in Company K, 26th Cavalry, C. S. A.[12]

Margaret was inconsolable. Each day she left the Steamboat House with an armload of flowers and spent many hours weeping at the grave site. Nannie and Maggie feared for their mother's health, both physical and mental. Nancy Lea begged her to leave Huntsville and stay with her in Independence.[13] As soon as Margaret was able to compose herself, she decided that Independence would be the place to carry out her husband's wishes concerning the education of their sons, so she made a trip there and stayed for a while with her mother.

Margaret wrote Sam that the children were "much occupied with their studies" and "improving." She said that Charles Power was aiding her in every way that he could, but she was a great deal perplexed about her business, and needed to talk things over with Sam. She asked him to request a furlough, and confided to him that there were financial problems: "I suppose I must stay here for a while, but our expenses will be alarming. Provisions are so scarce and so high that I can not see how I am to get along, but 'the Lord will provide.'"[14]

Provisions were scarce for the Confederate Army in Texas also. When Margaret heard her friend Ashbel Smith was in command of the Second Texas Regiment camped at Velasco, she worried about the troops spending the cold winter on the open beach. She wrote Smith offering him a large tent for the men in his regiment who most needed shelter and gave directions for obtaining it from Cedar Point.[15]

Margaret's finances were worse than she had expected. The Houston fortune had once stood as high as one-hundred-fifty thousand dollars, but when the assets were inventoried in December of 1863 by Thomas Carothers, the amount had dwindled to almost half that. Much of their property had been sold to pay debts, and because of the War, other things had sunk in value. Furthermore, many of the assets consisted of notes owed to Margaret by persons who shared her financial problems and could not pay her.[16]

Sam could not get a furlough to come to Independence, so Margaret traveled to Cedar Point and arranged a visit in Galveston with him. Maggie, who was not in school because she was recovering from an illness, went with her. Sam was greatly disappointed that his mother had not brought Andrew, as evidenced in her letter to Mollie: "Give my love to Andrew and tell him I regret very much not bringing him with me. . . . Tell him to be a good boy and learn well and next time if possible I will certainly bring him."[17]

On her way back, Margaret made a stop in Houston. From here she wrote to Sam of her concern that he was moving away from the church. "In a few days from all accounts, you are to meet the enemy, and if you should fall in battle what will be the condition of your soul?" She went on to advise him that it was better "to sacrifice a few sinful pleasures than to be cast with them into hell." She was anxious to hear from him on the subject.[18]

During her stay in Houston, Margaret was able to talk with another old friend, Major Eber Cave, who had also offered to give her financial advice. Major Cave came to Independence, examined Margaret's assets, and made arrangements for her to trade some of the land from the Independence farm for the Root House in town. This was a large colonial house around the corner from Nancy Lea's cottage. It stood just down the road from the Rocky Street Baptist Church that Houston had joined nearly ten years before, and about a mile from the two schools which the Houston children would attend. It was two stories of graceful architecture. The front door opened onto an entrance hall and stairway to the upper floor. To the left was Margaret's bedroom and to the right was the parlor. On either end of the house were great chimneys, so that each room had a big fireplace. Upstairs were the girls' room on one side and the boys' on the other. In keeping with the customs of the time, the kitchen was not attached to the house. It was a separate room some ways from the house to prevent the danger of fire.[19]

And so, shortly after Houston's death, the family possessions were loaded for their last journey and moved to Independence. Margaret was pleased to find a house so close to her mother's. It must have also been a consolation that Varilla and Antoinette and Charles Power were close by. Margaret had Eliza and Jeff help her settle into her new home, but she had to make the move without the help of the faithful Joshua. He had been out of town on one of his blacksmith's jobs when he learned that the Houstons were moving. He rode day and night to reach Huntsville, but much to his disappointment, the family had already left.

Joshua gathered up all of his cash and began a sad trip to Independence. A few days after Margaret was settled in her new home, he rode up on his mule and knocked on the back door. After supper was over and the younger children had been put to bed, Joshua asked to speak to Margaret. He took out a well-worn leather pouch and emptied his life savings onto the dinner table. As Margaret looked on in astonishment, he told her that he had heard she was having money troubles and he wanted her to have what money he had earned to "take care of the chilluns." Unable to speak at first as tears ran down her cheeks, Margaret silently gathered the gold, almost two-thousand dollars' worth, into the pouch and placed it back in the worn black hands. "May the Lord bless you," she whispered to Joshua, "but you know what the General would want you to do with this money. You must promise me that you will use it to educate your children."[20]

Joshua returned to Margaret from time to time between his jobs to do whatever he could to help her. He kept his promise to her, and sent his children to school. One of his sons became president of Sam Houston Manual Training School of Huntsville. Joshua himself became a fine citizen in the Huntsville community, respected by both black and white alike. When he died he became the first black to be buried in the Huntsville cemetery, and he sleeps today near his former master.[21]

Sam wrote home faithfully every chance he could. He sent Margaret a poem called "A Soldier's Prayer." She wrote to thank him, with some advice for expanding his fine talents:

You . . . must cultivate these whenever you have leisure by reading select authors and writing your own thoughts. Avoid a trashy book as you would a viper for nothing saps the intellect more completely. I think a well written history contributes as much towards expanding political genius as any other sort of reading.

She immediately realized the foolishness of talking to him about reading history and writing poetry "when perhaps this very moment you may be engaged in a deadly conflict with the enemy."[22] She then turned to more serious matters and wrote that her daily prayers were that he be prepared if he must fall in battle. As to her affairs at home, she wrote:

In a little while we shall all be in Eternity. There seems to be a work for me to do in this world. My duties are many and arduous, but blessed be God! He gives me strength for my day. They are often wearisome to spirit and body, but I would not have them otherwise than they are for me, for God has ordained that they should be so and He knows what is best for me.[23]

When Margaret had visited with Sam earlier, she had taken the opportunity of giving him some subtle advice on a love affair. She felt that the girl, who was younger than Sam, was also more serious than he was. Margaret had not come right out and stated her objections, and Sam had written his mother that she was being mysterious. She replied:

As to my being mysterious, I do hope you did not think I intended any insinuation against your young friend. Oh, no . . . I have no doubt she is worthy of any gentleman, but marrying is a serious business, and if you enter into it with any prospect of happiness, you must begin with a good store of real, sincere, and devoted affection. . . . If I could believe that you really loved her, I would not dare to oppose it.[24]

Sam took his mother's advice to write the young lady "in as delicate a manner as possible" and tell her that as there seemed to be no speedy end of war in sight, and as he was in the army for the war, that he felt it "his solemn duty to release her" from all obligation to himself. The matter was ended, and Margaret later advised him to "beware of the fair sex hereafter, and do not get into any more scrapes." She hoped he would not be unhappy, and confessed that she blamed herself a good deal over the whole thing "for to tell you the truth, I rather encouraged it, because I thought it would keep you out of the army."[25]

Margaret was able to enjoy her own mother's companionship for only a few months after her move to Independence. Soon after the first of the year Nancy had become bedridden with what was described as a "stomach affliction." This was complicated with a bad cold from which she never fully recovered, and she died on February 7, 1864. She was laid to rest in her pre-war coffin and interred in the vault she had so carefully supervised. This second blow within a few months was too much for Margaret and she collapsed. It was more than a week before she could write to Sam:

> Ere this I suppose you have received the sad news of your Grandma's death. Maggie gave you an account last week of her peaceful and happy departure. . . . I delivered your last message to her not many hours before her death. She expressed much pleasure and always spoke of you with the greatest affection. Her remains were put in her metalic [sic] coffin and deposited in her vault. The attendance was large, and I am told the scene was very impressive, but I am sure you will not be surprised to know that I had not the strength to be present.[26]

In her double grief, Margaret turned all her energies toward devotion to her children. Sam was once again fighting on the front, and this time he carried the San Jacinto sword. All of Margaret's fears were for him. She felt that he was fighting for a lost cause, but Sam's letters were optimistic. He often sent drawings he had sketched of the battles. He spent his leisure time writing poetry and sent her a poem. Maggie wrote that she thought it was "perfectly beautiful and should be published."[27] Margaret would write that she had reason for not sending it to the *Tri-Weekly Telegraph*:

> I would have sent it to Cushing, but he had not published the last one I sent him. He may not have received it, for I am sure he has published articles inferior to it, but this I could not determine. I hope you will continue to improve your talent.[28]

Sam's poem was called "The Southern Flag," and it reads in its entirety:

> Flag of the South whose golden folds
> Shine with a nation's stars new-born,
> More beauteous than the eastern sky
> When crimsoned by the flush of morn.
>
> God bless the banner of the free,
> Born 'mid the battle's deafening roar.
> Bath'd with the maiden's purest tears
> And red with southern heroes' gore.
>
> 'Tis thine bright flag when booming guns
> Scorch the damp earth with their hot breath—
> 'Tis thine to lead with southern sons
> Sweep to victory or death.
>
> And where the deafening cannon roar
> And bugles wake the stilly night
> When prancing chargers rear and sore
> And all pant wildly for the flight.
>
> And when death's dreadful missiles fly
> When the cowards shrink and brave men die
> 'Tis then bright flag, thy splendors shine.
> Flag of the South, thy fate is mine![29]

Sam amply demonstrated that he had inherited his mother's literary talents, and Margaret sent "A Soldier's Prayer" to the *Texas Christian Herald* to be published. At about the same time, Maggie was also demonstrating some literary ability. She became the editor of the "Violet," a handwritten newspaper put out by the students of Baylor. Two years later, her sister, Mary Willie, followed her in the same job.[30]

Sam wrote to his mother after a battle under his flag at Mansfield, Louisiana: "Through the mercy of an all wise Providence I am permitted to write to you after a hard fought and bloody battle. . . . Truly God is good and is on our side. Who can prevail against us?"[31] There were more battles and anxious moments for Margaret. She reminded Sam that after a battle she was "of course very anxious and unhappy" until she could hear of his safety. She begged him, "Do not forget this and write immediately." She wrote him the family news that Sallie and Thomas Power had plans to run the blockade at Galveston in the hopes of finally making it to England. Varilla was moving into her daughter's place to take charge of the house and servants. She described Sam's brothers as "promising boys."[32]

Finally the fighting seemed to be over in Louisiana, and Martin Royston arrived home for a visit. Margaret was greatly disappointed that Sam had not come with his cousin. She wrote him that aside from everyone wanting to see him, she felt that it was very important the he should come home and "look into their business matters." She suggested that now might be the time to come:

> From what I can learn, there is not probability of any fighting in [Louisiana], at least for some time to come, and I should think Gen'l Wharton could spare you now better than at any other time. If your services were required on the field, you know I would not ask such a thing.[33]

Margaret continued to send frequent letters to her son. She had heard of a wonderful report of him given by a Captain McMahan. She commented on it to Sam:

I do thank my Heavenly Father with my whole heart that he has given me such a son. If the Capt. has not overrated your virtues (and I do not believe he has) nothing but the grace of God could have made you what you are.

She urged Sam to read the New Testament through regularly, beginning at the first and reading as many chapters as he could every day. She went on to tell him of how her faith had sustained her:

A few months ago when the great sorrow first fell upon me and crushed my spirit in my loneliness and desolation, I could not see how I could ever guide my little flock through the dreary wilderness. But now I can truly say . . . "the Lord helped me." Not one of his precious promises has failed.[34]

She had earlier written Sam the news of his brothers:

Andrew . . . has taken a great fancy to spruce up and visit the girls at the Clark's. . . . Willie and Temple are the sweetest little companions for me in the world. They are such perfect opposites that it makes their conversation very spicy and interesting.[35]

Now Margaret was writing her oldest son that Andrew was "growing rapidly" and that he was "very boisterous and unmanageable." She needed help in handling him:

I need you at home with him very much. I have been thinking seriously of sending him to Johnson's school in the mountains beyond Austin. . . . It is a mixed school, girls and boys. I would like to have your opinion on the subject.[36]

In fact, Andrew would attend several schools. He had been very close to his father. Perhaps he needed a firm male hand or maybe he was just at an awkward age. At any rate, he was quite a handful for his mother. He neglected his studies, and according to his sister Maggie, he admired the older girls.[37] But regardless of how much Margaret needed his advice at home, Sam could not come. All furloughs had been stopped.

Margaret wrote him with the sad news of his friends, including the son of Brother Baines, who had been reported slain in Virginia:

> I suppose we will hear of a great many more, as the Texas brigade was cut all to pieces. Oh how can I ever thank my Heavenly Father sufficiently for sparing my boy through so many dangers, while so many of his youthful associates have fallen. Oh my son, your life has been spared for some purpose. Take care that you do not bury your talent.[38]

No doubt Margaret's anxieties were multiplied when she received a letter from Sam telling of his recklessness during battle:

> . . . it almost seems now that . . . the bursting shells had a music for me—I was proud that I could ride fearlessly through it all, and show to my friend and foe that I was not afraid to die. . . . Ma, it was not for myself alone—I was proud of my name and I wanted to show the world that the blood of a Houston ran untainted.[39]

It must have been a great relief to Margaret when Sam's next letter came and he was still in Louisiana. He assured her that he was in fine health, although many around him had sickened and died. He wrote:

> I haven't the most remote idea as to the military movements. Some think that we (our Battery) will remain in the rear, as we haven't horses to draw it through the mud of a campaign. But I dont want that to be the case.[40]

Despite Sam's feelings, he would not participate in further campaigns. In the spring of 1865, the war was coming to a close. On June 4, 1865, Sam was among the Confederate soldiers surrendered by General F. Kirby Smith at Alexandria, Louisiana.[41] He hurried back to Independence. With him he brought the first news of President Lincoln's assassination and the first newspaper to Independence which told of the tragic event.[42]

But even with her happiness in having Sam home, Margaret had not ceased to grieve for Houston. In September of 1865, she picked up her pen and wrote a poem expressing her feelings about her husband, as well as her father and brother Vernal, both long since deceased:

> Welcome gentle shades of even,
>   To this weary care-worn brain,
> Bringing thoughts of Heaven,
>   And the rest which doth remain. . . .
>
> While above my tranquil head,
>   Lengthening shadows softly fall,
> Let me converse with the dead
>   And the hallowed past recall. . . .
>
> Come to me my buried Love
>   In all thy solemn beauty!
> From thy radiant home above
>   And rouse my soul to duty!
>
> Oh Love, my heart is weary,
>   In its loneliness and pain!
> The way seems long and dreary.
>   Tell me shall we meet again?
>
> But thy children gather round,
>   And my sorrows I must hush,
> For the merry step must bound
>   And youth's joy I would not crush.

God hath helped me hitherto,
   Truly may his servant say,
And his hand will guide me through
   Safely through life's thorny way.[43]

About the same time Margaret renewed her interest in an old project. She had always felt that General Houston's life story should have been written when he was alive. Of course, one book, *The Life of Sam Houston: The Only Authentic Memoir of Him Ever Published*, had been published some years before by C. Edwards Lester. Margaret had often acknowledged that Lester's book was the only reliable account of her husband, but it was by no means a complete story. She requested that Dr. William Carey Crane undertake to write the biography, and she turned over to him all of Houston's papers. She made only one stipulation about the book; it was to have at least one chapter setting forth General Houston's religious character.[44]

At first Dr. Crane hesitated, afraid that he was not competent. Finally Margaret convinced him, and trunks of documents were brought from the barn and the attic. Margaret agreed to help him. Personal letters were separated from the journals and historical letters. Margaret gave Dr. Crane a list of her husband's friends and associates who might be willing to help him. He began his work with enthusiasm, reading page after page of Houston's literary remains—enough, he said, to fill a dozen volumes.

Dr. Crane wrote to the men Margaret had suggested. On October 17, 1865, he wrote to Governor A. J. Hamilton and outlined his plans for three volumes. He requested that Hamilton, as Houston's "personal and political friend" write an "estimate of Gen'l Houston[']s character." He asked for Hamilton's approval of the publication and permission to place the governor's comments in the introduction.[45] No record of a reply by Hamilton exists. Ashbel Smith and Dr. G. W. Samson both gave their help, but none of the other parties on Margaret's list would aid him. Crane reported that all "counselled delay." He did not make public the name of Houston's associate who had written him the following letter on March 23, 1866:

It does not seem to me that there is any pressing urgency to present the Life and Labors of Gen. Houston to the world. It is true that they will possess a paramount interest so long as the Republic or State, or Country of Texas ... shall possess an interest for men; yet even in this view there is an advantage in bringing out a book in an opportune time.[46]

When Margaret read the letter from someone she had supposed to be a friend, she became incensed. She ordered the fire in the parlor fireplace lit, and began burning letters and documents while the children and Dr. Crane watched in horror. There is no way of determining how many valuable papers were destroyed before her rage was spent. Dr. Crane sadly packed away his notes and the project was abandoned until "an opportune time" many years later.[47]

With the end of the Civil War and the beginning of Reconstruction, times were hard in Texas. Confederate money was worthless, and Union money was scarce. By 1866 Margaret's financial resources had dwindled considerably. She must have been greatly relieved when she received the news that the Reconstruction Convention had met and adopted resolutions of respect in honor of the late governor. An ordinance was passed appropriating money to pay Margaret Houston's salary for his unexpired term. This amounted to around seventeen hundred dollars, which was sorely needed by the Houston family.[48] The money, paid in gold, was quickly spent, but the leather pouch it had arrived in was preserved as a family memento.[49]

It must have also been gratifying to Margaret, as a further indication of respect, when A. J. Hamilton wrote to her that he was directed by the Convention to procure a full length picture of Houston to be hung in the House of Representatives. He asked Margaret's advice on which picture to use, mentioning that he had heard a good portrait was available in New York. Perhaps wishing to make amends for failing to cooperate on the Crane biography the governor commented:

> I cannot express to you how grateful it is to my heart that at last even General Houston's late enemies have been compelled in deference to public opinion to publicly acknowledge his eminent abilities, patriotism, and public service.[50]

Others were also showing an interest in Sam Houston. *Harper's New Monthly Magazine* published an article called "Last Years of Sam Houston" written by George Paschal. It had been written partially to pay tribute to Houston, but also to answer the question often asked outside of Texas as to whether Houston was still alive. No doubt Margaret was pleased with the tribute to her: "[Houston's] widow is a sterling woman, who had greatly influenced and improved his later years. In his darkest hours, she had been his best adviser."[51]

Despite Margaret's disappointment over her husband's biography, there were happier times ahead in the Houston home. The house was always full of young people. The older girls had many gentlemen callers, and it wasn't long before wedding plans were being made. Both Nannie and Maggie were engaged. Nannie had often said that she would only marry a man who could pay the preacher in gold and take her on a honeymoon to Niagara Falls. Joseph Stiles Clay Morrow could do both. He owned a mercantile business in Georgetown, and he had met Nannie when he came to Independence on business.[52]

The marriage ceremony was conducted by Dr. Crane on August 1, 1866, in the little Baptist Church. There were six bridesmaids, and the wedding was described as one of the social events of the reconstruction era in Texas. The material for the wedding dress had been purchased in New Orleans, and Mrs. Crane made the gown, a white moire silk with real Valenciennes lace, which had been featured in a current magazine.[53] After the ceremony the guests walked the block to Margaret's home, where the Houston's fine linen and silver had been brought out for the reception. At the end of the party, Nannie sat down at her rosewood piano to play and sing "Sad Hour of Parting."[54] The couple then left on a wedding trip to New York and Washington, where they were entertained at the White House by President Andrew Johnson.[55]

A few months later, on October 17, 1866, Maggie became the bride of Weston Williams in a ceremony also presided over by Dr. Crane, but in a somewhat smaller celebration. Maggie and Wes settled on a plantation called Labadie, which was about fourteen miles from Independence.[56]

Margaret rejoiced over the happiness of her two oldest daughters. Apparently each girl, as Margaret herself had done twenty-five years before, had wedded her "choice." Their husbands would be a help to Margaret both emotionally and financially. She would depend on them during the last year of her life, and in her letters to her daughters she always sent her love to their husbands.

When the Morrows returned from their trip to the East, Nannie was expecting a baby. Margaret insisted that Nannie remain with her in Independence. On June 4, 1867, Margaret's first grandchild, Maggie Houston Morrow, was born. There would be many more grandchildren, but little Maggie would be the only one which Margaret would live to see. The Morrows begged Margaret to come live with them in their big house in Georgetown. Because she preferred living in her own home, and because she did not want to move that far away from Maggie, Margaret refused the offer. She did, however accept their offer to take the boisterous Andrew back with them to attend school in Georgetown.[57]

Andrew needed a positive male role model, and in Joe Morrow he found one. Margaret later wrote, "I am truly glad that Nannie feels such a maternal interest in my dear Andrew. I know you both will give him good advice."[58] Margaret gave her son some parting advice in the last known poem she ever wrote. It was entitled "To Andrew, His Mother's Farewell." In it, she seems to be aware that her days on earth were numbered, although she was just forty-eight years old.

> Farewell my boy, my darling boy,
>   I leave you in God's care
> By day and night, in grief or joy
>   He will be ever near.

When evening shadows fall again
  Thy mother will be gone,
Remember, Oh remember then
  That great and Holy one,

Who dwelleth in eternity
  Within that glorious light
Which mortal eye can never see,
  Undimmed by cloud or night. . . .

When gazing on the starry heavens
  Think of that home above,
Where dwell the spotless and forgiven
  And all is light and love.

There may we meet my precious child
  When life's sad scenes are o'er
And in the Blessed Savior's smile
  Rejoice forever more.[59]

In addition to his taking care of Andrew, Margaret also depended on Joe Morrow for financial and business advice. In the fall
of 1867, Sam had decided to attend medical school at the University
of Pennsylvania. Margaret was determined to find the money for his
tuition, but wrote Joe that she "had hard work to raise the money."
She had tried to mortgage her house, but when this failed she
rented Cedar Point to a Mr. Evans. A friend, George Davis, borrowed
two hundred dollars for Margaret on her verbal promise to pay it at
the end of the year. Margaret wrote Joe of her situation: "That
money must be paid, let the sacrifice be what it may. As yet I can
collect nothing, and I am in need of money. My house is ruining for
want of repairs. What shall I do?"[60] In the same letter, Margaret
requested that perhaps if Joe or Nannie could represent her
situation to George Baines, perhaps he would find a way to pay the
long overdue note for which Houston had once knocked off the
interest. She also told Joe that she had stopped one of his wagons

348

en route to Georgetown and had taken the liberty of appropriating two of his bacon sides. She explained that she had not paid for them "for the simple reason that I had not the money."

Margaret had another worry also. She was greatly concerned about Maggie, who had lost a baby and never regained her health. Margaret wrote to Nannie that her sister was "the mere shadow of herself."[61] Anxieties were compounded by an epidemic of the dread yellow fever which had first appeared in the port city of Indianola.[62] It was now spreading throughout Texas. Margaret sent Willie and Temple to Georgetown to be with Nannie, and she went to Labadie herself to take care of Maggie. From there she wrote Nannie that in an epidemic which claimed one hundred nine residents of Huntsville, "nearly all our friends have died of the yellow fever." Among them were Frances Evans, Mrs. Yoakum, Dr. Kittrell, and Dr. Keenan. Margaret described Labadie as a "pleasant quiet place," and she was not making immediate plans to leave there. She reported on what she had heard about the situation at Independence:

> . . . there is such a constant communication with Brenham that I do not think it safe. Fevers, too have originated in town which seemed very much like yellow fever, but the physicians know so little about it that they can not decide.[63]

Margaret wrote that she was anxious to see her grandchild, Nannie's "little darling," and felt that she could not bear to be away from her a day longer. She expressed her gratitude that all of her family were in good health:

> While the pestilence is sweeping around us the Lord seems to shield me and my dear ones from its breath. One in the far North, four in the pure air of Georgetown, and the rest spared even in the sight of the fearful doings. I am amazed at the Lord's goodness and mercy. Oh, Why am I so blessed while so many households are made desolate![64]

Margaret returned to Independence in November. The family made plans to gather in Georgetown for a Christmas holiday. Margaret wrote Maggie begging her to come early to Independence: "Do my darling come and stay with me just a little while. . . . We have all been so happy at home. The children are better than I ever saw them. Oh do come up right away."[65] Margaret did not tell Maggie of a strange occurrence which happened a few days before when she had awakened from a restless sleep. She apparently did tell Nettie: "I had the strangest dream last night. I thought I saw Ma standing at the foot of my bed, and she said, 'Margaret, in two weeks you will be with me.'"[66]

Within a few days Margaret developed the symptoms of yellow fever. Her frail body, which had so often fought off the ravages of malaria, asthma, and pneumonia, as well as surviving the tumor operation, could no longer sustain her. Nettie and Mary Willie frantically searched for a doctor, but one was not available. They watched helplessly as their mother weakened and slipped into a coma. On December 3, 1867, just two weeks after her strange dream, Margaret Lea Houston was dead at the age of forty-eight. Beside her bed was the book she had been reading, *An Alarm to Unconverted Sinners: In a Serious Treatise on Conversions* by Reverend Joseph Alleine.[67]

Because of the fear of contagion, there was no way that Margaret could be buried in the cemetery in Huntsville as she had always wished. There was not even time to open Nancy's vault. Margaret's servant Bingley was sent to dig a grave beside the vault, where Margaret was laid to rest as quickly as possible. Only Nettie, Mollie, Bingley, and another servant were present at the burial. There was not even a minister to perform the funeral service. A simple white headstone would later mark the grave of the woman who was twice First Lady of Texas.

Such was Margaret's influence that when Dr. Crane's book on Sam Houston was published nearly twenty years later, he respected her wishes about Houston's religious character. He also devoted one chapter to Margaret herself. In commenting on Margaret's personality, character, and influence on her husband's life, Dr.

Crane wrote what was perhaps the eulogy which he could not give at her funeral:

> As a woman, Mrs. Houston was as remarkable as was General Houston as a man. True to principle, firm in her convictions, spiritual in her ideas of religion, devoted to her husband and her children, she considered the strict performance of the great duties of domestic life as an achievement of moral heroism. The good of the land were always welcome to her fireside, and cordially entertained at her hospitable board. While thus absorbed in home duties, Mrs. Houston was busied with her pen; her private letters and her magazine contributions all being tinged with the one aim of her life; as the moral and religious guide of her children, and [as] the guardian angel of her husband's private and public life.[68]

---

[1] Franklin Williams Collection, Huntsville, Houston to Margaret, January 29, 1850.

[2] The Bible may be seen at the Sam Houston Memorial Museum, Huntsville, Texas.

[3] Mrs. Ike Barton McFarland, "All Texas Mourned Death of General Sam Houston," *Houston Press*, August 1, 1935.

[4] Ibid.

[5] "Monument to Gen. Sam Houston Erected by State of Texas," *Dallas Morning News*, April 22, 1911.

[6] Sam Houston, *Writings*, vol. 8, 348–09, An Editorial Appreciation of Houston, E. H. Cushing, July 29, 1863.

[7] Ibid.

[8] B. H. Carroll, "Scenes About the Grave of General Sam Houston," *Houston Chronicle*, April 22, 1911.

[9] Sam Houston, *Writings*, vol. 8, 339–40, Will of Sam Houston, April 2, 1863.

[10] Ibid.

[11] Ibid.

[12] Maye Wynne McFarland, "General Sam Houston and Young Sam's Confederate Record."

[13] Madge W. Hearne, family story.

[14] Houston Correspondence, Texas State Archives, Margaret to Sam Houston, Jr, October 15, 1863.

[15] Ashbel Smith Papers, Barker History Center, University of Texas, Margaret to Ashbel Smith, October 26, 1863.

[16] Sam Houston, *Writings,* vol. 8, 341–44, Inventory of the Estate of Sam Houston, December 2, 1863.

[17] R. E. McDonald Collection, Dallas, Texas, Margaret to Mary Willie Houston, November 16, 1863.

[18] Sam Houston Papers, Barker History Center, University of Texas, Margaret to Sam Houston, Jr., November 24, 1863.

[19] The house is now a museum in Independence.

[20] Madge W. Hearne and Marian W. Whittemore, family story quoting Maggie Houston.

[21] Hunt, 124.

[22] Franklin Williams Collection, Huntsville, Margaret to Sam Houston, Jr., January 6, 1864.

[23] Ibid.

[24] Sam Houston Papers, Barker History Center, University of Texas, Margaret to Sam Houston, Jr., January 18, 1864.

[25] Ibid., Margaret to Sam Houston, Jr., February 18, 1864.

[26] Ibid., Margaret to Sam Houston, Jr., February 16, 1864.

[27] Sam Houston Papers, Barker History Center, University of Texas, Maggie to Sam Houston, Jr., February 18, 1864.

[28] Franklin Williams Collection, Huntsville, Margaret to Sam Houston, Jr., May 30, 1864.

[29] Madge W. Hearne Papers, San Antonio, "The Southern Flag," n.d.

[30] Laura Simmons, *Out of Our Past,* (Waco: Texian Press, 1967), 58.

[31] Sam Houston Papers, Barker History Center, University of Texas, Sam Houston, Jr., to Margaret, April 11, 1864.

[32] Ibid., Margaret to Sam Houston, Jr., May 13, 1864.

[33] Franklin Williams Collection, Huntsville, Margaret to Sam Houston, Jr., May 30, 1864.

[34] Unpublished Correspondence, Sam Houston Papers, Barker History Center, University of Texas, Margaret to Sam Houston, Jr., July 1, 1864.

[35] Ibid., Margaret to Sam Houston, Jr., January 18, 1864.

[36] Ibid., Margaret to Sam Houston, Jr., July 1, 1864.

[37] Ibid., Margaret to Sam Houston, Jr., February 18, 1864.

[38] Houston Correspondence, Texas State Archives, Margaret to Sam Houston, Jr., July 9, 1864.

[39] Sam Houston Papers, Barker History Center, University of Texas, Sam Houston, Jr., to Margaret, July 5, 1864.

[40] Ibid., Sam Houston, Jr., to Margaret, August 15, 1864.

[41] Mae Wynne McFarland, "General Sam Houston and Young Sam's Confederate Record."

[42] Hunt, 125.

[43] Margaret Houston Album, an untitled poem, September 25, 1865.

[44] Crane, *Life and Select Literary Remains of Sam Houston of Texas*, 3-4.

[45] William Carey Crane Papers, Texas Collection, Baylor University, Waco, Texas. Crane to A. J. Hamilton, October 17, 1865.

[46] Crane, *Life and Select Literary Remains of Sam Houston of Texas*, 3.

[47] Madge W. Hearne, family story quoting Maggie Houston Williams.

[48] Executive Records, Register Book 281, 179, Texas State Archives, A. J. Hamilton to Margaret Houston, April 16, 1866.

[49] Hightower, *Houston Chronicle*, April 22, 1923. The current location of the pouch is unknown.

[50] Friend, 354.

[51] George W. Paschal, "Last Years of Sam Houston," *Harper's New Monthly Magazine*, April 1866, 630-635.

[52] Jennie Morrow Decker, family story.

[53] Mary Reid, "Fashions of the Texas Republic," *Southwestern Historical Quarterly*, 45 (January 1942): 250–51. The wedding dress is in the collection of the Sam Houston Memorial Museum, Huntsville. See also Murray, 236.

[54] Murray, 236.

[55] Mrs. S. L. Shipe, "Recollections: Mrs. Sam Houston," *Dallas Morning News* (Dallas, Texas), n.d.

[56] Madge W. Hearne Papers, San Antonio, notes by Madge W. Hearne, n,d, See also wedding notice exhibited in Independence Baptist Church Museum, Independence, Texas.

[57] Jennie Morrow Decker, family story.

[58] Sam Houston Papers, Barker History Center, Margaret to J. S. C. Morrow, September 3, 1867.

[59] Margaret Houston Album, n.d.

[60] Sam Houston Papers, Barker History Center, Margaret to J. S. C. Morrow, September 3, 1867.

[61] Ibid., Margaret to Nannie Morrow, October 2, 1867.

[62] D. W. C. Baker, *Texas Scrapbook*, (Austin: The Steck Company, 1935), 467.

[63] Sam Houston Papers, Barker History Center, Margaret to Nannie Morrow, October 2, 1867.

[64] Ibid.

[65] Ibid., Margaret to Maggie Williams, November 23, 1867.

[66] Marian Williams Whittemore, family story quoting Maggie Williams.

[67] Madison, 128, quoting a letter from Mary Willie Houston to Andrew Jackson Houston, January 15, 1868 (in the possession of Meredith Spangler).

[68] Crane, *Life and Select Literary Remains of Sam Houston of Texas*, 255.

Sam Houston, Jr., age 22, as a medical student at the University of Pennsylvania, Philadelphia, in 1868. Courtesy of Sam Houston Regional Library and Research Center, Liberty, Texas.

On July 1, 1864, Margaret wrote to Sam after receiving a "fine report" on him from his commanding officer in the Confederate Army, "I do thank my Heavenly Father with my whole heart that he has given me such a son." On September 3, 1867, she wrote Joe Morrow that, although she was in a financial bind, Sam's tuition "must be paid, let the sacrifice be what it may."

Independence home of Margaret Lea, where she died December 3, 1867.
Courtesy of Texas Baptist Historical Center Museum, Independence, Texas.

On September 3, 1867, Margaret wrote her son-in-law, Joseph Morrow, of
her financial troubles: "As yet, I can collect nothing, and I am in sad need
of money. My house is ruining for want of repairs."

Independence home of Nancy Lea where she died February 16, 1864, at the age of 84. The woman in this photo, taken before 1900, is probably the Houston servant who was allowed to live in the home until it was torn down. Courtesy of Madora McCrocklin, Independence, Texas, and the Texas Baptist Historical Center Museum, Independence, Texas.

A neighbor said of Nancy a few years before she died: "The most lively imagination could not portray the early pioneer or the first settler more satisfactory to the mind's eye than was presented in the person of this old lady." [Mrs. S. Shipe. *Sunday Supplement*, 1905.]

Epilogue

Margaret Lea Houston was an inspiration to her children during her lifetime, and in death she left a void in a closely knit family. Some years later a biographer would write of her:

> In her maternal relations Mrs. Houston displayed qualities of surpassing power and tenderness through which she inspired in her children sentiments of profound reverence and affection. They never felt the power; they knew only the love that guided them. . . . All through [her] life her children counseled with her as a friend and sought her advice.[1]

Nannie and Maggie saw to it that the younger children were cared for. Joe Morrow, as executor of her estate, took care of all the business matters. He and Nannie remained in Georgetown and raised the younger Houston sons, who at the time of Margaret's death were thirteen, nine, and seven years old. Maggie and Weston Williams purchased Margaret's home from her estate, and Nettie and Mary Willie lived with them while going to school in Independence. Sam married and raised a family, but after his wife died he returned to Independence and made his home with Maggie until his death.

The faithful Eliza divided her remaining years between Nannie and Maggie, helping to raise Margaret's children, as she had promised so long ago, as well as the many Houston grandchildren that were arriving. No matter which sister she was with, she longed for contact with the other. Since she could not write, she had to depend on others to send letters for her. A few years before Eliza's death, Nannie wrote to Maggie, apologizing for her own weakness when it came to writing letters:

She did not come right out and ask me, for she had great sympathy with my weakness, but she "hinted around" until I did not have the heart to remain obtuse! Aunt Eliza could not be more devoted to your interest if you were her own child, and it would be downright cruelty if someone did not write for her. Often I think of a remark which dear Wes made about her—that "she was an example to all of us." She never forgets the comfort or fancies of any one and is a mother to everything on the place.[2]

The Houston children were also devoted to Eliza. Maggie had moved to Houston after Weston's death, so Eliza was with the Williams family when she became seriously ill. The physician indicated to Maggie that there was no hope of recovery. While Eliza was still conscious, Maggie held her aged hand and told her that she was going on a long journey and she would not be coming back.

Eliza answered that she understood because her feet had "already touched the chilly water of the Jordan." She then asked if she could be buried in the little family plot at Independence beside the mistress she had so loved. Maggie promised that this would be done. Eliza died on March 9, 1898. She was taken to Independence and buried beside the former First Lady of Texas, with her "family" attending. Margaret's children placed a marker on her grave.[3] It reads, "Aunt Eliza—Faithful unto Death."

Maggie and Wes Williams lived in Margaret's home in Independence for many years, and all five of their children were born there. The house remained in the Williams family until 1983 when it was sold to Frankie and Gene Slaughter of Houston. The Slaughters lovingly restored the old home and opened it as a museum in 1986.[4] Nancy Lea's home gradually deteriorated and was finally torn down in the early 1900s. The land where it stood is still owned by Maggie's descendants. Across the street, the little Baptist Church is still in use today, with a flag marking the Houston pew. Nancy's bell may be viewed there in the museum next to the church.

Nothing remains of the Cedar Point or Raven Hill homes, but the homes in Huntsville have been preserved. On May 3, 1929, through the efforts of the students and faculty of the Sam Houston

State Normal College, the Woodland Home was opened as a museum.[5] In 1936, as part of the celebration of the Texas Centennial, the Steamboat House where Houston died was moved to the same location, and a handsome brick museum was added to the site.[6] Houston family members began to donate artifacts to the complex.

For many years the simple tombstone purchased by Margaret Houston was the only one that marked Sam Houston's grave in Oakwood Cemetery. Over forty years after his death, the state of Texas raised the money for a suitable monument, and invited William Jennings Bryan to be the speaker when it was put in place. On April 21, 1911, the seventy-fifth anniversary of the battle of San Jacinto, thousands gathered at the gravesite for a ceremony described by a reporter as having all the "pomp and ceremony becoming an occasion of such magnitude." In deep contrast with the day on which Houston was laid to rest, "The day was fitting in every particular, the sun shone bright and there was not one single circumstance to mar the splendor of the undertaking."[7]

On the front of the imposing granite monument designed by the sculptor Pompeo Coppini, is a quotation from Andrew Jackson: "The world will take care of Houston's fame." On the side facing the grave is an inscription written by Nettie Houston Bringhurst in which she paraphrased what Margaret had written so long ago in the family Bible. It reads:

A brave Soldier, a fearless statesman
A great orator, a pure patriot
A faithful friend, a loyal citizen
A devoted husband and father
A consistent Christian and honest man

After making his speech at the gravesite, William Jennings Bryan was so moved that he agreed to give his famous "Prince of Peace" lecture at Sam Houston Normal School at no charge. With the proceeds, the students paid all debts on the Woodland home, which had been purchased by the history classes, and gave clear title to the state.[8]

Plans were discussed during the Texas Centennial for moving Margaret's grave to Huntsville. As the only surviving Houston child, Andrew Houston was much in favor of it. Most of the grandchildren agreed, as one of Maggie's daughters wrote, that in this instance the only object of the Texas Centennial Commission was to honor Margaret: "[The Commission] felt that as Houston was receiving so many honors they would beautifully assist [Margaret] in sharing them." However, one grandson was strongly opposed to the move, and the Commission could not agree on a decision.[9]

So Margaret's grave remained at Independence. At some undocumented point in time Nancy Lea's stone vault began to crumble. Her coffin was removed and buried beside Margaret. The Houston descendants continued to contribute funds toward the care of the small cemetery, worried that with the city of Independence fast disappearing, future generations might forget the little cemetery.[10]

Margaret was not forgotten, although it would be almost ninety-eight years after her death before a tribute and eulogy was delivered at her grave. On May 15, 1965, a ceremony was held as an official State Historic Monument and a roadside marker were unveiled at the graveyard. No doubt Margaret Lea Houston would have preferred to sleep through eternity beside her beloved husband, but one can not help but feel that she would be pleased with the marker placed at her grave to honor both her and her mother. It reads: "Women of character, culture and staunch devotion to their families and church, each in her own way greatly influenced the career of Sam Houston and the course of Texas history."

---

[1] Elizabeth Brooks, *Prominent Women of Texas*, (Akron, Ohio: Werner Company, 1896), 1415.
[2] Madge W. Hearne Papers, San Antonio, Nannie Morrow to Maggie Williams, July 29, 1891.
[3] Madge W. Hearne, family story.
[4] Frankie Slaughter in conversation with the author, March 1, 1986.
[5] Ruth Garrison Francis, "Sam Houston's Home Now State Museum," *The Dallas Morning News*. May 5, 1929.
[6] C. C. Springfield, "Sam Houston's Home at Huntsville"

[7] "A Monument to Houston," *The Houston Post,* April 22, 1911.
[8] Jean Houston Baldwin Collection, Sam Houston Regional Library, Liberty, an untitled clipping from *The Houston Post,* January 15, 1933.
[9] Madge W. Hearne Papers, San Antonio. Madge W. Hearne to Andrew Jackson Houston, January 5, 1938.
[10] Ibid.

Aunt Eliza with the Williams family shortly before her death in 1898.
Photograph in the possession of the author.

Clockwise from Eliza: Sam Houston Hearne, Madge W. Hearne, Franklin
Williams, Marian Williams, Royston Williams, Maggie Houston Williams,
and Houston Williams.

Eliza had asked to be buried in Independence next to Margaret. This was
done, and her tombstone reads "Faithful until death."

1 Ruins of Nancy Lea's house
2 Graves of Mrs. Houston & Mrs. Lea
3 Original tomb of Mrs. Lea

Ruins of Nancy Lea's house and graves of Nancy Lea and Margaret Houston, circa 1900. Courtesy of the Texas Baptist Historical Center Museum, Independence, Texas.

Nancy Lea was buried, according to her wishes, where she could hear the sound of "her bell." Today a marker at the gravesite describes Margaret and Nancy as "women of character, culture, and staunch devotion to their families and church. Each in her own way greatly influenced the career of Sam Houston and the course of Texas history."

Nettie Houston, January 16, 1873, shortly before her twenty-first birthday. Courtesy of Sam Houston Regional Library and Research Center, Liberty, Texas.

In a poem entitled "Our Daughters," written March 14, 1856, Margaret wrote:

> My beauteous gifts, how carefully
> Their tender branches I must train
> That each fair plant on earth may be
> a household joy! . . .

Andrew Jackson Houston, about age 18, while a cadet at West Point, circa 1872. Courtesy of Sam Houston Regional Library and Research Center, Liberty, Texas.

As his father had earlier predicted, Andrew grew up to be quite a teller of stories. On June 12, 1858, Houston had written Margaret, "Andrew has a turn for drollery and will, I am fearful, be an anecdotist."

William Rogers Houston, about age 6, circa 1864. Courtesy of Sam Houston Regional Library and Research Center, Liberty, Texas.

Temple Lea Houston, about age 4, circa 1864. Courtesy of Sam Houston Regional Library and Research Center, Liberty, Texas.

On January 18, 1864, Margaret wrote to Sam, Jr.: "Willie and Temple are the sweetest little companions for me in the world. They are such perfect opposites that it makes their conversation very spicy and interesting."

A painting of Margaret Houston commissioned after her death by Nannie
Houston Morrow. Original in the possession of Mrs. E. A. Everitt, Houston,
Texas. Courtesy of Sam Houston Regional Library and Research Center,
Liberty, Texas.

Appendixes

THE ESTATE OF MARGARET HOUSTON
(From the Washington County Probate Records, 1868.)

Inventory and Appraisement of the Real and Personal Property and Effects of the Estate of Mrs. M. M. Houston, dec'd made this the 7th day of February A. D. 1868 by J. C. S. Morrow, Administrator, and by George B. Davis, George Breedlove, and Thos. W. Morriss, Appraisers.

Real Estate in Washington County
Thirty nine (39) Acres Land & improvements lying in the west limits of the town of Independence near "Baylor Female College" better known as the "Hines' Homestead": @ $25 per acre   975.00

Fifty (50) Acres and improvements, lying near or adjacent to the South West limits of the town of Independence @ $20 per Acre   1000.00

Forty (40) Acres timbered land unimproved, a portion of the "Hines" timbered survey @ $7 per Acre   280.00

One Block—No. 22 and improvements in the town of Independence
                    500.00

Lots No. 3, 4, & 5 in Block No. 4 in the town of Independence—"Mrs. Houston's Homestead"   2000.00

Personal Property

One Ambulance & Harness @	150.00
Two Mules @ $100 each	200.00
Five Bureaus each @ $8	40.00
Two Wash Stands each @ $3	6.00
Six small Tables each @ $2.50	15.00
Two Ottomans each @ $1	2.00
Two Heavy Bedsteads each @ $10	20.00
Two Light Pine Bedsteads each @ $5.00	10.00
Seven Matrasses [sic] each @ $6.00	42.00
One Small Matrass [sic] @	3.00
One Spring Mattrass [sic] @	15.00
Four Feather Beds each @ $20.00	80.00
Ten Feather Pillows each @ $1.50	15.00
Four Feather Bolsters each @ $2.50	10.00
Five Bed Quilts each @ $5.00	25.00
Seventeen White Counterpanes each @ $3.00	51.00
Five Prs. Bed Blankets each Pr. @ $7.50	37.50
Nine Bed Sheets each @ $2.00	18.00
Five White Linen Table Cloths each @ $2.00	10.00
Nine Pillow cases each @ $.30	2.70
Five Split Bottom Chairs each @ $1.00	5.00
Four Hide Bottom Chairs each @ $1.00	4.00
Fourteen Cane Bottom Chairs each @ $.75	10.50
Three Shuck Bottom Chairs each @ $1.00	3.00
One Hide Bottom Rocking Chair @	3.00
Two Large Glass [blurred] Stands each @ $5.00	10.00
Three Basins each @ $2.00	6.00
One Set Table Ware @	30.00
One Bathing Tub @	3.00
One Library @	200.00
Two Wardrobes each @ $5.00	10.00
One Large Round Dining Table @	8.00
One Large Pine Dining Table @	4.00
One set Cooking Utensils, Tubes, etc. @	30.00

Two Parlor Sofas each @ $10.00	20.00
Four Parlor Chairs — damaged each @ $1.00	4.00
One parlor Rocking Chair @	5.00
One Parlor Centre Table @	25.00
One Seat Matting @	8.00
One set about 4000 Shingles @	40.00
One Plain "Silver Service" consisting of the following articles: One Silver Coffee Pot, Two Silver Tea Pots, One Silver Sugar Bowl, One Silver Castor Complete & one Silver Cream Pitcher, One Silver Slop Bowl, all @	500.00
Two Plated Silver Tea Pots, One Plated Silver Sugar Bowl, & One Plated Silver Cream Pitcher @	30.00
One Plain Silver Cup	12.00
One Plain Silver travelling Water Cup @	8.00
One Pr. Silver Sugar Tongs, Eleven Silver Table Spoons, Twelve Silver Dessert Spoons, Nine heavy Silver Tea Spoons, Six light Silver Tea Spoons, and Twelve four pronged Silver Forks	150.00
One Pr. Ear Rings @	5.00
One Silver Spectacle Case	5.00
One Santa Anna Gold Snuff Box	125.00
One Gold Watch Buckle & Key @	200.00
One Pr. Gold Spectacles	25.00
One Pr. Gold Eye Glasses @	8.00
One Gold Pen & Pencil Combined @	8.00
One gold [blurred]	2.00
One Gold Ring without Set	3.00
One chain of Gold Lumps @	50.00
One Breast Pin Set with hair & Rubies in Gold @	15.00
One Gentleman's Gold Breast Pin @	6.00
One harp Breast Pin @	3.00
One Silver Knee Buckle Set with Brilliants	2.00
Amount Brought Over	$7,097.70

List of Notes due the Estate E. W. Cave—note
date July 1st 1867, due at $600 at 10% int.—in
hands of G. B. Davis as a lateral security for $700.00
Credit on above note Jany 30th, 1868 103.27
E. W. Cave—Note date July 1st 1867, due at
9 mos. at 10% int. for 700.00
Credit on above note Jany 30th 1868 361.11
E. W. Cave—Note date July 1st 1867, due at
12 months at 10% inst. for 700.00
G. W. Baines—Note date Jany 1st 1858, payable
on demand to Sam Houston at 8% int for 300.00
Credit on above note, August 20th 1867 100.00
H. Clark—Note date Dec. 1st 1865 at 10%
int due Jany 1st 1866 for 628.20
January credits on above Note leaving bal.
due September 1st 1867 271.07
Reason Brown & John Stribling—note date
April 20th 1867 due Dec 1st 67 for 105.00

The State of Texas
Washington County
    We the undersigned appraisers do solemnly swear that the foregoing inventory is a just and fair valuation and appraisement of the Real and Personal Property belonging to the "Estate of Mrs. M. M. Houston, dec'd" to the best of our knoweledge [sic] & belief.
    F. W. Morriss
    George W. Breedlove} Appraisers
    G. B. Davis

Same to be subscribed before
me A. D. the 8th day of Feby 1868
Ashbury Daniel J. P. W Cty

372

DESCENDANTS OF SAM AND MARGARET HOUSTON

(Compiled by A. R. Teasdale, Jr., Dallas, Texas.)

I. Sam Houston, Jr., married Lucy Anderson
   Margaret Bell Houston m. Mark L. Kauffman
      Katrina Kauffman
   Nettie Houston
   Harry H. Houston m. Mary Edna Davis
II. Nancy Elizabeth Houston m. Joseph Clay Stiles Morrow
   Margaret Houston Morrow m. Robert Alexander John
      Alfred Morgan John m. Grace Spaulding Keehnel
      Marguerite Eleanor John m. Lester R. Ford
         Lester Randolph Ford, Jr.
         Margaret Houston Ford
      Jean Houston John m. Franklin Thomas Baldwin
         Jean Houston Baldwin m. Marion Price Daniel
            Marion Price Daniel, Jr., m. (1)Dianne Wommack
            Thomas Houston Daniel
               m. (2) Vickie Carroll Moore
            Franklin Baldwin Daniel
            Marion Price Daniel
            Jean Houston Daniel m. David Murph
               Marilyn Jean Murph
               Daniel William Murph
            Houston Lea Daniel m. Charlotte Whitehurst
               Timothy Houston Daniel
               John Price Daniel
            John Baldwin Daniel
         Franklin Thomas Baldwin, Jr.,
            m. Marion Frances Scheider
            Susan Jean Baldwin
            Sally Ann Baldwin
            Franklin Thomas Baldwin III

Robert John Baldwin m. Gloria Van Pelt Abbott
    Robert John Baldwin, Jr.
    Franklin Terry Baldwin
    Margie Clare Baldwin m. (1)Thomas R. Jennings
        Martha Jean Jennings m. M. Neal Guentzel
            Amy Elizabeth Guentzel
            Neal Andrew Guentzel
            Gary Robert Guentzel
        Mary Frances Jennings
            James Scott McMahon
            William David McMahon
                m. (2) James G. Sargent
        Margaret Ann Sargent
    Jack Lea Baldwin
    Frances Elizabeth Baldwin m. Dudley Bryon Foy, Jr.
        Elizabeth Anne Foy
        Dudley Bryon Foy III
Ruth Elizabeth John m. Elbert E. Seale
    Margaret John Seale m. Wayne A. Hodges
        John Gordon Hodges
    Elbert E. Seale Jr.
Isabel Mary John m. Griffith Conrad Evans
    Griffith Conrad Evans, Jr., m. Arlene Westbo Callahan
    George William Evans II
    Robert John Evans
Roberta Alexander John m. Edward Leslie Hogan
    Edward Leslie Hogan, Jr.
    Robert John Hogan
    Anne Houston Hogan m. William Mitchell Irish IV
        William Mitchell Irish V
        Kathryn Anne Irish m. John Patrick Scott
            Mary Elyse Scott
        John Rommel Irish
Rose Stuart John
Edward Brooks John m. Maude Evelyn Boyd
    Edward Brooks John, Jr.

Bettie Ann John m. William H. Schoellkopf
Kathleen Schoellkopf m. Paul Mauceli, Jr.
Terry Schoellkopf
Larry Schoellkopf
Dorothy Elben John
Katherine Lea John
George O'Brien John m. Rowena MacLaughlin
Elisabeth Loe John m. Paul Strong
Emily Preston Morrow m. Davis E. Decker
Stiles Morrow Decker m. Madeleine G. Loomis
Stiles Morrow Decker Jr. m. Lucie Randolph Smith
Randolph Morrow Decker
Joel Porter Decker
Joel Porter Lomis Decker
Jennie Belle Morrow m. Davis E. Decker
Margaret John Decker m. (1) Evan Peter Aurand
Evan Peter Aurand m. Patricia Riley
Margaret Lucille Aurand m. Terrence Keith Young
Dennis Houston Young
Peter Aurand Young
Henry Spiese Aurand Jr. m. Marietta Elizabeth Wade
Evan Peter Aurand II m. Claudie Kueker
Kevan Houston Aurand
Melissa Wade Aurand
m. (2) Jerry Everitt
Preston Perry Morrow m. Viola Louise Thompson
Louis Gleason Morrow m. Geraldine Arden
Dale Preston Morrow m. Carol Hooper
Steven Dale Morrow
Glen Robert Morrow
Emma Louise Morrow m. Franklin Donald Rose
Elizabeth Ann Rose
Susan Carol Rose
Charlotte Elizabeth Morrow m. Larue Ruston Rice
Joseph Thompson Morrow m. Adelheid (Heidi) Shroeder
Temple Houston Morrow m. Frances Augusta Carl

Carl Houston Morrow m. Nelle Larue Tillery
Houston Lee Morrow m. Barbara Alice Wood
Michael Houston Chadwick Morrow
Stephany Ann Morrow m. Bryan Scott Gill
Ann Frances Morrow
Nancy Larue Morrow m. James Rollo Edwards
Robert Karl Edwards
Otho Cecil Morrow m. Mary Frances Harrison
Temple Stuart Morrow m. Eunice Nadine Shelton
Carl Dickson Morrow m. Joan Rutter
Connie Lea Morrow m. Gregory Loy Maze
Brenda Ann Morrow m. Karl Eric Meynig
Temple Houston Morrow, Jr.
Frances Earl Morrow m. (1) Eugene Gary Potter
Eugene Gary Potter, Jr., (adopted by his step-father and
took the name Gene Gary Clement) m. Marilyn Boydstun
m. (2) Walter Carl Clement
Robert Mark Clement
Pamela Lucille Clement
Carl Scott Clement
Elizabeth Paxton Morrow m. Gail Hamilton Loe
Robert Houston Loe
Dorothy Elisabeth Loe
III. Margaret Lea Houston m. Weston Layfayette Williams
Sam Houston Williams
Madge Houston Williams m. Roy White Hearne
Sam Houston Hearne m. Eleanor Louis Woolford
Marian Weston Hearne m. Clarence Eugene Thornall
Madge Houston Thornall m. Charles Stanley Roberts
Catherine Lea Roberts m. Bryce Jacobson
Brett Houston Jacobson
Charles Randall Roberts
Nancy Lea Thornall m. William Joseph Burch
Duncan Kyle Burch
Andrew Wesley Burch
Bonnie Lea Burch

Penny Thornall m. (1) Lynn Hughes
Lindsey Lea Hughes
m. (2) David Remick
David Royston Remick
Franklin Weston Williams m. Annie McKeever
James Joseph McKeever Williams
Charlotte Gynne Williams m. James Andrew Darby
James Andrew Darby Jr. m. Holly Harrison Willis
McKeever Andrew Darby
Weston Willis Darby
Anne McKeever Darby m. Jay Ralston Kennett
Joanne Gynne Kennett
James Ralston Kennett
Richard Joseph Kennett
Charlotte Zue Darby m. John Stanley Taylor
Darby Anne Taylor
Emily Gynne Taylor
James Royston Williams m. Stella Root
Marian Lea Williams m. Claire R. Whittemore
IV. Mary Willie Houston m. J. S. Morrow (cousin of J. S. C. Morrow)
John Houston Morrow m. Ada Maie Griffin
Meredith Houston Morrow m. Henry Claypool Madison
Henry Claypool Madison, Jr. m. Paulette Louise Ayres
John Morrow Madison
Lara Louise Madison
Andrew Temple Morrow
Margaret Mary Morrow
Maude Louise Morrow m. J. B. Heitchew
Houston Heitchew
Jesse Lea Morrow m. Robert E. McDonald
Mary Louise McDonald m. Arthur Robert Teasdale, Jr.
Margaret Lea Teasdale m. Howard Houston Harley
Teresa Jean Teasdale m. Dennis Michael Young
Matthew Houston Young
Lisabeth Su Teasdale m. Kirk Charles Dallas
Bryce Caulfield Dallas

Collier Teasdale Dallas
Margaret Lea McDonald
V. Antoinette Power Houston m. William Bringhurst
Sam Houston Bringhurst
Charles Raguet Bringhurst
William Stuart Bringhurst
Nettie Houston Bringhurst m. Frank Bush
Margaret Lea Bush
Anna Katherine Bringhurst
VI. Andrew Jackson Houston m. (1) Carrie Glenn Purnell
Ariadne Houston
Marguerite Houston
Carrie Marie Houston
m. (2) Elizabeth Hart Good
Josephine A. Houston m. David Augustus Paulus
David Augustus Paulus, Jr.
Elizabeth Houston Paulus
Anne Cyrene Paulus m. John Pritchett Smith
David Hill Smith m. Roberta Rudat
Brenda Dawn Smith m. Jeffery Charles Tomek
Rosanne Smith
Catherine Q. Paulus m. John Benjamin Hightower
John Buckner Hightower m. Judith Ann Bagley
Christopher Paulus Hightower
Elizabeth Ann Hightower m. (1) William C. Bennett
Jeffery Todd Bennett
Stacy Lynn Bennett
m. (2) Dan Theodore Stathos III
Dan Theodore Stathos IV
Andrew Houston Paulus
Josephine Vaughn Paulus m. William Bankhead Hotchkiss
Nancy Vaughn Hotchkiss m. Jimmy Burch Aston, Jr.
Jennifer Elizabeth Aston
Amy Gail Aston
Charles William Hotchkiss m. Marcia Jane Love
Mary Majorie Paulus m. (1) Francis McDougal

(2) Franklin Murray
John Franklin Murray
Pam Murray
VII. William Rogers Houston (died unmarried)
VIII. Temple Lea Houston m. Laura Cross
Temple Lea Houston, Jr., m. Ivy Nichols
Sam Houston III m. Ruth Helen Nilson
Margaret Theresa Houston
Laura Helen Houston m. Virgil Hannafious
Gary Allan Hannafious
Houston Lee Hannafious
Eleanor Lea Houston
Sam Houston IV m. Virginia Rose Mikeska
Stephen Ray Houston m. Jean Anne Fowler
Andrew Scott Houston
Kevin Mark Houston
Temple Houston
Richard Coldon Houston m. Elizabeth Richardson
Richard Douglas Houston
Mary Houston m. Ivol Burnham
Laura Louise Burnham m. Gordon William Johnson
Gordon Howell Johnson
Susan Lynn Johnson
Carl Houston Burnham
Ivol Eugene Burnham

GENEALOGY OF THE LEA AND HOUSTON FAMILIES

LEA FAMILY GENEALOGY:

Temple Lea	b. November 9, 1773	d. January 28, 1834
m. Nancy Moffett	b. May 1, 1780	d. February 7, 1864

Children of Temple and Nancy Lea:

I. Martin Lea   b. June 27, 1799   d. March 26, 1843
    m. Opphia Kennon
    Children:
    1. Robertus   b. 1834
    2. William Jones   b. 1836
    3. Henry Clinton   b. 1838

II. Varilla or Virilla Lea   b. November 17, 1801   d. Dec. 22,1881
    m. Robertus Royston
    Children:
    1. Young Royston   b. 1819
    2. Robert Royston   b. 1824
    3. Sarah Ann   b. 1825 (married James Power)
    4. Serena Royston   b. 1827
    5. Neantha Royston   b. 1829
    6. Martin Royston   b. 1834

III. Henry Clinton Lea   b. October 7, 1804   d. November 7, 1854
    m. Serena Rootes   b. October 5, 1808
    Children
    1. Lucy Ann Lea   b. November 10, 1830
    2. Sumpter Lea   b. February 26, 1835
    3. Martin Lea   b. September 16, 1838
    4. Henry C. Lea   b. 1841
    5. Martha J. Lea   b. April 6, 1844
    6. Mary W. Lea   b. April 7, 1849

IV. Vernal Lea   b. June 26, 1816   d. December 17, 1852
    m. Catherine Davis Goodall
    Children:
    1. Temple Lea   b. July 3, 1847   d. April 13, 1853
    2. Margaret Lea   b. March 6, 1849   d. January 19, 1872
    3. James V. Lea   b. January 12, 1851
    4. Marie   b. September 20, 1852

V. Margaret Moffett Lea   b. April 11, 1819   d. December 3, 1867
    m. Sam Houston May 9, 1840
    Children:
    1. Sam Houston, Jr.   b. May 25, 1843   d. May 20, 1894
       m. Lucy Anderson
    2. Nancy Elizabeth   b. Sept. 6, 1846   d. March 6, 1926
       m. Joseph C. S. Morrow
    3. Margaret Lea   b. April 13, 1848   d. March 12, 1906
       m. Weston Lafayette Williams
    4. Mary William   b. April 9, 1850   d. Dec. 14, 1931
       m. J. S. Morrow (a cousin of Joseph C. S. Morrow)
    5. Antoinette Power   b. January 20, 1852   d. Dec. 5, 1932
       m. William Bringhurst
    6. Andrew Jackson   b. June 21, 1854   d. June 26, 1941
       m. Carrie Glenn Purnell
       m. Elizabeth Hart Good
    7. William Rogers   b. June 25, 1858   d. March 8, 1920
    8. Temple Lea   b. August 12, 1860   d. August 15, 1905

VI. Antoinette Power Lea   b. February 10, 1822   d. January 24, 1891
    m. William Bledsoe
    m. Charles Power
    Children:
    1. Thomas R. Power   b. January 26, 1848   d. Dec. 23, 1878
    2. Margaret Houston   b. September 17, 1852 d. August 26, 1854
    3. Emily Antoinette (Lillie)
                b. January 13, 1859   d. August 17, 1873

HOUSTON FAMILY GENEALOGY:

Children of Samuel and Elizabeth Paxton Houston:
I.   Paxton (died young; never married)
II.   Robert (officer in U. S. Army; never married)
III.   James (merchant in Blount County, Tennessee)
IV.   John (lived in Memphis, Tennessee)
V.   Sam (married Eliza Allen; Margaret Lea)
VI.   William (married Mary Ball of Kentucky)
VII.   Isabella (died young)
VIII. Mary (married Matthew Wallace; William Wallace)
IX.   Eliza (married S. A. Moore; moved to Texas)

Appendix D

THE WOODLAND HOME, HUNTSVILLE, TEXAS

Mrs. W. A. Leigh, who was the daughter of a Houston neighbor, Dr. W. A. Rawlings, knew the Houston family and was a frequent guest at the Woodland home. In 1935 she drew a map of the grounds and wrote a description of Margaret's flower gardens. Both are now at the Sam Houston Memorial Museum in Huntsville, Texas.

> Extending east and west were flower beds, on which grew Flags beside the fence. Jonquils, narcissi, Easter flowers [were] on the borders. A short distance from the gate, on the east, there was a pomegranate bush, about equal distance another pomegranate bush. The flower bed on the west was similarly adorned.

> A broad walk [led] from the front gate to the entrance of the house. On either side of this were flower beds, two on each side separated by a narrow walk. On each corner of the square beds grew a myrtle; between the myrtles grew Purple Lilacs. Within the squares [were] Roses and on the borders Jonquils, Narcissi, Easter flowers.

Mrs. Mae Wynne McFarland, who also grew up in Huntsville, added a note below Mrs. Leigh's description: "It also had some single hyacinths—white and blue and a clump of flowering almond."

MAP OF HOUSTON'S WOODLAND HOME, HUNTSVILLE, TEXAS as it was when they lived there
(From a diagram drawn by Mrs. W. A. Leigh)

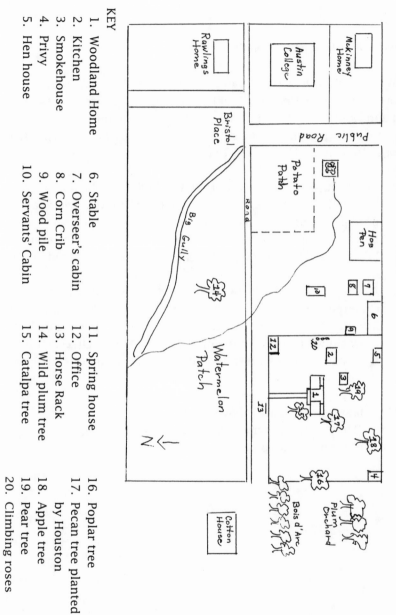

KEY

1. Woodland Home
2. Kitchen
3. Smokehouse
4. Privy
5. Hen house
6. Stable
7. Overseer's cabin
8. Corn Crib
9. Wood pile
10. Servants' Cabin
11. Spring house
12. Office
13. Horse Rack
14. Wild plum tree
15. Catalpa tree
16. Poplar tree
17. Pecan tree planted by Houston
18. Apple tree
19. Pear tree
20. Climbing roses

A SELECTION OF POEMS BY MARGARET HOUSTON
(From her Album of Poems, Verses, and Diary Entries, now in the possession of Mary Willie's granddaughter, Meredith Spangler, of El Paso, Texas.)

Shortly before her marriage in 1840, Margaret wrote this poem to her
cousin, Sarah Ann Royston, expressing her feelings about leaving Alabama
to make her home in Texas:

To Sarah Ann

Sweet girl, whenever of early days
I muse, and recollections roam
O'er merry childhood's sunlit ways,
'Tis then thy gentle image comes

And point[s] to many a well loved scene,
Far—far removed, but ne'er forgot,
The mount, the stream, the rustic green,
To each prefixed some hallowed spot.

Come hither, let us speak once more,
Of those sweet hours that came to past [sic],
Like fairy dreams, that glimmered o'er
Our paths each brighter than the last.

Ah me! those joyous hours are gone,
And with them many a cherished friend
And now the hour is hastening on
That other ties as dear shall rend.

Yes, I must leave the household band
That e'en in childhood loved me well.
Far—far within the stranger's land,
Midst unfamiliar scenes to dwell.

And yet the beauteous West I love
O'er its broad plains bedecked with flowers
Of glowing buds, the wild deer rove
And sleep within its moonlit bowers.

Farewell e'en now my spirit sighs
To wander where the "Lone Star's" light —
Gleams out from the pure cerulean skies
And gilds a land of verdure bright!

A Poem written January 28, 1841, and sent to her husband.

Musings

Oh I would linger yet awhile
Upon the green earth's shore.
The stream of death is dark and wild
Its dismal waters roar.

Yet in my heart that scene of gloom
No terror can awake,
Nor is it earth with all its bloom
That draws my spirit back.

No, there's an eye that fondly beams
Upon me in my sleep,
A form beloved that haunts my dreams
I think on him and weep.

Oh I would linger with him yet,
Who knows the dark snares now
That may his lonely path beset
The grief, the tearless woe!

Yes I would linger yet awhile
His lonely heart to cheer,

And break the artful tempter's wile
That would his soul ensnare.

On July 12, 1849, Margaret recorded in her album this poem called
"Truth," which reveals many of her religious convictions and ideals.

Truth

There is a star, whose Heavenly ray,
The spirit doth illume,
Its light direct from endless day,
Dispels the deepest gloom.

Dark errors, spectres of the mind
Before its brightness flee,
And tho'ts and passions unrefined
Conscience amazed doth see.

This is the star that ever throws,
Its radiance o'er that way,
Which brighter and yet brighter grows,
Unto the perfect day.

Impartially, its light doth fall
Upon the sons of earth.
It gilds the rich man's pictured wall
And cheers the cottage hearth.

The prisoner in his dungeon lone,
Its piercing ray hath found.
The monarch, on his glittering throne,
Hath humbly bowed him down.

The light of truth! 'tis that which throws
Its beams o'er youth and age,
O'er small and great, the light which glows
Upon the sacred page.

Yes, and this orb of heavenly day
Shall rise in luster bright,
Where e're the sun with gladdening ray
Dispels the shades of night.

The knowledge of the Lord shall fill
The earth, with joy and peace.
O'er forest wild and vale and hill,
Dark Error's reign shall cease.

Margaret's poetry often reflected a love of nature and its effect on her life. The following poem was written in Huntsville on April 15, 1856:

To the Whip-poor-will

Thou'rt come again thou lone night-bird,
Whose mournful song is never heard
Until the balmy spring hath breathed
Upon the waking earth and wreathed
The cottage door and woodland bower
With many a smiling bud and flower.

Thou recluse of the feathered throng
Dost never mingle thou [sic] sad song,
With those sweet carols of the grove
That breathe of joy and hope and love.
A spirit of the darksome wood,
Thou seemest in thy solitude.

Each morn the mock-bird's joyous lay
With cheerful welcome greets the day,
But silent is thou [sic] gloomy tone,
Until the fleet-winged day is gone.
Wouldest tell us by that mournful cry
That shortly, spring's sweet bloom must die?

Soon doth the heart that lesson learn,
And oft-times feel as 'twere the urn
Of blighted hopes and withered flowers,
Yet quickly through the spring time hours,
With all their beauteous dreams depart.
Their sunshine still within the heart

May linger till the winter's snow
Falls softly o'er the careworn brow,
And many a night-bird's mournful tone
Hath sung the dirge of pleasures gone.
The heart may still in freshness glow,
Though cherished hopes have fallen low.

In the spring of 1862, while living at Cedar Point, Houston and
Margaret learned that Sam, Jr., had been wounded while fighting in the
Confederate Army. It was reported that he had been captured and was in
a Union prison. On July 30, 1862, Margaret expressed a prayer for her
oldest child's safety:

A Mother's Prayer

Oh thou 'neath whose omniscient eye
The footsteps of the wanderer roam,
Far from his own loved native sky,
Far from the sacred ties of home!

A captive on some hostile shore,
Perchance his young heart pineth now,
To join the household band once more,
That round the evening altar bow,

Or mid the cannon's roar again,
And gleam of flashing steel, perchance
Upon the bloody battle plain,
Hath met the deadly foeman's lance.

I cannot tell my dim eye now
His wandering may no longer trace,
But oh! 'tis sweet to feel and know
Through every scene in every place

Thy glorious Eye doth follow him!
On toilsome march, mid prison gloom,
On Southern soil, through Northern clime,
Or mid the cannon's dismal boom,

His life is safe beneath thy sight,
As though a mother's love could soothe,
And for the weary head each night,
With tender hand, his pillow smoothe!

But for the guardian care that kept
My patriot boy on Shiloh's plain,
His youthful form would now have slept,
With thousands of the noble slain,

And can I doubt thy power and love?
Oh Father, let me doubt no more!
Each cloud of unbelief remove
And hide me, till the storm is o'er!

Into thy hands, Oh God, I yield
My first born treasure and my stay!
Be thou his guardian, guide and shield,
And save him, in the last great day!

After Houston's death Margaret struggled against grief and financial ruin. In a poem titled "Evening Thoughts," written at Independence on September 25, 1865, she expressed her despair and also remembered her father's and brother's deaths:

Welcome gentle shades of even
To this weary care-worn brain,
Bringing with thee thoughts of Heaven,
And the rest which doth remain.

To the people of our God,
Who through faith have gained the shore,
And beyond the billowy flood,
All their griefs and toils are o'er.

While above my tranquil head,
Lengthening shadows softly fall,
Let me converse with the dead
And the hallowed past recall.

Father, brother, let me hear
The early admonition,
And the unforgotten prayer,
The deep heart-felt petition.

In the world's bewildering maze,
I have wandered far since then,
But the memory of those days
An unfailing shield hath been.

Brother let thine image rise,
From the early grave oh come!
Tell me of our native skies
Of our far-off childhood's home!

Ah those beauteous skies I knew
Sometimes wept through darksome cloud,
And our favorite flowers too
'Neath the tempest meekly bowed.

And I know thy soul doth rest
In a land of cloudless skies,
Ever with the pure and blest,
In the Saviour's paradise.

But oh Brother since you left
Loving ones that night in tears,
I have oft times been bereft,
Grief hath dimmed these many years!

Come to me my buried Love
In all thy solemn beauty!
From thy radiant home above
And rouse my soul to duty!

Oh Love my heart is weary
In its loneliness and pain!
The way seems long and dreary,
Tell me shall we meet again?

But thy children gather round,
And my sorrows I must hush,
For the merry step must bound,
And youth's joy I would not crush.

God hath helped me hitherto,
Truly may his servant say,
And his hand will guide me through
Safely through life's thorny way.

SELECTION OF HOUSTON FAMILY LETTERS

The first letter written by Margaret Moffette Lea to Sam Houston

Marion, Perry County, July 17 [1839]

Your letter from Nashville was received on last night. Strange as it may seem, it is my first news of you since your departure from Mobile. The one written from Columbus was never received. I remained in constant expectation of it, but at length I concluded that the mail had been miscarried. At last however, I have heard from you and the tidings are truly welcome I assure you. My answer may be taken as a strong evidence of that, for it is the first I have addressed to any gentleman.

We are once more in our native county, and Marion—our own Marion is still happy and flourishing. Surrounded by its green hills, groves, and bowers, it is like a sweet wood-nymph untarnished by the wiles and cold deception of the world. I am in the midst of my childhood's friends, and greeted on every hand with gentle words and soft endearing epithets and I am happy; quite happy. Ah no—there are those absent whose station within my heart remains unfilled. Alas it is ever thus through life! Happiness is a grand union of tender associations, ties, and friendships. Let but the smallest of these be removed, and the whole is incomplete. What being can ever be so blessed as to embrace all at once? And even if that were accomplished, would it not be in constant dread of severing some link of the beautiful chain?

I have taken my seat in the library. For several reasons it is a favorite resort. Now in the early morning it looks out upon a range of wild hills, still slightly obscured by the mist of the night, and in the evening, the sunset rays will beautifully gild their rich verdure. How solemn the place! Sacred to holy meanings and communion with the genius of ages gone-bye [sic]! I am in the midst of a band of heroes, ideal and real, and sages with their wisdom and philosophy are here and orators and poets with their dusty laurels. A majestic host! And yet though it may seem sacreligious, my heart is not with them today. It is like a caged bird when weary pinions have been folded weeks and months—at length it wakes from its stupor, spreads its wings and longs to escape, but ah, my heavy words still weigh it down, it cannot go forth.

Last night I gazed long upon our beauteous emblem the star of destiny, and my thoughts took the form of verse, but I will not inscribe them here, for then you might call me a romantic star-struck young lady, you know I would not like it at all to be put in that sublime class of individuals.

I regret that it will [the words "be out of my power" are crossed out] not be possible for me to see you at the Blount-spring [a community in southern Alabama known for its mineral springs]. Marion is but a trifling journey from that place and we will expect you to perform it. Mr. Bledsoe and my sister [Antoinette Bledsoe], mother [Nancy Lea], and some others of my relations will set off for Texas in Oct. Those of my family who remain are unwilling, under existing circumstances, that I should accompany the others until you have visited Marion. It is natural that they should wish to see you, and I agree with them in the course upon which they have decided. Therefore if you do not take Marion in your homeward route, the probability is that you will not [see] your rustic Esperanza [Spanish for "the one hoped for," a named given Margaret by Houston] for ages (months I mean) to come. My brother Henry met with Gen. Parsons in the Cahaba [a river in Perry County, Alabama] a few days since. He is to make us a visit very soon. Dear good old man, he speaks so affectionately of you! I have become much attached to him, and will suffer no one to question his bravery in my presence. Well, I believe I have no more to tell you now except that you must write to me immediately and constantly until I see you. I fear if Dr. S. does not return to Mobile shortly, the preference will be to Meritt. I do not prefix Superior. That is for the young lady to decide.

[The remainder of the letter is water-spotted and blurred. It contains a postscript in another handwriting, probably that of William Bledsoe, which is also blurred.]

The following letter was written by Margaret after eight months of marriage. During this period the Houstons had actually been together for less than half of that time.

Galveston, Jan 27th [1841]

My Love,

Capt. Todd called this morning & informed me that a Mr. Dawson was going up to Austin, and would take a letter for me. I am glad of the opportunity, for although I have written to you constantly, I apprehend that you do not get my letters as I never receive any acknowledgements. I have sent a letter to the care of Judge Moreland which you will perhaps receive with this. I have nothing amusing to tell you, for I have been so ritual of late that the fluctuations of society have left me several degrees in the lurch. I write to you therefore merely because you are very dear to me and because I love to tell you my thoughts & feelings, although they may be tame & uninteresting. If you have rec'd my letters, I fear you are vexed at my urgent entreaties for you to come home. You must not be, my Love, for indeed I am very lonely without you. I ought to have known however that it would disturb you and that the prudent course would have been to conceal my illness & low spirits from you. I confess that selfishness and the desire of being with you prompted me against my better judgment to tell you everything. But my husband will surely forgive this weakness which originated in devoted love for him! If you do not—I have no other excuse to offer, and if I promise you to exercise more firmness here after, you will not believe me—for I made the same promise when you returned from the red lands! It has been so long since I saw you that the past seems almost like a dream but such a dream! so bright—so beautiful. Shall we ever see such happiness again? I trust we shall.

I rec'd a letter from Mr. Bledsoe a few days ago. He mentioned that he & sister A. had some idea of coming down with you. I should be delighted if they could as it would be a great source of comfort to have her with me at this time. Almost every day brings us some new rumour of war. It will at least serve as a subject of conversation and that is what the people often need. It is now several weeks since I have been out of the house. Oh how beautiful and tempting is the blue sky and even the bare prairie! How often in other days has my heart bounced with rapture when I could roam through the balmy woods and breathe the pure air of Heaven! But alas I did not know what a blessed privilege it was until entirely deprived of it. I vainly imagined that while I live the flowers would never cease to bloom— the wild birds to sing for me. Perhaps the sweet spring may bring back the same hopes. I sometimes grow fretful and impatient, but I think I am resigned to any fate that may await me. I have a merciful God to deal with, and though he should bid me go down to an early grave, my spirit can say "thy will be done." But I will not dwell on this subject. My Love do you find time to read the bible? I trust that you do and that its holy precepts may sink deep into your heart. I would have you read the history of our blessed Saviour again & again and to meditate much upon his character.

My love, so write to me oftener. I am so happy when I get a letter from you! But when days & weeks pass away without one cherishing word, my heart feels as if it would burst with grief. Oh shall I ever be with you again and see you and hear you speak! I shall be wild with joy. I am sure if my heart was probed at this time, there would not be found much patriotism in it, for I almost hate the duties that keep you from me. Mother & bro. V. send their love to you. Dearest do not forget [sic].

Your own devoted
M. L. Houston

[on outside of letter]

It is 6 years today since my dear father died.

"I know that he's gone where his forehead is starred

With the beauty that dwelt in his soul!"

but this day always brings to me a loneliness of heart that nothing can dissipate. I mention the circumstances because you have always simpathised [sic] with my feelings toward that sainted being. How sad is such simpathy! It enables us to realize "the joy of grief" and the very sorrow that else would render life lonely & desolate becomes a link of union that makes life desirable. Dear noble husband, how often do I need thy gentle simpathy! Sometimes when my heart is filled with gloom, I try to imagine what you would say to me, and there is even pleasure in that. How much sweeter would be the reality! Present me to our friends Mr. & Mrs. Toland. Tell her I am expecting an answer to my letter. Dearest farewell.

Margaret wrote this letter to Houston while he was away in Austin serving as the president of the Republic of Texas and dealing with a hostile Congress.

Houston, Jan 3rd [1842]

Dearest Love,

I rec'd your invaluable letter tonight by Mr. Green, and although it is way past my usual hour for retiring I must answer it tonight as he will be off in the morning. I wrote to you this morning by a Mr. Fisher, but the letter was realy [sic] so hurried and incoherent that I am now ashamed of it and at this time I am so out of spirits, that I can hardly write at all. Mr. Green tells me that congress will not adjourn within less time than six weeks, and this is my grievance. Surely my love your patriotism is undergoing a severe test and doubtless will come out like the refiner's gold. Mine has been pretty much shaken by recent events and I must confess that my predominant thought has been that my husband was wasting his time and energies upon an ungrateful people! But perhaps it is wrong to indulge such feelings. If you think so Love, I will try to overcome these. Many thanks for your poetry. Your muse is certainly very [word is blurred] to visit you in the midst of the turmoil and impractical bustle which must necessarily reign in Austin at this time, and I am certainly much indebted to her for reminding you of your absent Maggy. If she is so fortuitous at this time, what may we expect when we again roam through the sweet wild woods around our home! Indeed Love, I was delighted with the sentiments entertained in your lines, particularly the conclusion! I had heard of "jumping at conclusions" but I must confess I thought that a pretty sudden leap. Never the less, I was highly flattered and I never consider my Husband a poet as well as a hero, statesman, and I believe a philosopher, but I do not know exactly about the latter! Nous aerrosis!? The good people of Texas have certainly determined to ascertain. I hear nothing of the seat of government being moved and it is a subject in which I am not altogether uninterested. It would be a source of consolation to me to know where in the future home is to be that I might draw plans for it and indulge visions which though they may never be realized, would at least amuse me for the moment. But even this is denied us. We are slaves of the public and must await its pleasures. My Love I am almost sorry that I have said so much. I know that it is my duty to soothe you in your deep disappointments and trials as much as possible, but at this moment I am so indignant at the recent acts of congress that I can not restrain my feelings. If the seat of government should not be moved, I must confess to you candidly that I

397

wish you to resign immediately. Of course this will not decide your course of conscience in a case of such importance, but I must say what I think and feel!

If you are to serve the people for nothing I think you ought at least to have the privilege of performing the labour in safety and in some civilized spot. But dearest if you are satisfied it will all be right with me for your happiness is mine! My Love, can it be that there is realy [sic] probability of a Mexican invasion! May Heaven avert such a calamity! Oh my husband I can not endure the thought. It is too dreadful! I can not be happy until I see you again and hear from your own lips that the danger no longer exists. Dearest one portion of your letter gives me more pleasure than any others. It was that you were trying to rise above the dreadful practice of swearing. Oh continue those efforts. I entreat you Love by all the sacred happiness we have enjoyed together, by every hope of future happiness do not profane the name of him who has been so merciful to us. Are we not more blessed than others? In vain we look around for that communion of hearts that God has suffered us to enjoy. And oh do not in return ask his name as an expression of anger or to embellish the unjust! Dearest husband, my constant prayer to God is "that you may be saved." Oh that I knew some argument that would drive you to the feet of the saviour! How freely would I yield this fleeting breath and lie down in the cold grave if it would purchase your salvation. But it can not be. If you will not fly to Jesus for refuge there remaineth no more sacrifice from sin but a certain fearful evoking for of judgment and fiery indignation which shall devour the adversaries. Oh how can I rest one moment while my husband is exposed to the wrath of God!

Cold luke warm heart of mine, too long hast thou been swayed by earthly hopes and drawn away from my Heavenly Father by the blessings of his own hand! Dearest each night and morn, I will pray for you with my whole heart and at these calm and peaceful hours, will you not "visit" with me? and Oh I entreat you to throw aside every worldly thought at such a time and pray with a heart free from distractions! It is late, very late at night and hearts more joyous than mine are lulled into gentle sleep and yet I would write until the east again puts on her rose-tinted morning garb for how can I sleep. My heart is troubled like the glorious sea, and no gentle husband is near me to hush by his bright looks of affection, the darkness and clouds from my spirits or by his soft words to still the boisterous words of grief. I am figurative you will say but dearest it is no exaggerated picture. I do feel as if my heart was bursting & deep midnight stillness is reigning around me. My own one thou are not here and oh how silent is the spot in which thy voice is not heard! How dark and dreary the scene, if I behold thee not! Dearest my heart finds relief in the expressions of its deep feelings and I know you will not treat them lightly. Last night I was happy for I dreamed much of you. We meandered arm-in-arm through a lovely country and thick hanging bows above our heads were filled with a thousand bright birds and our path was fringed with innumerable strange and beauteous flowers. We meandered on and on but felt no fatigue for we were happy. Oh may it promise a vision of our journey through life. Dearest talk no more of wars and sacrifices for your country. It must not be. You are mine and mine alone and you must not —oh no you can not leave me again! I am constantly surrounded by friends, but oh I feel desolate for you are not with me and oh what solitude is like the loneliness of a crowd! Write often dearest and oh do hasten home.

Your devoted wife
M. L. Houston

This is the first letter Houston wrote to Margaret after he became a senator.

Washington, 31st March 1846

My Dearest,

Three nights since, I arrived here. Sunday passed quietly as I could make it. Tho' to be absolutely quiet was impossible. People would call, and did call. On Monday my colleague (with whom I am perfectly cordial) presented my credentials to the Senate where I took the Oath, and my seat. So Texas is fully represented in the Senate, and persons say as ably as any State of the Union. Ably I say because we are the tallest gentlemen from any State, and in all respects as sizeable. Already I wish to get home and be my own "single side."

Were I pleased any where else than at home, I might be pleased here. Every person renders to me respect, so far as it is in their power, and nothing pleases me so much as the inquiries which are made about you, and the character which they tell me that they have heard of you. This is done by old familiars, who more than rejoiced to see me. You have at least as much popularity, if not more than I have myself. Some wish me to tell them just how you look. The ladies, what few I have seen have not failed to say "Gen'l is she pretty? But I know she is!" and many things of this sort, and my modesty permits me to say "I think so." To be thus writing, is to me very painful. If I could only be so blessed as to be present with you, I would thus be happy. My love, you can have no idea of the pain which I endure in absence from you and our dear Boy. Of him, too, I have much to answer, and it is done with the most pleasure, because say what I may of him, I am compelled to blend a portion of it with "his mother!" You will think this is a love letter my dear, unless I change my tone to narrative.

Well, to day we had a fine speech from General Cass, and I will send you a copy, so soon as it is out in pamphlet. On the Oregon Subject, there is a pretty equal division, and it may be that the vote of the Texian Senators will decide the question in favor of the notice. This evening I was at the Drawing room of the President, or as they are called, "Mr. Polk's drawing rooms." When I first came, as well as to night, I was most kindly received, by both the President and his Lady. She is quite what you would desire to see her, and does not appear to be older than twenty-five, or eight years, tho' she must be forty-five. She is not quite so tall as you are, but very much of your person, and of course, I think her very genteel. Not by any means flashy, tho' quite cheerful & pleasant. The ladies, most of them, I was introduced to, or I might say (if you will pardon me) were introduced to me, as I ask no introduction. Now my dear, do not get angry. I really did not promenade with any one, nor did one of them touch my arm. You will be provoked at them, will you not, for treating me with so much disrespect? If they do so again, I will not complain to you of their neglect. But should they do otherwise, I will tell you of it. Now I will assure you dearest that my course is taken, and it will be not to lose one moment from business that I can possibly avoid. We will have incessant labour to perform, and could I when the toils of the day are over, only have the pleasure of sitting down with you, and Sam, and passing the evening, I would be in the enjoyment of earth's greatest happiness. You will perceive that my hand write [sic] is still affected by my wound, tho' I do not suffer any pain from it. My health is good, and I was not fatigued by the journey. In passing the mountains I saw piles or banks of snow several feet deep, and there was quite a fall of snow upon us. This to you would seem strange. I put on two pair of socks, lest I might be cold.

I came to this place in the Cars, and I assure you my love, in times past I have enjoyed more pleasant rides when my earthly all was mounted or packed upon Bruin! I sigh for the return of those rural scenes, days of happiness which [I] declare I would not exchange for the "White House" for life. You need entertain no fears my dear that I will ever desire to remain in public, and all the demonstrations which can be offered will never induce me to desire a contrary course. If in the enjoyment of home, I can not find happiness, then on earth there is none for me. You dearest, are the sole repository of my love and my hopes! You and your love are to me every thing, and without you earth would be cheerless. Your happiness will be ever the choicest object of my care. To our dear Boy I must write, and he is to write me a letter on his slate, and read it to you.

My son! I am far from you. Days and nights will come & pass by before your poor Papa can see his son. Pa loves his dear boy (his great big boy) and hopes that he is a good boy. Does his son say his prayers, and pray for his pa, & ma, and Grand ma? does he obey his Ma, and not get mad? Does he love the Good Father, and his son Jesus Christ? My Dear Son, be a good boy, and make your dear Ma happy! You must write to pa and get Ma to send pa the letter. Pa will not forget the pretty dress for you. Pa loves his dear boy too much to forget any thing which he wants. Your Father loves you my dear Boy.

During his years in the Senate, Houston frequently wrote letters to his children and encouraged them to write to him. The following letter to his third child, Maggie Lea, is preserved in the Barker History Center, The University of Texas, Austin, in the Sam Houston Papers.

Washington
23rd Dec 1858

My Dear Daughter,

I am in the Senate, and tho' all is bustle and noise I cannot deny myself the pleasure of thanking you for your two pretty little letters. I admire your efforts to write well, and while you cherish a wish to write, as you do, you will improve. To excel in anything, it is only necessary to persevere, and practice will insure success. Notwithstanding the pleasure which your letters gave me, I was much distressed to hear that your Dear ma was not well, and had suffered so much that it was necessary to sit up with her. I feel pained, tho I hope that she is now well, that I had not the gratification of sitting by her every moment of her illness, and waiting upon her, for I am sure that I could have to some extent have mitigated her suffering. It has been otherwise ordered by Providence, and I submit to the dispensation, with prayers that her health is now restored and that she may enjoy better health than she has done for years past.

So distant as I am from the object of my affections, that I do not expect to enjoy an hour of pleasure until I can, God willing, embrace my family. All things around me claim no love, no tenderness, no thrilling emotions of affection and love!

Thus I am cut off from what, to me, is life's treasure. If it were in my power I would gladly fly to the dear objects of my affection. I will anxiously look every moment of my life for letters from home. I never cease to think of home & family only when I am sleeping, and that seldom, until near morning dawns.

My Dear Daughter, you ask me to come home. I am sure my Dear, that no one at home can be more anxious to see me, than I am to be with them. Every hour that I pass from home, I regard as a blank in my existence. This is my feeling when I reflect on my absence, but I feel additional regrets of the most painful character, when I fear that your Dear Ma may be languishing in a bed of sickness. This thought deprives me of all limits to my sorrow and distress. Surrounded as I am by business, and busy men, might be supposed to divert my thoughts from home and private affairs, but it is not so. In the midst of business, my thoughts recur constantly to my home.

I was pleased that you gave me so lively a description of our Dear Little Willie. He must be quite an interesting chap, and I would be charmed, if I could only have the happiness to dandle him on my knees or see him jump with his joyous face. Give many kisses to your Dear Dear Ma, Sisters & brothers.

Affectionately Thy Father
Sam Houston

On February 28, 1859, Houston rose on the Senate floor to make his last lengthy speech before that body. In it he defended himself against an attack by Dr. N. D. Labadie who charged that Houston was not responsible for the victory at San Jacinto. W. C. Crane described it as a "speech refuting calumnies produced and circulated against his character as commander-in-chief of the army of Texas" (see Crane, *Life and Select Literary Remains of Sam Houston of Texas*, pp. 578-99). Within minutes of completing it, he wrote Margaret the following letter:

Senate Chamber, 28th Feby 1859

My Dear Love,

I feel relieved at this moment having made my speech that I promised. The galleries were crowded, and many it seemed could not get in. The galleries are said to contain no less than 2500 people. I am candid in saying I was not satisfied with the effort, tho, I am assured by kind friends that the audience were delighted. When I sat down there was considerable applause in the Galleries, and no call to order was made. Gov. Fitzpatrick was in the chair, and we are very kind in our feelings. The speech was the last I ever expect to make of an official character. Indeed I intend that shall be the very last unless on some incidental debate that may arise. If I shou'd live, I may on some occasion speak to the people, and I may speak in Court, as I propose in the case of Col. Forbes.

I feel that a burden has fallen from me. Now my thoughts are all with you and home. I hope my Love, when you see the speech, you will be pleased with it. I felt the pressure of amount of time, and I was not prepared as well as I wished to be, & these things may cause me not to be pleased with my speech as well as I wished to be.

Since writing the above we have had a recess from 5 o'clock to half past six. I went to dinner and was greeted by Ladies and gentlemen on my speech! If every person is pleased with it, why shou'd I not be so also? I have my Dear, borne myself in such sort at this session, that I believe there will be a universal regret at my leaving the Senate, as that which can be felt for the departure of any other member of the national councils. This will be gratifying to me, and the extenuation of the world will become a matter of course gratifying to you & may stimulate our children & cause them to love and estimate characters properly. All this causes me no regret that I am to leave here, and retire to my family. No indeed My Dear, it is regarded by me as an act of emancipation from toil and a furlough that I may pass the residue of my days. You my Love, promise me your smiles and your affection to beguile the hours at home. These I prize far above Sceptres and thrones. I wish my Dear, that I were near enough to you to receive the smile or the evidence of affection!

Well I am too distant for either, but I will anticipate the enjoyment of both. This is the last day of this and I do not anticipate a return from here until the seventh day of March, and then I may have occasional detentions on my way home. I must look out for the best sheep so that I may be able to get the best in the U.S. to cross on our Texas stock. I would have to pass thro Ohio & then I may go to Louisville by way of Cincinnati, and from thence to Nashville to see the flock of Mark Cockerell, the greatest raiser of sheep in the U. S. I hope it will not detain me more than a week. If I get you a fine mule, I will have to take my buggie [sic] from Alexandria. This will cause me a few days more than if I were to go by stage. The articles ordered for Miss Nannie are procured and some fine things for you that Ladies tell me not to let you know of until you are surprized by them. They are not finery that will wear out.

I ordered a pretty cap for Willie to be selected. I must take Willie Rogers one or there will be a renting in the family, if I am a good judge at this distance. I think Willie can be well dressed that the children would be willing to wear very common clothing. I hope we will be able to clothe the little fellow comfortably.

I anticipate pleasure in making his acquaintance & securing his friendly esteem & intimacy, if I am spared to meet the dear little fellow. And to see him in his Dear Mother's arms, and both in health.

Love to all
Thy Devoted
Houston

Bibliography

Primary Sources

Books:

Houston, Sam. *The Autobiography of Sam Houston.* Edited by Donald Day and H. H. Ullom. Norman: University of Oklahoma Press, 1954.

Lester, Charles Edwards. *The Life of Sam Houston; The Only Authentic Memoir of Him Ever Published.* New York: J. C. Derby, 1855.

_____. *Sam Houston and His Republic.* New York: Burgess, Stringer, and Co., 1846. (These two books were both dictated to the author by Sam Houston, and so are considered primary sources.)

Manuscript Collections:

Baldwin, Jean Houston. Collection. Sam Houston Regional Library, Liberty, Texas.

Crane, Royston. Scrapbook. Texas Collection, Baylor University, Waco, Texas.

Crane, William Carey. Papers. Texas Collection, Baylor University, Waco, Texas.

Daniel, Jean and Price. Texas History Collection, Sam Houston Regional Library, Liberty, Texas.

Everitt, Mrs. E. A. [Peggy]. Collection. Sam Houston Regional Library, Liberty, Texas.

Friend, Llerena B. Collection. Sam Houston Regional Library, Liberty, Texas.

Hearne, Madge W. Collection of Houston letters jointly owned by her granddaughters, Madge Thornall Roberts, Nancy Thornall Burch, and Penny Thornall Remick, San Antonio, Texas.

Hearne, Madge W. Collection [of letters to Sam Houston]. Barker History Center, University of Texas, Austin, Texas.

Hearne, Madge W. Collection. Texas State Archives, Austin, Texas.

Hearne, Madge W. Papers, photographs, and correspondence in possession of the author, San Antonio, Texas.

Hearne, Sam Houston. Collection. Barker History Center, University of Texas Library, Austin, Texas.

Hearne, Sam Houston. Collection. Sam Houston Regional Library, Liberty, Texas.

Houston, Andrew Jackson. Collection. Sam Houston Regional Library, Liberty, Texas.

Houston, Sam. *The Writings of Sam Houston.* Edited by Amelia Williams and Eugene Barker. 8 vols. Austin: University of Texas Press, 1938–43.

Houston, Andrew Jackson. Collection. Texas State Archives, Austin, Texas.

Houston Family Correspondence. Texas State Archives, Austin, Texas.

Houston, Margaret. Album of poems, verses, and diary entries, 1839–1865. In the possession of Meredith Morrow Madison Spangler, El Paso, Texas.

Houston, Margaret Bell. Papers. Sam Houston Memorial Museum, Huntsville, Texas.

Houston, Sam. Papers. Barker History Center, University of Texas, Austin, Texas.

Irion, Robert. Papers. Barker History Center, University of Texas, Austin, Texas.

Jones, Anson. Papers. Barker History Center, University of Texas, Austin, Texas.

Loe, Dorothy E. Collection. Sam Houston Regional Library, Liberty, Texas.

McDonald, Mrs. R. E. Collection of Houston letters in the possession of Mary Louise Teasdale, Dallas, Texas.

Penland, Sam. Collection. Rosenburg Library, Galveston, Texas.

Smith, Ashbel. Papers. Barker History Center, University of Texas, Austin, Texas.

Williams, Franklin. Collection of Houston letters, 1839–1861. Sam Houston Memorial Museum, Huntsville, Texas.

Williams, Franklin Weston. Collection of Sam Houston materials. Woodson Research Center, Rice University, Houston, Texas.

Yoakum, Henderson. Diary. Texas State Archives, Austin, Texas.

Miscellaneous:

In addition to written recollections of the Houston family and its descendants, the author has drawn upon her own recollections of family stories told to her throughout her life by the following family members: Nancy Thornall Burch, Charlotte Williams Darby, Jennie Morrow Decker, Peggy Decker Everitt, Madge Williams Hearne, Sam Houston Hearne, Andrew Jackson Houston, Margaret Bell Houston, Sam Houston IV, Penny Thornall

Remick, Meredith Madison Morrow Spangler, Charlotte Darby Taylor, Mary Louise Teasdale, Marian Hearne Thornall, Marian Williams Whittemore and Franklin Williams. In the chapter notes, these sources are listed by the storyteller's name, then the words "family story."

County Records:

Perry County (Alabama) Court Records, 1835.
Perry County (Alabama) Marriage Records, 1840.
Walker County (Texas) Court Records, 1850–51.
Walker County (Texas) Deed Records, 1847–58.
Washington County (Texas) Court Records, 1867–1869.

State Records:

Executive Records, Register Book 281, Texas State Archives.

Individual Documents:

Lea, Temple. Will. Photocopy of original Perry County Will Book A, 57–58.

Houston, Sam and Margaret Moffette Lea. Marriage License. Photograph of the original furnished by Sam Houston Memorial Museum, Huntsville, Texas.

Leigh, Mrs. W. A. Map of Houston home and gardens in Huntsville, n.d. Sam Houston Memorial Museum, Huntsville, Texas.

Leigh, Mrs. W. A. and Mrs. M. A. Park. Notorized document detailing Sam Houston's funeral, dated 28 March 1938. Sam Houston State University Library, Huntsville, Texas.

Genealogy Records:

Lea Family Records. Stake Genealogy Library, San Antonio, Texas.

Teasdale, A. R. compiler, "Gen'l Sam Houston 1793–1863: Descendants," a computer print-out, Dallas, March 3, 1991.

Secondary Sources

Books and Articles:

Baker, D. W. C. *Texas Scrapbook*. Austin: The Steck Company, 1935.

Baker, William Mumford. "A Pivotal Point." *Lippincott's Magazine* 26 (November 1880): 559–66.

Banks, C. Stanley and Grace McMillan. *The Texas Reader*. San Antonio: The Naylor Company, 1947.

Binney, Ludie Anders. "Personal Recollections of Sam Houston." *The Alcalde* (Sam Houston State University Yearbook), 1929.

Blackburn, Mary Ellis. "Her Farewell to Sam Houston, A Kiss Shortly Before His Death." *San Antonio Express*, (San Antonio, Texas), July 5, 1936.

Brooks, Elizabeth. *Prominent Women of Texas*. Akron, Ohio: Werner Company, 1896.

Brown, John Henry, ed. *Encyclopedia of the New West*. Marshall, Texas: U. S. Biographical Publishing Company, 1881.

_____. *History of Texas 1885-1892*. St. Louis: L. E. Daniel, 1892.

Brown, Rosa. *Texas Scrapbook*. Houston: Concord Press, 1945.

Bruce, Henry. *Life of General Houston*. New York: Dodd, Mead and Company, 1891.

Bryson, Harold Clayton. "The Women Who Made a Man of Sam Houston." A research paper, typescript, June 1936. Texas Collection, Baylor University. Waco, Texas.

Burford, Patti McLeary. "General Houston's Daughter." *The Ladies Home Journal* (November 1895): n.p.

Burleson, Georgia J., ed. *The Life and Writings of Rufus C. Burleson.* Waco, Texas: Georgia J. Burleson, 1901.

Carroll, B. H., Jr. "Scenes About the Grave of Sam Houston." *Houston Chronicle* (Houston, Texas), April 22, 1911.

Carroll, Mrs. James V. "My Mother Saw Sam Houston." *Banner Press* (Brenham, Texas), March 2, 1936.

Crane, William Carey. *Life and Select Literary Remains of Sam Houston of Texas.* Philadelphia: J. B. Lippincott, 1885.

_____. "Sam Houston's Wife." *Houston Post,* (Houston, Texas), August 28, 1884.

Crews, D'Anne McAdams, ed. *Huntsville and Walker County, Texas: A Bicentennial History.* Huntsville: Sam Houston State University Press, 1976.

Daniel, Jean Houston and Price Daniel and Dorothy Blodgett. *The Texas Governor's Mansion.* Austin: The Texas State Library and Archives Commission and the Sam Houston Regional Library and Research Center, 1984.

Daughters of the Republic of Texas. *Fifty Years of Achievement.* Dallas: Banks Upshaw and Company, 1942.

Dickenson, Johnnie Jo, compiler. *Walker County Texas 1850–1860 Census.* Huntsville: Dickenson Research, 1989.

Dietrich, Wilfred O. *The Blazing Story of Washington County.* Brenham, Texas: Banner Press, 1950.

Dixon, Sam Houston. *The Poets and Poetry of Texas.* Austin: Dixon and Co., 1885.

Dressman, Fran. "Victorian Lady Tames Texas' Hero." *Beeville Bee-Picayune* (Beeville, Texas), August 21, 1986.

Ellis, Joseph Henry Harrison. *Sam Houston and the Related Spiritual Forces.* Houston: Concord Press, 1945.

Farrell, Mary D. and Elizabeth Silverthorne. *First Ladies of Texas.* Belton, Texas: Stillhouse Publishers, 1976.

Fitzhugh, Bessie Lee. *Bells Over Texas.* El Paso: Texas Western Press, 1955.

Flanagan, Sue. *Sam Houston's Texas.* Austin: University of Texas Press, 1964.

Foster, Margaret Hadley. "Mrs. Margaret Lea Houston, Wife of the Hero of San Jacinto." *The Gulf Messenger,* 10 (September 1897): 337–342.

Francis, Ruth Garrison. "Sam Houston's Home Now State Museum." *Dallas Morning News* (Dallas, Texas), May 9, 1929.

French, Janie and Zella Armstrong. *Notable Southern Families.* Bristol Tennessee: King Publishing Company, 1928.

Friend, Llerena. *Sam Houston: The Great Designer.* Austin: University of Texas Press, 1954.

Habekotte, Bess. "Restoration of the Nancy Lea Rock Vault." Brenham, Texas: Washington County Historical Association, 1970. A printed handout at the Independence Baptist Church and Museum, Independence, Texas.

Harris County Historical Society. *Houston—A History and Guide.* American Guide Series. Houston: Anson Jones Press, 1942.

Harry, Jewel Horace. "History of Chambers County." Master's thesis, University of Texas, 1940.

Hartwell, Joan M. "Margaret Lea of Alabama, Mrs. Sam Houston." *The Alabama Review* 17 (October 1964): 271–79.

Hatcher, Mattie Austin. *Mary Austin Holley.* Dallas: Southwest Press, 1933.

Henson, Margaret and Kevin Ladd. *Chambers County: A Pictorial History.* Norfolk: Donning Company, 1938.

Hightower, Rebecca. "General Sam Houston's Daughter Relates New Facts About Life and Work of Texas' Great Leader." *Houston Chronicle* (Houston, Texas), April 22, 1923.

Holcombe, Hosea. *A History of the Rise and Progress of the Baptist in Alabama.* Philadelphia: King and Baird, 1840.

Houston, Andrew J. *The San Jacinto Campaign.* Houston: Gulfport Printing Company, 1935.

Howser, James R. and H. Harris. *The Howser Family History.* n.p.: Howser Family, 1986.

Hunt, Lenoir. *My Master.* Dallas: Manfried, Van Nort, and Company, 1940.

Jackson, Pearl Cashell. *Texas Governor's Wives.* Austin: The Steck Company, 1915.

James, Marquis. "Epic Sequel to a Blighted Marriage." *American Legion Weekly* 8 (March 5, 1926): 4–5, 12–15.

_____. "On the Trail of Sam Houston." *Texas Monthly* 6 (July 1930) : 1–8.

_____. *The Raven.* Indianapolis: Bobbs-Merrill Company, 1929.

Jones, Katherine M. *Heroines of Dixie*. Indianapolis: Bobbs-Merrill Company, 1955.

King, Frank. "Who Saw Sam Houston?" *Brenham Banner Press* (Brenham, Texas), March 16, 1936.

Kilman, Ed. "Steamboat House is Monument to Sam Houston." *The Houston Post* (Houston, Texas), June 16, 1935.

Link, J. B. ed. *Texas Historical and Biographical Magazine*. Austin: privately printed, 1891.

Little, Mrs. John L. "Stories of Pioneer Texans Retold." *The Beaumont Enterprise* (Beaumont, Texas), March 24, 1946.

Madison, Meredith. "Margaret Lea Houston." Master's thesis, University of Texas at El Paso, 1960.

McAshan, Marie Phelps. *On the Corner of Main and Texas: A Houston Legacy*. Houston: Hutchins House. 1985.

McFarland, Mrs. Ike Barton. "All Texas Mourned Death of General Sam Houston." *Houston Press* (Houston, Texas), August 1, 1935.

McFarland, Mae Wynne. "General Sam Houston and Young Sam's Confederate Record." n.d. An unidentified newspaper clipping in the Sam Houston vertical file, Daughters of the Republic of Texas Library, San Antonio, Texas circa 1936.

Montgomery, Robin. *The History of Montgomery County*. Austin: Jenkins Publishing Company, 1975.

Morrow, Temple Houston. "Bullet Marks Psalm in Bible Given Sam Houston, Jr. by Mother." *Dallas Morning News* (Dallas, Texas), March 5, 1939.

Murray, Lois Smith. *Baylor at Independence*. Waco: Baylor University Press, 1972.

Murry, Ellen N. "Promise in a Lonely Land." *Texas Libraries* 45 (Winter 1984): 140–141.

Orr, Lyndon. "The Wives of General Houston," *Famous Affinities of History, The Romance of Devotion*. Vol. 3. New York: Harper & Brothers, 1909.

Patlow, Miriam. *Liberty County and the Atascocito District*. Austin: Pemberton Press, 1974.

Paschal, George W. "Last Years of Sam Houston." *Harpers New Monthly Magazine* 32 (April 1866): 630–635.

Phares, Ross. *The Governors of Texas*. Gretna: Pelican Publishing Company, 1976.

Pickrell, Anna Doom. *Pioneer Women in Texas*. Austin: The Steck Company, 1929.

Pinkney, Pauline. *Painting in Texas: The Nineteenth Century*. Austin: University of Texas Press, 1967.

Raines, C. W. *Year Book of Texas*. Austin: Gammel Statesman, 1902.

Reid, Mary. "Fashions of the Texas Republic." *Southwestern Historical Quarterly* 45 (January 1942): 244–254.

Rose, Ben L. *Report of Research on the Lea Family in Virginia & North Carolina Before 1800*. Richmond, Virginia: Printing Services, Inc. 1984.

_____ and Margaret M. Marty. "The Lea Ancestry of Margaret Lea, Wife of Gen. Sam Houston." Addendum #2 to *Report on the Lea Family in Virginia & North Carolina Before 1800*. Typescript, 1987.

Schmidt, Charles F. *History of Washington County*. San Antonio: Naylor Company, 1949.

Shipe, Mrs. S. L. "Recollections: Mrs. Sam Houston." *Dallas Morning News* (Dallas, Texas). An undated clipping, Daughters of the Republic of Texas Library, San Antonio, Texas.

Shuffler, Henderson. *The Houstons of Independence*. Waco: Texian Press, 1966.

_____. "The Women Who Changed Sam Houston." *Texas Parade Magazine*, (December 1965): 18–20.

Simmons, Laura. *Out of Our Past*. Waco: Texian Press, 1967.

Smither, Harriet, ed. "The Diary of Adolphus Sterne." *Southwestern Historical Quarterly* 31 (July 1927): 63–83.

Springfield, C. C. "Sam Houston's Home at Huntsville." *Texas Parade Magazine*, (January 1951): 8–9.

Terrell, A. W. "Recollections of General Sam Houston." *Southwestern Historical Quarterly* 16 (October 1912): 113–136.

Thomas, Anne. "Sam Houston's Strong Convictions Caused Turmoil in Later Years." *Texas Weekly Magazine* (October 25, 1981).

Toland, Gracey Booker. "Austin Knew His Athens." San Antonio: Naylor Publishing Company, 1938.

Waldrop, Charles P. "The Conquest of Sam Houston." *American History Illustrated* 21 (January 1987): 37–43.

Walker County Genealogical Society and Historical Commission. *Walker County Texas: A History*. Huntsville: Curtis Media Corporation, 1986.

Wallis, Jonnie Lockhart and Laurence Hill. *Sixty Years on the Brazos*. Waco: Texian Press Reprint, 1967.

White, Olive Branch. "Margaret Lea Houston, Wife of General Sam Houston."
Naylor's Epic Century Magazine (April 1936): 28–30.

_____, "Robert E. Lee In Texas." *Naylor's Epic Century Magazine* (February
1938): 12–14.

Williams, Alfred M. *Sam Houston and the War of Independence in Texas.*
Boston: Houghton-Mifflin Company, 1893.

Amelia Williams. *Following General Sam Houston.* Austin: The Steck Company, 1935.

Wisehart, M. K. *Sam Houston: American Giant.* Washington: Robert B. Luce,
1962.

Wooten, Mattie Lloyd. "Pioneer Women of Texas." *Southern Magazine* 2
(May 1935): 7.

Youngblood, Frances. *Historic Homes of Alabama and Their Traditions.*
Birmingham, Alabama: Birmingham Publishing Company, 1935.

Newspapers:

Commercial Bulletin (New Orleans), May 23, 1836.
Daily Herald (San Antonio), December 27, 1859.
Dallas Morning News (Dallas), April 22, 1911.
_____, April 14, 1927.
_____, November 14, 1937
_____, March 5, 1939.
_____, April 3, 1949.
Houston Post (Houston), April 22, 1911.
_____, January 15, 1933.
_____, March 26, 1936.
Houston Press (Houston), April 17, 1924.
Marion Herald (Marion, Alabama), May 16, 1840.

Red-Lander (San Augustine, Texas), October 28, 1841.

Republican (Jacksonville, Alabama), July 13, 1842.

San Antonio Express-News (San Antonio), April 15, 1978.

Texas State Gazette (Austin), April 4, 1854.

Vertical Files:

Friend, Llerena. Sam Houston Memorial Museum, Huntsville.

Lea, Nancy. Daughters of the Republic of Texas Research Library, San Antonio, Texas.

Houston, Margaret. Daughters of the Republic of Texas Research Library, San Antonio, Texas.

Houston, Sam. Daughters of the Republic of Texas Research Library, San Antonio, Texas.

_____. Houston Public Library, Houston, Texas

_____. Sam Houston State University Library, Huntsville, Texas.

_____. San Antonio Public Library, San Antonio, Texas.

_____. Texas Collection, Baylor University, Waco, Texas.

Houston, Sam. Biographical File, Barker History Center, University of Texas, Austin, Texas.

Houston, Sam. Scrapbook, Barker History Center, University of Texas, Austin, Texas.

Index

Houston, Margaret Lea (Maggie), 165–67, 169, 171, 174, 192, 195, 223, 226, 227, 245, 254, 258, 262, 274, 278, 287, 292, 295, 296, 311, 314, 318, 324, 334, 335, 338–40, 342, 346, 347, 349, 350, 357, 358, 360, 362

Houston, Mary Willie (Mollie), 204, 208, 226, 231, 245–47, 258, 262, 274, 278, 335, 340, 350, 357

Houston, Nancy Elizabeth (Nannie), 141, 159, 162, 164, 165, 171, 192, 195, 219, 226, 235, 236, 245, 256, 257–58, 262, 270, 274, 278, 287, 311, 314, 317, 318, 321, 334, 346– 49, 357, 367

Houston, Sam—
assassination threats, 45, 86, 88, 98, 293, 308; baptism and first Communion, 252, 253, 260; Battle of San Jacinto, 1, 6– 7, 18, 36, 39, 117, 165, 276, 286, 307, 333, 338, 359; biographers, 128–29, 344–45, 346, 350–51; birth, 2; boyhood, 2–3; challenged to duels, 62– 63, 253; character traits, 23, 37, 40, 53–54, 61, 66, 68, 70, 74, 87, 97–98, 100, 102, 104, 106, 118, 127, 189, 234, 323, 344, 350; Cherokee life, 3, 5, 6, 21, 106; children and family life, 56, 97, 99–100, 102, 136, 141, 145, 165, 172, 191, 195, 204, 211, 213, 218, 225, 227, 228, 231, 235, 241, 260, 270–

71, 273, 274, 277, 291, 292, 296, 297, 298, 316–17, 333, 373–79. *See also* children's names; courtship and engagement to Margaret Lea, 23, 25, 31 n.19, 33, 51, 52; custodian, Republic of Texas archives, 128; death, final illness and, 322–24, 331–33, 359; descendants, 373–79; early legal and political career, 4, 100, 166; family background, 2; first met Margaret Lea, 14, 18, 20, 22, 51, 84; governor of Tennessee, 4–5, 30, 285; governor of Texas, 279, 280–99, 303, 304; governor of Texas, unsuccessful campaign, 262–64, 269–70; inaugural ceremonies, 64, 69, 78, 285, 286, 303; "Journal of my Administration" ("Big Book"), 182, 193, 200 n.1; law partner, 25; law practice, 17, 28, 38, 40, 42, 43, 55, 57, 112, 118, 152, 175, 191, 192, 231, 255; library, 253, 307, 333; marriage to Eliza Allen, 5, 10, 21, 23, 29–30, 37; marriage to Tiana Gentry, 6, 21, 23; *Memoirs*, 86; military service, 3–4, 6–7, 78, 131–34, 143–44, 251, 310; monument, 359; "Old Chief," 28, 279; "Old Sam," 88; physical appearance, 15 n.19, 21, 40, 87, 96, 139, 178, 246, 247, 249, 267, 283, 303; president, Republic of Texas, first term, 9–10, 17, 65; president, Republic of Texas,